The Rough Guide to Cult TV

Flipping like  like a cork

Credits

Text editor: Paul Simpson

Contributors: Helen Rodiss, Jo Berry, Angie Errigo, Chris Hughes,
Damian Hall, Marianne Gray, Steve Morgan, Simon Kanter,
Derek Winnert, Lloyd Bradley, Ann Oliver, Chris Lepkowski, Kim Newman,
David Butcher, Richard Lowe, Chas Chandler

Production: Ian Cranna, Michaela Dooley, Sue Weekes
Picture editor: Dominique Bocaly Picture researcher: Simone Smith

Thanks to: Julie Christie, Pictorial Press, Cathrine Keen, Michelle Draycott,
Julia Bovis, Helen Prior, Wolfgang Harles, Mark Ellingham

Picture adjustment: Helen Prior
Cover design by Peter Dyer

Designed by Jon Butterworth
Printed in Spain by Graphy Cems
Dedicated to: Jack Simpson, the Rodisses, Teenage Kicks, the future Mr Dooley,
Scott, Ren & Stimpy, Hugo Butler and Diane Keen

Publishing Information

This edition published October 2002 was prepared by
Haymarket Customer Publishing for Rough Guides Ltd,
80 Strand, London WC2R ORL

Distributed by the Penguin Group

Penguin Books Ltd, 80 Strand, London WC2R ORL
384pp, includes index
A catalogue record for this book is available from the British Library
ISBN 1-84353-009-0

Contents

1. Through the square window...**5-12**
What makes a television show cult? Complete with
a vox pop on the subject, in homage to Nationwide

2. Cult shows.. **13-82**
The 56 cultest shows on the box, only some of
which star a log lady, all-in wrestling and Terry Collier

3. Genres.. **83-284**
The guide to cool programmes in different genres: from action
heroes to game shows to shows that made us all go zzzz…

4. Cult heroes...**285-336**
Those who have inspired us, from Tony Hart to
David Letterman via John Le Mesurier

5. Stuff..**337-358**
Memorabilia, books, websites, lists, music, more memorabilia
and a list of props requested of the BBC

6. The back stories..**359-371**
What 'kemo sabe' really means, the full story on the Monkee
auditions, the Pugwash rumours: TV myths exposed

7. TV listings...**372-375**
Strange TV programmes from around the world,
as described by the people who made them

Index... **376-383**

Closedown..**384**

Photo credits

Cover: Getty Images, Pictorial Press www.pictorialpress.com,
Hulton Getty, Moviestore Collection, Rex Features, Famous, Corbis,
Channel 4, Fox TV, Sky One, Hallmark Channel, Challenge TV, Paramount
Comedy, UK TV, UK Gold, SCI FI, BBC, Channel 5, Decca Records, Trunk
Records, HBO, Jarrod & Sons Ltd, IB Tauris, Rev-Ola Records, Capitol Records,
Fremantle Media Enterprises

Through the square window
What's cult on the box and what's not

'I hate television. I hate it as much as I hate peanuts but I can't stop eating peanuts'

Orson Welles

Are you sitting comfortably? Then we'll begin. There is, alas, no hard scientific formula for deciding whether a TV programme is cult or not. You can pore over the definition in the *Oxford English Dictionary* (which will invoke such ideas as religious worship, homage and fashion) but ultimately whether a show is cult or not is as personal a decision as whether you preferred **Jenny Hanley** to **Valerie Singleton**, or **World Of Sport** (with its breathtaking coverage of the World Target Clown Diving Championships from Florida) to **Grandstand**.

But certain qualities help define what's cult. An obvious and irritating sign is that 'Four Yorkshiremen' moment when your peers quote huge chunks of dialogue to each other and titter. But one besotted viewer does not a cult make; it takes at least two to swap allusions and in-jokes.

Swift and irrational condemnation by the legendary **Mary Whitehouse** once helped many shows become cult. Since she departed to the green room in the sky, the *Daily Mail* has done its best. But it's not the same. The indignation needs to be dispensed by a woman who looks like the result of a genetic experiment involving **Dame Edna Everage** and **Barbara Woodhouse** to be truly effective.

Nor is a show's cult status directly related to its quality. A cult programme can be inspirationally great (like **The Singing Detective**), so weird that even regular viewers aren't sure what'll happen next (**Spike Milligan**'s *Q* series) or, like **Crossroads**, as cheesy and as full of holes as Switzerland's annual output of Emmental. It takes a certain nerve to set a soap opera in

7

the glamour-free zone that is the Midlands, shooting every scene in one take even if the set began to shake, and start a glorious tradition whereby characters aren't written out but simply forgotten. In 1967, **Benny Wilmott**, a teenager who ran the coffee bar, was told by **Meg Richardson** to 'go out and buy a bag of sugar', an errand from which he had still not returned when the show closed 20 years later.

A cult show is usually an original. In 1971, American humorist Fred Allen noted, 'Imitation is the sincerest form of television.' The industry's default mode is to repeat a success until the repetitions stop being successful, which is why most of the time it's the originals we cherish, **Monty Python** rather than **The Goodies**, **Morecambe And Wise** not **Hale And Pace** (whom Victor Lewis-Smith accurately described as 'the world's only known comedy double act consisting of two straight men'). For most of us, **Hamish Macbeth** is a work of subtlety and **Monarch Of The Glen** is a poor copy with the quirkiness removed to make space for extra shortbread.

Catchphrases help, be they as blatant as 'Nice to see you to see you...' (there is something almost Pavlovian in the way we all feel obliged to

'Dear Biddy, What I really want to do is direct...' Petra secretly felt she was more than a mere entertainer

shout 'nice!') as apparently innocuous as 'Are you sure that's wise?' or even 'Hands that do dishes can be soft as your face.'

A programme's cult value isn't just determined by the show itself – we play our part. Children's susceptibility to media influence is debated by sociologists, leader writers, programme-makers and politicians. Yet the influence, good or ill, is obvious in the number of programmes, one-liners and slogans that enter our young brains to pop up at random for the rest of our lives. For Britons of a certain age, there was a time in their lives when **Biddy Baxter** was one of the most important people in the world, almost as eminent as the prime minister, a remote god-like figure who moved in mysterious ways to produce the wonder that was **Blue Peter**. Many of the shows which have stuck with us were those we saw before we grew up (or before we reached the age at which we are officially deemed to have grown up): **Roobarb**, **Tiswas**, **The Demon Headmaster**, et al. This isn't always true, but it's true an awful lot of the time.

Peanuts, paranoia and panics

A few misguided souls still mock the very idea that television, a medium famously described as 'chewing gum for the eyes', could create anything as powerful as a cult. **Orson Welles**, who knew a thing or two about the power of the media (and, for that matter, Californian wines and Domecq sherry), got closer to the truth with his peanuts analogy.

Often, the very people who insist on television's terrifying triviality, proclaim it is a deeply subversive force. Moral panics about television date back to 1948 when the *New York Times* sighed: 'the wife scarcely knows where the kitchen is, let alone her place in it, Junior scorns the afternoon sunlight for the glamour of a darkened living room and father's briefcase lies unopened in the foyer. The reason: television.' The bad publicity never stops: various studies have blamed/credited TV for making viewers paranoid, soothing stressed battery hens and causing a rise in accidents in the home through endless DIY series.

The most significant study was conducted in Germany and the UK in the early 1990s, in which 80 families were paid £40 a week not to watch telly. The pay-per-non-view experiment soon ended as the families gave the money back because without TV they had nothing to talk about. Too bloody right. Where would the art of conversation be if we couldn't speculate about when **Mulder** was going to kiss **Scully**, how long **Vanessa** would last in **Celebrity Big Brother**, and whether **Jerry Springer** really wanted to do a show called 'I Married A Horse'? (Answer: No, but he did make a programme called 'Seven Months Pregnant And Still Stripping'.)

The boredom-killing business

The final word goes to **Howard Beale**, the newsreader who threatens to commit suicide on air in the 1976 movie **Network**. In one of his shorter speeches, he observes: 'Television is not the truth. Television is a god-damned amusement park. Television is a circus, a carnival, a travelling troupe of acrobats, storytellers, dancers, singers, jugglers, sideshow freaks, lion tamers and football players. We're in the boredom-killing business.' There are times when TV seems to be in the boredom-generating business (dogs saying 'sausages' on **That's Life**, **Ray Stubbs**, every TV series 'starring' **Cannon and Ball**) but at its best, the box kills boredom almost as effectively as **Domestos** is said to kill all known germs. Anyway, inspired by the man-in-the-street sequences in **Nationwide**, et al, we asked some folks to choose their favourite TV shows. This is what we found.

VOX POP

Stars of big and small screen (and stars with no screens involved at all) say what turned their TVs on:

Tina Baker (GMTV star and soap pundit)
Coronation Street is my comfort blanket. A Hobnob, Horlicks and Hayley Cropper is bliss.

Sanjeev Bhaskar (The Kumars At No. 42)
I was addicted to the first two series of *Moonlighting* which played with the conventions of television in a way I'd never seen. The third series was also worth watching because of the tension between Bruce Willis and Cybill Shepherd.

Peter Boyle (NYPD Blue, Lois & Clark, X-Files)
Knight Rider. In every episode, David Hasselhoff is trapped by bad guys and says, 'Rescue me!' to his car – which shoots out so fast from a parking lot that it makes a guy walking by with groceries throw his bags up in the air… It's not the series I like, just the waiting for that shot – differing angles, sometimes, but it's always the same shot.

Rory Bremner
Spitting Image. Satirically it hit the spot. It also gave a voice to disenfranchised groups while the Tories were in power.

David Cassidy
The Sopranos is without doubt the best TV show ever. The supporting cast is phenomenal, especially Steve van Zandt from Bruce Springsteen's backing band, who's never had an acting lesson in his life. It's sheer genius.

George Clooney
As a kid I thought *The Lone Ranger* was God. He was cool, independent, a real man.

Martin Clunes
Men Behaving Badly, because men are like that.

Minnie Driver
My favourite TV show is *The Office*. I am a huge Christopher Guest fan – he was the beginning of agonisingly funny faux documentaries, and Ricky Gervais seems to be his British counterpart. The show is just so brilliantly observed.

Jenny Eclair
Malcolm In The Middle – I approve hugely of any family that puts the fun into dysfunctional.

Rupert Everett
I love watching *Blind Date*: it has become so ruthless. They used to go off to have a lovely time. Now they all hate each other from the moment they arrive in Budapest or Inverness, and then they're so rude about each other afterwards.

Emma Freud
Ruby Wax is brilliant and brave. Some of the things she's tried didn't really work, but at least she doesn't just stick to the safe chat-show formula of two sofas and a coffee table.

Mariella Frostrup
The only series I've ever watched religiously was *Dallas*. I was at a reasonably idle stage of life and couldn't get enough of JR, Sue Ellen, Bobby, the poison dwarf and square-jawed Jock. I wondered if real life would ever be so glamorous.

James Gandolfini
As a kid the only show that I ran home to see was *Kolchak: The Night Stalker*, which I found out recently was written by David Chase, the creator of *The Sopranos*!

John Hannah
When I was growing up, I tried never to miss *The Sweeney*. I particularly liked it when the villains got off. It seemed to make it more real. That does happen in cop shows now, but then how can you tell who the villains are today anyway?

David Jason
Reilly: The Ace Of Spies. You only have to watch that programme to understand why British television shows are probably the best in the world.

David E Kelley (creator of *Ally McBeal*)
The Sopranos. I rushed out after they won the Golden Globes. Someone said: 'You must be a sore loser!' but I just wanted to get home in time to watch it.

Nicholas Lyndhurst
The Sweeney – my favourite as a kid. The chemistry between Dennis Waterman and John Thaw was fantastic, as was the theme. Guess what? I was in an early episode as an extra who nearly gets run over by a car full of baddies.

Miriam Margolyes
The Weakest Link panders to my sado-humiliation fantasies. Anne Robinson is a highly skilled performer, using contempt and malevolence to entertain – I die laughing. I would NEVER go on the show.

Morrissey
Coronation Street. It's the campest thing on TV.

Barry Norman
Frasier. Unlike most sitcoms, it's thoughtful, intelligent and brilliantly written.

Su Pollard
The Golden Girls – it's so wonderfully written. People like the sex-mad Blanche and Dorothy coping with her dozy mother really do exist. And I love *Batman* with all that KAPOW! and 'Holy mackerel!' – it's so camp.

Shaggy
Sex And The City. I like watching the four women talking about men, because you know what they're thinking.

Isla St Clair (*Generation Game* hostess, 1978-82)
I know *The Winds Of War* wasn't supposed to make you laugh, but the acting was hilarious.

Billy Bob Thornton
As a teenager I never missed the 1960s rock programmes *Hullaballoo* or *Shindig*. They kept me up on all the British rock bands who were coming to America.

Tina Turner
Fawlty Towers. It's simply the best TV comedy ever.

Jessie Wallace (Kat Slater in *EastEnders*)
Daffy Duck. I watched him all the time when I was growing up. He was horrible sometimes, so I never felt sorry for him when he'd get his beak whacked round his head for the millionth time. I like his lisp, though – it's cute.

Michael Winner
Come Dancing. Unquestionably it's the best – and the worst. I love the fact that they make those dreadful costumes, though they've stopped giving you as much detail as they used to – like the number of sequins.

56 cult TV programmes

The cultest of the cult shows

'America needs to be more like The Waltons and less like The Simpsons'

George Bush

It's still cool to decry the telly but as American comedy writer **Michael Elias** noted, there is no proof that the TV industry's output is any worse than, say, a year's modern art: 'There are 3,432 hours of prime-time programming on American TV every year. If you hung the equivalent number of oil paintings from the same year in full view people might not be so impressed by art either.' Given the ordeal programmes endure before they reach our screens, it's a miracle we take any of them to our hearts. By the time **ER** made its debut, creator **Michael Crichton** could have founded a new hospital. Others, like *Black Adder*, survive only after recasting and a swift chop of the budget. Here are **56** shows that made it onto the small screen (and into our hearts) with their personality and flaws intact.

Note: If these shows are available on video or DVD, we have added the letters "VHS" or "DVD" to the credits.

★ The Avengers ★

ITV 0 **VHS, DVD**

The Avengers hooked 1960s audiences with a supremely stylish blend of espionage, tongue-in-cheek humour and surreal sci-fi. Ingenious masterminds and hand-to-hand action scenes (with women more than holding their own against men) were combined with bizarre plots, a knowing sense of the absurd, and topped off by immaculate dress sense and witty banter. The casting was just as inspired. You can have fun spotting future stars like **Charlotte Rampling, Donald Sutherland** or **Christopher Lee** (as robot scientist Dr Frank N Stone) in lead roles, or the likes of **John Cleese,**

Ronnie Barker or **John Laurie** in wonderfully eccentric supporting parts.

Patrick Macnee really did make the role of dapper John Steed his own. The show was slated to replace *Police Surgeon* and Macnee, as sidekick to Ian Hendry's Dr David Keel, was left to his own devices. The actor (told by his mum that he was a cousin of quintessential Englishman David Niven) created a cultured, droll agent who relied on wits more than weapons. Producer Sydney Newman, inspired by a news story from Kenya about a woman whose family was attacked by terrorists, made Steed's partner female. In the early 1960s, leatherclad **Honor Blackman** using martial arts to defeat her male opponents was revolutionary stuff – Cathy Gale was the first truly liberated female character on television.

Blackman's replacement – **Diana Rigg** – played Emma Peel. The name was derived from 'man-appeal', which she had buckets of, along with a relaxed charm and teasing wit – one arch of her eyebrows conveyed far more than any scripted joke. With some (literally) fantastic storylines and the chemistry between Steed and Peel, *The Avengers* hit its creative and commercial peak, being sold to 120 countries. Things were never as good after Rigg left in 1967. Her successor **Linda Thorson** played Tara King as a ditzier, more conventionally feminine character but lacked Rigg's gift for humour. The show petered out after two more seasons – the weak 1970s resuscitation, co-starring **Joanna Lumley** (Purdey) and a second sidekick, **Gareth Hunt** (Gambit) was as original as its title *The New Avengers*. 'It was bad and ordinary, unimaginative and not interesting,' Macnee sighed later.

+ + + + + + + + + + + +

★ Bagpuss ★

BBC1 1974 **VHS, DVD**

Almost everyone knows that only 12 episodes of **Fawlty Towers** were ever made, but it comes as some surprise that the ubiquitous **Bagpuss** called it a day after 13. Like *Fawlty Towers*, it has been rerun many times (almost 30 on the BBC alone), proving essential viewing for many generations.

Created and produced by **Oliver Postgate** and **Peter Firmin**'s

As Emma Peel, Diana Rigg had plenty of men appeal. Except, for some reason, with train drivers

Smallfilms, *Bagpuss* combines live-action animation of an endearing cast of characters with a simple narrative formula offering scope for songs and stories. In each episode, Emily (played by Firmin's daughter) drops into her shop (which didn't sell anything) to deposit an unidentified object someone has mislaid. Bagpuss, her magical candy-striped cloth cat, wakes up, followed by the mice on the mouse organ, Madeline the rag doll, Professor Yaffle and Gabriel the toad. Together they identify the item, fix it up and put it in the shop window in case the owner strolls by. A carved wooden bookend in the shape of a woodpecker, Professor Yaffle scorns the mice. But they get their revenge – once conning him into thinking they could make chocolate biscuits out of bread crumbs and butter beans.

As **Ricky Tomlinson** has proved, we like our TV heroes baggy and a bit loose at the seams, so Bagpuss had it made. Tales like 'The Bony King Of Nowhere' provide a real sense of bygone comforts. *Bagpuss* was voted Britain's favourite children's TV show in a 1999 poll, leading to 100 lines of merchandise and a comfortable retirement for all concerned.

✛ ✛ ✛ ✛ ✛ ✛ ✛ ✛ ✛ ✛ ✛ ✛ ✛

★ Banana Splits ★

BBC1 1969–71 **VHS**

First there were the **Beatles**. Then the **Monkees**. And then, in this unique case of evolution in reverse, came the **Banana Splits**. Their ancestry was at its most brazen with the drummer, **Bingo**, whose name rhymed with **Ringo** and whose looks were loosely modelled on **Mickey Dolenz**. Sorry Mickey. The Splits songs were Tin Pan Alley's Fab Four retreads. The classic 'I Enjoy Being A Boy' included the 'I Am A Walrus'-style verse 'I live in a purple plum mansion/In the midst of a strawberry stream/And mellifluous bells ring out softly/From a hill of vanilla fudge cream.'

Flipping like a pancake, popping like a cork, **Drooper**, **Bingo**, **Fleegle** and **Snorky** could be guaranteed not to get rebellious like Mickey, Davy, Mike and Pete. Anybody could wear those furry outfits, a painful truth Dan 'Drooper' Winkless soon discovered. When the Splits staged their very own concert tour, local actors were hired to save fees and expenses.

Yet **William Hanna** and **Joseph Barbera** hired the best voices: **Paul**

Winchell (aka Dick Dastardly) supplied Fleegle's drawl, while **Daws Butler** (Huckleberry Hound, Yogi Bear) was the voice of Bingo. Snorky, who only honked, is officially 'voiced' by **Don Messick**, but Messick denies it. **Allan Melvin** voiced Drooper, the guitar-playing lion who answered the mail. To finish the Fab Four/Furry Four analogy, Snorky is the quiet Beatle George Harrison, Fleegle/McCartney and Drooper/Lennon.

To watch the *Banana Splits* is to realise just how weird American TV can be. The phrase 'Hold the bus!' was the signal for the Splits to behave as if they had been driven mad by a mailbox which wouldn't give Fleegle the mail, a bin which wouldn't accept Drooper's trash, and the odious **Sour Grape** girls. It was all too much for America's **TV Guide** which huffed: 'This is a fine program for the one-and-under set, for two-and-older you might be better off with straight commercials.'

> 'Dear Drooper, who invented spaghetti?' 'Spaghetti was invented by a guy who used his noodle'

In their ruthless determination to provide entertainment, the Splits also showed cartoons of the **Arabian Knights, The Three Musketeers**, and an adventure called **Danger Island**, famous for the cry 'Oh oh Chango it's danger island!' and because **Richard Donner**, director of **Lethal Weapon**, got his start on it. Let's end with a Dear Drooper letter (they were, **Winkless** insists, real fan mail): 'Dear Drooper, who invented spaghetti?' To which Drooper replied sagely: 'Spaghetti was invented by a guy who used his noodle.'

✛ ✛ ✛ ✛ ✛ ✛ ✛ ✛ ✛ ✛ ✛ ✛

★ Batman and The Six Million Dollar Man ★

ITV 1966–68) **VHS, DVD**   ITV 1973–79 **VHS, DVD**

Holy bat bulges! 'Muscular older man takes teenage boy under his wing, sort of thing,' said Burt Ward, musing on the show that made him an unlikely sex symbol. 'What's so unnatural about two guys running around wearing tights and living together?' Certainly the friendship between millionaire-cum-superhero Bruce Wayne (West) and his side-kick-cum-boy-wonder Dick Grayson (Ward) didn't seem any odder than anything else in this sublimely ridiculous series.

19

The central relationship, the costumes, the gadgets (far funnier than Bond's, especially the soluble batsuit tablets: just drop them into a full glass and wait for the suits to form), the cartoon words ('Kapow!'), the double entendres ('Hi Robin, my name is Pussycat but you can call me Cat') – all seemed of a piece. While West and Ward deserve an award for keeping a straight face through scenes where they only escaped by the skin of their shark repellent spray, acting honours must go to **Stafford Repp** as **Commissioner O'Hara**, Gotham's dumb Irish police chief – such consistent, measured stupidity is rare indeed.

'What's so unnatural about two guys wearing tights and living together?'

Ward and West did some stunts to save money ('There were many occasions, I was tied down and the special effects guys were setting dynamite and I would smell liquor on their breath,' recalls Ward) but the show still became too costly to survive, despite good ratings. To the end *Batman* was broadcast with a warning to kids not to fly off their sofas in emulation of the winged wonder. Holy fork in the road!

Five years after The Caped Crusader went off air, **The Six Million Dollar Man** arrived to hog prime-time viewing, and his powers were almost as ludicrous as Batman's gadgets. Being rebuilt after a crash (remember they had the technology) astronaut Steve Austin (**Lee Majors**) emerged with bionic legs which enabled him to run faster than cars, a bionic right arm to lift the heaviest weights, and fab new eyes with infrared vision which could see farther and through anything.

Based on Martin Caidin's novel *Cyborg*, Austin was sent on dangerous, or just strange, missions which required his super powers. One week he chased evil spies, the next wrestled with Bigfoot. Austin had no Robin-style sidekick although he would share quality screen time with Jaime Sommers, aka The Bionic Woman (hey, even Batman could call on Batgirl). **Lindsay Wagner** (not dissimilar in looks to Majors' real-life love Farrah Fawcett) was hired as Sommers, his childhood sweetheart and victim of a freak parachuting accident necessitating bionic surgery. She died when her body rejected the new limbs but the fans ensured that Sommers was resurrected in her own series. The bionic twosome wed in the 1994 TV movie *Bionic Ever After* which also gave us a bionic dog, Max. This being the 1970s – an era of rampant inflation – there was also a seven million dollar man, Barney Miller, built so that Austin could have a break.

Despite the fact that everyone over a certain age can recite the 'We can rebuild him' intro by heart, the series only ran for five seasons. The producers couldn't decide if Austin was a new James Bond or Superman. Adults didn't like the cut-and-paste style of filming, and penny-pinching Universal didn't help, insisting that submarine shots be taken from *Ice Station Zebra*, and robotic noises recycled from *How To Frame A Figg*.

None of this bothered the kids, who demanded action figures of their hero – and his fantastic body parts. One seven-year-old from Philadelphia pretended he was blind in the hope of getting a bionic eye. When that didn't work, he tried to stop his parents' car with his foot in the hope of gaining a bionic leg. All he got was a letter from Lee Majors explaining

Grey is not an especially flattering colour if you're a superhero with love handles

that the show wasn't real – the 1970s equivalent of the Batman 'don't try this at home' warning. In case you're wondering, with inflation, the Six Million Dollar Man would cost $24.4m to make today.

+ + + + + + + + + + + + +

⋆ Black Adder ⋆

BBC1 1982 –89; 1999 **VHS, DVD**

Black Adder is that rarity: a comedy whose most indelible impression on our collective memory was the quietly tragic scene where the protagonists steeled themselves for certain death in the madness of World War I.

As with many works of genius, *Black Adder*'s merits were dismissed at first. The original pilot never aired and the BBC almost cancelled it before it began, but after some changes, including the replacement of the original Baldrick (Philip Fox) by **Tony Robinson**, a classic was born. Rewriting history from the 15th-century War of the Roses (with Richard III defeating Henry VII for once) through the reign of George IV (where he gave his patronage to Samuel Johnson's dictionary, despite it being published 56 years before George's accession), it all ended abruptly during World War I with the lasting image of Black Adder with two pencils stuck up his nose.

Although best remembered for Black Adder's sardonic wit ('The eyes are open, the mouth moves, but Mr Brain has long since departed, eh Perce?'), the series also boasted a host of worthy adversaries, created by **Richard Curtis**, **Rowan Atkinson** and from series two, **Ben Elton**. (If **Michael Grade**, then at the BBC, had had his way, there wouldn't have been a second series: 'not enough laughs to the pound' he said; he was placated only when location shooting was ditched for a cheaper, studio-bound format).

Black Adder's dung-smelling, turnip-loving servant Baldrick was the butt of much of the humour – 'To you, Baldrick, the Renaissance is just something that happened to other people, isn't it!' – but **Hugh Laurie**, **Stephen Fry** and **Tim McInnerny** also contributed a whole variety of great sitcom characters. (Laurie is best remembered as Prince George: 'You know, Black Adder, for me socks are like sex. Lots of it about and I never seem to get any'). There were appearances too by **Peter Cook**, **Miranda Richardson** (Queenie in Series 2) and **Robbie Coltrane** (Samuel Johnson in Series 3).

Two years after the Millennium special, *Black Adder Back & Forth*, there are still cries for a fifth series. Curtis has resisted such calls – 'There are only four gospels, for God's sake' – but it's got to be more fun than *Notting Hill 2* (but then *Notting Hill* was, itself, *Four Weddings And A Funeral 2*).

+ + + + + + + + + + + +

★ Blake's 7 ★

BBC1 1978–81 **VHS**

Created by *Dr Who*'s Terry Nation, *Blake's 7* was a rare British effort at adult space drama – a tough, cynical, pulp sci-fi adventure that veered between camp and poetic. At its worst it was like psychedelic panto, but at its best – including the third season's bleak cliffhanger 'Terminal' and much of the twisting final season – it was cracking stuff.

Hero Roj Blake (**Gareth Thomas**) was a resistance leader framed by Federation administrators on Earth for crimes he didn't commit. Bound for a penal planet, he escaped and assembled the original seven: himself, computer genius embezzler Avon, smuggler Jenna, cowardly thief Vila,

Blakes 7: Costumes from Abba's wardrobe, props found at the bottom of a BBC cupboard. Triffic

muscleman Gan, telepath Cally and Zen – the computer of the fortuitously appropriated *Liberator*, a very cool spaceship of mysterious alien origin.

The fanatical Blake made it their mission to destroy the Federation, a hopeless quest that saw them embroiled with double-crossing criminals, bizarre aliens and mad scientists. Losses, including Blake and the *Liberator*, saw the arrival of weapons expert Dayna, mercenary Tarrant (no relation to Chris) and the beautiful crackshot Soolin, plus portable brainbox Orac and obsequious computer Slave, on a new ship *Scorpio*, under the ruthless leadership of sexy, sneering Avon (**Paul Darrow**). Their outrageous nemesis was power-mad supreme commander Servalan (Jacqueline Pearce).

The costumes may have been reminiscent of **Abba**'s 'Waterloo' period, and the favoured locations quarries and industrial estates (innovation being at odds with a tight BBC budget). But when the four-year fight between the rebel band and their corrupt Federation foes culminated in tragedy with the cast's massacre at Christmas 1981, fans felt truly bereft.

+ + + + + + + + + + + + +

★ The Borgias ★

BBC2 1981

For those who weren't there the first time, the only way to relish the glory that was **The Borgias** is to relive the dialogue. 'As vice-chancellor of the

> **'Your horse and your foot await.'**
> **'My horse?'**
> **'And your foot'**

Holy Church, should you not be here to welcome the King of France?' 'By the bones of Christ!' 'Rimini has fallen. We must take Ferrara unaided.' 'Ferrara unaided! Are you mad?' 'Your horse and your foot await.' 'My horse?' 'And your foot.' 'Help me retake Urbino.' 'Retake Urbino! Are you mad?' 'God is good to us, my friends!' 'The man lies!' Repeat ad nauseam, with minor variations, for seven episodes.

The series earned a Vatican censure, which it deserved – if only for the dialogue. The excess of historical detail may be due to scriptwriter **John Prebble**, author of such not-at-all risible historical books as *Culloden*, but he probably wasn't responsible for the stand-out scene, when the cast crawled half-naked on the floor picking up chestnuts with their mouths.

The wonder, after watching just one episode, was how the 15th century's most infamous family held on to power long enough to occupy the Papacy and inspire Machiavelli's *The Prince*. As depicted, they were the kind of family who inspired others to homicidal rage, not by their crimes but with their conversation. All concerned (especially producer **Mark Shivas**) had hoped this would follow in the sandals of *I Claudius*, but it ended up rivalling *Up Pompeii* for cheap laughs.

+ + + + + + + + + + + +

★ Buffy The Vampire Slayer ★

SKY/BBC2 1998– **VHS, DVD**

After a 1992 US film based on his script had been a box office flop, Joss Whedon reclaimed the idea for *Buffy The Vampire Slayer* (a cheerleader is trained to stake creatures of the night) and remade it for TV. Thus was a cult TV series born and **Sarah Michelle Gellar** launched as a pin-up.

Gellar, who'd made her acting debut as a child in the daytime soap *All My Children*, was cast as the quick-quipping blonde who moves with her mother to sleepy Sunnydale, only to find her vampire-slaying skills are needed because the town is built on a hellmouth (a gravitation point for ghoulies, demons et al). To help her as best they can, Buffy has a Watcher (think father-figure with an unhealthy knowledge of the undead) in the stiff-upper-lip British librarian Giles (**Anthony Stewart Head**) and a few pals: Willow (who goes from computer nerd to amateur witch), Xander (her best friend), mysterious vampire and Buffy's amour **Angel**, and later, Anya (an ex-vengeance demon) and Tara (another amateur witch).

Whedon's blend of vampires, demons, killer robots and the adolescent world certainly appealed to teens, but a deliberate policy of sharp dialogue and adult situations also earned a much older following. 'Because the series was set in a high school, we originally targeted school and college age viewers,' he says. 'But my target audience has always been me.' With six successful series (in which Buffy has died twice, gained a teenage sister, lost a vampire lover and sung through an entire episode), plus a spin-off series *Angel*, there must be a lot of people like Whedon out there.

+ + + + + + + + + + + +

★ Captain Scarlet And The Mysterons ★

ITV 1967-68 **VHS, DVD**

'This is the voice of the Mysterons.' The baddies from Mars had a voice as deep as the Marianna Trench – a voice which, if you were less than ten years old when you first heard it, seemed to embody evil. Yet the voice of the Mysterons (**Donald Gray**) was also the voice of good guy **Colonel White**, commander of **Spectrum**, Earth's security command.

There may have been a social message in the fact that the organisation protecting the Earth was called Spectrum. **Gerry Anderson** had always wanted to bring black characters into his supermarionation shows but sales to the American South had worked against such a move. By 1967, TV politics had changed and Trinidadian **Lieutenant Green** and Japanese **Harmony Angel** joined the cast – although the baddy was still called **Captain Black** (also voiced by the versatile vocal cords of Donald Gray).

'Tell me, have any of you seen Captain Burnt Sienna recently?'

Captain Scarlet was designed to be as 'serious' as any TV show whose characters spoke with the aid of strings could be, so despite the presence of five gorgeous female pilots known collectively as the Angels (far more charismatic and sexy than the human ones Charlie recruited in the 1970s) there was little love interest or even humour. And for an organisation with such a mighty mission, Spectrum didn't have that many agents on its books: its palette evidently only ran as far as **Captain Magenta** and **Captain Ochre**. Sadly, there was to be no room for Captain Burnt Sienna.

The Mysterons themselves were never shown because Gerry feared extra-terrestrial life would be found soon and he didn't want his Martians to become obsolete. As a result, the Mysterons were much scarier than the villains in **Thunderbirds** or **Stingray**'s inept

> **The baddies from Mars had a voice as deep as the Marianna Trench**

Aquaphibians who wouldn't scare plankton in their Terror Fish craft.

The most memorable part of the show was the title sequence: the Mysteron onion-ring like Os, the smashing glass and the cry of a cat which had somehow got embroiled in this war of the worlds. As the Mysterons made the basic tactical error of saying just how they would terrorise Earth, the outcome of each episode was never in doubt. But as long as the Angels took flight, it didn't really matter.

+ + + + + + + + + + + +

★ The Clangers ★

BBC1 1969–74 **VHS, DVD**

After their success with **Noggin The Nog** and **Pogles Wood**, writers and animators Oliver Postgate and Peter Firmin were commissioned by the BBC to create a new prime-time children's show in colour. Colourful language was what Auntie got. Postgate's technique was to write a script then whistle the words to resemble human speech as closely as possible. But when a door stuck and **Major Clanger** whistled, 'Oh sod it! The bloody thing's stuck again', Postgate was summoned by the BBC and told to moderate the Clangers' language. In the end he convinced the troubled management that, 'If people have nice minds they will hear, "Oh dear me."'

The Clangers prepare a trip to Earth to see that nice Mr Armstrong who lives at Cape Canaveral

The Clangers first aired in 1969, just as America landed on the moon. After inviting children to picture what life on other planets might be like, the series showed them long-nosed, pink, mice-like creatures who whistled to one another, ate green soup and blue-string pudding, and spent their days putting space trash to good use. They shared their charming world and entertaining adventures (which usually mixed a cosy moral tale with droll humour) with such imaginative creatures as **The Soup Dragon**, **The Iron Chicken**, and the **Froglets** (who travelled in a magic top hat).

Offscreen, the show had strong family roots. Postgate, responsible for the storylines, was inspired by his twin sons' belief that a soup-eating giant called Edward lived behind the moon, while the Clangers – based on a character called the Moon Mouse who had appeared in *Noggin The Nog* – were knitted by Firmin's wife. The show – which fascinated parents as much as kids – lasted three seasons, and included a special edition to tie

28

in with the 1974 general election in which a Froglet tried to get elected. The creatures also appeared on *Dr Who*, when **The Master** spotted what he thought was an interesting life form, only to be told they were puppets.

+ + + + + + + + + + + +

★ CNN International ★

cnn 1991–

How can an entire channel possibly be cult? As anyone who has dipped a toe into the self-referential world that is **Cable News Network** will tell you, it has always marched to its own peculiar beat. True, it hasn't been quite as eccentric since founder **Ted Turner** joined with Time Warner. And, like many news organisations, it has been slapping on the make-up of late, trying to tempt a younger audience. But none of this matters because CNN is still a parallel universe where even the weather is odd.

Consider the cities with which CNN gives a flavour of Earth's climate. Oslo and Copenhagen are listed, but not Stockholm. Berlin but not Brussels? And why does St Louis (pop: 348,189) make it while Memphis (pop: 650,100) doesn't? Are secret meteorological criteria at work, or is someone at HQ in Atlanta just throwing darts at a map of the world?

This isn't the only CNN mystery. Nobody has satisfactorily explained the semi-continuous presence of **Larry King**, an 'interviewer' who has all the characteristics of the classic American journalist (braces, striped shirt and stoop all out of *Hold The Front Page*), except as a curiosity.

In the old days, the channel gave viewers a break from its ceaseless news bombardment by cutting to brochure-style shots of Marriott Hotels (real or ersatz) around the globe but now the ad department actually sells ads, this glossy variation on the old potters wheel is a too-rare sight.

All of which may make it sound as though CNN is not to be cherished but it definitely is. If you want to know if the Kazakh energy minister had to resign in that bribery scandal, CNN is the network for you. The channel even has a 30-minute programme called *Inside Africa* in an age when its rivals don't get much closer to that continent than Gibraltar.

For superficial males, CNN offers the finest selection of thinking man's crumpet since Joan Bakewell's heyday with **Saxon Baines**, **Willow Bay** (no, it's not a beach in *Home And Away*: she anchors CNN's LA bureau) and **Rosemary Church**, all gorgeous and you instinctively sense, much cleverer than you. Female viewers aren't as fortunate, having to make do with the less obvious charms of **Jonathan Mann**, who looks as if he might have been booted out of the Munster family for being too normal.

CNN is not without absurdities: one lowlight is *Pinnacle*, a series about people who have reached the top and are addicted to phallic symbols. But even at its worst, it's still better than the amateurish **News 24** or the slick but dull **Sky News**. Oh, and it breaks the odd news story, too. Someone called Saddam Hussein has been known to give it an interview or two.

+ + + + + + + + + + + + +

⋆ Cracker ⋆

ITV 1993–96 **VHS**

Writer **Jimmy McGovern** and producer **Gub Neal** had envisaged their anti-hero **Cracker** as a thin, wiry man, and chose **Robert Lindsay** to star. They ended up with **Robbie Coltrane** but the switch proved to be the making of *Cracker*. Coltrane was intelligent, warm and charismatic – and a cynical, cruel, fatally flawed oral compulsive. Anti-hero Fitz freely

> **'I smoke too much,
> I drink too much,
> I gamble too much,
> I am too much'**

admits his vices (McGovern based them on his own): 'I smoke too much. I drink too much. I gamble too much. I am too much.' But rather than do anything about them, he contents himself with goading and bullying the suspects about their inadequacies.

With Fitz as a psychologist, McGovern combined the classic whodunnit of police dramas with the psychological why-he-dunnit. The interrogations were the show's set pieces but the classic cop clichés were still on hand. Fitz had an unhappy, complex private life. His ally in the force was not a dependable unquestioning type like Morse's Lewis but Penhaligon (or Panhandle)(**Geraldine Somerville**) – strong-willed, ambitious and female, with whom, inevitably, he was drawn into an affair.

McGovern's writing defined the series. Fresh from *Brookside*, with the advice of **Alan Bleasdale** still fresh in his mind – 'keep that (mouth) shut and these (ears) open. You're far too inexperienced to be mouthing off' – McGovern realised his best bet was to write from his roots. He began by basing Fitz and DS Jimmy Beck (**Lorcan Cranitch**) on parts of his own personality. McGovern's gritty realism, often mistaken as glamourising violence, was at its most compelling in 'To Be A Somebody' in which the deranged Albie (**Robert Carlyle**) seeks revenge for the **Hillsborough** disaster. This started McGovern's obsession with the tragedy which would later lead to a powerful one-off two-hour drama.

The show ended with a one-off special in 1996, with Coltrane eager to move on (to *Harry Potter* no less) and McGovern convinced there were no more big issues on which to base each episode. Fitz's big speeches had also begun to tremble on the edge of cliché, which would have been a pity. On form, *Cracker* was as weighty and hard to ignore as Coltrane himself.

✢ ✢ ✢ ✢ ✢ ✢ ✢ ✢ ✢ ✢ ✢ ✢ ✢

★ Crossroads ★

ITV 1964–88; 2001–

It was the butt of a billion cheap gags; its characters disappeared as mysteriously as planes in the Bermuda Triangle, and its sets wobbled like a floating voter. But *Crossroads*, the Midlands soap set in a motel far stranger than Norman Bates', ran for 24 years and at its peak attracted audiences of 16 million. It never enjoyed the street cred or witty dialogue of **Corrie** but it had its own treasures, such as Brummie char **Amy Turtle** (Ann George) who made an art of line-fluffing, and plots, from terrorism to test-tube babies, that made us believe that if the extraordinary could happen in a village like King's Oak, it could happen on our doorsteps too.

But it didn't matter if walls moved, actors missed their lines or if a receptionist answered the phone before it rang (to be fair, this only ever happened in **Victoria Wood**'s send-up **Acorn Antiques**). Holding it all together was matriarchal Meg, played by **Noele Gordon**. *Crossroads* centred on Meg (originally Richardson, later Mortimer and in between Ryder but she found out hubby Malcolm had tried to poison her) and her two children, Jill (**Jane Rossington**) and Sandy. By the end only Jill was left. **Roger Tonge** (Sandy) died in 1981. Meg was controversially written

31

out the same year, tearfully waving goodbye on the QE2. Jill, never adept at choosing men, was one of three originals (the others being **Doris Luke**, played by Kathy Staff, aka Nora Batty, and **Adam Chance**, played by Tony Adams) in Carlton's 2001 revival, but she was killed off by Adam on their wedding day (she'd married and divorced him in the original).

Many thought that the soap would die with Meg. It almost did. Meg's co-owner, heartthrob David Hunter (**Ronald Allen**), was axed in 1985. Later owners Nicola Freeman (**Gabrielle Drake**, sister of cult singer-songwriter Nick) and Tommy 'Bomber' Lancaster (**Terence Rigby**) failed to save the show. But no British drama series had sustained a punishing five-day schedule before (retakes were frowned on) and few have tried since.

✛ ✛ ✛ ✛ ✛ ✛ ✛ ✛ ✛ ✛ ✛ ✛ ✛

★ Dynasty ★

BBC1 1981–89

Nobody was ever in any doubt as to how they felt about **Dynasty**. The plotlines, the shoulder pads, the villainess (**Joan Collins** as Blake Carrington's ex-wife Alexis) all demanded a reaction. The sheer relentless ludicrousness was impressive. Even the minor plotlines (Adam trying to kill Jeff by redecorating his offices with poisonous paint) were daft in this 20th-century fairytale world, full of beautiful people, sparkling jewels, and an apparently endless supply of long-lost relatives.

Hoping to rival *Dallas*, *Dynasty* (originally titled *Oil* – or should that be unoriginally titled?) featured the wedding of oil baron Blake Carrington (**John Forsythe**) to his secretary, Krystle Grant (**Linda Evans**). Krystle was a perfect (Nancy) Reaganite heroine, beautiful, submissive, bland and so virtuous it made you queasy – yet ambitious enough to seduce the boss. While Blake and Krystal struggled with the difficult business of being very rich and almost as idle, daughter Fallon was having an affair (her marriage to Jeff just a business deal), and his gay son Stephen was having an affair – with a woman – prior to Blake killing Stephen's gay lover, Ted.

All this was before Alexis arrived in Denver, bent on revenge. Alexis was exactly what TV had been lacking: **a queen bitch**. Her introduction as the nemesis to Krystle and Blake had two consequences: 1) it ensured that

Dynasty's infernal triangle: A queen bitch, a murderer and a woman so virtuous it made you queasy

one of the main characters had some character and 2) made *Dynasty* the highest-rated show in America, despite *Dallas'* 'Who Shot JR?' cliffhanger.

Despite all the plot twists (affairs, murders, rapes, terrorist plots, and even a fight between Krystle and a doppelganger), it was a simple kiss – between Krystle and Daniel Reece (**Rock Hudson**) that generated the most intense publicity. Just before dying from AIDS in 1985, Hudson had gone public with his illness and America, convinced that Hudson had put Evans at risk of contracting the disease, rose in ill-informed outrage.

True to form, *Dynasty* went out in a blaze of glory. With Krystle on her way to Switzerland for a brain operation, and Collins having announced that season nine would be her last, it seemed *Dynasty*'s days were over. The show ended with Alexis, Dex (**Michael Nadar**) and Blake all lying in pools of their own blood. In true soap opera style, despite being thrown from a balcony and shot, they still managed to return for a reunion in 1991.

Dynasty proved a hard act to follow for its principals. Forsythe couldn't find another saga to suit, Evans ended up launching a line of fitness centres and Nadar took the Hollywood route of drink-driving, drug-dealing and going into rehab. Joan Collins, though, became a legend. Alexis had ensured that her previously suspect acting career (*The Stud*, anyone?) was forgotten.

33

+ + + + + + + + + + + +

34

Celine Dion won Eurovision in 1988, possibly because the judges mistook her for David Essex

★ Eurovision Song Contest ★

BBC1 1956–

The Eurovision Song Contest's fanfare of 'Te Deum' might be horribly apt for some (try saying it out loud), but for millions from Lisbon to Ljubljana, that Saturday night in May is still the musical extravaganza of the year. Invented by Frenchman Marcel Baison, it aims to promote peace and unity through song. In truth, thanks to blatantly political voting and the odd boycott, it has never led to much harmony, on stage or off. In 1974, Portugal's entry was even used as the signal to start a revolution.

It all started in Switzerland in 1956, with just seven countries entering. Royaume Uni joined in a year later when Patricia Bredin finished seventh. It would be a decade before Albion prevailed, thanks to **Sandie Shaw**'s 'Puppet On A String' (a song she hates to this day). **Lulu**, **Brotherhood Of Man**, **Bucks Fizz** and **Katrina & The Waves** have since joined the roll of honour; Britain has also scored 15 second places, among them **Cliff Richard** belting out 'Congratulations' in figure-hugging blue crushed velvet. Ireland are the all-time champs with seven wins (four in the 1990s), as satirised by **Father Ted**. Norway have yet to get the hang of Eurovision, though the phrase 'nul points' is never actually used during the contest.

The fall of the Berlin Wall gave the Communist bloc not only freedom and Levis but the chance to enter Eurovision, forcing the organisers to introduce promotion and relegation to limit the number of entries. The 1990s saw various bids to update the event, with phone voting and a more modern approach to selecting songs (thank you, **Jonathan King**) but it remains, as **Terry Wogan** has it, 'a monument to magnificent foolishness'.

✦✦✦✦✦✦✦✦✦✦✦✦✦

★ The Fall And Rise Of Reginald Perrin ★

BBC1 1976–79 **VHS**

It was Labour MP **John Stonehouse** who did a 'Reggie Perrin' for real, leaving his clothes on a beach to fake his own death and vanishing in the summer of 1974 – after David Nobbs had written his novel but before it had been published. Yet, 25 years later, when a Somerset father did the same, he was said to have done a 'Reggie Perrin' not a 'John Stonehouse'.

Reginald Iolanthe Perrin's tale of crushing responsibility, utter boredom and longing for a second chance is as relevant today as in the 1970s. Yet the sitcom had a troubled journey to the screen. Nobbs' first attempt, a tragic play, was deemed too depressing. He then wrote a novel which Granada wanted to turn into a drama starring **Ronnie Barker** but Nobbs' agent insisted it should be a sitcom. The **BBC** then bought it, an executive called Jimmy Gilbert meeting Nobbs to discuss casting. 'Anyone in mind for the role?' asked Gilbert. 'Yes, Ronnie Barker,' said Nobbs. 'Good, **Leonard Rossiter** it is then,' said Gilbert.

Filming was tough technically, the farting armchairs often farting several seconds after the characters had stood up. But the cast, from Rossiter down, made what could have ended up as mere whimsy very credible indeed. **Pauline Yates** as Perrin's wife, **John Barron** as Reggie's boss CJ and **Geoffrey Palmer** as the brother-in law Jimmy who was always having a 'cock-up on the catering front' stood out from a very strong cast.

The catchphrases, especially CJ's 'I didn't get where I am today', helped steer the viewer through what is, by the standards of today's sitcoms, a massive ensemble cast. Reggie's excuses for his tardiness (he wasn't always 11 minutes late, he was 17 and 22 minutes late in series two) were almost as popular, the best being 'escaped puma, Chessington North'.

Nobbs took a risk in not trying to be funny all the time, especially in the episodes after Perrin's fake death, and he had a wonderful ear for dialogue. At one point CJ confessed, 'I didn't get where I am today by thinking. My father caught me thinking once and do you know what he said to me? "CJ," he said – we were never close.' Lines like that explain why Reginald Iolanthe Perrin will never be left to rest in peace.

✛✛✛✛✛✛✛✛✛✛✛✛

★ Father Ted ★

Channel 4 1995–98 **VHS, DVD**

Father Ted is a religious satire where the inside of a church is never shown. Instead, the laughs are based around three resident priests (one stupid, one alcoholic and the hard-done-by eponymous hero trying to live with both) and their neurotic tea-making housekeeper Mrs Doyle.

(Her first name, Joan, was dropped at the last minute.) Variations took the form of trips away (usually in a naff caravan), eccentric parishioners and visiting priests/nuns/alcoholic gameshow hosts.

Playing hyperactive Father Noel was the making of **Graham Norton**, while Father Larry Duff became a star in the style of *South Park*'s Kenny by incurring some terrible misfortune – from driving off a cliff to being stampeded by donkeys – every time Ted rang his mobile. Yet the show was at its funniest in the interplay between the three priests, especially when Dougal (the sublime eejit played by **Ardal O'Hanlon**) waxed theological: 'That whole loaves and fishes thing is mad. You're not supposed to believe it, are you Ted?'

> **'That whole loaves and fishes thing is mad. You're not supposed to believe it, are you Ted?'**

Much of *Father Ted*'s surreal comedy drew on real life. Dougal and Ted competing in the Eurovision Song Contest with 'My Lovely Horse' was an allusion to the rumour that, having won the Contest three times in a row, Ireland couldn't afford to host it again and lost deliberately. And the *Stars In Their Eyes* contest was based on Ireland's *All Priests Roadshow* – even the dancing priest was based on a real-life man of the cloth in Northern Ireland. There are obviously some things you just can't make up.

Dermot Morgan (Ted) always said the third series would be his last, but his untimely death in 1998 necessitated a rewrite. He died five days before the last series was aired, and the writers replaced the final scene, which was to show a depressed Father Ted joining suicidal Father Kevin on a windowsill, with a montage of clips from the series.

✛ ✛ ✛ ✛ ✛ ✛ ✛ ✛ ✛ ✛ ✛ ✛

★ Fawlty Towers ★
BBC2 1975–79 **VHS, DVD**

'This is a very boring situation. The script has nothing but very clichéd characters and I cannot see anything but a disaster if we go ahead with it.' That was the verdict of one BBC executive, in a memo which has done many rounds of Auntie's light entertainment department. *The Daily Mirror* agreed, dismissing the show with the words 'Long John, short on jokes'.

At first, the executive and the *Mirror* were almost proved right: the first series attracted just three million viewers. Yet word of mouth made the second one a hit and reruns have graced top 20 ratings almost ever since.

The tangled origins of the show are told elsewhere (see p370) but the series had one very simple root: John Cleese's psyche. In university at Cambridge, his future colleague Eric Idle noted, 'John's always had that streak – half-caught by the English class system, half despising it.'

Fawlty, as the incompetent, fawning hotelier with the frighteningly competent wife Sybil (the unforgettable **Prunella Scales**) was initially grotesquely servile to his VIP guests but quickly came to detest them when his flattery went unrewarded. Even Fawlty's famous rudeness ('Whose fault is it then, you cloth-eared bint? Denis Compton's?', 'Is this a piece of your brain?' etc etc) can be seen as a cathartic release for Cleese, who admitted he was badly bullied at school because 'I had a lot of problems asserting normal healthy aggression.'

> **'Whose fault is it then, you cloth-eared bint? Denis Compton's?'**

Cleese's comedy works in mathematical fashion with his then wife and co-author **Connie Booth** providing some of the strange emotional juxtapositions Terry Gilliam brought to Python's comedy. Booth always liked the episodes where Fawlty did something utterly unexpected, like smacking himself on his bottom and saying 'Who's a naughty boy then?'

Each episode took six weeks to write and film, partly because the scripts were twice as thick as a typical sitcom script – also why the episodes lasted 40 minutes. With such complexity, the claustrophobically simple setting of a fictional Torquay hotel helped, despite the misgivings of many BBC execs who urged Cleese to take the story outdoors whenever he could.

At times, Fawlty's pain was almost too much to bear. He 'won' about as rarely as Tom did in *Tom And Jerry* and, at his worst, reminded us of our direst moments of sycophancy. BBC memos notwithstanding, Fawlty was a wonderfully rounded character, and his rage was always understandable, whether he was thrashing his broken-down Mini with a tree or high-kicking his way across the ground floor in his haste to impress the German guests with his impersonations.

Booth and Cleese called it a day, as writers and as husband and wife, after just 12 episodes. He still talks about a possible movie. 'I love the idea of Basil being invited to meet Manuel's family and getting to Heathrow and spending 14 hours waiting for the flight. He finally gets on the plane and a terrorist tries to hijack the flight. Basil is so angry he overcomes the terrorist. When the pilot says "We have to fly back to Heathrow," Basil says, "No! Fly to Spain, or I'll shoot." He arrives in Spain, is immediately arrested, spends the holiday in jail, and is released just in time to go back on the plane with Sybil.'

But Cleese insists he'll never make it. You can't really blame him.

✠ ✠ ✠ ✠ ✠ ✠ ✠ ✠ ✠ ✠ ✠ ✠ ✠

★ The flashing Blade ★

BBC 1 1969 **VHS, DVD**

Along with **Belle And Sebastian** and **White Horses**, this was one of the perennial summer holiday imports in the late 1960s and early 1970s with which Auntie tried to encourage millions of young children to switch off their TV set and do something more interesting instead.

The real star of this swashbuckler, set in a long-forgotten war between France and Spain, was its infectious theme tune about derring-do with the compelling couplet 'As long as we have done our best and no one can do more/And life and love and happiness are well worth fighting for' ('well worth fighting for' being repeated ad nauseam as the tune fades and the horses gallop into the distance).

Almost as impressive were the horses on which the Flashing Blade, aka Francois da Ricci (**Robert Etcheverry**) and his loyal aide Guillot (**Jacques Balutin**) evaded the Spanish. Due to some technical quirk, or a budget as tight as the Blade's perm, the horses set the kind of pace usually associated with Formula 1 racing cars.

The formula for each episode was almost as predictable as a Grand Prix. Ricci and Guillot, allegedly in town to help the French save the fort of Casal from Spanish siege, would stage a few pranks, this action being interspersed with some stock footage of a few Spanish cannon firing at castle walls. Yet while many dubbed imports of this decade exhibited the

39

kind of time-lapses later featured in the camerawork for BBC wildlife series, the dubbing on *The Flashing Blade* was usually impeccable.

Etcheverry sported the kind of haircut usually seen on the lead singer of Chicory Tip, while Balutin had a hint of Marty Feldman about his face. Balutin is a famous French comic actor, whose niche in TV history is doubly secure. Apart from his mugging in this classic, he also provided the voice of **Starsky** in the French dubbed version of *Starsky And Hutch*.

++++++++++++

★ Hamish Macbeth ★

BBC1 1995–97 **VHS**

Comedy dramas notoriously generate precious few laughs and not much tension. *Hamish Macbeth*, as perverse a programme as you're ever likely to stumble on at 7.15pm on BBC1 on a Sunday, was an intriguing exception to

the rule. Not many shows in this slot would dare build an episode around the Scottish villagers' horror at the slow realisation that they have dined on the lobsters that dined on the corpse of Bad Georgie McRobb. Or, for that matter, have the undertaker's conniving nephew hide in a coffin – only to be incinerated at the local crematorium.

Much of the credit goes to writer **Daniel Boyle** and star **Robert Carlyle**. The somewhat unpromising raw material was a series of reasonably selling crime books. Boyle remembers laughing at the name: 'It's so arch. It's like

Hamish Macbeth, an unusually arresting TV copper

calling an Irishman Paddy Murphy.' But with Carlyle's help, he created a memorably low key cop who, the actor noted, 'went to any length to avoid being credited with solving any crimes.'

The people of Lochdubh are as tightly knit as the inhabitants of Walton Mountain, the essential divide being between locals and outsiders rather than those on different sides of the law. When Hamish is briefly replaced, his laidback approach gives way to something closer to David Blunkett's idea of law and order. The inevitable result is that the whole village is under arrest. It's not that they're bad people: as one character says of Whisky Bob: 'He's a good man when he's sober, Hamish, but that's as rare a sight as Halley's comet.'

Carlyle's enigmatic Hamish is key. He had never wanted to be an actor until a brief encounter in a bookshop. 'I didn't realise *The Crucible* was a play until I bought it. When I started reading it, I realised it was an interesting way to disguise yourself. This would be a good way of changing who you actually were.' *Hamish Macbeth* was one of his more successful disguises, but one he stopped wearing after three series, just as the word spread about this successful combination of, as Carlyle put it, 'shortbread and cannabis'.

✛ ✛ ✛ ✛ ✛ ✛ ✛ ✛ ✛ ✛ ✛ ✛

★ Harry O and The Rockford Files ★

BBC1 1974–77   BBC1 1975–82 **VHS**

James Garner and **David Janssen** were both small on the big screen and big on the small screen. Both had already had worldwide TV hits (Garner in **Maverick**, Janssen in **The Fugitive**) and were naturals to front leftfield private eye series in the 1970s. Garner's **Jim Rockford** was an (innocent) ex-con who lived in a trailer on a Malibu beach, while Janssen's lamed retired cop **Harry Orwell** had a beach house near San Diego. Both characters owed a debt to the twin peaks of fictional Californian detectives: **Raymond Chandler**'s Philip Marlowe and **Ross MacDonald**'s Lew Archer. Like them they often helped sexy but troubled women. Both also had irate cops to placate: Dennis Becker (*Rockford*) and Manny Quinlan/KC Trench (*Harry O*).

> **Harry's car was always out of action. He chased suspects on the bus**

41

★ Calling Jim Rockford... ★

The best of Jim's answering machine

'Mr Rockford, you know what to do if you are attacked and killed? Ask for Albert Kimcee at grand opening of Happy Dawn School of Secret Arts. Win a free lesson.'

'It's Betty. I'm calling all the neighbours because Spotty is loose. If you see him, call me. Oh, don't wear musk cologne. Leopards have a thing about that.'

'It's Pete. Hope you enjoyed the cabin last week. Only next time leave the trout in the refrigerator, huh? Not in the cupboard.'

'Jim, Joel Myers at Crowell, Finch and Merriwether. We're going to court tomorrow with that Penrose fraud case but the steno misplaced your 200-page disposition. Could you come down tonight and give it again?'

Jim, Rocky and an answering machine

There were distinguishing differences, however. Harry O would do a case for free (he could afford to on his disability pension). Rockford charged $200 a day plus expenses – not that anybody saw him get paid – though he once took a distressed damsel's case for what he called his 'special sucker rate' of $23.74. And while Rockford (like Garner) was happiest spinning his car in a chase, Harry O's car was always out of action and he often chased suspects on the bus.

But the biggest difference was the ambience of the shows. *The Rockford Files* had a sunny, warm, atmosphere from the moment the fantastic theme tune kicked in and the first guest star (cue **Dionne Warwick** or **Isaac Hayes**) dropped by. Rockford was happy to go fishing with father Rocky and to acquire a surrogate family: attorney Beth Davenport and former cellmate Angel Martin (**Stuart Margolin**).

Harry O was more downbeat. The character was loosely based on Clint Eastwood's **Dirty Harry**, although Janssen played him as grumpy Harry. (Janssen had beaten **Telly Savalas** to the part, but Savalas's consolation was the title role in **Kojak**.) *Harry O* wasn't big on guest stars but it did give **Martin Sheen** and **Farrah Fawcett Majors** their big breaks.

Aficionados insist that Jim Rockford and Harry O are the greatest private eyes ever to nail villains on the small screen. That might be overstating it a bit. Garner carried his show, becoming (as **Barry Norman** once put it) television's first superstar. In both cases, though, there was a casual, but instinctive, avoidance of cliché which made them very easy to watch.

+ + + + + + + + + + + + +

★ Homicide: Life On The Streets ★

Channel 4 1993 –99 **VHS, DVD (US formats only)**

How safe are the streets of Baltimore? Detective Munch is on the stairs having a screaming row with one of his ex-wives. Detective Lewis believes it's justifiable homicide if destruction of a Funkadelic album is involved. Neatness fanatic Frank Pembleton can get anybody to confess to anything. The man in charge is Lt Giardello (**Yaphet Kotto**) – a big black man with an awful syrup who seems to get around without moving his legs and cusses, frequently, in fluent Sicilian. And let's not forget Detective Crosetti, who spent most of his days trying to solve Abe Lincoln's murder, then topped himself.

Homicide: Life On The Streets, the brainchild of **David Simon** (who wrote the book on which it is based) and **Barry Levinson** (executive producer) went way beyond dysfunctional. Other TV cops hang out in bars, these guys bought one. On one occasion, other officers from their precinct – sent to close down a hippy photo exhibition for obscenity – found the material featured a much younger, very stoned and stark naked Detective Munch, who became a station-house legend. And Detective Bolander once spent most of an episode figuring out that the 'coffoon' the woman he'd just met said she slept in was in fact a coffin.

The series also broke several moulds. There were few car chases and even less gunplay – in the only shootout of note half the squad were killed. The glamour factor was non-existent, and the criminals were more doggedly hunted than caught. The very antithesis of *Miami Vice*, *Homicide: Life On The Streets* kept itself edgy with a very subtle set of internal tensions that manifested themselves in behaviour as unexpected as it was inappropriate. The cops might have spent their working hours solving murders, but they spent their lives behaving like real people – ie they were all a bit mad and they didn't really like each other that much. Oh yes, and **John Wilkes Booth** was framed. Apparently.

+ + + + + + + + + + + + +

★ Interceptor ★

Channel 4 1989–90

Television is at its crassest when trying to stop a popular series running out of steam. When a bunch of smart arsed execs got together to give **Treasure Hunt** a fresh new slant the end result was humiliating, zero rating, total failure. Yet the need to fill countless hours of digital TV schedules has brought their strange recreation, **Interceptor**, into rehab.

In the original **Treasure Hunt** newsreader put-out-to-grass Kenneth Kendall strutted around a pseudo library with a couple of posh smart alecs issuing jumpsuit-clad Anneka Rice, her chopper pilot and myriad cameramen with instructions to help her find a treasure buried somewhere in Miss Marple land. Anneka wheezed her way down grass tracks, cadging lifts on tractors and invariably unearthing the bounty with (gasp) seconds to spare. Hurrah!

Fast forward to the late 1980s. Anneka is now failed British tennis pro Annabel Croft, a sort of Surrey Kournikova dressed like she's auditioning for a part in **Howard's Way**, while Kendall looks increasingly like a bloke from the land time forgot.

Gone is the kindly old gent in his study: Croft is in the field issuing orders to two upper-class prats in jumpsuits lost in Miss Marple land. The contestants must find hidden keys and touch hands before time is up in order to win £1,000. Sound familiar? Ah, but here's the rub. This time the toffs are chased by The Interceptor, a glowering, granite jawed Scot in a three-quarter-

Croft scans the horizon for upper-class twits

length leather coat who barks orders at his hapless chopper pilot and waves a 'zapper gun', which if it connects with the twits' backpacks, means the money box can't be opened and the loot stays locked away.

This utterly hilarious series – which featured Interceptor vs the RAF, Interceptor vs the Army on Salisbury Plain, and Interceptor vs the river police in a *Live And Let Die*-style speedboat chase across the Norfolk Broads – has now been resurrected by a desperate Challenge TV. The series ends when the great man is finally arrested by a cop and gives his name as 'Interceptor' ('No, your name sir'. 'I told you, In..ter..ceptor'). Another series, please. Oh go on, go on, go on, go on.

✛ ✛ ✛ ✛ ✛ ✛ ✛ ✛ ✛ ✛ ✛ ✛ ✛

★ Kolchak: The Night Stalker and The X-Files ★

ITV 1983–85   BBC1/2 /SKY 1994–2002 **DVD**

This is a tale of two shows which redefined the sci-fi genre: one (**The X-Files**) is the most famous TV series of the last decade. The other (**Kolchak: The Night Stalker**) has achieved limited fame, partly because **Chris Carter**, creator of Mulder and Scully, has acknowledged his debt to it.

In its context of American TV in the 1970s, **Kolchak** was the equivalent of Leonardo da Vinci doodling the first helicopters – so far ahead of its time it never stood a chance. But 17 years later, inspired by Kolchak's freaky investigations (and *The Twilight Zone* and *Close Encounters)*, Chris Carter would give us a show which almost defied genre classification.

An FBI agent stubbornly probing strange, unsolved cases – sardonic, idiosyncratic Fox Mulder (**David Duchovny**) – was teamed up with a sceptical redhead scientist – Dana Scully (**Gillian Anderson**) – in pursuit of the truth. The show was a sensation for its stylish noir ambience, exciting storytelling and teasing chemistry between deadpan Mulder and doubting Scully. Mulderisms – 'The truth is out there' – abounded, and websites, imitators and spoofs proliferated as the pair crept through murky locales with their flashlights. The show also had a nice line in psychic saddos and scary mutants (such as the liver-craving rubberman Eugene Toombs).

Kolchak (**Darren McGavin**, who guested in *The X-Files*), a seedy reporter with the world's toughest news beat, met similar perils. One

45

week he'd be in a sewer with a monster; the next he had to shoot his old aunt in the stomach with a crossbow (in reality she was a figure projected by an evil spirit). But his editor never believed him and the beasts turned into dust which blew away, leaving Kolchak as frustrated as Fox Mulder.

Kolchak was a (relatively) simple tale of man against monster but for kids in America, it was like *Halloween* every week. But **The X-Files** was also compelling for its ongoing, nigh-unfathomable story arc – 'the mythology' (expanded in a 1998 feature film), in which Mulder's personal obsession with alien abductions and the mysterious disappearance of his sister in childhood led to the discovery of heinous biological experiments, killer bees, black oil contagion and shape-shifting assassins. The vast cosmic conspiracy helped the show to endure through nine seasons.

Kolchak, in contrast, lasted just two seasons, even though its debut TV movie got 75 million viewers. ABC didn't like kicking its weekend off with this weird horror/humour hybrid although later, post-**Star Wars**, a rerun on CBS was a big hit. *Kolchak* was the kind of series where a nurse looked up from a corpse to say 'A well done autopsy is a thing of joy forever.' (The mordant tone could owe something to the fact that **David Chase**, creator of **The Sopranos**, wrote for the series.) Let's leave the last word to Kolchak, as he told a distressed citizen: 'We all have rats, sir. You should see the one I work for.' Mulder would know just what he meant.

✛ ✛ ✛ ✛ ✛ ✛ ✛ ✛ ✛ ✛ ✛ ✛ ✛

★ The League Of Gentlemen ★

BBC2 1999–   **VHS, DVD**

Royston Vasey may be 'comedian' **Roy 'Chubby' Brown**'s real name but it's best known as the setting for the disturbing but deeply funny *The League Of Gentlemen*. Co-writer and actor **Mark Gatiss** explained that the name was chosen because: 'It sounds like an ordinary town, but with something wrong.' For 'something wrong' read spectacularly quirky, darkly obsessive, incestuous, macabre, grimy, twisted and just plain sick.

The hilariously hideous characters and the dark storylines which parody small-town English culture are of infinite appeal – for fans. From Edward and Tubbs, the inbred, stranger-fearing Local Shop keepers, Barbara the

At moments like this, you realise why the local corner shop is in danger of extinction

mid-sex-change-cock-up cabbie and Pauline the sadistic, pen-befriending restart officer to the toad-obsessed, absurdly regimented Dentons (based on relations of Dyson), there are fantastic freaks aplenty. Enough, in the second series, to send Papa Lazarou ('You're my wife now') and his mutant circus scurrying from the town in fear. Alarmingly, most characters are based on the creators' own experiences and all are played by the four writers (apart from Gatiss, the script duties are shared between **Reece Shearsmith, Steve Pemberton** and **Jeremy Dyson**, who opted out of acting to produce). There's a pinch of David Lynch about it all and the four include pastiches of such horror films as *The Shining*.

The show began life at the London Fringe in 1995, moving to Radio 4, BBC TV and the stage, its progress helped by its brilliant balance of far-fetched weirdness and the hauntingly familiar. You laugh, but nervously. Many now wonder if their neighbour conducts clandestine toad-mating ceremonies every third Tuesday of the month. As the sign by the Local Shop says, 'Welcome to Royston Vasey. You'll never leave.'

+ + + + + + + + + + + +

The Lone Ranger

BBC1 1956–62 **VHS**

At the end of almost all 221 episodes of this classic series, someone would ask the identity of the masked hero who had saved the populace from evildoers. Someone else would then look puzzled and say 'I don't rightly know his real name but I've heard him called… the **Lone Ranger**.'

The most astonishing thing about this show is that it's still so famous, even though many of us weren't alive when it first ran on British TV. The masked man was a former Texas Ranger who had survived an ambush. For no obvious reason, he pretended to be dead and start a new life under a pseudonym, wearing a mask as he sought to 'rid the west of outlaws'.

The Ranger was usually played by **Clayton Moore**. (He was dropped for a couple of seasons to stop him getting cocky but the public spotted there was a different man behind the mask and Moore was recalled.) **Tonto**, the native American (played by **Jay Silverheels**, a real Mohawk chief's son and an ace boxer and lacrosse player whose real name was **Harold Smith**) had found the injured Ranger and nursed him back to life. The two then saved a wild stallion from a berserk buffalo and the grateful horse duly became the Ranger's trusty steed Silver.

The series theme, **Rossini**'s rollicking *William Tell Overture*, was a vital part of the show's success, adding to that reassuring sense that you were getting an infinitesimally different version of the same experience week in, week out. As did the catchphrases – a lively online debate continues about the real meaning of 'kemo sabe' [see p364]. The Ranger's cry of 'Hi ho Silver, away!' also became the hook for a tonguetwisting single in 1979 by a UK band called **Quantum Jump**. Regularly used by **Kenny Everett** in one of his TV series, the song ('The Lone Ranger') was a top five hit, despite – or because of – its jokey allusions to homosexuality (one line noted 'Kemo Sabe never ever had a woman') and drugs. At the same time, two successful Lone Ranger action figure ranges were launched in the US. For reasons nobody has really fathomed, the masked man is still a star.

+ + + + + + + + + + + +

⋆ The Magic Roundabout ⋆
BBC1 1965–71, 1974–77/Channel 4 1992 **VHS**

Drug-fuelled animated antics, French political satire or something to keep the little darlings quiet just before dinner? The idea that *Play School* presenter **Eric Thompson** conned the BBC into running a show about drugs, or (worse) foreign politics, is not without its appeal but *The Magic Roundabout* would be a classic even if taken at face value.

The BBC commissioned a superbly colourful stop-motion animation French kids programme, *Le Manege Enchanté* (complete with creator Serge Danot's French narration) to run for five minutes before the early evening news. Rather than hire a translator they paid Thompson to write new scripts, which he did by making up stories to fit the animation. Thompson's witty and often droll commentary made what had started life as simple, mild-mannered kids entertainment soon became a favourite with children and their parents alike.

Each character acquired a new name and personality. Pollux the Maltese Terrier became **Dougal**, a sarcastic, arrogant ('I'm here, let joy be

49

The Magic Roundabout: Revenge for De Gaulle's 'non' to British membership of the EEC? Possibly...

unconfined') shaggy dog with a sugar habit (Thompson said Dougal owed a lot to **Tony Hancock**). Flappy lost his Spanish accent and became Dylan a hippy rabbit; Ambroise (the epitome of relaxation) became Brian the Snail, the real brains of the group ('Snails are under-estimated'); and Zebulon became Zebedee, a kind of jack-in-the-box obsessed by bedtime.

Whether or not Dougal really did represent **Charles De Gaulle**, his sugar cubes LSD and Brian's sudden spinning amphetamines, was a secret Thompson took to his grave. A deeper mystery is why Channel 4 insisted on re-recording the shows with **Nigel Planer** (admittedly, his Neil in *The Young Ones* was a human Dylan), rather than just running the originals.

+ + + + + + + + + + + +

★ Marion And Geoff and A Small Summer Party ★
BBC2 2000–01 **VHS, DVD**

Though the 10-minute dramatic monologues were called *Marion And Geoff*, neither appeared in the shows. The only character was Marion's estranged husband Keith Barrett, a lonely, hapless minicab driver, played by the previously unknown **Rod Brydon**. All the darker for being shot by a lone camera fixed to the taxi dashboard, the series consisted entirely of Keith talking cheerily through his daily kicks in the teeth. Geoff has moved in with his wife and two kids, and a dodgy radio stops him getting any fares. Despite all this, the garrulous Welshman remains disturbingly sanguine. 'I don't feel like I've lost a wife,' he says. 'I feel like I've gained a friend. I would never have met Geoff if Marion hadn't left me.'

Co-written by Brydon and **Hugo Blick**, with associate producer **Steve Coogan** adding finishing touches, *Marion And Geoff* was an instant word-of-mouth hit. In September 2001, fans were treated to a one-off 50-minute special, *A Small Summer Party*. The programme introduced a distant Marion and a manipulative Geoff (Coogan), plus bemused neighbours, reluctant relatives and confused kids ('my little smashers') as a celebration of Marion's success at work descended, torturously, into her elopement with Geoff – a conclusion inevitable to everyone but Keith.

Like the series it drew from, *A Small Summer Party* brilliantly tickled the elusive nerve that lies somewhere between humour and pathos. The point is perhaps best illustrated when Keith, the eternal optimist, gives his departing wife a beefburger 'in case you get hungry on the road'.

++++++++++++

★ Monkey ★

BBC2 1979–82 **VHS, DVD**

Based on the ancient Chinese legend 'Journey To The West', in which the mischievous Monkey (or The Monkey King) accompanies the priest Tripitaka from China to India to collect the Buddhist scriptures, **Monkey** was a huge hit with British 'children of all ages'. *Saiyuuki* (as it was called in Japan) became the most profitable show Nihon Television made, and like its **The Water Margin**, was snapped up by the BBC and adapted by David Weir, whose anglicised, amusing dialogue adds to its charm.

Former pop star **Masaaki Sakai** played Monkey with great charisma, flair for physical comedy and luxurious facial hair. Tripitaka, the 'boy' priest, was played by actress **Masako Natsume**, while the other principals were Pigsy the pig spirit (**Toshiyuki Nishida**) and Sandy the water monster (**Shiro Kishibe**). Monkey, Pigsy and Sandy were all immortal officials

51

of heaven who had been thrown out by Buddha for various misdemeanours.

Filmed in northwest China and Inner Mongolia, each new episode found the quartet beset by demons, awkward monarchs and the like. One-liners littered the script, a disco soundtrack blared, vigorous combat ensued (Monkey adored fighting), and a narrator would always tie it all up at the end, drawing a confusing Buddhist lesson from proceedings. Beneath the comedy and combat, *Monkey* stressed honesty, charity, and avoiding violence – unless, of course,

Monkey, funnier than the Goodies funky gibbon

it was called for in the script. But the real charm lay in the programme's special effects. For those brought up on *Star Trek* and *Blake's 7*, the shape-changing, cloud-flying and magic made *Monkey* loiter in the memory.

+ + + + + + + + + + + +

★ The Office ★

BBC2 2001– **VHS, DVD**

'I'm a friend first, boss second and entertainer third,' says **David Brent**, immodest boss of Slough paper merchants Wernham Hogg. In reality, the regional manager, played with unnerving ease by **Ricky Gervais**, is fantastically unfunny and brilliantly inappropriate. Yet he sees himself as wise and spiritual, adopting Des'ree's lyrics, 'Money don't make the world go round, I'm reaching up for the higher ground' as his credo. In short, he is a smug, leering, platitudinous and grotesque Boss From Hell.

Most of the material for **The Office**, the brainchild of Gervais and **Stephen Merchant**, was garnered during the former's seven-year stint as a student union entertainments manager. At London's Xfm radio he met Merchant, with whom he conceived Seedy Boss. Gervais' TV break came on Channel 4's *11 O'Clock Show* as an obnoxious social commentator a la

Alf Garnett, but the unsubtle character was eclipsed by **Ali G**. But by then *The Office* was well developed and Gervais, who hadn't acted, directed or written for TV before, persuaded the BBC to back his mockumentary.

The Office is built on the premise that every work place has at least one top-of-the-range twerp (often more), and everyone else wants to be somewhere else. Tim (**Martin Freeman**), the likeable deodorant-lacking dreamer, and Gareth (**Mackenzie Crook**) the skeleton-faced wannabe-soldier, who wonders if there will ever be a boy who can swim as fast as a shark, also star. The cumulative effect of such stapler-labelling banalities is both very funny and frighteningly familiar.

First screened in July 2001, *The Office* was an instant cult hit. Recorded without canned laughter, and helped by astute direction using a hand-held camera, this sardonic satire has clearly struck a chord. Brent was later used in a **Dixons** staff-training video as an example of how not to behave – very apt given one episode where Brent hijacks a trainer's audience to sing guitar-assisted, self-penned songs about Princess Diana and as-bad-as-it-sounds 'hot love on the highway'.

+ + + + + + + + + + + +

★ One Man And His Dog ★

BBC2 1976–99

After 23 years of whistling and cries of 'Come boy', the BBC axed **One Man And His Dog**. From the outcry you might have thought Auntie had demolished a Grade-1 listed building. In a way they had. The simple show – man, dog and sheep in perfect harmony (unless you were vegetarian) – with its quaint country settings, flat-caps and cute collies was television's version of Constable's *The Haywain*, a nostalgic treat from a rural Britain which in reality was changing faster than you could say 'Countryside Alliance'.

> **One Man And His Dog was television's equivalent of Constable's The Haywain**

The show was the brainchild of producer **Philip Gilbert**, who saw the appeal after stumbling across a sheepdog trial in Northumberland. Somehow the idea survived the cynical scrutiny of BBC execs and made its debut in 1976. Archetypal countryman **Phil Drabble** (personal credo: 'If a ferret bites you, it's nearly always your own fault') hosted it for 18 years before **Robin Page** took over, with **Eric Halsall** commentating.

The original format saw audiences introduced to three shepherds (often indistinguishable to the urban eye), each using their dog to guide a flock of sheep through a gate, into a ring and then into a pen – minus one poor lamb who had to learn not to follow the flock. Despite frequent cries of 'Oh, he's lost one', someone always won. In 1999 the BBC decided such quaint viewing had passed its sell-by date, citing dwindling figures. But, like fox hunting, it's not dead yet. In 2001 a Christmas special was aired, introducing a 'champion of champions' competition (sneered at by old-school competitors), but it could yet lead to a 21st-century revival.

✛ ✛ ✛ ✛ ✛ ✛ ✛ ✛ ✛ ✛ ✛ ✛ ✛ ✛

★ Porridge ★

BBC1 1974–77 **VHS, DVD**

'Norman Stanley Fletcher, you are an habitual criminal who accepts arrest as an occupational hazard and presumably accepts imprisonment in the same casual manner.' Thus did old lag Fletcher, guilty only of pilfering alcohol (albeit a lorry-load), find himself once more a guest of Her Majesty.

Porridge developed out of *Seven Of One*, a 1973 series of pilot sitcoms devised to find a starring vehicle for **Ronnie Barker** (the same series included the *Open All Hours* pilot). This prologue focused on the fractious relationship between officious head warder Mackay and Fletcher, with his been-there, got-the-arrowed-suit demeanour.

Only when the series began did we meet more of HMP Slade's residents. The best of these was undoubtedly Fletch's naïve cellmate Godber, played with endearing gormlessness by **Richard Beckinsale**. But one of *Porridge*'s strengths, alongside **La Frenais** and **Clement**'s dialogue and plotting worthy of a criminal mastermind, were the finely drawn supporting crooks. These included 'Orrible Ives (guilty of some unspecified sexual misdemeanour), McLaren aka 'Black Jock' (this *was* the 1970s) and a youthful **David Jason** playing septuagenarian Blanco, plus hapless warder Mr Barrowclough and the menacing prison overlord Harry Grout. Most episodes found Fletch on the wrong side of Mackay or Grout (or both), having brewed hooch inside his bed-frames or trying to find out who had filched his pineapple chunks ('soaked in a heavy syrup from the sun-kissed shores of Hono-bleedin'-lulu!').

Fletcher and Godber were reunited for an anaemic post-release spin-off *Going Straight*, but the Slade saga ended with a decent big-screen version of *Porridge*, in which Fletch and Godber 'accidentally' escaped from prison and frantically tried to break back in. Tragically, Beckinsale died just after filming wrapped. But the most impressive tribute of all to *Porridge* was the fact that real prisons were forced to amend their TV viewing hours so that inmates could

> **★ Best supporting players ★**
>
> **Overlooked but not forgotten. Yet**
>
> **Christopher Biggins** Before Christopher camped it up as a friend of Cilla's and a children's TV host permanently on safari in shorts so wide you could have fitted Terry Venables in the other, he was an actor who won plaudits as camp, cuddly but mad Nero in *I Claudius* and as camp, cuddly needlework-loving Lukewarm in *Porridge*
>
> **Max Wall** British comedian, more famous for silly walks than John Cleese, who is also the answer to a TV trivia question. Before he died in 1990, he found time to appear in *Crossroads*, *Emmerdale* and *Corrie*.
>
> **Lois Maxwell** The voice of Atlanta in *Stingray* got fed up waiting for Troy Tempest and stormed off to suffer similar indignity as 007's Moneypenny.

see the show, lest rioting break out. Fletch would have chuckled at that.

+ + + + + + + + + + + + +

★ The Prisoner ★

ITV 1967–68 **VHS, DVD**

'Questions are a burden to others; answers a prison for oneself,' was the kind of edict passed around the Village in *The Prisoner*. Questions were obviously a bit of a burden for the scriptwriters too – they left most of them unanswered. Those who think cheese-rolling and *The Wicker Man* are as weird as village life gets, clearly haven't seen **The Prisoner**, devised by its star **Patrick McGoohan** (fresh from **Dangerman**) and still on the world's screens thirtysomething years later.

The plot goes something like this: man packs in his job as a spy, goes home, gets gassed and wakes up in a perfect Italianate village where everyone is known by a number (six in McGoohan's case) and from which there is no escape (thanks to a huge weather balloon called Rover). But who are the unseen yet all-seeing dictators who run the place and want 'information' from him? Suspicious Number Six will not be 'pushed, filed, stamped, indexed, briefed, debriefed or numbered', not even if his captors try brainwashing and hallucinogenic drugs. He spends the next 16 episodes trying to fathom what the hell is going on – as do we.

The Prisoner relies on more symbolism than the *Highway Code*. Rover is said to symbolise the repression of a corrupt, faceless authority, the Village's symbol of a penny-farthing to stand for lack of progress, and the Village itself represents the triumph of a Big Brother-style (as in Orwell, not the TV series) government. Called the most challenging TV series ever shown, '*The Prisoner* was a journey to save an individual from moral decline into the anonymity of the melting community. It was the battle of the 1960s,' says assistant editor **Ian Rakoff** ('I am not a number, I am a free man!' thundered McGoohan defiantly). This may be true, but they could also have been having a laugh. Either way, it made for great telly.

+ + + + + + + + + + + +

★ Prisoner: Cell Block H ★

ITV 1989–93 **VHS**

If you're not a devotee, you'll probably have come across this channel-hopping in the small hours. Indeed, cynics maintain the programme is best viewed when the brain is dulled. This is not an opinion to be offered lightly. Fans of **Prisoner: Cell Block H** (it was called *Prisoner* in Australia but retitled elsewhere to avoid confusion with McGoohan's meisterwork) are not to be trifled with, as Carlton Television found when it pulled the show, and had its phone lines jammed by an organised group of 'Blockies'.

Carlton should have known better: Central TV, after screening all 692 episodes, had to start all over again due to public demand. Despite never being given a networked time slot (never mind a decent hour), this tacky Australian women's prison soap pulled in ten million viewers. Its mainly female cast and storylines of female interaction attracted a devoted women's following, while its no-holds-barred approach to prison life

'Come in Number Six, your time is up'

included groundbreaking matter-of-fact portrayals of lesbians. On the west coast of the US, where the show rated second only to **Charlie's Angels**, the death of openly lesbian inmate Freda 'Franky' Doyle (**Carol Burns**) prompted San Francisco's women bikers to organise a wake.

Cell Block H had a fantastic gallery of inmates: thumbsuckers, armed robbers, dumb blondes and an alcoholic, chain-smoking serial killer hell bent on escape. The ominous sight of warder Joan 'The Freak' Ferguson pulling on her black leather gloves prior to some new assault had genuine dramatic power, but the bizarre stories (meek librarians who turn out to have multiple personalities etc) got too much for creator **Reg Watson**, who fled to sunny Ramsay Street. Nothing he's done since, however, has captured the strange intensity of *Prisoner: Cell Block H*.

Prisoner: Cell Block H had as iron a grip on its audience as the cellmates did on each other

★ The Professionals ★

ITV 1977–83 **VHS, DVD**

Screeching tyres, shoot-outs, permed action men ready to kill against a multinational gallery of rogues, all served with a light sprinkling of sexual innuendo. Welcome to *The Professionals*, staple of ITV Sunday nights in the late 1970s and early 1980s. In February 1977 *The Avengers'* supremo **Brian Clemens** and executive producer Albert Fennell were asked by London Weekend Television to create a rival to Thames' *The Sweeney*. The pair devised a scenario whereby ex-MI5 head George Cowley (**Gordon Jackson**) led an organisation (Criminal Intelligence or CI5) which handled crime that endangered national security – and wasn't afraid to use underhand tactics. Enter one-time detective constable Ray Doyle (**Martin Shaw**) and former para William Bodie (**Lewis Collins**) as CI5's top two agents.

> **Clemens could teach someone to do a hand-brake turn in the Capri within ten minutes**

Anthony Andrews was cast as Bodie but he and Shaw were friends and didn't generate the 'abrasiveness' Clemens wanted. Shaw and Collins, though, had taken a dislike to each other while filming for **The New Avengers** and so seemed to have the 'perfect' relationship. Off camera, Shaw did little to hide his disrespect for Collins, who responded in kind.

All episodes began with a three-minute pre-credit sequence which often had little to do with the storyline. The plots in the 57 episodes varied from the sublime to the bizarre. One of the stranger gems was 'Discovered In A Graveyard' in which a wounded Doyle can't decide whether to live or die – all told via a dream while in a comatose state. One storyline involved the Ku Klux Klan, but Collins was uneasy about his character's racist tendencies and the episode has never been shown in the UK.

Clemens once claimed he could teach someone to do a hand-brake turn in one of the trademark Capris within ten minutes. The tell-tale tyre marks left on roads during filming tell a different story. Watch out too for now-famous actors making cameo appearances, including TV debutant **Pierce Brosnan**, the dubbing of foreign accents on to English actors during the crudely filmed first series, and continuity errors in many episodes.

The show was discontinued in 1981 (although the last episode wasn't shown until 1983 because of a backlog) when Collins and Shaw chose not to renew their contracts. Shaw even disowned the show's 'hardware before humans' policy. The show has not run on UK terrestrial TV since 1988, but has been screened (censored) on Granada Plus. A retread, **The New Professionals**, with **Edward Woodward** in the Jackson role, was a slur on the original's memory, despite having creator Clemens on board.

+ + + + + + + + + + + +

★ Ren And Stimpy ★

Nickelodeon; BBC2 1991–94 **VHS**

Laugh? Bewilderment was usually the first reaction on encountering **Ren and Stimpy**. What, after all, was a viewer raised on bland post-war cartoons to make of the dysfunctional relationship between a psychotic chihuahua (Ren) and a large cat with a blue nose (frequently picked), the braindead but blissfully happy Stimpy? Or an episode like the fairytale in which Robin Hood (Ren) rescues Maid Moron (Stimpy in drag) from the Sheriff of Dodge City's tower by climbing up her Rapunzel-like nose hair?

The true descendants of the artist-driven **Warner Bros** and **Tex Avery** cartoons of the 1930s whose protagonists were bad-tempered, scheming and violent, Ren and Stimpy were created by Canadian cartoonist **John Kricfalusi**. Having slaved in Hollywood animation factories, he founded his own company (Spumco) and hawked his radical manifesto – that cartoonists should create the story, not scriptwriters – until he found a sympathetic ear at the new **Nickelodeon** channel.

> **Farts, bloodshot eyes and bug-eyed rages: all part of Ren & Stimpy's appeal**

Nickelodeon were, though, taken aback by the reality of *Ren & Stimpy*, where farts, bloodshot eyes and Ren's bug-eyed rages were part of the appeal. Alarmed execs did water down some content but were mollified when this unlikely pair became a hit, and catchphrases like 'You *eeee*diot!' and 'What *eeee* it, man?!' appeared on answerphones across the US.

Kricfalusi's dedication to style (the music was taken from the 1930s jazz of **Raymond Scott**, the music behind **Bugs Bunny**, et al) and content –

leftfield characters like Powdered Toast Man, inspired lunacy (the 'Ask Dr Stupid' slot) and its own catchy ads – became a landmark in contemporary creativity. Sadly, the forces of reaction triumphed (Nickelodeon wanted Ren made nicer – doh!), and Kricfalusi left during series two. (Read a splendidly bilious – if not libellous – account of the whole sorry affair at *http://victorian.fortunecity.com/russell/105/storyp.htm*).

But Nickelodeon's victory was a Pyhrric one. Without Spumco's wild imagination and anarchic ideas, the show petered out in the hands of dull, corporate scriptwriters – the very people Kricfalusi had rebelled against. There's a moral in this story, and it's not very hard to spot.

✣✣✣✣✣✣✣✣✣✣✣✣✣

★ Ripping Yarns ★

BBC2 1976–79 **VHS, DVD**

On 8 January 1976, there was but one topic of conversation for schoolboys aged 13 and over. The big question heard in Britain's playgrounds that morning was 'Did you see **Tomkinson's Schooldays** last night?' To admit you hadn't seen the bit where Tomkinson picks up the ball in a rugby game and keeps on running, long past the point where he should have stopped to score a try, with the cries of his classmates and teachers fading into the distance, was as shameful as saying you liked the Bay City Rollers.

The show was the pilot of a series called *Ripping Yarns*, set in a bygone era when the British schoolboy was expected to show pluck, even if his elders did celebrate the end of term by nailing him to the school walls. That was the kind of thing that happened in *Tomkinson's Schooldays*, the *Tom Brown's Schooldays* spoof written by ex-Pythons **Michael Palin** (who played the lead) and **Terry Jones**, who stayed off-screen. School Bully was not an accusation but an official rank and **Ian Ogilvy**, bless him, looked far more at ease as a cad than he had as the new Simon Templar.

This being a satire of a certain kind of British adventure yarn, it all worked out well in the end, with Tomkinson rising through the ranks to become school bully. But the misery, the indifference – even the punishment – struck a chord with millions of 1970s schoolboys who had never got closer to a public school than reading the Tom Brown novel.

61

None of the other yarns equalled the impact of *Tomkinson's Schooldays* but all had virtues. The best were **'Crossing The Andes By Frog'** and **'Golden Gordon'**, a tragic tale of the last days of Barnstoneworth United, supported by Gordon Ottershaw (Palin) who comes home each week after their latest thrashing to wreck the living room in disgust. With its tales of forward lines of yore ('the mighty Davit once scored a goal with the back of his head from 28 yards') this yarn is familiar to anyone who asked their dad what football was like in their day.

The yarns ended after nine instalments. The policy of shooting on real film (and Palin and Jones's attention to period detail) meant they were just too expensive. Palin's likeable (if undemanding) **The Missionary** is a kind of companion piece. The untimely end did, at least, mean that the ripping yarns remained gripping to the last.

+ + + + + + + + + + + +

★ Roobarb ★

BBC1 1974–5 **VHS**

Announced by Johnny Hawksworth's ear-splitting electronic theme tune, **Roobarb** was a scruffy green animated dog who bounded into public life in October 1974 and was aired regularly on the BBC until the late 1980s.

He lived in a two-up two-down with a good-sized garden, and what he lacked in conventional intelligence he made up for with enthusiasm. Custard, the smarmy, disdainful pink cat next door, was his nemesis, and **Richard Briers** provided the voices. A typical episode would involve Roobarb embarking on some crackpot mission and retiring to his shed to invent something useful. Inevitably he'd fail to think things through and some mishap would follow, to the delight of the ever-watchful Custard.

The only other regulars were the birds who sat on the fence. As Roobarb's audience, they laughed and showed off their most un-avian teeth, one of the more memorable parts of the visuals. These came from award-winning animator **Bob Godfrey** (producer and director, also responsible for *Noah And Nelly On The Skylark*). Tight budgets meant Roobarb was drawn with magic markers on paper rather than acetate, giving rise to the distinctive wobbling or flickering style of animation.

Jim changes channels to avoid another Royle Family theme night. 'Theme nights my arse!'

Creator **Grange Calveley** did the key drawings and wrote the scripts for 30 original five-minute episodes, which drew on Calveley's dog of the same name, and Custard the cat next door. Yes, there really was a shed, a fence, a chestnut tree and a pond in the garden of Roobarb's St Albans home. Whether Calveley's dog ever decided, as Roobarb did, 'that the whole idea of being a loaf of bread had gone a bit stale', is unrecorded.

+++++++++++++

★ The Royle Family ★

BBC2/BBC1 1998–2000   **VHS, DVD**

When **Caroline Aherne** and **Craig Cash** moved on from Mrs Merton and Malcolm to create Denise and Dave in *The Royle Family*, they had another TV partnership in mind. The living-room-based sitcom saw the reunion of *Brookside*'s Bobby and Sheila Grant (**Ricky Tomlinson** and **Sue Johnston**) as Barb and Jim, although neither knew about the other's casting until they arrived for the first reading. The show also saw the start of a beautiful TV relationship for Ralf Little and Sheridan Smith (as Anthony and posh veggie girlfriend Emma), who would go on to their own series as Jonny and Janet in *Two Pints Of Lager (And A Packet Of Crisps)*.

The Royle Family was quickly taken to British hearts, moving from BBC2 to prime-time BBC1 after the first series. No longer could we complain of 'unreality' TV, where characters never watched telly, went to the loo or broke wind – each episode of the Royles revolved around these. With a plot that happens mainly off-screen, the show addressed the gritty issues of Northern working class life – births, deaths, marriages, shopping catalogues, phone bills and betting on *Antiques Roadshow*. Domestic life was only interrupted by friends and neighbours, the arrival of Anthony's girlfriend and a move to the bathroom for Baby David's labour pangs.

Aherne quit after series three, fleeing to Australia after turmoil in her own life. She returned in 2002 as the creator of the sitcom **Dossa And Joe**. A debate on the British monarchy in the first episode showed that, half a world away, the Royles had not been forgotten. 'Royal family? My arse.'

+++++++++++++

⋆ Seinfeld ⋆

NBC; BBC2 1993–98   **VHS, DVD**

In 1997, a 62-year-old Massachusetts man was diagnosed with 'Seinfeld syncope' after passing out three times while laughing at the antics of **George Costanza** in *Seinfeld*. The patient's arteries had furred up for the usual reasons (drink, diet, living in Massachusetts), and when he laughed, the pressure in his chest pushed down on his heart, cutting the flow of blood to his brain. Luckily, doctors improved his blood flow so he could watch the sitcom without blacking out.

> **'So please – a little respect, for I am Costanza, Lord of the Idiots!'**

Seinfeld is often called a show about nothing. More accurately, it is a show where nothing is learned. When the show ends, Jerry is still the kind of guy who ends a relationship because of the way his date eats peas. George is a loser with a grudge against the world. Elaine, with her truly excruciating dancing technique, is as commitment-shy as Jerry, and Kramer is still seeking a short cut to millionairedom, after the inexplicable (to him) failure of such bright ideas as a coffee-table book about coffee tables.

To those who think that America patented Dumbing Down TV, the most inexplicable thing about *Seinfeld* is its success. Thanks partly to the BBC's bizarre scheduling, Brits have warmed more to the schmaltzier glamour of *Friends*

Three idiotic peers. And one truly bad dancer

65

or the highbrow but sentimental *Frasier*. The three shows are tellingly differentiated by their handling of tragedy. The other friends are always there for the sufferer; the family (after a few squabbles) lovingly rallies round in *Frasier*, but in *Seinfeld*, the death of George's fiancee (poisoned by glue on the envelopes for the wedding invitations) is a lucky escape. When **George Steinbrenner**, the boss of the New York Yankees baseball team, tells George's father (mistakenly) that his son is dead, Costanza Senior can only reply: 'How could you trade Buhner?'

At times the four friends seem to do the minimum necessary to maintain their friendship; at others they go out of their way for each other. But they are as competitive as they are compassionate – witness the famous episode where Jerry and George argue over who is the bigger idiot. Costanza, for once, wins, saying: 'I just threw away a lifetime of guilt-free sex and floor seats to every sporting event in Madison Square Garden. So, please, a little respect, for I am Costanza, Lord of the Idiots.'

+ + + + + + + + + + + +

★ The Simpsons ★

Sky/BBC1/BBC2 1987– **VHS, DVD**

With only slight exaggeration, **The Simpsons** has been described as the defining document of life in the West these last 15 years. Creator **Matt Groening** first caught the eye as the author of a US comic strip called *Life In Hell*. It attracted Gracie Films, for whom (in 1985) Groening developed the idea of a dysfunctional animated family that became the first Simpsons shorts, shown on the *Tracey Ullman Show* in 1987. (The BBC, to its shame, cut these shorts out when it ran Ullman's show). Two years later the Simpsons had their own show, and 14 seasons (around 300 episodes) later, despite tensions with parent company Fox (manifested in sly digs at their expense written into the scripts) it should continue for some time, (more than can be said for Groening's subsequent creation, *Futurama*).

Each gloriously farcical storyline is as precisely engineered as a Swiss watch with fine running gags, one-liners ('We don't do animation live,' a snooty TV exec tells Homer, 'it would place a terrible strain on the animators' wrists'), movie and TV parodies, and inspired surrealism. The show's resilience owes something to its massive cast. If the family have hogged the limelight, the focus shifts to bit players like **Moe**, the bartender so ugly it's a wonder the glasses in his bar don't crack or **Chief Wiggum**, US TV's dumbest police chief since **Commissioner O'Hara** in *Batman*.

Thoroughly disapproved of by George and Barbara Bush (he prefers *The Waltons*, she reckons it's the dumbest thing she ever heard; quite a claim for someone who spent eight years so close to Ronald Reagan), the Simpsons can handle themselves in a duel of wits. As Bart said to Bush Senior: 'Hey, we're just like the Waltons — both families spend a lot of time praying for the end of the depression.'

✢ ✢ ✢ ✢ ✢ ✢ ✢ ✢ ✢ ✢ ✢ ✢ ✢

★ The Singing Detective ★

BBC1 1986 **VHS, DVD**

No matter how good **The Singing Detective** might be in your memory, to watch it again is a revelation of a kind. When it was first shown (thanks to the usual tabloid outrage eight million of us tuned in), the Monday morning post-mortem became a national ritual. What might this bizarre amalgam of **Raymond Chandler** pulp fiction and a coming-of-age tale straight out of an early **DH Lawrence** novel, with a soundtrack full of nostalgic, melancholy gems like 'Peg Of My Heart', actually mean?

A more cautious writer than **Dennis Potter** might have pulled back from using a song like 'I've Got You Under My Skin' in a series whose hero is suffering such severe psoriasis that his face looks, as one critic said, 'like meat that has been boiled and left out to rot'.

> **His face looked like meat that had been boiled and left out to rot**

But it's Potter's ability to take such risks — to have his hero (Philip Marlow, troubled author of out-of-print detective fiction) indulge in a sub-Chandler narrative in the pulp novel he's writing (or hallucinating) — that puts this drama in a class of its own.

Michael Gambon was justly praised for his portrayal of Potter's para- noid, bitter, and abusive hero. **Joanne Whalley** (pre-Val Kilmer) caught the eye, as actress and pin-up, as the sympathetic nurse. The songs are brilliantly interspersed, especially when the unruly OAP in the next bed to Marlow begins to croon 'It Might As Well Be Spring'. It's easy to miss the understated **Lyndon Davies**'s performance as the young Marlow. Sitting in a tree, watching his mother commit adultery, his expression is beautifully judged, tinged by shame and yet curious, as if he's trying to solve a difficult maths problem. The attention to detail is incredible: the hospital, where so much of the inaction takes place, looks like it has suffered the same continual, casual neglect as many of Britain's real hospitals.

The misogyny which marred some of Potter's work seems, at least, in character here for Marlow. Even after the puzzle has been revealed, Potter's imagination and wit (which has, at times, a Swiftian cruelty) means this is almost as compelling at second viewing. Potter once famously declared: 'television is the true national theatre' – a point he proved here. This is one series to mention whenever someone tells the gag about television being called a medium because it's never rare and seldom well done.

+ + + + + + + + + + + + +

★ Soap ★

ITV 1978–82   **VHS (US format only)**

US network **ABC** received 32,000 letters about the launch of this fantastic spoof of daytime soaps. Nine of them defended the show, the rest agreed with the religious minister who publicly insisted **Susan Harris**' sitcom was trying to 'tear down our moral values'.

The show focused on two small-town sisters, Jessica Tate and Mary Campbell. The Tates lived in a mansion – the only place they could find with enough closets to hide the family skeletons in. Jessica was played by **Katharine Helmond** in a style familiar to anyone who recalls her turn as Jonathan Pryce's mum in **Terry Gilliam**'s film *Brazil*. They also had a butler in **Benson** (Robert Guillaume) who, if the doorbell rang, would say with mock surprise 'You want me to get that?' The Campbells were poorer and dafter, with Mary's impotent husband Burt, a rubber-faced loon, kidnapped by aliens and his son Chuck thinking his ventriloquist's dummy was real – mind you, in one episode, where the men go on a binge, they left the dummy to pick up the tab.

Today, even *Soap*'s weirdest sub-plots – Burt's openly gay stepson Jodie (daring stuff for its time) – played by **Billy Crystal** – being hypnotised into believing he's an old Jewish man, Jessica about to be shot by a firing squad – would not seem that out of place in soaps like **Sunset Beach**. The show had such a voracious appetite for jokes and plot twists (not for nothing was the show's catchphrase 'Confused? You will be') that the later series were hit-and-miss, especially after Benson was spun off into his own series. But for years, *Soap* gave you a good reason to turn to ITV after 10pm on a Friday. Not many shows that have done that. Before or since.

+ + + + + + + + + + + + +

★ The Sopranos ★

Channel 4 1999– **VHS, DVD**

From bedroom to boat deck to back of the Bada Bing club, **The Sopranos** (created by **David Chase**) is sex and drugs and mystery – and misogyny

As 'singing' is frowned upon by some Italian-Americans, it's a miracle they produce so many great crooners

and waste management and vicious killers discussing hand cream. Intelligent modern TV drama at its best, it's a superbly written and mesmerisingly detailed saga of an Italian-American crime boss attempting to balance the needs of his family with the needs of the Family.

The Sopranos is misogyny, waste management and killers discussing hand cream

Set and largely shot in New Jersey, it has become a cultural phenomenon. At the time of writing, the fourth – and rumour has it, penultimate – season is awaited, but each of the first three series (39 episodes in all) has had its own distinct flavour.

Season one introduced a superb cast – Tony Soprano (**James Gandolfini**), wife Carmella (**Edie Falco**), his two adolescent children and his associates – while the storyline centred on the changing nature of Tony's business, his frequent anxiety attacks, his poisonous mother Livia and his clandestine visits to psychiatrist Dr Melfi (**Lorraine Bracco**). Season two meandered more, introducing Tony's grasping sister Janice and Richie Aprile, fresh out of jail. Richie took up the troublemaking slack from Tony's Uncle Junior (**Dominic Chianese**), who was facing an orange jumpsuit himself. Pulling back from the mayhem, the third season focused on Tony and Carmella as parents. It was no less of a gangster show for that, containing the usual dense web of sub-plots, inventive violence, dark humour and an inspired soundtrack.

Brilliantly exploiting our fascination with organised crime, *The Sopranos* is so popular (the New Jersey crime family it draws on use it as a recruitment aid) that Chase can't attend industry functions without being pestered for guest roles, and one casting call drew 14,000 non-professionals before degenerating into the kind of riot you need wise guys to control.

++++++++++++++

★ Star Trek ★

NBC; BBC1 1969–71 **VHS, DVD**

When **Gene Roddenberry** created *Star Trek*, nobody imagined it would become a popular culture phenomenon spanning five decades, a feature film franchise, successive TV series and a global multitude of Trekkies.

Leonard Nimoy was a popular singer of rare distinction. On the planet Vulcan

Intergalactic Romeo and champion of democracy Captain James T (for Tiberius) Kirk (**William Shatner**) romanced space babes, bluffed cosmic bullies and saved the day, the ship, and civilisation, with his quips. (He is loosely based on another liberal, womanising, authority figure of Irish descent: **John F Kennedy**, a blatant clue being the initials: JFK/JTK.) His half-Vulcan science officer Spock (**Leonard Nimoy**) glorified logic and mind-melded with recalcitrant guest aliens. Dr McCoy (**DeForest Kelley**) often pronounced 'He's dead, Jim,' engineer Scott (**James Doohan**) resolved warp drive crises, and glamorous Lieutenant Uhura (**Nichelle Nichols**) provided communications expertise and emblematic racial integration. (Shatner and Nichols delivered the first interracial kiss on US TV, albeit under the influence of alien mind control.)

Warm and humorous interplay characterised these adventures celebrating the *Trek* ethos: comradeship, courage, curiosity and moralising cultural imperialism. There were ingenious and prophetic ideas, from alternative universes, time warps and genetic engineering to mobile communicators, the electronic notepad and the hyposray. Nasa's first space shuttle was even named *Enterprise* in honour of its starship. By the time the show was axed after just three seasons, its lexicon and catchphrases ('Beam me up, Scotty') had passed into the public consciousness. The weirdest evidence of this was the 1980s UK number one hit single **Star Trekkin'** by The Firm, in which the phrases become a kind of mantra: 'It's worse than that he's dead Jim, dead Jim, dead Jim, it's worse than that.'

Roddenberry lived long enough to exult in **The Next Generation** (1987-1994), in which Captain Jean-Luc Picard (**Patrick Stewart**) continued to boldly go with a multi-cultural crew and android Data (**Brent Spiner**). Similar adventures have followed but none had quite the resonance with the general public enjoyed by the first two. **Deep Space Nine** (1993-1999) explored darker, topical socio-political themes on a remote station. **Voyager** (1995-2001) emphasised action aboard a stranded Federation starship led by Kathryn Janeway (**Kate Mulgrew**). The torch has now passed to a prequel, in which Captain Jonathan Archer (**Scott Bakula** – no we're not kidding) and the *Enterprise* boldly go where – well, you know.

+ + + + + + + + + + + +

★ The Sweeney ★

ITV 1975–82 **VHS, DVD**

Perhaps the most revealing aspect of *The Sweeney* came in the closing credit sequence. In close up, the time is checked on a watch – 22.50. Last orders. It could've meant there was just time to get one in after a hard day's nicking villains, or it could've meant it was all over for Skip and Guv – that there was no place in the modern world for these hard drinking, two-fisted, womanising, civil rights-restricting sartorial catastrophes. Indeed there might not have been, but their last round-up stretched itself out for four years from 1975 to 1978, during which time it completely revolutionised the way the British public perceived a) the bobby on the beat; and b) the police drama on TV. And if you weren't happy with it, then you could 'Shut it!' as well.

The idea that there's little difference between police and thieves was not particularly new yet it had rarely been handled so entertainingly as in *The Sweeney*, created by **Troy Kennedy Martin**. They were funny and they knew they were – after all, if you can't have a bit of a laugh after you've whacked hell out of first your motor and then sundry armed robbers, you might as well work in a bank.

In this world where women were 'birds' or 'brasses', 'drinkers' were where you met 'your snout' – and speaking of 'snout', 20 Piccadilly still

★ SKIP'N'GUV ★
Being a Flying Squad detective is all a question of attitude
After arrest 'Get 'em in, will you George?'
The burden of proof 'He's an active villain. Stands to reason he's up to something'
Canteen culture 'Ere guv, does this ham roll look alright to you?'
Ladies of the night 'Put 'em away, darlin'
PC 'A woodentop'
Snout 'Can I have one of yours, George? I'm out'
Special Branch 'Piss off, you're on our manor'
Themselves 'Ratman and Robbin'
Underage villains 'Round up the cavalry George. This might get a bit tasty'
Very violent villains 'Round up the cavalry George. This might get a bit tasty'
White collar villains 'Round up the cavalry George. This might get a bit tasty'
Women in policework 'On second thoughts, darlin', make it a triple'

Regan was known to get a bit agitated if police work interrupted his evening meal

came in a flat pack. If you weren't on the piss then it was there to be taken. Rules were made to be broken, shirt top buttons kept coming undone and when you're looking down the wrong end of a 'shooter', well. *The Sweeney* wasn't so much the sharp end of policing as a side-on shunt in a Ford Granada. British TV cop shows have only just recovered from it.

+ + + + + + + + + + + +

★ thirtysomething ★

ITV 1987–91 **VHS**

thirtysomething – 'skinny white people from hell' **David Letterman** called it – was the show yuppies never missed: the *Friends* of the 1980s, minus the gags and L'Oreal moments but with a dash of high drama and chintz decor.

There was someone for everyone: Hope, whose name mirrored her sickly sweet nature; Michael, the tortured thinking man; Elliot, the loveable philandering rogue; his long-suffering wife Nancy, with her angora knits and Indian patterned skirts; Gary, who looked like a rocker but was actually a cool yet sensitive professor (just like real life); Ellyn, the high-maintenance career woman; and Melissa, the flaky, single arty type.

The show took pride in handling 'real' issues, so coping with a child and a career, infidelity, fatal accidents and cancer were all crammed into four seasons. (Talk about car safety standards between Hope and Michael was cut, however, in case it offended advertisers.) Originally the producers had wanted to explore what happens to a group of friends when one of them dies, but after being bombarded with letters urging them to let cancer-stricken Nancy survive, they decided to kill off womanising Gary instead.

> **thirtysomething proved growing up hurt so much you wanted to suck your big toe**

Why *thirtysomething* ended in 1991 remains a mystery. Even the cast didn't know it was coming – **Melanie Mayron** (Melissa) found out in the press. The consensus is that the show had another season in it, which would have saved viewers from a pitiful conclusion in which Hope and Michael work things out and everyone lives happily ever after – except Gary.

Although it's now long gone, we have *thirtysomething* to thank for such adult-angst dramas as **Ally McBeal**, **My So Called Life** and **This Life**. But *thirtysomething* was unique – the show that proved growing up hurt so much sometimes you just wanted to suck your big toe.

+ + + + + + + + + + + +

★ This Life ★

BBC2 1996–97 **VHS, DVD**

If, in 1996, you were twentysomething, having a bad time at work with a love life largely in tatters, **This Life**, the late-night series about five trainee lawyers sharing a house in London was the perfect pick-you-up. By the end of its second 21-week run (which culminated in one of TV's greatest cat fights as 'Little Miss Perfect' Milly landed one on colleague Rachel because she'd revealed Milly's affair with her boss to boyfriend Egg), *This Life* was up there with the most talked and written about TV of the 1990s.

Launched almost surreptitiously in March 1996, it was written by a lawyer, **Amy Jenkins**, daughter of political columnist Peter Jenkins and step-daughter of *Guardian* commentator Polly Toynbee, and produced by **Tony Garnett**, best known for 1960s TV drama *Cathy Come Home*. The pedigree helped, and its hand-held camera action earned plaudits, but it was the performances by **Daniela Nardini** (as boozed up but aspirational Anna) and **Jack Davenport** (mean and moody Miles) which hooked us.

Anna's lines were legendary and included gems such as, 'I believe in booze. It's a great leveller.' An intelligent ladette, Anna was game for most things – and most people, including Egg's dad, although she drew the line at a full-blown lesbian affair. As such, she achieved that rare accolade of being both the guys' and the girls' favourite character. Successful Miles, who Anna had slept with (and still loved), was liked by both genders; girls fancied him and men wanted to be him. Egg, meanwhile, appealed to girls because of his sensitivity and devotion to Milly, and to guys because of his ultimate decision to follow his dreams even if it meant running a greasy spoon café.

After that final punch at Miles' and Francesca's wedding, it was hard to see where *This Life* went next. We glimpsed the return of Warren (Welsh, gay and hopelessly in love with motorbike courier Ferdy for ages), but we knew it was over. If only **Big Brother** inmates were this compelling.

+ + + + + + + + + + + +

★ Tiswas ★

ITV 1974–82 **VHS**

True anarchy is always hard to organise (just ask Mikhail Bakunin) which may explain why no programme – not even Chris Evans' **TFI Friday** – has come close to emulating this show – an acronym, with tongue firmly in cheek, for *This Is Saturday With A Smile*. On the BBC, **Noel Edmonds** was trying to arouse enthusiasm for a multi-coloured swap shop but compared to the flan flinging, the constant water dousings and the regularity with which guest stars were confined to a cage, Noel, Keith, Maggie and Mike seemed about as much fun as a Conservative party conference.

If you hadn't watched *Tiswas* before, the gleeful chaos could be disturbing. Why was **Chris Tarrant** having his hair washed as the show started? And why did they keep showing that clip of the two skeletons slugging it out from *Jason*

And The Argonauts? The best way to hang on to your sanity was to focus on **Sally James**, who always looked good, even in baked beans: the tolerant sister you never had and who, unlike the Philbinettes on BBC1, didn't look like the kind of girl your mum wanted you to be/deemed safe for you to go out with.

Many famous, or plain notorious, faces crossed our screens as *Tiswas* crept from the Midlands like a stain across the ITV network: **Jim Davidson, Jasper Carrott, Lenny Henry**. But the Independent Broadcasting Authority saw *Tiswas* as a virus which could infect other children's programmes. So the suits told ATV to make it more educational. Tarrant left to found the shortlived *OTT*, a late-night show which was not as funny as it thought it was – the wackiness seemed forced, as it never had on *Tiswas*. Without Tarrant, the new improved educational version petered out in 1982. Sally James had the last word, asking on voiceover: 'How'd you like that?' We liked it very much, thanks.

+ + + + + + + + + + + + +

Anarchy in the UK. With the added bonus: Malcolm McLaren wasn't involved this time

⋆ Trumpton ⋆

BBC1 1967 **VHS**

Although creator **Gordon Murray** burnt all the puppets and sets used in **Trumpton**, its most famous residents, Hugh, Pugh, Barney McGrew, Cuthbert, Dibble and Grubb never got anywhere near a fire, even though they comprised the town's fire brigade. But then anything as spontaneous as a fire was never on the cards in a community whose town clock had an obsessive-compulsive disorder: 'Here is the clock, the Trumpton clock. Telling the time steadily, sensibly, never too quickly, never too slowly.'

Originally planned to be part of *Watch With Mother*, *Trumpton* was the second in Murray's Trumptonshire trilogy, which began with *Camberwick Green* and ended with the overlooked *Chigley*, each focusing on everyday life in rural towns, only a short bus ride away from one another.

Writer **Alison Prince** was commissioned to write stories based around the Trumpton fire brigade, with one proviso – the stories could not include smoke, fire or water. (Nothing to do with upsetting small children: they were just difficult to animate.) Each of the 13 episodes focused on the adults and their role in the community, the most memorable being Chippy Minton (carpenter), Mr Clamp (greengrocer), Mr Antonio (a suitably Italian sounding ice-cream man) and Miss Lovelace (a hat-maker and absolutely no relation to Linda).

Despite the complete dearth of animals or children, *Trumpton* was

Yet another promotion from the Chigley tourist board

such a success that BBC Wales dubbed it into Welsh ten years later. **Brian Cant** was the man behind the mike, holed up in composer Freddie Philips' cupboard, which doubled as a recording studio. Cant worked with only a script and the odd instruction from Murray to pause. Cant was chosen for his tone of voice, which sounded to Murray like that of a young dad. The rumour mill has been in full swing ever since trying to locate the real Trumptonshire, but only Murray knows for sure.

+ + + + + + + + + + + + + +

⋆ Twin Peaks ⋆

Spelling Entertainment; BBC2 1990–91   **VHS, DVD**

A show co-created by filmmaker **David Lynch** (*Dune, Blue Velvet*) couldn't do anything but break rules. Lynch and Mark Frost's series may have looked like a detective story (who killed Laura Palmer?) but it was anything but. No ordinary crime series would make room for log ladies and dancing midgets, a man talking backwards, mind-boggling dream sequences or dialogue devoted to the appreciation of homemade cherry pie or chocolate bunnies. Into this bizarre, dream-like universe – set in the northern logging town of Twin Peaks – Lynch propelled Dale Cooper (**Kyle Maclachlan**), an FBI agent with the habit of talking into his dictaphone to his unseen assistant Diane, ostensibly to investigate the crime, but ultimately to be another cog in Lynch's machine of weirdness.

It took more than a series for Cooper, along with Sheriff Harry Truman (**Michael Ontkean**), to find who did kill Laura Palmer, during which time we were introduced to squeaky-voiced receptionist Lucy (Kimmy Robertson), teen temptress Audrey (Sherilyn Fenn, whose appearance in *Playboy* led US greetings card shops to boycott the *Twin Peaks* calendar), scheming Catherine (Piper Laurie) and the man who gave millions the shivers, Bob (Frank Silva, initially hired as one of the set decorators).

Easily the strangest show ever to be broadcast on mainstream TV, *Twin Peaks* ran for two years and was followed by Lynch's prequel movie, *Twin Peaks: Fire Walk With Me*. 'I have no idea where this will lead us,' Cooper said to Truman in one episode, 'but I have a definite feeling it will be a place both wonderful and strange.' Which is as close as you can get to

Cooper: 'Who's that lady with the log?' Truman: 'We call her the log lady'

summing up *Twin Peaks*. As Lynch said, 'I don't know why people expect art to make sense. They accept the fact that life doesn't make sense.'

+ + + + + + + + + + + +

★ Whoops! Apocalypse ★

ITV 1982 **VHS**

Freshly lobotomised American president **Johnny Cyclops** is at his desk in the Oval Office, dressed in the kind of attire often associated with Jimmy Savile and talking to his barking adviser (**John Barron**, CJ in *Reginald Perrin*). Through the window, we see a young man on a crucifix being erected on the White House lawn. Cyclops turns to his aide and asks: 'Don't you think that the Easter decorations are a little severe this year?'

Written by Andrew (**2.4 Children**) Marshall and David (**One Foot In The Grave**, **Jonathan Creek**) Renwick, *Whoops! Apocalypse* was a glorious, tasteless romp about the run up to the start of World War III. The gags came so thick and fast you suspected the writers had set themselves a mathematical challenge. You were just getting used to the idea that the deposed Shah of Iran was trapped on a Sealink ferry (what an episode of **Triangle** that would have made) when he was spirited away to a space shuttle on collision course with a Kremlin ruled by countless interchangeable Russian leaders all played by **Richard Griffiths**.

Marshall and Renwick's manic inventiveness was matched by a stellar cast which included **Geoffrey Palmer**, **John Cleese**, **Alexei Sayle**, **Peter Jones**, **Rik Mayall** and **Ed Bishop**. Apocalypse, assassination, religion, the rhetoric of US TV news – all was grist to the writers' mill. At one point, Cyclops is shot in the shoulder, at his adviser's behest, after appearing as a pair of celebrity knees on a US game show. But he fluffs the quips on cue cards he was to read to the media to show how brave he is. (Bear in mind this was only a year after the attempt on **Ronald Reagan**'s life.)

Give the 1986 movie of the same name (by the same writers) a wide berth but the series, shown in the Sunday 10pm slot for which Marshall and Renwick later devised the fine **Hot Metal**, was fast, furious and funny. 81

+ + + + + + + + + + + +

⋆ World Of Sport ⋆

ITV 1965–85

To those misguided souls who spent their formative Saturday afternoons watching **Grandstand**, **World Of Sport** may just be a relic from some old TV listings. But for the 17 years it was fronted by **Dickie Davies**, *World Of Sport* was no ordinary sports magazine show. The essential ingredient of any sports programme is, of course, sporting action. ITV didn't have much of that stuff, so they (and we) had to make do with a selection of the day's racing (the **ITV Seven** which mysteriously always included a race at Redcar), wrestling, contests between monster trucks and more wrestling.

The bags under Dickie's eyes were so vast, several wrestlers could have lived in them

If the show was subtitled 'International Sports Special' this was usually a sign that Australian rules football was on the menu. Then there were the results, delivered with none of the gravitas of BBC's *Final Score* but with an endearing naffness. (After nearly 50 years, ITV has yet to find an adequate colour combination in which to show these simple statistics.)

The show kicked off with a keyboard riff borrowed from *War Of The Worlds* before cutting to a dodgy-looking bloke with a Mallen streak in a hairstyle usually reserved for badgers, and sporting a blazer that screamed 'This man is a cad.' Then there were the eyes: 'He's got Dickie Davies eyes,' sang **Half Man Half Biscuit**, part in parody of Kim Carnes' smash Bette Davis Eyes and part in tribute. By the end of his reign, the bags under Davies' eyes were so vast several wrestlers could have lived in them.

Davies had the air of man who had just strolled into the studio after a few G&Ts to cast an eye over the odds and who, as soon as the afternoon was done, would return to his club for something he would undoubtedly call a 'freshener'. Unlike Steve Rider, Davies was no supermarionette; while he managed to link water-skiing and monster trucks with a straight face, he never suggested any of it mattered that much. That genial good humour also typified *On The Ball*, always more fun than *Football Focus*. Television sport has seldom been as addictively absurd since.

✦✦✦✦✦✦✦✦✦✦✦✦✦

The genres

From action heroes to shows that went zzzz...

'Ten per cent of television is honest'

Jean-Luc Godard

Television execs usually define their shows by genres. Most are named on the 'does what it says on the tin' principle that it wouldn't be a bad idea if medical dramas had something medical in the title. Sometimes, the naming process is more opaque, soaps being famously christened after the kind of companies which sponsored them. In this era of post-modern irony (which we've been in for so long television must soon reach post-post-modern irony), execs have devised terms like 'water cooler TV' (**Big Brother**, **This Life**, **Dick Emery** – one of those was a joke) to make the business sound more glamorous. Here is our selection (flawed, partial, subjective, meretricious etc) of shows, advertisements, public information films and personalities which come from Godard's ten per cent. If you think we've missed something, we could say 'Shaaaat it!' but, as we're not the Flying Squad, we'll invite you to email us at cult.tv@haynet.com.

★★★ Action heroes and superheroes ★★★

Everyone loves a hero, especially when they can be put in jeopardy each week while rescuing the feisty but forever in distress damsel. They come in all shapes and sizes (from part-man, part-machine to part-man, part-Flipper) with producers often relying on comic book heroes. In TV's

early days, the accent was on honour and heroism. By the 1970s, thanks to **The Six Million Dollar Man**, they had to be honourable, heroic and high-tech (or have a flashy car). In the rough, tough 1980s we were treated to a new breed of hero: men – often loners with a slightly dodgy past so they were forever bucking the system – who were good with their hands, cynical

ommers brought equal opps for bionics

85

about life, and ready with a quip and a set of jump leads to disarm a thermonuclear device. In the caring, sharing 1990s the traditional testosterone-fuelled hero vamoosed, leaving us with guys like **Fox Mulder** who got no further with his partner in nine seasons than a comforting hug. Even the bespectacled, clumsy **Clark Kent** did better than that…

The A-Team ITV 1984–88

On the run from the Army who thought they had stolen money, four mismatched (oh yes) Vietnam veterans were available for hire to handle bad guys and make quips. Unlike the Army, women hunted by suspicious-looking men never had much trouble finding Colonel John 'Hannibal' Smith (**George Peppard**, in cigar- and scene-chomping mode), jewellery-draped mechanic BA Baracus (**Mr T**), conman 'Face' Peck (**Dirk Benedict**), or lovably mad pilot **'Howling Mad' Murdock**. Together they outfoxed baddies and turned a shed full of garden equipment into a high-powered assault weapon. Nonsensically addictive.

Adam Adamant Lives! BBC1 1966–67

Seminal meld of swashbuckling and *The Avengers* in which Adam Llewellyn De Vere Adamant (**Gerald Harper**, British TV's favourite posh bloke before Nigel Havers) emerges from cryogenic hell in the Swinging Sixties to grapple with sundry villains. Well scripted (by, among others, **Brian Clemens**), stylishly directed (by, among others, **Ridley Scott**) and well cast (Peter Vaughan, John Le Mesurier, Deryck Guyler, Iain Cuthbertson, Patrick Troughton). The series even quit while it was ahead. Somebody needs to rediscover this very soon.

Airwolf ITV 1984–86

Helicopters were clearly the in-thing in 1984 – one US channel produced *Blue Thunder* (special unit cops in a chopper) while CBS had *Airwolf*, featuring Stringfellow Hawke (played by **Jan Michael Vincent**). A cello-playing loner (the name wasn't a great icebreaker), he stole back a super high-tech helicopter for the government but decided to use it for good deeds. Unintentionally funny thanks to an odd performance from

Alex Cord as government representative Archangel and a gruff one from **Ernest Borgnine** as Hawke's co-pilot. The series only lasted two years, but is now a staple of Saturday afternoon cable schedules the world over.

The Bionic Woman ITV 1976–79

First introduced in an episode of *The Six Million Dollar Man* (see page 19), the Bionic Woman proved girls wanted a superhero(ine) too. Yet Jamie Sommers (played by made-for-TV-movie stalwart **Lindsay Wagner**) only lasted two years, despite being given a bionic dog. In the 1980s TV movie *Bionic Showdown*, a young **Sandra Bullock** played a bionic girl.

The Champions ITV 1968–69

There were many unusual things about **The Champions**, not least that it was one of the rare shows to be cancelled before it had even been screened. Filmed in 1967, but not broadcast until 1969 in the UK (it was sold to the rest of the world first), this fantasy series about secret agents with superpowers anticipated such telefantasies as the **Six Million Dollar Man**. Heroes Craig (**Stuart Damon**), Sharon (**Alexandra Bastedo**) and Richard (**William Gaunt**) had had their senses (and psychic powers) mysteriously enhanced by a kindly Tibetan after their plane crashed. The show is a fine example of what Gaunt calls 'the white Jaguar' school of British TV. The same white Jag, usually hurtling down a lonely road towards a cliff, appeared in (among others) **The Champions** and **Randall And Hopkirk (Deceased)**. ITC accountants couldn't see why, if a character had to die, they couldn't save everyone money and effort by getting in the same car to set out on the same deadly ride.

Department S ITV 1969–70

Look up the word 'louche' in the dictionary and it will say Jason King. As played by Peter Wyngarde, the mystery-writer-cum sleuth was the real star of this camp creation (his colleagues were ciphers) and he soon got his own spin-off. The plots were even more outrageous than some of *The Avengers'* episodes and in some instances, such as the kidnap of an entire village by a crazed Colonel, anticipated **The X-Files** and **Jonathan Creek**.

The Fall Guy ITV 1982–86

In **Lee Majors**' second highly successful action series he starred as Colt Seavers, a Hollywood stuntman who earned pin money by working as a bounty hunter. Another Glen A Larson production (his other offences to be taken into consideration are **Buck Rogers** and **Manimal**), this featured Majors' 'memorable' rendition of the theme song 'Unknown Stuntman'.

The Flash ITV 1990

John Wesley Shipp – who went on to play Dawson's dad Mitch in the teen series **Dawson's Creek** – was the tanned, muscular actor hired to play The Flash in this 1990 series based on the DC Comics character. Scientist Barry Allen, clearly not having a good day, gets covered in chemicals and struck by lightning which, as it would, turns him into an ultra-fast, extra-strong superhero named The Flash. Unintentionally camp, the short-lived series is fondly remembered for its awful dialogue, mediocre plots, and career-worst performances from **Amanda Pays** as Barry's pal and *Homicide: Life On The Street*'s **Richard Belzer** as a TV reporter.

The Incredible Hulk ITV 1978–82

Every decade has a green small-screen icon. In the late 1960s, it was **The Green Hornet**. In the late 1970s it was the Incredible Hulk. **Bill Bixby** starred as Dr David Banner, tormented by the death of his wife (whom he couldn't save), who accidentally zaps himself with a few too many gamma rays and turns into a huge green muscleman (played by former Mr America **Lou Ferrigno**) every time someone annoys him. This doesn't do a lot for his social life (nobody must discover his secret) but, given the shirt-ripping prelude to every transformation, is probably good news for his tailor.

Knight Rider ITV 1983–87

A talking car (voiced by *St Elsewhere*'s William Daniels) out-acts **David Hasselhoff** who plays a cop who was killed but brought back to life by a millionaire. His benefactor also gave him a new identity (Michael Knight) and a souped-up Trans Am car fitted with a talking computer, KITT (Knight Industries Two Thousand) so he could right wrongs, save

Wonder Woman was always giving people lifts – even when she'd left her car at home

the good guys and run the bad guys over. A triumph of kitsch, the series doubtless inspired the designers of the Austin Maestro, the clunky family car that told you if your seatbelt wasn't fastened.

MacGyver ITV 1987–94

Middle-aged female TV viewers (especially Patti and Selma, Marge's sisters on **The Simpsons**) loved **MacGyver**, the one-man A-Team played by **Richard Dean Anderson**. He could make a bomb from a TV aerial and a clothes peg, was always polite to the ladies, and accepted whatever mission a body called The Phoenix Foundation gave him. Travelling only in the clothes he stood up in, he would make a weapon from whatever was handy (maybe the appeal to housewives was that he looked like he'd be a dab hand at fixing the washing machine).

The Man From Atlantis ITV 1977–78

Before Bobby Ewing, **Patrick Duffy** donned webbed hands and feet and green contact lenses to play Mark Harris, a young humourless survivor from the lost city of Atlantis. Instead of using his 'powers' (breathing underwater for long periods, looking good in very small trunks) to raise the *Titanic*, he had to battle his arch-nemesis, evil scientist Mr Schubert. This was the first US TV show bought by the People's Republic of China.

Manimal BBC1 1984

Simon MacCorkindale would probably rather forget his foray into action heroism in this awful but awfully compulsive crime adventure series. He played animal behaviourist Jonathan Chase, who could mutate at will into any species of animal (usually a hawk or tiger; we longed in vain for the day he'd become a three-toed sloth).

Wonder Woman BBC1 1978–80

Initially aimed at young girls, *Wonder Woman* began life in 1974 as a TV movie starring **Cathy Lee Crosby**. By the time beauty queen **Lynda Carter** was cast for three more and the subsequent TV series, the producers must have realised men were watching. Carter was busty and scantily clad in a stars-and-stripes outfit, virtually a swimsuit with a golden utility belt, fighting for her rights in her satin tights. The first season had Wonder Woman (originally from female-only Paradise Island, she used the alias Diana Prince in the US) fighting Nazis. But when the series switched US networks in 1977 it was updated, with **Debra Winger** co-starring as Diana's younger sister, Wonder Girl. Wonder Woman is often seen as a feminist icon yet producers took four inches off her real height: her 'official' height of 5ft 6in was supposed to make her more feminine.

★★★ Adverts ★★★

By the time you're 35, you'll have spent two months of your life watching TV commercials, so it's no surprise that some have acquired cult status. The first advert on British TV aired at 8.12pm on 22 September 1958, ITV's premiere night. It was for **Gibbs SR toothpaste** and featured a tube encased in a block of ice, accompanied by the obligatory RADA-style voiceover. 'It's tingling fresh! It's fresh as ice! It's Gibbs SR toothpaste – the tingling fresh toothpaste that does your gums good too!'

Although our molars might be in tingling health, many feared that commercial television might rot our minds (and this was before **Man O' Man**). ITV's first chairman, Charles Hill, announced Hamlet would not 'interrupt his soliloquy to tell us of the favourite brand of toothpaste used at Elsinore.' Next morning, Bernard Levin wrote in the *Guardian*: 'I feel neither depraved nor uplifted. The advertising has been entirely innocuous. I have already forgotten the name of the toothpaste.'

From brown bread to Blade Runner

In the five decades since, TV ads have become part of our culture, and proved a remarkable training ground for talent. **Jonathan Ross** made his screen debut advertising Raleigh Bikes. **Patsy Kensit** has never surpassed her performance in the Birdseye Garden Peas commercial and **Sarah Michelle Gellar**'s pitch for Burger King was a bigger test of her thespianry than Buffy. And if **Ridley Scott** had never thought of the 1930s' Hovis kid cycling up a hill ('It were like takin' bread to top o' t'world!'), he might

91

never have made *Blade Runner*. TV ads have bred many unsung cult heroes. Like **Jenny Logan**, the demented dancing housewife who insisted we 'Do the Shake 'n' Vac and put freshness back' in the 1980s and **Gary Myers**, the 007-style Cadbury's Milk Tray Man who went to superhuman lengths to deliver a box to his paramour.

Soft drinks were selling hard in the 1970s, with the Real Thing teaching the world to sing along with the **New Seekers**. But the ultimate cult pop star was R White's secret lemonade drinker, perennially sneaking downstairs for an illicit swig, accompanied by the magnificent jingle penned by dance-band singer Ross McManus, aka **Elvis Costello**'s dad. Not forgetting the Cresta polar bear ('It's frothy, man!'), and Um Bongo ('A hippo took an apricot, a guava and a mango, he stuck it with the others and danced a dainty tango'). They drink it in the Congo, you know.

If you fancied something stronger, you could follow George the Hofmeister Bear, dropped for – shock horror – appealing to under-age drinkers. For more cosmopolitan palates, there was the 'any time, any place, anywhere' sophistication of Martini, with **Lorraine Chase** being wafted abroad from Luton Airport. Best of all, there was **Joan Collins** and **Leonard Rossiter** pitching for Cinzano, with Joanie inevitably getting a tumbler-full down her blouse ('Getting your head down, sweetie?'). The ads were dropped because the performances were so funny that nobody could remember what they were actually advertising.

Men From Del Monte, Mars and Henry McGee

No such problems for Mr Kipling and his exceedingly good cakes, Captain Birdseye and his fish fingers or the elusive Man From Del Monte (he say yes). Terry Wogan promoted Flora as 'the margarine for men', while the yellow lads from Country Life insisted that you'll never put a better bit of butter on your knife, or on your Nimble bread once you've piloted that hot-air balloon back down to earth. Meanwhile, from 1973, the For Mash Get Smash metallic Martians mocked us for eating, gasp, real potatoes. And let's not forget Heinz Baked Beans for, as the mighty **Half Man Half Biscuit** once noted: 'A million housewives every day, pick up a tin of beans and say… what a remarkable example of synchronicity.'

The cult cereal killer is Sugar Puffs spokesyeti, the **Honey Monster**, co-starring with **Henry McGee** in the 1970s and baffling pub quizzers in the 1990s as the only player to score for Newcastle and keep goal for Man United in the same season. His closest rivals are Tony the Tiger (Frosties: 'They're grrrrreat!') and Ready Brek's Central Heating For Kids campaign (depicting youngsters with a comforting Sellafield glow).

Back in the 1970s, once you'd shaved with a Remington (which **Victor Kiam** liked so much he bought the company – if true, Mrs Kiam must have winced every time he tried a new product in case he said 'Hon, you know I like these toenail clippers so much…'), you had three choices. You could splash some Brut 33 all over, as recommended by ''**Enery Cooper**', slap on some Old Spice, or don Hai Karate, if you weren't petrified by the thought of being assailed by buxom **Valerie Leon** and her cohorts (but at least the smelly stuff came with tips on self-defence).

The least successful ad ever was probably the early 1960s campaign for Strand cigarettes, featuring a trilby-clad, trench-coated loner with the tagline 'You're never alone with a Strand.' Sadly, viewers didn't want to buy a product for social outcasts although it did inspire **Bryan Ferry** to write 'Do The Strand'. Very recently, **John Cleese**'s Value To Shout About campaign for Sainsbury's tanked, largely because check-suited, bowtied, bellowing Cleese was bloody irritating, and because it portrayed the supermarket's staff as idiots. But the undisputed worst commercial of all time must be the one for **Ferrero Rocher**, its non-ironic kitsch take on intercontinental glamour ('Monsieur, wiz zees Ferrero Rocher you are really spoileeng us!') rapidly becoming a chocolate-coated cult all by itself.

★★★ Animals ★★★

Barbapapa BBC2 1973

No one knows what kind of animal Barbapapa is. But, like the rest of his family, he's made up of pink ectoplasm and can transmogrify as fast as he can say 'All change'. It's a gift kids the world over grew to envy, which may be why so many of us remember those tones, hovering somewhere between dull and dulcet. He started out as the star of such

French children's books as *Barbapapa, La Maison De Barbapapa* and *L'Ecole De Barbapapa* – you get the picture. But how many of you recall the rest of the family? Barbamama, Barbabravo, Barbazoo, Barbabelle, Barbalala, Barbabeau, Barbabright, and Barbalib. Bad girl Barbarella, alas, is never mentioned after falling foul of the pink patriarch.

Champion The Wonder Horse BBC1 1956–57

Produced by **Gene Autry**, this tale of a boy, a wonder horse and a dog called Rebel on the southwest frontier was one of those shows which peaked too early. Indeed, to be exact, it peaked in the opening credits, when the wonderful theme tune blazed out, sung by **Frankie Laine**.

★ What animals like to watch ★

Cats
In January 1999, **Whiskas** launched a new TV ad campaign. Nothing unusual in that, except it spent £600,000 creating an ad that would actually be watched by cats. The 40-second ad showed fish, mice, birds and a ball of string. Whiskas also ran a 10-second pre-ad, urging owners to line up their cats in front of the set to watch the new ad. Cats do watch TV, usually from very close to the screen and attracted by movement, although studies also show cats are as likely to watch shadows on a set as the programmes. In tests, six out of ten cats showed they preferred this new Whiskas ad by, for example, twitching their ears or tapping the set.

Chickens
Tests at Edinburgh's Roslin Institute have proved that letting battery chickens watch around **30 minutes of soaps** a day on TV made them 'more rounded, less self-conscious and lay larger eggs'.

Gorillas
Nico and Samba, two West African gorillas at Longleat, preferred to watch **David Attenborough** and **Tom And Jerry**. Nico liked **Planet Of The Apes** so much he ran around the cage collecting food before it was on, in the time-honoured fashion of males of every species about to plonk themselves in front of the set for a while.

Deputy Dawg BBC1 1963–64

Dopey canine deputy defends hen coop from various varmints, says 'Just one cotton-pickin' moment' a lot, and entertains us all.

Hector's House BBC1 1968–70

How did 'big silly old Hector' get a mortgage? This teatime favourite was originally the French show *La Maison De Tu Tu*. **Joanna Lumley** provided the voice for Zaza, Hector's co-habitor, a cat in a red pinafore. Kiki the frog was the neighbour who seemed to live in their home.

Lassie ITV 1956–73

Lassie was television's first gender bender. She was actually a he with a patch of fur over his testicles. Apparently the problems associated with having a bitch on heat were more serious than having a sex-starved dog. This didn't stop the gender-bending dog from saving the world. 'Lure Of The Wild' is a favourite episode, mainly because when Lassie is running down the road you can see the shadow of the cameraman's truck. **Cloris Leachman** started out on this show, bless her.

White Horses BBC1 1968

This Yugoslavian import came round about as often as the school summer holidays. Those who are old enough will be able to sing the theme song (sung by **Jackie**, a number ten hit and since covered by indie bands with varying degrees of irony). Rather like *Champion*, the show went downhill from there, downhill into Enid Blyton land as Julia (**Helga Anders**) and Uncle Dimitri (**Helmuth Schneider**) saved the horses from being nicked, lost or made into glue.

★★★ Animation ★★★

Animation, for the purposes of this guide, is broadly defined as stuff for grown ups and little grown ups – ie the diminutive and the over-tens. The children's cartoon section starts on p107. **The Simpsons**, as the definitive adult animation series, is in one of our 56 top shows on p66.

Beavis And Butthead Christmas specials sure beat Perry Como's Christmas turkeys

Beavis And Butthead MTV 1993–97

Mike Judge created and provided the voices for two incredibly dumb, heavy-metal-loving teens (Beavis is the blond in the Metallica T-shirt; Butthead has braces and an AC/DC top) for a crudely animated cartoon short that caught the eye of MTV. **Beavis And Butthead** premiered as a series and became a cult hit as kids tuned in to watch the snickering adolescent slackers critique music videos, lust after voluptuous neighbours, and set fire to things. (When a five-year-old boy set fire to his family's home after watching the show, the series was switched to a later hour and the boys no longer carried their lighters.)

Clerks Disney 2000

Kevin Smith turned his first movie, the black and white comedy *Clerks*, into a colour cartoon. Six episodes were made but only two shown in the US (all are now available on video). Each followed the adventures of convenience store clerks Dante and Randall (voiced by **Brian O'Halloran** and **Jeff Anderson**, who played the characters in the movie), while Kevin Smith recreated his character Silent Bob. Deemed too risqué for TV, the series attracted a host of guest voices, including **Matt Damon** as himself, Judge Reinhold as The Honourable Judge Reinhold, and **Alec Baldwin**.

The Critic Bravo 1995

Movie critics got their own hero of sorts with this animated comedy about film critic Jay Sherman, a fat, balding, whiny and neuroses-filled man who has a young son, Marty, and a pitying ex-wife. Each week Jay has to review movies he hates for his show, which gave the series' creators the chance to launch well-aimed jabs at movies and TV. **Jon Lovitz** supplied the voice of Jay while **Nancy Cartwright** (the voice of Bart Simpson) is the voice of his ex-wife. The show was made by the same TV company as *The Simpsons*, and Jay turned up as guest critic at a festival organised by Marge Simpson.

Dr Katz Paramount 1995–

Voiced by comic **Jonathan Katz**, this was a loony toon for adults, about a shrink who once treated a woman for her fear of adverbs.

Duckman BBC2 1995–

Deliciously twisted adult cartoon about a useless private eye who happens to be a duck (voiced by **Jason Alexander** of *Seinfeld*). Created by the team behind **Rugrats**, and featuring an innovative cartoon style, music by Frank Zappa and cynical humour, this was definitely not for children ('Remember kids, when you get to prison attach yourself to the biggest, toughest, meanest-looking goon you can find. You don't wanna wind up as just anyone's bitch!').

• Phil Hartman •

You might remember him as Troy McClure, Springfield Z-list celeb and star of such documentaries as *Man Versus Nature: The Road To Victory*. Or you might remember him as the bloke from *Saturday Night Live* who, when he was just 50 with greater fame beckoning, was shot by his third wife Brynn in June 1998, minutes before she turned the gun on herself.

As an impersonator of grinning, vacant, handsome actors he was as good as anyone, except possibly the occupant of the Oval Office for most of the 1980s. His motto was 'don't go too far with the caricature' and he made all his impersonations, be they of Phil Donahue or McClure or down-at-heel attorney Lionel Hutz ('Mrs Simpson, your sexual harassment suit is exactly what I need to help rebuild my shattered practice. Care to join me in a belt of scotch?') utterly believable – even, in McClure's case, oddly sympathetic, which took some vocal talent.

Family Guy Sky 1999

The family guy in question in this hilarious series from Seth McFarlane (who had written for **Cow And Chicken**) is pudgy, stupid but loveable Peter Griffin, who muddles through life with the help of his wife Lois, eternally embarrassed daughter Megan, dim-witted son Chris (voiced by *Buffy The Vampire Slayer*'s **Seth Green**) and cynical talking dog Brian. Stealing the show is baby Stewie, who unbeknown to the family is highly intelligent and secretly plotting to annihilate them and take over the world.

God, The Devil And Bob BBC2 2000

God (voiced by **James Garner**) and the Devil (voiced by **Alan Cumming**) have made a bet. The Devil can choose one human, and if that man can't prove to them that there is still human decency in the world, God has to scrap the world and start over. The person the Devil chooses is Bob (*Third Rock From The Sun*'s French Stewart), a car factory worker who can see and hear the Devil (trying to tempt him) and God (offering words of wisdom) but no one else can. It's up to Bob to stay sane and decent to save the world in this often sharp comedy that ran for one season.

King Of The Hill Channel 4, Sky 1997–

When Hank Hill meets his idol **Willie Nelson**, it is a tender moment. 'Hey Hank,' says Willie, 'your son Bobby's been telling me all about you. I hear you like playing guitar and you've got a narrow urethra.' A seductive adult companion to *The Simpsons*, this creation by **Mike Judge** (of *Beavis* fame) and **Greg Daniels** (from *The Simpsons*) offers an amusing insight into the kind of suburbia where the neighbours' idea of a good time is comparing power tools. Best line? Hank on discovering a ra-ra costume in his son's room: ' Bobby – there had better be a naked cheerleader under your bed!'

South Park Channel 4 1997–

Controversy raged on both sides of the Atlantic when **Trey Parker** and **Matt Stone** launched their cartoon about four foul-mouthed kids. Set in the Colorado mountain town of South Park, each episode follows the antics of Kyle, Stan, obese Cartman and Kenny (who has a tendency to die

Dale and Hank: shooting the breeze and comparing the width of their urethras

horribly in each episode, leading another character to exclaim 'Oh My God! They killed Kenny!') and their friends Chef (voiced by soulman **Isaac Hayes**) and repressed teacher Mr Garrison. Packed with foul language and rude plotlines (Cartman's mother being shown to be a slut, Satan and Saddam Hussein having an S&M gay affair), the series has often been criticised (why? it's really funny) but remains popular and idiosyncratic.

Teenage Mutant Ninja Turtles BBC1, BSkyB 1988–95

Starting life as a napkin doodle by **Kevin Eastman** and **Peter Laird**, the Teenage Mutant Ninja Turtles were a group of, naturally, mutant turtles (they lived in the New York sewers where they had been exposed to a weird substance) with a fondness for pizza and kicking butt (under the instruction of Splinter the rat). Named Leonardo, Michaelangelo, Donatello and Raphael, the team became a huge success when the animated series was launched in 1987, leading to a 1990 live action movie and another series.

99

In Japan and some European countries, the series had to be renamed *Teenage Mutant Hero Turtles* as 'Ninja' was deemed too violent. Cowabunga fever has now abated somewhat, but for a time it was almost as global a phenomenon as *Big Brother* madness.

★★★ Arts ★★★

Inside The Actor's Studio Performance 1995–

You may take a while to warm to **James Lipton** as he interviews his endless procession of seriously famous guests but even the duller episodes offer minor revelations, such as **Faye Dunaway**'s prim refusal to say her favourite curse word (the closest she gets is 'shoot!'). The best, especially the interviews with **Mike Myers** and **Anthony Hopkins**, are so intriguing you're disappointed to spend only an hour in their company.

Rolf On Art BBC1 2001

Rolf and **Vincent van Gogh** once came first and second when an opinion pollster asked the British public to name an artist. So it was good to see them reunited in *Rolf On Art*, the series which irritated critics and pulled in six million viewers. We side with *The Times*' Paul Hoggart: 'I may find Rolf's cheesy, folksy manner about as appealing as a poke up the nose with a wet paint brush, but I did learn things that I did not know before.'

Watercolour Challenge Channel 4 1998–

Hannah Gordon offers low-key continuity in this strangely addictive show which does for water colours what *Changing Rooms* did for home décor. Three amateur painters spend four hours at their easel, have their work appraised by an expert and, if they're lucky, win some art supplies. The complete antidote to hype, this series will run and run.

Without Walls – Dennis Potter Channel 4 1994

A reviewer on epinions.com sums this up succinctly, if slightly unfairly: 'Pros: Potter; Cons: Bragg'. Interviewed weeks before his death, Potter talks frankly about Rupert Murdoch, after whom he named his cancer;

divine beings ('God is a rumour') and his uneasy relationship with his dad. This is one of the few programmes to remind you that, as **Orson Welles** put it, 'the chat show is the only art form invented by TV.'

★★★ Banned ★★★

Television is not an uncontroversial medium although it's not always easy to say what will trigger a controversy and why – as you will discover.

The Ed Sullivan Show CBS Television 1957

Ed Sullivan, who dominated American TV in the 1950s, had sworn he wouldn't touch a new hip-swinging singing sensation called **Elvis Presley** with a barge pole. But when the Pelv helped a rival show stomp on Ed's ratings, Sullivan did the dirty deal. On Elvis' last appearance with Ed Sullivan, he started to sway and Sullivan, standing in the wings, imme-diately made a sweeping motion with his hand to tell the camera-man to shoot above Presley's waist. Elvis later recalled: 'There was Sullivan in the wings staring at me mumbling "Son of a bitch" and I didn't know what he was saying so I was saying "Thank you very much, Mr. Sullivan."'

Family Fortunes ITV 1978–
Hard to imagine this innocuous game show upsetting the author-ities but Central TV soon learned, the hard way, that they had to screen the questions asked of 100 randomly selected mem-bers of the British public. In the first pilot, seven of the 100

'And let's hear it for the Thicke family...'

asked to 'Name a dangerous race apart from the Grand Prix' replied 'Arabs'. Later in the first series, the producers had to cut the laughter from the studio audience, which greeted the Thicke family from Ireland. Sadly, Mrs Thicke lived down to her surname. Asked to name something which 100 people had identified as blue, she mulled it over and said: 'Would it be me cardigan by any chance?'

I Dream Of Jeannie   ITV 1966–70

Lucky astronaut Tony Nelson (**Larry Hagman**) landed back on Earth on a desert island, there to meet his own personal genie called Jeannie (**Barbara Eden**) who was supposed to be 2,000 years old but didn't look a day over 25. The series was made in 1966 and although the Rolling Stones were singing about spending the night together, NBC decreed that Eden could wear a bikini but viewers could not see her navel. Footage was checked to make sure no contemplation of Eden's navel was possible.

World Cup   Iranian TV 1994

Iranian television showed edited highlights of the 1994 World Cup, edited to cut out scenes of female spectators wearing Islamically incorrect outfits. So, while the players were shown sweltering in the 90 degree heat in a stadium like Orlando, Iranian TV cut from the action to crowd scenes taken from an Iranian League game played the previous winter where spectators wore gloves, woolly coats and hats.

★★★ Breakfast ★★★

The great breakfast TV war started in 1983 when TV-AM entered mortal combat with Frank and Selina on BBC1. Despite enlisting two skydivers, 917 pigeons, 1,000 crewmen of *HMS Hermes* and 6,000 Bristolians for its credit sequence, TV-AM's ratings soon began to sink until **Roland Rat** emerged as an unlikely saviour. The revamp, led by **Greg Dyke**, led, almost seamlessly (in terms of content if not corporately) to the **GMTV** we love or loathe today. Oddly, having won the ratings war with Uncle Frank, the BBC now offers a rather self-important news-based service.

The Big Breakfast Channel 4 1992–2002

Worth watching for Chris and Gaby, Johnny and Denise, Zig and Zag ('Hello to all you mums, dads, brothers, sisters, and small kitchen utensils'), Richard Bacon and the late Paula Yates' interviews. Strangely compelling when **Sharon Davies** was presenting, although her shoulders were more charismatic than she was. The best ideas (egg on your face: guess the mystery celeb with the egg covering their physog) were the kind of wheezes Kelvin McKenzie would have come up with if he'd understood television. Bad as it could be, *BB* looks better than ever compared to the fast sinking *RI:SE*. The punctuation device in the middle of the word was a gimmick last used by L!ve TV. Which is, of course, now ext!nct.

And finally… a list of people you've probably forgotten you've shared breakfast with: Toni Arthur, Russell Grant, Debbie Greenwood, John Noakes, Naval Commander David Philpott, Jeremy Beadle, Richard Keys, Diana Dors, Fern Britton, Eve Pollard, Danny Baker, Ruth Madoc, Derek Jameson, Kevin The Gerbil and Colin The Flea. Scary.

★★★ Canned ★★★

Just six shows that dared to be different, a daring which sealed their fate.

Cows Channel 4 1997

Despite being the brainchild of one of Britain's funniest stand-up comedians, six years in development and production by the team behind **Coogan's Run**, *Cows* never got past a single, one-hour pilot episode. **Eddie Izzard** saw the show as 'like *Planet Of The Apes* with a *Simpsons* sensibility'. Audiences struggled with the idea of **Pam Ferris** (then popular as Ma Larkin in *Darling Buds Of May*) dressed in a prosthetic cow costume preparing for her son's wedding to a human. *Cows* may have been simply ahead of its time – talking cows attempting to become a Tory MP (as one episode was due to feature) being just what television is missing today. But in 1997 it was received, as Izzard put it, 'like a long-lost relative who turns up at the wrong house with an overdue Christmas card.'

Hardwicke House ITV 1987

Bullying by staff and pupils, under-age sex, corruption, a standout scene where a second year is force fed raw liver and has his head flushed down the toilet... it's easy to see why this Central TV sitcom (with a cast which included **Roy Kinnear**, **Pam Ferris**, and **Tony Haygarth**) proved controversial. This being Thatcher's Britain, the outcry was loud enough for ITV to pull this after just two episodes. A scandal really.

Jossy's Giants BBC1 1984

Jossy's Giants dealt with the exploits of shellsuited Geordie Jossy (**Jim Barclay**) as an ex-footballer coaching a floundering northern youth team, the Glipton Grasshoppers (the worst television football team name, ever). It offered something for everyone – cute lads in shorts for the girls, football for the lads (including a cameo by **Bryan Robson** – as unconvincing as his performance on the bench in his last season at Middlesbrough), and a catchy theme tune: 'Here go Jossy's Giants/Football's just a branch of science'. And it was written by darts and pool commentator **Sid Waddell**, who once said: 'Even hypotenuse would have trouble working out these angles.'

Police Squad ITV 1982

You could be forgiven for thinking that *Police Squad*, which led to the *Naked Gun* movie trilogy, was a smash. But the small screen antics of Detective Frank Drebin lasted a mere six episodes. Packed with quirky touches that ensured immediate cult status, each episode featured a special guest star being murdered – **Lorne Greene** and **William Conrad** were knifed, Florence Henderson was shot and **William Shatner** poisoned. Leslie Nielsen's deadpan wit – 'It took me two weeks to find Stella's apartment. She had neglected to give me her address' – complimented the intricate visual gags. The final episode was to have featured **John Belushi** as the doomed special guest, but he died shortly after filming and it was never shown.

Springhill Channel 4 1996

Springhill was a curio. Co-created by **Frank Cottrell Boyce** (the former *Living Marxism* columnist who wrote the script for *24 Hour Party People*), the show focused on the return of Eva Morgan into the lives of the Freeman family of whom (we finally learned) she was the real mum. (Mind you she nearly began an affair with one of the sons.) Writers **Paul Cornell** and **Gareth Roberts** (*Dr Who* graduates) showed their love of sci-fi when the series ended with the youngest son running off into the hills to search for his lost mum and escape the devil woman/housekeeper who was chasing him. They don't make 'em like this any more. Although ITV tried in 1997 with the altogether ooky **Wokenwell** (doomed to fail in a Sunday evening slot normally reserved by ITV for **Heartbeat**), in which three policemen in a small northern town deal with minimal crime with help from their wives. That this wasn't *Last Of The Summer Wine* country rapidly became apparent when a severed human hand was found next to a wedding cake.

★★★ Chat shows ★★★

Chat shows are a good excuse not to talk to members of your family and spend just enough time in a celeb's company for them not to become annoying. **David Letterman**, who towers above this genre like a tall towering bloke with a top ten list in his hand, is profiled on p312. His only British rival is **Parkinson**, although even he's less compelling now he's forced to interview Posh Spice every week and not Richard Burton or Mohammed Ali. Jonathan Ross' **The Last Resort** (Channel 4) was also a work of genius, albeit short lived.

Aspel & Company ITV 1984–93

Aspel was born to be draped across a sofa, lobbing anecdote-cueing 'questions' at guests straight off the showbiz-plug-circuit conveyor belt. Nine years of Aspel as host produced just one memorable incident but it will live long in the memory: **Oliver Reed**'s appearance on 19 February 1987. Reed had threatened to show his tattooed penis backstage and then entered 'through the set' according to his fellow guest **Clive James**, bellowing out The Troggs' 'Wild Thing' and took it from there. 'You have a great talent. Why do you drink?' asked James. 'Because the people I like most are in pubs,' said Ollie.

Clive Anderson Talks Back/All Talk Channel 4, BBC 1989–99

Anderson's brand of snide, point-scoring humour has its appeal – though not to the **Bee Gees**. When **Jeffrey Archer** congratulated him on his quick wit, Anderson said: 'I hadn't realised you were a critic as well as a writer, Jeffrey… there's no beginning to your talents.' Archer unwisely replied, 'I always say the old ones are the best, Clive,' to which Anderson harrumphed 'Yes, I've read your books.' What Clive lacked, however, was any curiosity about his subjects, unless they were **Goldie Hawn**.

Knowing Me Knowing You BBC2 1994

Not strictly a chat show – spoof hosts are one thing, but team them up with spoof guests and it's a sitcom – but any review of TV chat shows is

---

★ Chat is a four-letter word ★

E is for emu. This relentlessly pesky puppet, plaything of Rod Hull and popular on children's TV during the 1970s, was responsible for the only instance in which the unflappable Parky lost his cool. Emu pecked and prodded his long-suffering host before grabbing him and knocking him to the floor. Billy Connolly was also on that show and Emu made the mistake of swiping at The Big Yin. Connolly grabbed Emu's throat, and growled: 'If you do that again I'll break your neck and his (ie Hull's) arm.'

I is for insulting, blue rinse ladies. Dame Edna Everage, Housewife Superstar, warped creation of Australian comic genius Barry Humphries, was the first spoof chat show host, the first female chat show host and the first to host a show that wasn't a pluggers' delight. Sadly, she became a slave to the double entendre, Mrs Nudge Nudge Wink Wink.

N is for not very good hosts. Richard and Judy, Joan Rivers, Danny Baker, Harold Wilson. The producer Iain Johnstone knew he had a struggle with Harold Wilson's short lived BBC2 show when he told Wilson 'We'll do the show at 7pm' for the Labour legend to reply, 'Haven't we just done it?'

Q for questions. Many are memorable: Jay Leno's to Hugh Grant ('What were you thinking of?'), Mrs Merton asking George Best whether it was 'all that running around playing football that makes you so thirsty?' But Gloria Hunniford, of all people, came up with the all-time classic. Stranded on a sofa with Brigitte Nielsen (she of the silicon breasts), she popped the one question all of us wanted to ask: 'Is it true they blow up on planes?'

incomplete without reference to this murderously precise pastiche. A hilarious lampoon of every lunkheaded twerp who's ever donned a 'tasteful' V-neck jumper and risen from his seat as some gormless actress slunk down the staircase, it did for a certain brand of chat-show host what **Smashie and Nicey** did for the old-style Radio 1 DJ (ie rendered them obsolete). Unlike Smashie and Nicey, the show's power lies not in gross caricature but in being so nearly believable (in its original form as a Radio 4 series, listeners, thinking it to be genuine, rang in to complain).

Russell Harty BBC 2 1974

Mildly camp, mildly amusing, mildly intelligent and mildly eccentric, Russell was an accepted part of the TV furniture. Attacked by the mayor of his home town – 'You may be big in London, but you're bugger-all in Blackburn' – he was also the hapless victim of Amazonian songstress Grace Jones who took umbrage when Russell turned his back on her, and lamped him. Blows rained down before the flailing host, dignity in shreds, restored order. A small price to pay for a place in TV history.

TFI Friday Channel 4 1996–2000

Painful as it may be to acknowledge, the Ginger Whinger's show, in its heyday, was quick, bright, cocky and unhinged to just the right degree. Now carving out a second career as Mr Billie Piper.

★★★ Children's cartoons ★★★

Bod BBC1/2 1975–76

A short, bald kid wearing a yellow dress wanders around, meeting the same people – Aunt Flo, PC Copper – over and over again This 'action' was interspersed with *Alice In Wonderland*-style events. Strange, unfathomable, and brilliant. Narrated by John Le Mesurier.

Dangermouse ITV 1981–87, 1991–92

A cartoon rodent take on **Patrick McGoohan**'s *Danger Man*, the show added a new dimension to children's cartoons with classic tales of secret agents complemented with Pythonesque imagery and narrated asides, and sophisticated humour that adults and kids could enjoy. It was the work of a motley crew of talents, including *Screen Test* presenter Brian Trueman, comedian **Mike Harding**, **David Jason** as DM and **Terry Scott** as Penfold. The show went on to become the first successful animated export to the US. Fascinating fact: Dangermouse had 730 white suits and eye-patches.

Doctor Snuggles ITV 1980

Contrary to popular belief, the strangely-trousered chubby doctor was not created by **Douglas Adams**. Pre-dating Adams' success, *Hitchhiker's Guide To The Galaxy*, he and co-writer **John Lloyd** were hired by Jeffrey O'Kelly to help flesh out a new story idea he had, inspired by his pet chameleon, Mooney Snuggles. Mooney became Dr Snuggles and O'Kelly re-wrote Adams' work influenced by poet **Ted Hughes**. **Peter Ustinov** become the voice of O'Kelly's amiable doctor.

Dogtanian And The Three Muskehounds ITV 1985

Swashbuckling doggy-style in this cute canine re-working of the **Alexandre Dumas** novel set in 17th-century France. Most people just remember the breakneck speed in which it was dubbed, and the catchy theme tune, 'One for all and all for one/It's a pretty story/Sharpening everything with fun/That's the way to be.'

Galaxy High ITV 1987

If you managed to reach 9am on a Saturday morning having resisted the temptation to smash up the TV to shut up **Timmy Mallet**, you would have been rewarded, if briefly – only 13 episodes were ever made – with American space cartoon **Galaxy High**. Galaxy high school was attended by kids throughout the Milky Way, with humans Doyle Cleverlobe (annoying Philip Schofield lookalike) and Aimee Brighttower mingling with creatures from other planets, including multiple-mouthed Gilda Gossip and Booey Bubblehead (she had a bubblehead). Like most American shows there was a touching message – all the kids got along well despite their obvious differences – but it worked.

Hergé's Adventures Of Tin Tin BBC1 1962–64

By the time the narrator (**Peter Hawkins** of *Pugwash* fame) had finished reminding you what happened last week and asked the cliffhanging questions which marked the climax of this five-minute cartoon, there really wasn't much time for Tin Tin and his dog Snowy to do anything.

The Jackson Five ITV 1971

After The Archies, and before Jacko went solo and wacko, the Jackson 5 had a cute, cuddly, cartoon series, as easy to watch as A-B-C.

James The Cat ITV 1984

James was a sanctimonious, big, fat, black and white cat who, whilst chasing birds and butterflies around the garden, bragged to his Corner House companions. He shouldn't have been loveable, but his owners had abandoned him, leaving him to the mercies of an odd set of mates who included Dennis, a pink Chinese dragon with a Welsh accent, an ex-employee of the Emperor of China and Rocky, a rabbit from the Bronx who used to be a boxer. With friends like these…

Danger Mouse was almost as much of a neverstoptothinkamouse as Fingermouse

Jamie And The Magic Torch ITV 1978

'Jamie! Jamie! No two nights are the same/And life is one long glorious game with Jamie/Jamie and the Magic Torch.' If this doesn't ring any bells, just think Donny Osmond crossed with Rick Astley (wearing disastrous yellow bell-bottom pyjamas). As its name suggests, Jamie had a magic torch capable of taking him and his best friend, Wordsworth the dog (he only had a shadow of a mother to make matters worse) to Cuckooland. The animation was trippy and no one seems to know what it all meant. Rumours are a big-screen version is in the offing.

Ludwig ITV 1977

Ludwig, a mechanical violin-playing egg, lived in the woods, saving his pals from various perils while being spied on by a mysterious man in a deerstalker with binoculars. Just your run-of-the-mill kids' cartoon then.

Moomins will go to any extreme to escape their loud tuba-playing neighbours, the Hemulens

Marine Boy BBC1 1969–70

In this ecologically sound Japanese cartoon, Marine Boy battled to save the seas from the nefarious schemes of Captain Nazi et al with a selection of 007-inspired gadgets. But it was full of tension and comedy: Would Marine Boy's Oxygum run out of oxygen before he saved the waves? And why was Marine Boy voiced by female landlubber **Corinne Orr**?

Mary, Mungo And Midge BBC2 1971

Captain Pugwash creator **John Ryan** paid homage to the public inform-ation film with this toon about the perils of urban life. Mary's main fear was lifts so each episode included free useful advice on pressing the right button. This may be why it only last-ed 13 episodes – there's a limit to how much even Mary (human), Mungo (dog) and Midge (mouse) can tell you about lifts. Best remembered for Richard Baker's sanguine narration.

Moomins ITV 1983

Not to be confused with *Moomin*, the Japanese animated version of the children's books by **Tove Jansson**. The Moomins, who rose to the dizzy heights of their own theme park in Finland, were mouthless white trolls who lived amid a dark Scandinavian forest. They shared their lives with the equally odd Snork Maiden (did she and Moominpappa have improper relations? I think we should be told), Snufkin, a wandering musician, and the Hemulens, a group of loud, tuba-playing bores (heck, we've all had

★ Hanna Barbera ★

Given the productivity of William Hanna, a former engineer, and ex-banker Joseph Barbera, we couldn't include all their creations. But we made room to squeeze in these…

The Flintstones
Before John Goodman of course.

Hong Kong Phooey
One side mild-mannered (aren't all super-heroes) police station janitor, kung-fu, street-wise super dog on the other. And don't forget his sniggering cat sidekick. Actor and musician Scatman Crothers brought him to life.

The Jetsons
Space age update of the stone age Flintstones.

Secret Squirrel
007 spoof with a rodent secret agent and his Peter-Lorre-like sidekick Morocco Mole.

Snagglepuss
Sartorially elegant lion, always with matching collar and cuffs and never losing his cool. Heavens to Murgatroid indeed.

neighbours like that). Sadly overshadowed in the UK by the Japanese version: you probably need to have grown up in the daylight-deprived winters of Finland and northern Poland to best understand the appeal.

Mr Benn BBC1 1971–

The 13 episodes of this children's animation have been resurfacing on the Beeb for 30-odd years. In them, our eponymous hero goes into a costume shop and tries on an outfit which transforms him magically into anything from a cowboy to a balloonist. The very simplicity of **David McKee's** premise has sparked many to ponder whether the show has religious, Freudian or political roots (was Mr Benn part of a plot to undermine Anthony Wedgwood Benn?). Until McKee tells us otherwise, the sanest explanation is probably the best: this is just a children's TV show.

A Homepride reject?

Murun Buchstansangur Channel 4 1982–85

Nobody's quite sure what Murun Buchstansangur was. The nearest scientists and aficionados have come is to say he was small enough to live in a crack under a kitchen cupboard. Small enough, also, to be squeezed into four-minute fillers on Channel 4's schedule.

Pingu BBC1/2 1990–

Those who learned conversational Clanger thrilled to the linguistic challenge posed by this baby penguin/anarchic genius, who had a strange fixation with toilets. Must be something to do with long Swiss winters.

The Pink Panther Show BBC1 1970–71

The coolest cat on the block, created solely for the opening credits of the Blake Edwards 1963 movie, *The Pink Panther*, earned better reviews than the film and a show of his own. The original remains the best, with the opening scene of the sports car (the one with the pointy nose) and which saw the panther battling the inspector. A mysterious character who, in Mexico and Spain is, for reasons best known to them, portrayed as a girl.

Rugrats Nickelodeon, BBC 1996–

The title is American slang for kids. The soundtrack is by Mark Mothersbaugh of Mormon punk band **Devo**. And there's Chucky, who's a spotty, short-sighted, ginger-haired coward. And we love him to death.

Scooby Doo, Where Are You? BBC1 1970–72

Okay, the follow-up with nephew Scrappy Doo should have been scooped up by the owners and flushed away for public health reasons, but the original kept us laughing for more years than we'd care to admit, given that it was always the same plot. Yet if repetition is an art form, the regularity with which the culprit tore off their mask and spluttered about 'pesky, meddling kids' must make *Scooby Doo* a work of genius.

Wacky Races BBC1 1969–70

No explanation needed really. Based on the 1966 Blake Edwards' film, *The Great Race*, the cartoon version had all the essential elements: a fab theme tune, a wealth of oddball characters and brilliant animation. Villain Dick Dastardly was voiced by **Paul Winchell**, who aside from also being the voice of Tigger, was an amateur inventor who patented an artificial human heart. **Don Messick** (also Scooby Doo and Boo Boo among others) was the wheezing voice of Mutley, while **Daws Butler** (Yogi Bear) gave voice to Pat Pending, Peter Perfect and the Ant Hill Mob.

Willo The Wisp BBC1 1982

Without **Kenneth Williams** this would have been a non-starter. The stories may have been threadbare but

---

★ Animated cuties ★

Not human but still sexy...

1 Daphne, Scooby Doo
No wonder Fred was so bloody smug.

2 Lady Penelope, Thunderbirds
If you fancy a bit of posh (with a small p), few were as delectable as Lady Penelope.

3 Penelope Pitstop
Beautiful, classy, with her own wheels and stupid: an unbeatable combination.

Over to you ladies...
As most puppets of the supermarionation era were modelled on Cary Grant, there wasn't much to choose between Troy Tempest, Captain Scarlet or, for girls who always fall for the wrong guy, Captain Black. Alan Tracy, the blond one, obviously appealed to the butler's daughter (Tin Tin). The rest of us can't see the attraction.

the sneering Williams managed to give each of the 2D characters a personality of their own. An instant success, it reached the top 50 of the BARB chart – relatively unheard of for a kids' programme. A new series is on its way, **James Dreyfus** having the hard task of replacing Williams.

★★★ Children's drama ★★★

The Adventures Of Robinson Crusoe BBC1 1965

Robert Hofman played Robinson Crusoe and Fabian Canalos was his sidekick Friday, but most of us just remember the theme, the time-lag delays in dubbing and the beach. Nothing much seemed to happen but something made us feel obliged to watch it anyway.

Box Of Delights BBC1 1984

'Herne The Hunter, keep your lions away from my unicorns.' You don't hear that very often on telly anymore. **Box Of Delights** was a quaint Edwardian children's drama, with the lion, the witch and the wardrobe replaced by a pack of angry wolves disguised as clergymen (what else?). **Patrick Troughton**, aka Doctor Who 2, played the kindly hobo who persuades Kay Harker (Devin Stanfield) to take care of his box of delights while Robert Stephens excelled as the baddie trying to steal it. Included a promising cameo by Nick ('Every Loser Wins') Berry as a pirate rat.

Children Of The Stones ITV 1977

Spooky goings-on in Wales, with the good folk in the small town of Milbury under the spell of a group of Neolithic stones. Each episode saw father (**Gareth Thomas** of *Blake's 7*) and son (Peter Denim) drawing closer to discovering the truth behind the circle of stones' psychic powers. An instant hit, kids seemed to like a show which portrayed a father joining in with junior's imaginings, rather than grounding him for telling tales.

Daktari BBC1 1966–69

The title is Swahili for 'doctor' – not that it matters much as Marshall Thompson (as Dr Marsh) is, like every other human actor – even Erin

Moran (Joanie in *Happy Days*) – out-acted by Clarence the cross-eyed lion and Judy, the chimp who'd had her teeth extracted after biting several actors during *Lost In Space*. Dr Marsh wore a cravat, possibly a bit formal for a doctor running a game reserve in deepest, darkest Africa.

Dark Season BBC1 1991

Commissioned to replace **Maid Marion** whilst Tony Robinson took time off, *Dark Season* was dubbed the kid's *Dr Who*, not least because it was conceived by Russell Davies, a devout *Dr Who* fan. Three precocious school friends, led by Marcie (Victoria Lambert) – wise beyond her years and with Doctorish qualities, try to stop a computer achieving world domination. Davies denies any intentional links to his favourite show but devoted fans have noted direct quotes from *Dr Who*, such as 'Nothing in the world can stop me now!' from 'The Underwater Menace'. This Who nonsense aside, it also marked the debut of a red-headed **Kate Winslet** as Reet. Davies later headed to more controversial climes with *Queer As Folk*.

The Demon Headmaster BBC1 1996–98

The **Dr Who** of the 1990s, in which **Terence Hardiman** is the demonic head ('Childhood is such a useless waste of time') who has the power to brainwash his pupils and wants to take over the world. Who does he think he is – a James Bond villain? Only young bright spark Dina Hunter (Frances Amey) can resist his powers and foil his plans. Gripping stuff, even if you're no longer school age.

Follyfoot ITV 1971–73

Young Dora (Gillian Blake) is sent to live with her kindly uncle whilst her parents swan off round the world. Fortunately for Dora, her uncle, the Colonel (played by **Desmond Llewelyn** when he wasn't being Q), owns a farm full of neglected horses. Thirty-nine episodes were made before **Arthur English** went off to star in *Are You Being Served?* and Steve Hodson had a hit single with a little help from the Bee Gees with 'Crystal Bay'. Also boasted a catchy theme tune ('Down in the meadow where the wind blows free/In the middle of a field stands the lightning tree'). **Flambards** (starring Christine McKenna) was another variation on the theme, slightly nastier and with planes providing the escapism rather than horses.

Here Come The Double Deckers BBC1 1970

Originally rejected by the BBC who opted instead for the imaginatively titled *Adventure Weekly*, this British troop became a huge success in the US, when the corporation decided to take the series after all. Although many of the stories were taken from old Children's Film Foundation films, the **Double Deckers** were refreshingly not just another Famous Five/Scooby Doo rip-off. There were no mysterious or supernatural plots, just a bunch of kids having fun in their gang clubhouse courtesy of London Transport. It saw early appearances by a few stars, including **Peter Firth** (Scooper), and **Brinsley Forde**, who became the lead singer with Aswad.

Jonny Briggs BBC1 1985

More of a dramatic comedy than full-blown tear-fest, Jonny started life as a **Jackanory** story. Apart from the drama of not being able to pronounce his consonants and having the same moniker as *Corrie*'s Mike Baldwin in real life, Jonny had to cope with whinging sister, 'Our Rita', weird brother Humphrey and dog Razzle. Best remembered for Jonny's classmate who began every sentence with, 'My mam – who's a nurse'. Poor Jonny (Richard Holian) hasn't been seen on our screens since.

Kids From 47A ITV 1973–75

With Phil (*Brookside*) Redmond and Lynda (*Prime Suspect*) La Plante (then Lynda Marchal) writing, it was never going to be the most cheerful of shows. When widow Ma Gathercole died at the end of the first series, her four kids were left to fend for themselves coping with bills, life and growing up. It might have flown in the face of social services practice, but it made for decent drama in which, ahem, issues were even addressed.

Land Of The Giants ITV 1968–72

Wonderful **Irwin Allen** telefantasy in which bread was made from four-foot slabs of rubber to convince us that Captain Steve Burton and his crew really had landed on a planet where everything was 12 times normal size. Part of the appeal was that after the show was over, you could just go to the woods and pretend you were Captain Steve Burton.

Last Of The Mohicans BBC1 1971

Sunday late afternoon in the 1970s was the BBC's slot for series based on old classics which would appeal to kids and grown ups. This dramatisation of the James Fenimore Cooper novel was rather more efficient (and less pretentious) than the Daniel Day Lewis movie, with **Philip Madoc** as Uncas and **Joanna David** in the cast. **Tom Brown's Schooldays** was probably the pick of the rest in this slot.

Little House On The Prairie BBC1 1974–82

Laura Ingalls Wilder wrote the autobiographical books this show was based on, featured as one of the daughters (played by Melissa Gilbert) and narrated the show. **Michael Landon** did almost everything else (write, produce, direct and star as the father), especially cry in an open field – we blame the pollen count. The show lasted one season after he left to save souls in **Highway To Heaven**. (Mind you, it couldn't have helped that he was replaced by an ex-American footballer, Merlin Olsen.) Heart-warming in the extreme, the show had soapy moments, as when Mary Ingalls lost her sight and married her blind tutor who then regained his, (sigh!). It just lacked a 'Goodnight John Boy'-style catchphrase.

The Littlest Hobo BBC1 1966

London, the German Shepherd, had a heart of gold and more slush than you'd get if there was a sudden unseasonal thaw in Greenland.

Lizzy Dripping BBC1 1972–75

Lizzy Dripping, the lass whose skirts were slipping, according to the theme, did what every bullied schoolkid wanted to do, got a witch to sort out her enemies. **Tina Heath**, who played the skirt-slipping heroine, later achieved fame as a pregnant **Blue Peter** presenter. There was even a sequel *Lizzy Dripping Again*, more imaginative than *Lizzy's Still Dripping*. Just.

The Red Hand Gang BBC1/2 1977–78

More kids acting like adults, this time solving mysterious crimes. The show only ran for one season of 12 episodes but, thanks to a catchy theme tune and stereotypical characters (a leader, a brainbox, a streetwise kid, baby of the group and a mascot called Boomer), the show had kids all over Britain leaving their own red hand prints wherever they went. Bizarrely, mascot Boomer faired best, being given his own show in 1980, although kiddie heart-throb **Matthew Laborteaux** (Frankie) did go on to star in the more wholesome *Little House On The Prairie* as Albert.

The Singing Ringing Tree BBC1 1964

Produced in East Germany in 1958, this was later dubbed and serialised by the BBC to counter the accusation it was buying too many American shows. A Brothers Grimm fairytale, it saw a haughty princess robbed of her beauty, the spell only undone when she changed her ways and started to help people. The tree was magical, but only in the presence of true love. For all its odd European style, dramatic accompanying score and OTT acting, it is probably best remembered for scaring kids in the 1960s half to death with its bulbous-eyed fish, evil gnomes and a princess with the hots for a grizzly bear. Parodied by the **Fast Show** team in 'The Singing Ringing Binging Plinging Tinging Plinking Plonking Boinging Tree'.

★★★ Children's shows ★★★

Adventure Game BBC1/2 1980–86

A strange breed, this was one of the few children's TV shows which didn't actually feature children. Instead C-list celebs of the likes of **Keith Chegwin** and **Noel Edmonds** were put through their physical and mental paces in a series of *Crystal Maze*-style challenges. The games were fantastic, best of all being the Vortex finale where contestants tentatively crossed an hexagonal lattice – the thrill of seeing Cheggers zapped into oblivion made it all worthwhile. Remembered fondly in 1980s revival shows, although perhaps not by newsreader **Moira Stewart** who presided over the action in fetching spaceman outfits.

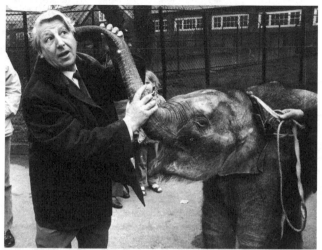

'What did you say? Nellie the elephant did what exactly?'

Animal Magic BBC1 1962–83

Two generations of kids grew up watching Johnny Morris converse with such friends as Wendy the elephant and Dotty the lemur, only for the show to be cancelled after 21 years when pretending that animals were humans wasn't deemed the thing to be done. Shame on the corporation. For animal magic, Morris tops the time John Noakes pretended the elephant had trod on his foot on **Blue Peter**, although when the zookeeper skidded across the studio in elephant dung – that was worthy of Chaplin.

Blockbusters ITV 1983–93

Watched by millions, if only initially because it nabbed the crucial teatime slot, one swotty kid took on two not-so-swotty kids competing for either a *Blockbusters* jumper or some kind of outdoor activity in foreign climes (no one told Bob that swotty kids aren't generally into sports).

119

Led to constant repetition of 'Can I have a P please Bob?' by sniggering teenagers, the Bob in question being the headmaster-like Bob Holness.

Blue Peter BBC1 1958–

Sting may have saved the rainforest but the 'Here's one I prepared earlier' *Blue Peter* team have done their bit when it comes to re-using the world's resources (washing-up bottles, coat hangers, a 'pair of Val's knickers' even). But then they are the ultimate do-gooders, raising huge amounts for charity in their legendary appeals (will half a million parcels of scrap metal, three hospital trucks, six emergency doctors cars and two jet injectors do you?) and filling vital gaps in our education on historical figures like Anne Frank. The teatime perennial has had its share of scandal (presenters dabbling in drugs and appearing in blue movies) but seems as

★ That Saturday morning feeling ★

Faced with an audience of kids glad not to be at school and grown-ups too hungover to change channels, TV programmers have experimented on Saturday mornings as if we were all lab rats. Who can forget the pairing of Tommy Boyd with Isla St Clair, although Big Daddy had been the original choice to host? Anyway, here's our pick of the best.

Tiswas (1974–82) See p76 for more on Saturday's finest hours.

Number 73 (1982–88) A welcome relief from Mike Read's listless *Saturday Superstore*. Best bit: Sandy Toksvig's Sandwich quiz (kids added layers to their sandwich when they got a question correct). Worst bit: probably the fact that this replaced *Tiswas*.

Going Live (1987–92) Despite the boy-next-door image, Philip Schofield could make you laugh, fluffing his lines in good spirit and happy to be upstaged by Gordon the Gopher. Don't bring back Trev and Simon.

SMTV: Live (1998–present) Wiped the floor with the BBC in the ratings war but as good as the Geordie duo of Ant and Dec were, the key to its success was realising that it wasn't just kids watching. How many kids' TV programmes allow their hosts to mock losing contestants on their game shows (Challenge Ant) or, worse, make them cry when they come up with the wrong answers (Wonky Donkey)? A classic.

squeaky clean as ever. Presenters, dogs, cats have come and gone but the person who embodied the show was its producer **Biddy Baxter** whose 'stomach lurched every Monday and Thursday for 26 years as the show began,' she has said. Still, when she left in 1988, she got a piece of double-sided sticky tape and a *Blue Peter* badge. Over on ITV was the hipper **Magpie**, in which Mick Robertson was children TV's answer to David Essex (well, he had the hair) and Jenny Hanley was eye-candy for boys. David Jason briefly appeared as Captain Fantastic, reprised from the series *Do Not Adjust Your Set*.

Cheggers Plays Pop BBC1 1977–82

The first game show to fully embrace the use of gunge and pumping presenters full of E-numbers to get that hyperactive look. Although known of late for his embarrassing naked TV stint, Keith Chegwin was once deemed a genius by kids, based on his skilful run and skip entrance.

Chorlton And The Wheelies ITV 1976–79

Chorlton was a dragon recruited by the king and queen of Wheelie World to fend off the miserable witch Fenella with his happy smile and cheery Lancashire ways. If you don't remember any of this, worry not, the show's psychedelic look and surreal air was more conspicuous than the plot. Some critics say *Chorlton* was racist because all the good guys were English, whereas Fenella was Welsh, her sidekick telescope was Irish and her book of evil spells, undoubtedly, German. Or maybe narrator **Joe Lynch** simply ran out of regional English accents to use.

Crackerjack BBC1 1955–84

A classic depending on when you watched it. **Crackerjack** began as a variety show for kids with games (Double Or Drop), special guests (including such bizarre combinations as **Gary Numan** and **Basil Brush**) and daft sketches hosted by Leslie Crowther and Peter Glaze, but ended up as a pantomime reject bin with Stu 'I could crush a grape' Francis assisted by **The Krankies**, showbiz's most disturbing husband and wife team – with the possible exception of Paul Daniels and Debbie McGee.

Do Not Adjust Your Set ITV 1967–69

This zany kids' sketch show was appreciated more by adults, kids merely sticking around for the catchy song at the end, 'Oh the Elephant goes miaow/And the pussycat moos like a cow/And the tiny little dog goes oink like a frog/And the lion goes bow wow wow (wow wow wow).' The show starred half of the Pythons, **David Jason** in his television debut and music from the Bonzo Dog Doo-Dah Band.

The Flumps BBC1 1977

Grandpa, father, mother, Perkin, Posie and Pootle Flump made up this family of cute round furry creatures, each character resigned to a stereotype: father the breadwinner, mother the cleaner, Pootle the mischievous baby and in the final episode, grandpa the senile OAP who gets himself lost. Although they never spoke (each episode was narrated by Gay Soper), they looked as if they lived in 'grim up north' land, with their brown surroundings and grandpa's flat cap. A cult classic with just 13 episodes.

The Herbs BBC1 1970–72

A joint effort from the talents that brought us *The Wombles* (Ivor Wood) and *Paddington* (Michael Bond), **The Herbs** matched a surreal setting with equal measures of dry sardonic wit. The garden could only be entered using the magic word, Herbidacious, and each character had their own signature tune ('I'm a very friendly lion called Parsley…'). Although Parsley and Dill the Dog are best remembered, we met Bayleaf the gardener, Constable Knapweed and a rather fat feathery owl called Sage.

Jackanory BBC1 1965–96

The demise of the popular storytelling show left parents very uncomfortable. More than 700 books were read during its lifetime including *The

Hobbit to mark the 3,000th episode and Prince Charles' own, *The Old Man Of Lochnagar* read by the prince himself. **Bernard Cribbins** holds the record for most appearances (111). Maybe it was canned because (and this is only our opinion) in an age where mutant turtles ruled the airwaves, some bloke sitting in a chair reading a story just seemed a bit dull.

John Craven's Newsround BBC1 1972–90

Although simply known as *Newsround* for the last 12 years, this was **John Craven**'s show before he went back to nature with *Countryfile*. Meant to run for six weeks, the show endured, thanks to children's natural curiosity about which chunky-knit sweater Craven would wear next. Even managed a scoop when the *Challenger* space-shuttle disaster occurred.

Rainbow ITV 1972–92

Despite being aimed at pre-schoolers, *Rainbow* remains one of the most talked about programmes amongst 20–35 year olds. What exactly *was* Zippy? Why did George's head change on a regular basis and why did he wear pyjamas in bed yet nothing during the day? Matthew (Sooty) Corbett was an original member of the all-singing, all-crap Rod, Jane and partner trio, replaced by **Roger Walker** (*Eldorado*'s Bunny) and then Freddy who, although no one knew his full name, was the most popular.

Record Breakers BBC1 1972–

Classic BBC fare, at its best helmed by **Roy Castle**, himself a tap-dancing record breaker (24 beats a second) and aided by politically suspect clever clogs Norris and the late Ross McWhirter. The truly mysterious aspect of this show was the source of Castle's energy: if only scientists had found a way of manufacturing it we wouldn't have had to worry about the oil embargo.

Rentaghost BBC1 1976–84

Originally called *Second Chance* (deemed not child-friendly enough) **Rentaghost** was as the name suggests, ghosts renting themselves out to avert minor disaster. But they weren't just your regular band of ghosts (if

Michael Staniforth brought everything he'd learned at the Actors Studio to Rentaghost

there is a regular sort), and included a court jester, Timothy (gadzooks) Claypole, Nadia Popov who popped off whenever she sneezed and Dobbin, a pantomine horse. The series, which starred **Lynda La Plante** in earlier episodes as Tamara Novek, set new standards for bad jokes and hammy acting, and made **Christopher Biggins** a household name.

Runaround ITV 1975–81

Proof that Mike 'diamond-geezer Frank Butcher' Reid was once a kids' TV presenter. Here he fired questions at contestants before he shouted 'Goooooooooo' and they ran around (geddit?) until they decided which screen held the correct answer, or which had most people standing next to it. He never seemed this sinister in Albert Square.

Tales Of The River Bank BBC1 1960–64

The adventures of Hammy the Hamster and his chums Roderick the Rat, GP the Guinea Pig et al, narrated by **Johnny Morris**. The idea of animals piloting their own speed boat is unlikely to get past animal welfare these days, so treasure any repeats.

Why Don't You? BBC1 1973–95

Precocious brats who wanted us to spend our school holidays 'usefully', ie baking cakes and making puppets from tennis balls. The full title was *Why Don't You Just Switch Off Your Television Set And Go Out And Do Something Less Boring Instead*? which inevitably led to letters from other precocious brats pointing out if they did that, they wouldn't be able to watch the show.

Worzel Gummidge ITV 1979–81

Although based on the books of Barbara Euphan Todd, Worzel the friendly scarecrow was largely based on **Jon Pertwee**'s desperate attempts to escape his Time Lord alter ego. Despite the classic weird-creature-befriends-recently-traumatised-kid storyline, Worzel was a bit of a ladies'

★ The greatest TV bears ★

They're big, they're furry, they're on the telly and they've enriched our lives.

1 Yogi Bear
Smarter than the average.

2 Bear In The Big Blue House
Groovy, laid back, hipster of a bear, never needs an excuse to click his fingers and croon.

3 Paddington
Never have duffle coats, marmalade sandwiches and hard stares been so cool.

4 The Hair Bear Bunch
Yogi Bear turned psychedelic, this bunch were locked in conflict with zookeeper Mr Peevley who was, like the name says, permanently peeved.

5 The bear on the Andy Williams show
Did he ever get any cookies?

125

man, toying with the affections of Aunt Sally (Una Stubbs), Saucy Nancy (saucy Barbara Windsor) and Dolly Clothes-Peg (Lorraine Chase). The swapping of heads bit was often just too eerie for younger viewers.

★★★ Christmas ★★★

Turkey, trimmings, the Morecambe and Wise Christmas special, the Queen's speech (impossible to ignore if gran was over), a morning show in which **Jimmy Savile** or **Noel Edmonds** visited the sick – surely they were miserable enough already, being in a hospital on Christmas Day – to remind everyone that there were those less fortunate than we. Christmas night: the big family movie, **The Sound Of Music**. And on Boxing Day afternoon, the second half of the not-to-be-missed Christmas edition of **Top Of The Pops**, which would play all the year's number ones – usually just as your mum would call you to the dining table. And then we could all settle down to watch James Bond. That was the traditional Christmas fare in this country until horribly recently – with **Only Fools And Horses** carrying the burden of responsibility for the quality of the British Christmas which Eric and Ernie had shouldered for so long. But there have been a few other highlights, with **Robbie The Reindeer** deserving of honourable mention.

A Ghost Story For Christmas BBC1 1971–78

These days, the BBC schedule is too stuffed with festive versions of existing shows ('and now Craig Charles presents a special festive edition of **Robot Wars** – Reindeer Wars!') to fit in a cracking Christmas ghost story, just like the BBC used to make. In the early 1970s, the Beeb shot eight of acclaimed Victorian ghost-meister MR James' creepiest short stories to be shown over eight consecutive festive seasons. Subtle, unsentimental and often entirely lacking in the usual trappings of

Robbie on the run, trying to evade a hospital visit from Rolf Harris

figgy pudding, they were a welcome antidote to the gluttonous excesses elsewhere on the schedule. So can we have some more, please?

Mike Yarwood's Christmas Show BBC1 1970s

Can we ever forget that instant when he turned to the camera and said 'And this is me…'? That was his worst impression of all, certainly less convincing than his attempt at Frank Sinatra.

Perry Como's Christmas Specials BBC1 1970s

The care that went into these shows, mainly into the selection of the jumpers, cannot be overestimated. Perry, enjoying something of a revival in the 1970s after his worldwide smash 'It's Impossible' sung in familiar trancelike fashion, was a sucker for Christmas songs, exotic locations and for celebrity friends like Eydie Gorme and Steve Lawrence whose celebrity credentials most of us were obliged to take on trust. Or, if he was barrel-scraping (as in his 1980 Christmas in the Holy Land special), **Richard Chamberlain** would guest. Yet the crooner kept his success in perspective: 'I've done nothing that I can call exciting. I was a barber. Since then I've been a singer. That's it.' So there you have it.

★★★ Cops ★★★

As 37.2 per cent of TV series feature the police (we made the figure up but you get the picture) this section could be a book of its own. So we are forced to merely mention in passing such luminaries as **Taggart**, **Z Cars** (although it was ahead of its time for many years), and **Between The Lines** (or *Between The Sheets* as it was dubbed). True greats **The Sweeney** and **Homicide** are featured in more detail on p73 and p43 respectively. This section is for cops who have a badge: those who don't need no stinking badges to solve crimes may be found in the detectives section.

21 Jump Street Sky One 1987

The Renegades (starring Patrick Swayze) had tried out the concept of young cops going undercover to stop teen crime back in 1983, but 1987's

21 Jump Street made the idea work, partly due to **Johnny Depp** in his first lead role as hunky rebel cop Tom Hanson and to the rock music soundtrack.

24 BBC2 2001

The 21st century has seen revitalised careers for some of the first and second generation Brat Pack, who had almost disappeared in the 1990s. **Charlie Sheen** took over from Michael J Fox in *Spin City*, **Rob Lowe** won acclaim with Charlie's dad Martin in *The West Wing*, and, best and unlikeliest of all, **Kiefer Sutherland** made audiences sweat for 24 episodes of the ground-breaking *24*. As Jack Bauer, head of an LA crime unit investigating a possible assassination attempt on a presidential candidate, Sutherland perspired, ran, grappled with bad guys, saw his wife and child kidnapped and was pursued by his own colleagues – all in real-time (each episode covered one hour in Bauer's day from hell). With tense scripts, edge-of-your-seat direction and superb performances from Sutherland, Dennis Haysbert (as Senator Palmer), Leslie Hope (as Bauer's wife Terri), Dennis Hopper and Lou Diamond Phillips, this reinvented the cop genre.

Cagney And Lacey BBC1 1982–88

The female cops in *Cagney And Lacey* wore flat shoes, frumpy skirts and cardies, and were not at all the sort of gals to give men fantasies about being handcuffed. **Tyne Daly** and **Sharon Gless** starred as Mary Beth Lacey and Chris Cagney (Loretta Swit played Cagney in the pilot TV movie but was replaced by Meg Foster, who herself was dumped after a few episodes because research suggested she wasn't feminine enough). One was a grumpy mum with a doormat for a hubby (John Karlen), the other an alcoholic with baaad taste in men. The series was nearly cancelled after its first year, but viewer complaints brought it back and it ran for five years from 1984, finally clawing its way up the ratings in the US and UK.

Car 54, Where Are You? ITV 1964–65

The first sitcom about police officers (*Barney Miller* followed in 1975), *Car 54…* featured the antics of bumbling patrol cops: short, dim-witted Toody (**Joe E Ross**) and tall, slightly smarter Muldoon (**Fred Gwynne**,

Herman in *The Munsters*) working out of a Bronx police precinct. The series featured cameo appearances from Rocky Graziano and Sugar Ray Robinson. An ill-advised attempt to make a movie version failed in 1994.

CHiPs ITV 1979–87

You could watch this series about two himbos in the California Highway Patrol while eating your tea, reading a newspaper or defusing a small nuclear device. (Sample dialogue: 'You know, he robs stranded women. He's bad news.') Partners Jon Baker (**Larry Wilcox**, who quit in 1982 after rows with his co-star) and 'Ponch' Poncherello (**Erik Estrada**) faced countless crises and crashes (Estrada was seriously injured in one bike stunt) and handled the tough ethical questions which have perplexed law enforcement officials through the ages: dilemmas like, what do you do when you stop a speeding van full of nude female volleyball players?

Columbo ITV 1972–79, 1991–94

Peter Falk will forever be linked with the raincoat-wearing detective who asked suspects about their shoes. But the character was created seven years earlier for a show called *The Sunday Mystery Hour* (in which Columbo was played by Bert Freed), and when the script for the TV movie *Prescription: Murder* floated around Hollywood in 1968, Falk only got the part because **Bing Crosby** became unavailable. Falk has since played the shuffling detective in this how's-he-gonna-prove-it series more than 70 times (his third movie, *Columbo: Murder By The Book,* was directed by a very young Steven Spielberg in 1971). In 1992, Falk was given a fresh raincoat to wear; the original was said to be at the Smithsonian Museum, but Falk insists it is in his wardrobe. If you find Columbo intensely irritating, don't worry – it is deliberate, he is loosely based on the inspector who brings down Raskolnikov in *Crime And Punishment*.

Dempsey And Makepeace ITV 1985–86

Hilariously bad attempt by the British to make an American-style action cop show in the mid-1980s. **Glynis Barber** (previously comic book character Jane) played icy posh blonde Detective Sergeant Makepeace, teamed with gruff, unconventional Brooklyn cop Lieutenant Dempsey (**Michael Brandon**). Naturally, despite being complete opposites and always at each other's throats, the partners fancied each other rotten – Barber and Brandon found romance in real life too and are now married.

Due South BBC1/2 1995–99

Even if she was largely referred to as 'Meg', it's hard not to smirk when you spot a character called **Inspector Margaret Thatcher**, especially when she's 'strong-willed, career-oriented' and er, 'attractive'. Aside from this, the story of a Canadian mountie who moves his patch to Chicago (though it was filmed in Toronto), had plenty of appeal. Its quirkiness often stemmed from lead **Constable Benton Fraser** (Paul Gross), who was blessed with a well-developed set of senses (making him good at tracking) and an ability to communicate with a deaf husky-cum-wolf. Despite a loyal fan base, it was one of those shows which swapped channels, skipped weeks and changed days – pesky schedulers being what they are.

Grushko BBC1 1994

With **Brian Cox** as the eponymous hero, confronting the Russian Mafia in Moscow, this could have been a cheap Gorky Park knock-off. But it was better than that, thanks in large part to Cox's performance, some decent scripts and good support from the likes of Mark McGann.

Hill Street Blues ITV 1981–84 Channel 4 1987–89

Before launching this series, NBC execs asked their psychologist how many storylines an audience could retain in their head at any one time while watching a show. The suits said three, the shrink said between five and nine. The fact the question was raised proves just how different **Hill Street Blues**, created by **Stephen Bochco** and **Michael Kozoll**, was. **Daniel J Travanti**, as Captain Frank Furillo, was one of the first TV cops not to expect to win the war on crime, just to manage it. And defence attorney Joyce Davenport (**Veronica Hamel**) was that rarity: a successful, sexy, female character whose private life was not an obvious mess. Without this series, *NYPD Blue* et al would have found airtime much harder to get.

Inspector Morse ITV 1987–2000

If **Inspector Morse** (**John Thaw**) is so clever, how does it take him two hours to solve crimes that Jessica Fletcher (*Murder She Wrote*) and Kojak can solve in less than an hour? Especially as, by the time he has finally cracked the case, the field of suspects has usually been reduced by successive murders to the point that it was bleedin' obvious the survivor did it? Such cavils aside, this is a deeply pleasurable stroll around Oxford, a city which is (from the evidence here) far more dangerous than the south side of Chicago. Thaw and **Kevin Whateley** (as Sergeant Lewis) played off each other beautifully. Part of the appeal was that the series wasn't in a rush to explain Morse and Lewis: there were always mysteries to be solved about them (and not just the hyped business about Morse's first name).

Kojak BBC1 1974–78

The bald head. The lollipop. 'Who loves ya, baby?' Right from the start in 1973, when Telly Savalas took on the role of the righteous New York cop Theo Kojak, his look, mannerisms and catchphrase became part of TV history. With his partner Bobby Crocker (Kevin Dobson, later Mac in **Knots Landing**), Kojak tackled crime and made an icon of Savalas. He even released an album featuring his hit spoken version of 'If'. The only downside, presumably, was that if he went out in public without a lollipop he looked underdressed. Savalas (godfather of *Friends* star **Jennifer Aniston** and stepdad to *Knots Landing*'s Nicolette Sheridan) made TV movies in the role until 1990 and died in 1994.

NYPD Blue Channel 4 1994–

Notorious, when it began in 1993, for its steamy sex scenes (**Dennis Franz** nude in a shower!) and X-rated language, *NYPD Blue* has proved its worth many times over. In the first season, Franz (as alcoholic cop Sipowicz) starred with **David Caruso** as John Kelly, but Caruso soon decided he was such a big star that he was due a hefty pay increase. The producers demurred and Caruso left during the second season to pursue a movie career that has still to materialise. **Jimmy Smits** (late of *LA Law*) became Sipowicz's new partner; other cast members in this gritty drama

131

Tennsion had a harder stare than Paddington

have included **Sherry Stringfield** (of *ER*). The series has inspired several British me-toos including **The Cops** (BBC2, 1998) and **Out Of The Blue** (BBC, 1995) both of which had merit.

Prime Suspect ITV 1991–96

Single-minded police woman Jane Tennison (**Helen Mirren**) is successful at work, despite the chauvinism of some of her colleagues, but a disaster in her private life. Sounds so much of a cliché it's hard to explain how compelling this series was. The claustrophobia of a major investigation, the conflict of personalities and the stroppy yet alluring central character are devices many cop dramas have used since but are all done brilliantly here – thanks to **Lynda La Plante**'s writing, Mirren's mesmerising performance and some fine turns by (amongst others) **Tom Bell**.

Rosie BBC1 1975–81

Whimsical charming sitcom about a young copper (**Paul Greenwood**), from the pen of whimsical **Roy Clarke** which, unlike most of his *Last Of The Summer Wine*, was whimsical and amusing. Greenwood, who reappeared as Superintendent Yelland in *Spender*, co-wrote and sang the theme tune.

Starsky And Hutch BBC1 1976–81

132 Merseyside police chief Kenneth Oxford was mightily relieved when this show ended, noting 'When it was showing, my police on patrol duty were adopting sunglasses and driving like bloody maniacs.' A work of genius by

Aaron Spelling, this show starred two then-unknown actors. To enable even the laziest viewer to tell them apart one was tall, thin and blond with straight hair and often sported a brown leather jacket (**David Soul**), and the other was shorter, stockier, with frizzy black hair and had distinctly dubious taste in chunky knit cardigans (**Paul Michael Glaser**). Each week they infuriated their boss Captain Dobey, possibly because the only way they knew how to solve crimes was to call on the sartorially outrageous Huggy Bear (**Antonio Fargas**) who would nod a few times, and solve the crime with a sentence that invariably began 'The word on the street is…' Quite violent in its early days, the show soon turned almost as soppy as Soul's best-selling ballads.

Wiseguy ITV 1987-88

Shown on prime-time in the US, this was buried in the late-night British TV schedules – a sad fate for a seriously innovative cop show. Rather than have a different drama and bad guy in each episode, *Wiseguy* was shown in story 'arcs', as deep undercover cop (he served time in jail so that bad guys would believe he was one of them) Vinnie Terranova (**Ken Wahl**) spent up to ten episodes trying to infiltrate an organised crime group without breaking his cover, before taking on another case. The cast of baddies included Patti D'Arbanville and young tyro **Kevin Spacey** as a deranged businessman called Mel Profitt who enjoyed a bizarre relationship with his sister (Joan Severance).

★★★ Costume Dramas ★★★

Anne Of Green Gables Channel 4 1985

Writer-director **Kevin Sullivan**'s version of Lucy Montgomery's famous tale of a fiery red-headed orphan growing up on Prince Edward Island was not the first attempt to bring it to the small screen, but it is widely cited as being the best. His success is partly down to **Megan Follows** as our heroine although in fact Shuyler Grant (grand-niece of Katharine Hepburn) was actually Sullivan's original choice. Follows' nationality helped win her the role.

133

Fortunes & Misfortunes Of Moll Flanders ITV 1997

Heaving breasts galore, with the then relatively unknown **Alex Kingston** perfectly cast as Daniel Defoe's hard working and feisty prostitute, Moll Flanders. Despite a fantastic performance by Kingston as the fair maiden battling to survive on the wrong side of the law whilst going through husbands faster than Zsa Zsa Gabor (life in *ER* would be a cinch after this), and an energetic script by Andrew Davies, most people tuned in in the hope of catching Kingston with her kit off. An unlikely prospect you might think for a prime-time drama from Granada, but Moll took her job seriously – the series contained 17 sex scenes.

Gulliver's Travels Channel 4 1997

Ted Danson's English accent is about as convincing as Robert Redford's in *Out Of Africa* but you soon forget about that, such is the brilliance of this production, the effects by **Jim Henson** and, to be fair, Danson's performance. Far better than TV mini-series have any right to be.

★ Don't lose the plot ★

Don't want to watch them but like to know what's occurring? Let our synopses help you

Emma
Single woman wants marriage in the days before computer dating.

Jane Eyre
Doomed love between governess and sinister rich bloke with wife from Barking.

Jude The Obscure
Miserable carpenter tops himself.

Ivanhoe
Love triangle in chain mail. Not as kinky as it sounds.

The Prince And The Pauper
You've seen *Trading Places*.

Poldark BBC1 1975

Based on a series of novels, set in the 18th century, by Winston Graham (previously better known for his novel *Marnie*, which Hitchcock turned into a movie starring Sean Connery). Ross Poldark (**Robin Ellis**) returns to his home to find his true love betrothed to his cousin and his family estate and the town in tatters. Accordingly he sets out to restore order and win back his love, despite encountering the odd complication, like getting hygienically challenged servant girl Demelza (**Angharad Rees**) pregnant. Costume drama fare with the usual dastardly or heroic men and swooning women, it became vastly popular on Sunday evenings. The series was revamped in 1996 with John Bowe taking over from Ellis, but sent few hearts a-flutter.

Pride And Prejudice BBC1 1995

Much-loved reworking of Jane Austen's classic take on the foibles of the 19th-century social classes. One of the few – if not the only – costume drama to boast a devoted cult following (their letters doubtless to thank for a recent rerun). Despite a superb script, by **Andrew Davies**, and Alison Steadman and David Bamber never cast better as Mrs Bennett and Mr Collins, **Colin Firth**'s dashing portrayal of Mr Darcy was all it really needed to be a success (although his enthusiasm for the role is doubtless on the wane, as he can't make a Hollywood movie without reference to his alter ego). The only blot on its copybook was that its success inspired a host of me-toos, including series that serve mainly to remind you that not all the Brontes were that good at writing novels.

★★★ Crime ★★★

Banacek ITV 1975–77

George Peppard was smooth insurance investigator Banacek (no first names required) in this series loosely based on the Steve McQueen movie, **The Thomas Crown Affair**. Sporting his trademark turtleneck, sports jacket and cigar, Banacek was the chauffeur-driven freelance employee of the Boston Insurance Company, who never failed to solve mysterious thefts and disappearances. It was a huge hit with Polish Americans – thanks to the Polish proverbs strewn throughout each episode ('Read the whole library my son, but the cheese will still smell after four days') – but nobody else. Yet statisticians claim if you switch on the telly any weekday afternoon, your chances of catching an episode are better than one in ten.

Crane ITV 1962–65

Crane (**Patrick Allen**) was a crim with a heart of gold. Having upped sticks in an effort to escape the rat-race life he led as a respectable businessman, he moved to Morocco, running a bar which doubled as his own private smuggling depot. He was not without morals: he only dealt in cigarettes and alcohol – no guns or drugs – and helped the local law fight the real low-life of Casablanca – like that café owner Rick who was always pining for Ingrid Bergman. Allen guested in almost every show on TV and starred in three seasons of *Crane* but he is best known as a voiceover supremo, his dulcet tones featuring as the four-minute warning man on Frankie Goes To Hollywood's, **Two Tribes** and as the bloke who was always telling us to buy Barrett homes.

David Cassidy – Man Undercover ITV 1982

Sandwiched between **The Partridge Family** and the resurrection of Cassidy's pop career, this was evidently a forgettable experience for star and audience alike. Despite having the show named after him, it didn't even get a mention in the star's autobiography. The fact that the diminutive pop star was to play Officer Dan Shay – a married father (hence a distinct lack of pubescent female interest) – and LAPD undercover cop, should have been a warning sign (how fantastical does a concept have to sound to be put in the bin?). A spin-off from the *Police Story* movie 'A 'Chance To Live', Officer Shay was in his late twenties but was young enough to pass for a teenager, hence he often went undercover as a student. Not exactly a hardcore crime drama but certainly amusing.

The Dukes Of Hazzard BBC1 1979–85

Bo and Luke Duke (**John Schneider** and **Tom Wopat**) were baddies but underneath it all just good old boys never meaning no harm, as **Waylon Jennings** congenially suggested in the theme. The real stars were the Dodge Chargers and the cut-off jeans sported by Daisy (**Catherine Bach**). Boss Hogg (Sorrell Brooke) was the kind of supporting character who aspired to be one-dimensional. The episodes when Schneider and Wopat were replaced, after a pay row, are as dull as Hogg's suit was shiny.

The Fugitive ITV 1964–67

When Dr Richard Kimble (**David Janssen**, who went on to be Harry O) finally confronted the one-armed man who really killed his wife, the show

'I'm not a crook' – a popular television catchphrase back in 1972

earned the largest recorded audience for a single episode with 72 per cent of US viewers watching it (it took *Dallas*' 'Who shot JR?' episode to break that record). The show was based on the real-life 1954 trial of Dr Sam Shepard, livened up with a dash of Victor Hugo's **Les Miserables**. William Conrad narrated with customary gravitas.

The Gangster Show BBC2 1972

That was how this 105-minute adaptation of Bertolt Brecht's *The Resistible Rise Of Arturo Ui* was billed on TV, with Nicol Williamson excelling as the Hitler figure who rises to power with Mob help. Coincidentally or not, it was screened on the very night Richard 'I am not a crook' Nixon beat George McGovern in the US presidential election.

Club tropicana socks are free – fun and sunshine there's enough for everyone

Law And Order BBC2 1978

You can understand why this crime drama caused a bit of a fuss. Writer **G F Newman** was of the opinion that: 'The person who becomes a policeman has almost exactly the same pathology as the criminal.' Newman had failed to make much impact on **Z Cars** – possibly because he went so far as to suggest decent old Frank Windsor (Sergeant Watt) might take a bribe – so he created **Law And Order**. The gritty drama-documentary style made events onscreen seem all the more disturbing, while the antics of Detective Inspector Pyall (Derek Martin) made *The Sweeney* look like *Dixon Of Dock Green*.

Maelstrom BBC1 1985

Described by one viewer as, 'a little bit like watching an Oslo Film Authority documentary on the wonders of Formica' this unique Norwegian/British collaboration was, depending on which camp you were in, so bad it was good or genuinely offbeat and intriguing. **Maelstrom**'s convoluted plot featured an advertising executive inheriting a house in the fjords, only for the series to spiral into tales of freaky dolls and congenital madness. It did wonders for Norwegian tourism with shot after shot of breath-taking forests and glacial lakes, however entertaining TV this does not make. *Maelstrom* was actually brought to the screen by **Blake's 7** director, **David Maloney** who brought along **Paul Darrow** (Avon in Blake's 7) for the ride, opposite **Ann Todd**, the veteran star and former wife of David Lean in her final role (but probably not the one she hoped to be remembered for). Bizarre, at times mind-numbingly slow but strangely compelling viewing, if not necessarily for it's entire six hour run. In Norwegian mythology, a maelstrom is a monster whirlpool off the island of Lofoten.

Miami Vice BBC1 1985–90

It could have been just another cop show. But the style created by Michael Mann (who went on to direct movies like *Heat*) made Miami one of the stars, filling TV screens with images of pastel-coloured buildings (brown and red ones were reportedly banned), chrome, glass,

139

endless beaches, sun and bikini-clad women. Thrown into the mix were the interracial pairing of **Philip Michael Thomas** as former New York street detective Tubbs and **Don Johnson** as cool Crockett, who lived on a boat with his alligator Elvis and wore shoes with no socks, a T-shirt with a pastel suit and rolled-up sleeves. The soundtrack was pure MTV – Jan Hammer provided the opening music and instrumental interludes, Phil Collins' 'In The Air Tonight' became a haunting theme for Crockett (if not for anyone else). Collins, Miles Davis, Leonard Cohen and **Sheena Easton** (as Crockett's ill-fated love) all got acting roles, but the good times ended when NBC ran it against **Dallas**.

Minder ITV 1979–94

Originally envisaged as a new vehicle for **Dennis Waterman** after *The Sweeney*, **Minder** could have been retitled *The George Cole Show*. What began as a violent thriller ended as a comedy following low ratings and complaints about its violence. Cole made Arthur Daly, small-time con-man and king of the dodgy deal, one of the best comic characters of recent decades, cementing his own 'mockney' vocabulary into the English language, particularly such phrases as, 'A nice little earner', and 'her indoors'. When Waterman finally called it a day in 1991, the virtually unknown (then and now) **Gary Webster** was brought in as a replacement for another three years.

★ Bumfights ★

It's not on TV yet but it can't be too long. Proof that the reality TV craze is spinning into realms unimaginable even to the most extreme sci-fi writers. In the opening scene of the video *Bumfights* (of which 250,000 copies have already been sold in the US at $22 a copy), one homeless man, his pants falling off his backside, pummels a foe into the corner of a public toilet while another rips his front teeth out with pliers. This fine work by wannabe film directors Ray Leticia and Ty Beeson has been so successful that, despite qualms about what the hour-long video says about the homeless (or the people who buy it), a sequel is already planned.

Murder One Sky, BBC2 1996

Deemed by creator **Steve Bochco** to be his easiest sale to a network, but you have to wonder why a show which held its own in America against the mighty *ER* would have its format and lead star changed for its second series. What began as unique – the entire 23-

episode series focusing on one trial, with **Daniel Benzali** as bald legal eagle Theodore Hoffman – moved into standard legal drama territory, with **Anthony LaPaglia** replacing Benzali (removed because he was follically challenged), and three rather than one trial investigated. What was once dark, gritty and absorbing, ended up as a lame homage to *LA Law* but without Harry Hamlin.

The Saint ITV 1962–69

The show which ensured Roger Moore could always top up his tan. Moore starred as wealthy haloed hero, Simon Templar, stealing from the rich and saving lives at every turn. Novelist Leslie Charteris had first tried to develop a TV spin-off with **David Niven**. When Lew Grade became involved the show took off: **Roger Moore** was cast after original choice **Patrick McGoohan** turned down the role (he didn't approve of Templar's womanising ways). Where Bond had his Aston Martin, Templar had the Volvo P1800, although he was meant to drive a Jaguar, the car manufacturer foolishly turning down the free publicity in return for donating a car. Moore returned to similar territory with **Tony Curtis** in **The Persuaders**, camp 1970s nonsense brilliantly done, with a fine 'dum dum di dum' **John Barry** theme, Moore's self-designed safari suits and a parade of 1970s pin-ups, including **Joan Collins**, **Susan George** and **Anouska Hempel**.

Widows ITV 1983

Having had enough starring opposite a precocious red-haired brat in kids' show *Educating Marmalade* and a court jester in *Rentaghost*, actress Lynda Marchal changed her name and profession to become writer **Lynda La Plante**. *Widows* was her first commissioned script. Following the widows of three armed robbers and a drug addict, the women decide to finish the job their husbands had begun, successfully holding up a security van before flying off to Rio with the dosh – an unusually upbeat ending for La Plante. Hard to believe that the recent US revamp, despite being scripted by La Plante, will be as good, not least because we're supposed to accept **Brooke Shields** as an armed robber.

★★★ Daytime TV ★★★

Daytime TV used to be viewed by TV execs in the same way the Russian government regarded the Siberian tundra: as a vast space which may contain hidden treasures but was too arduous and expensive to exploit. Daytime has also suffered from Lord Reith's view of telly which, heavily simplified, was that it could play a valuable role but should not make unemployment too enjoyable or distract housewives unduly. The success of **This Morning** (with Richard and Judy) has changed things but daytime is still a time when budgetary constraints are more obvious than quality.

Belle And Sebastian BBC1 1967–68

Enduring proof of the effect children's TV can have on popular beat combos. Sebastian was an abandoned gypsy boy and Belle, who he befriended, was a wild white dog of whom everyone else, having read Jack London's *White Fang*, was understandably suspicious. Apart from Belle and Sebastian, the inhabitants of this Alpine village seemed to suffer from deep existential angst, massive hangovers, constipation or all of the above.

Crown Court ITV 1972–84

If you were throwing a sickie from school in the 1970s, it was usually permissible to emerge looking suitably groggy at about 1pm to tuck in to a meagre lunch of arid toast and turn on the telly to see how **Richard Wilson** (alias Jeremy Parsons QC) was doing. But this being **Crown Court**, you'd have to stay off for three days to see the verdict. Among the up and coming talent processed by the court were Colin Firth, Bob Hoskins, Ben Kingsley, Juliet Stevenson and, as a writer, David Yallop, author of papal conspiracy fest *In God's Name*. This was one of the first fruits of the IBA and BBC decision that TV companies had to broadcast in the afternoons.

The Flowerpot Men BBC1 1952–54

142

Watch With Mother's second offering was a much richer experience than the first, **Andy Pandy**, who behaved as if he'd been on a white-knuckle ride to hell if he sat on a swing. But Andy didn't get up to too much partly because the panel which advised the BBC on such programming worried that if kids were watching telly, mum would be free to do 'other things'. When fears that British mums would use the 15 minutes respite offered by *Andy Pandy* to jump into bed with the window-cleaner proved unfounded (15 minutes isn't a lot of time but remember this was before the discovery of foreplay), the **Flowerpot Men** were allowed to live more dangerously. They had their own special language allegedly – although as their conversation consisted of 'Flobbadob' or 'Luggalug', either Bill and Ben were yet more evidence of the failings of British education or they had the smallest native vocabulary known to man or garden accessory.

★★★ Dennis Pennis ★★★

For two years, comedian Paul Kaye's alter ego **Dennis Pennis** embarrassed and humiliated some of the top names in film and TV. The nature of the

joke meant Pennis was always going to have a short shelf-life, but he ruffled plenty of feathers. **Joan Collins** got his measure and avoided Pennis like the plague but he still managed to shout, 'Hey Joan, you look like a million lire', (about £25). **Steve Martin** may be one of Kaye's comic heroes but even he could not escape Pennis ('How come you're not funny any more?'). But perhaps his funniest question was aimed at **Demi Moore**: 'If it wasn't gratuitous in any way and it was tastefully done, would you consider keeping your clothes on in a movie?'

A world famous Pennis

★★★ Detectives ★★★

Remember, these people don't need no stinking badges to fight crime. They're private eyes, mystery writers, lawyers, chefs (Richard Griffiths in **Pie In The Sky**) and part-time violinists, but they do, obviously, need

143

'Y'know Frank, you're kinda cute, in an overfed walrus kinda way'

a gimmick (see opposite). The more seminal detective series (**Harry O**, **The Rockford Files**, **The Singing Detective**) are profiled at length in our cult of the cult selection on p41 and p67 respectively. *Murder She Wrote* is not at all cult, but give **Jessica Fletcher** (Angela Lansbury) her due for trying to solve the Kennedy assassination in one episode.

77 Sunset Strip ITV 1958–64

Efrem Zimbalist Jr – whose daughter Stephanie starred in *Remington Steele* – and **Roger Smith** played two private detectives whose offices were located at 77 Sunset Strip in Hollywood. The show's hipness quotient was initially boosted by its great flinger-clickin' theme tune, and teenage girls galore fell for the brilliantined good looks of Kookie (**Edd Byrnes**), who worked at a parking lot and became a private investigator too. Byrnes even had his own minor chart hit with 'Kookie, Kookie, Lend Me Your Comb' – a duet with **Connie Stevens** – but although the producers tried to ring the changes, audiences proved increasingly reluctant to lend the series their eyes and it died a natural death.

★ The gimmicks file ★

Whether you're a cop, a private eye or a lawyer, you can't fight crime on the small screen if you don't have a gimmick. Here's our useful guide…

Fashion accessories

A mac like Columbo's can be useful but if you really want to get ahead get a hat (a cowboy one like McCloud's or a homburg like Kojak's). Lollipops (Kojak again), Hawaiian shirts (Magnum), or an ocelot called Bruce (Honey West) can help you stand out from the pack.

Physical disabilities

You can be lame like Harry O, obese like Cannon, wheelchair-bound like Ironside, even blind like Mike Longstreet (James Franciscus).

Psychological flaws/wounds

You can be a recovering alcoholic (Bergerac), a secret drug addict (Sherlock Holmes), recovering from a mysterious breakdown (Shoestring) or simply grumpy for no apparent reason (Harry O, Morse). Sometimes, you'll have suffered tragically (like the recently bereaved Jack Frost). At best, your personal life will be a disaster (Morse, Frost, Tennison).

Specialist area of expertise

You have to have one – and preferably one that has nothing to do with your job. Chandler's Philip Marlowe, the prototype for many American TV tecs, could play chess. Holmes could play the violin, Cannon was a gourmet (Henry Crabbe – Richard Griffiths in *Pie In The Sky* – was happier chasing recipes than crooks), while Morse was a dab hand at crosswords. Judging by his opening credits, Petrocelli, the 1970s lawyer played by Barry Newman, liked building walls, although as the wall never seemed to get any higher, maybe he didn't like doing it that much.

Talking cars and other similar phenomena

Get an answering machine like Jim Rockford, a talking car like Michael Knight in *Knight Rider* or, failing that, a special high-tech helicopter (James Farentino and Dana Carvey in *Blue Thunder*). Or, failing *that*, get a computer-generated buddy (as Desi Arnaz Junior did in *Automan*).

But remember

Always be a maverick. Nobody ever solved crimes by obeying rules, filling in forms, being nice to the superintendent, or having a tidy desk.

Adventures Of Sherlock Holmes ITV 1984-85

The detective as tortured artistic genius, as played to perfection by **Jeremy Brett**, whose interpretation of Baker Street's most famous resident makes **Basil Rathbone**'s movie impersonation look like competent hack work. Played by Brett, Holmes was a camp, arrogant, impetuous, cantankerous old devil who could be more intimidating with an eyebrow than most cops can be with truncheons. A work of elementary genius.

Boney ITV 1975–76

Caucasian Kiwi actor **James Laurenson** played aboriginal Detective Inspector Napoleon Bonaparte in a black-and-white-minstrels, blacked-up kind of way, using his bushman skills to track the crims. Unusual for its time and point of origin, and too left of field to survive.

Cannon BBC1 1972–78

William Conrad starred as Frank Cannon, the 'overfed walrus' (his words, not ours) ex-cop turned private 'tec in this **Quinn Martin** production. Known for his culinary skills, **Cannon** – one of the few TV private detectives who didn't live on the edge of bankruptcy – didn't have the build for punch-ups, so the series was packed with well-planned car chases (with Frank in his swish Lincoln Continental) and smart scripts.

Charlie's Angels ITV 1977–82

Aaron Spelling created this hugely successful series about three female police academy graduates who go to work for mysterious unseen benefactor Charles Townsend (voiced by Dynasty's **John Forsythe**). **Farrah Fawcett**, **Kate Jackson** and **Jaclyn Smith** were Charlie's original angels, solving crime, usually without a bra (hence the phrase 'jiggle TV') but with the help of Charlie's aide Bosley. Fawcett left after a series to be replaced by Cheryl Ladd. In 1979 Kate Jackson also left, replaced first by Shelley Hack and then Tanya Roberts – no, we don't know who they are either. Spelling tried to update the series in the 1980s (with an unshown pilot called *Angels 88*), but the movie smash may have renewed the franchise.

Big hair, big belt, big lapels: who says the 1980s were a fashion disaster zone?

Hart To Hart ITV 1980–85

'When they met, it was moidah' or so housekeeper Max (gravel-voiced **Lionel Stander**) told us about his obscenely happy bosses, husband and wife Jonathan (**Robert Wagner**) and Jennifer Hart (**Stefanie Powers**) at the start of each episode of this fluffy Aaron Spelling hit. The Harts were millionaires whose business prospered even though they were always up to their pretty necks in murder, espionage and international intrigue, which had to be solved in time to get home for dinner (prepared by Max when he wasn't petting family dog Freeway).

Hazell ITV 1978–79

Half-scripted by **Terry Venables**, with a theme by Roxy Music's **Andy MacKay** and starring Pamela Stephenson's first husband **Nicholas Ball** as the eponymous gumshoe, this series had echoes of Philip Marlowe (the voiceover, the noirish feel, the seedy streets – albeit of London, not Los Angeles) but with added mockney (Hazell's favourite phrase being 'Kin ell'). A shortlived show that deserved better.

Magnum, PI ITV 1981-87

If it wasn't for **Magnum**, **Tom Selleck** would have been Indiana Jones. The actor was picked for the lead in *Raiders Of The Lost Ark*, but he couldn't get the time off from his day job as Thomas Sullivan Magnum, a Vietnam veteran who becomes a private eye in Hawaii, employed by mysterious unseen Robin Masters (voiced by **Orson Welles** until 1985). Filmed in Hawaii, the series often mentioned Steve McGarrett (of *Hawaii Five-O*) but Jack Lord never appeared. In one season's finale Magnum was killed by a man driven mad by the PI's shirts, but when the series was unexpectedly renewed, it proved, as with Pammy Ewing, that it had all been a dream.

Moonlighting BBC2 1986–89

A ground-breaking detective/comedy show, **Moonlighting** often had its characters talk directly into camera to address the audience (creator **Glen Larson** described it as 'the show that knows it's on television'). Ex-beau of Elvis and Peter Bogdanovich, **Cybill Shepherd** played Maddie Hayes, a former model who finds her accountant has taken all her money. She's left with one remaining investment: the Blue Moon Detective Agency, run by fast-talking David Addison (**Bruce Willis**, who at this point had only a couple of bit parts to his name). The dialogue between the odd couple (scripts were 50 per cent longer than other series) was packed with double entendres and wit. Each character often talked over the other, and the innovative plots included a hip update of *The Taming Of The Shrew*. After two years' sparring, the duo realised what we'd known all along – a twist usually credited with ruining the show, although the principals' reported mutual animosity and Shepherd's pregnancy were as much to blame.

Remington Steele BBC1 1983–84/C4 1986–87

This is the role which earned **Pierce Brosnan** his shot at 007. (He was approached to play Bond in *The Living Daylights* in 1986, but was still under contract to *Remington Steele* so the role went to Timothy Dalton.) The series' premise was simple: Laura Holt (**Stephanie Zimbalist**) was a private investigator who got very little business under her own name, so she set up an agency run by the fictitious Remington Steele, only for a stranger (Brosnan) to walk in one day claiming to be the real Steele. The two team up, and before the series ended… go on, have a wild guess. Great puns in the episode titles ('Thou shalt not Steele'). Not.

Shoestring BBC1 1979–80

Trevor Eve was the 'private ear' DJ Eddie Shoestring, who always seemed to be about to go mad again (well, it can't have been easy driving that Cortina) while solving crime in the West Country. **Daniel Day Lewis** made a brief appearance in one episode and Leslie Crowther's daughter Liz played the station receptionist. After 21 episodes, Trev said enough and one of the small screen's more engaging sleuths was no more.

Vegas ITV 1978–81

TV stalwart **Robert Urich** became the coolest detective on the box as Dan Tanna, complete with 57 Thunderbird car and a bevy of female friends. Yes, this was another Aaron Spelling creation. Each week Dan walked past showgirls and through plush casinos, often just to to improve the scenery rather than for the sake of the plot. Urich put on his gumshoes again in **Spenser: For Hire**, a tedious adaptation of the Robert B Parker novels.

★★★ Doctors ★★★

We've always been suckers for a handsome doctor with a plausible manner, be it Dr McCoy, Dr Ross or Dr David Owen. Indeed Holby now supports two prime-time TV dramas. Although our image of doctors has changed for the worse in recent years, in American and British dramas (**Cardiac Arrest** excepted) they are still heroes. In the healthy **ER** and the now ailing **Casualty**, the hospitals are staffed with fantasy workmates, who usually rally round in a way real colleagues or relatives seldom do.

A Very Peculiar Practice BBC2 1986–88

This **Andrew Davies**-scripted comedy drama was almost as strange as its title. **Peter Davison** played an idealistic young doctor arriving at a university where his colleagues were either drunk (**Graham Crowden**), manipulative and machiavellian (**David Troughton**), or convinced that illness was a male plot against women (**Barbara Flynn**). There weren't many belly laughs but the series was too unsettling to be dull. The arrival of **Joanna Lanska**, as a Polish student, marked that point in British TV history when Polish babes were deemed exotically erotic – on *Brookside* poor old Terry was besotted by Anna Wolska. That vogue soon passed.

Dr Quinn Medicine Woman ITV 1993–

She was called Mike Quinn, even though she was really Michaela, a switch which disturbed the good people of Colorado Springs when they realised their new doctor wasn't a bluff drunken Irishman but a do-gooding rebellious surrogate mum with a wardrobe full of expensive, but sensible, dresses. This show, always on somewhere in the digital TV universe, fills the same psychological need as **Little House On The Prairie**. Heck, there's even a Michael Landon stand-in, tousle-haired Byron Sully (**Joe Lando**), although he does keep a pet wolf. Quinn herself (**Jane Seymour** who, judging from her eternal youth, has a really nasty self-portrait in the loft)

★ How to tell your medical dramas apart ★

Casualty
The British medical drama in which management are an arse-covering, penny-pinching John Bird and John Fortune bunch who would prefer that if patients die, they do so as cheaply as possible, in line with the targets in the five-year hospital trust plan and without suing. Luckily, the staff led, physically and morally, by ever-present nurse **Charlie Fairhead**, all pull together to do the best possible job as plane crashes, riots and terrorism cut a swathe through Holby's citizenry. Fairhead and his ever-rotating cast of sympatico docs and nurses get all the riff-raff.

Chicago Hope
The American medical drama set in Chicago which has more up-to-date facilities (and close-ups of pumping blood and diseased organs) than the other one (**ER**) but less charisma (who would you invite to a dinner party – **Mandy Patinkin** or **George Clooney**?). Created by **David E Kelley**, though it might have been more fun if it had been inspired by DeForest Kelley ('It's worse than that he's dead, Dr Geiger').

ER
The American medical drama set in Chicago which is as almost as gloriously shambolic and tightly budgeted as **Casualty** but whose staff have more intriguing quirks and a cynical line in jargon (D&Ds – death and doughnuts, a term for conferences where doctors eat doughnuts and discuss patients who died). Dr Ross and Nurse Hathaway's romance is more Rhett/Scarlett than Baz and Charlie's in *Casualty*.

Holby City
The British medical drama in which the management is **Anton Meyer**, sharper than most surgical instruments and the consultant we'd all like to treat us when we're stricken with a serious, unidentifiable disease. His colleagues do the best possible job, unless Sandy is hungover and Chrissie is being an adulteress. Luckily, the patients have more interesting afflictions than in *Casualty*, which helps the staff focus on the job, but Alex and Sam's love story is about as inspiring as a disciplinary hearing.

is a fine example of a character whose anachronistic belief in 20th-century liberal values gives us the cheap thrill of feeling incredibly enlightened. Just sit back, chortle at the chauvinists and bigots of Colorado Springs and congratulate yourself on how far the human race has come.

St Elsewhere Channel 4 1983–89

Nothing became this medical drama (set in a Boston hospital) like its leaving of the airwaves. For its final episode, the producers came up with a new spin on the Pam-dreamed-Bobby's-death scenario in *Dallas*. This time it turned out the entire six-year series was a dream by a character's autistic son. And as the credits rolled, viewers saw the MTM cat, the TV studio's spoof MGM logo, on a life support machine: at the end it was shown flatlining. Often seen as the missing link between fodder like **Marcus Welby MD** and more characterful stuff like **ER**, it also gave **Denzel Washington** his break. **Hill Street Blues** with gauze on, but lower ratings.

★★★ Documentaries ★★★

7 Up ITV 1964–

When he's not making Hollywood blockbusters with the likes of Sigourney Weaver, director **Michael Apted** interviews ordinary folk with ordinary lives. What began as an episode of **World In Action** is now the only programme television audiences pencil into their diaries seven years in advance (each episode actually features a voice-over reminding viewers to tune in, in seven years' time). As a researcher for Granada TV in 1964, Apted interviewed a selection of seven-year-olds, each with distinctly different backgrounds and personalities, about their views on life. In 2000 **42 Up** aired, with each of the original characters, minus two. By 2007 the group will doubtless be in the throes of mid-life crises.

The Ascent Of Man BBC2 1973

The speech presenter **Dr Jacob Bronowski** gave at Auschwitz will not be forgotten easily. 'Into this pond were flushed the ashes of some four million people and that was not done by gas – it was done by arrogance, it was done by dogma, it was done by ignorance. When people believe they have absolute knowledge, this is how they behave.'

The Impossible Job Channel 4 1994

A documentary designed to raise sympathy for cruelly vilified ex-England boss Graham Taylor which proved that he was surrounded by yes men (**Phil Neal**), that striker Nigel Clough didn't understand his tactical talks and that he swore a lot. Phrases 'Do I not like that?' and 'Can we not knock it?' became common speak. For a while. Classic viewing.

Mythical Monsters Channel 4 2001

The exact opposite of **Walking With Dinosaurs**: bugger all footage of Bigfoot but lots of academic-looking chaps talking calmly and wisely about the evidence for such creatures existing. Compelling.

Reputations BBC2 1995–

The broadsheet approach to TV biography, as opposed to Channel 4's **Secret Lives** (whose success is based on the simple truth that the dead can't sue for libel). **Reputations** has usually done a marvellous job of cramming complex lives into 50 minutes although of late, especially in its less than convincing portrait of Jimi Hendrix, it has begun to flag. On a scale of historical revelations, telling us Hendrix took a lot of drugs is on a par with *Secret Lives*' disclosure that Errol Flynn was a bit of a lad.

When Louis Met BBC2 2002–

Louis and the Hamiltons, Louis and the Daniels, Louis and Max Clifford, Louis and Jimmy Savile, how's about that then? As it happens, Theroux's **Weird Weekends** on BBC2 was more original, although he's usually very watchable. He is, though, the kind of broadcaster best seen six times a year. He should learn from the eclipse of his old boss **Michael Moore**, host of the brilliant **TV Nation**, now famous for the alleged size of his expense claims. A few years ago, he upset **Newt Gingrich** (by asking him where the coast was after finding Newt's congressional district got public funds for its coast guard; Gingrich was as pissed off as a Newt) but he lost it somewhere.

The World At War ITV 1974

'Utterly brilliant. Powerful and evocative. The most compelling documentary series ever made concerning war.' That's what the bloke from Whitley Bay on the Internet Movie Database says. And he's right.

★★★ Double acts ★★★

Those comic double acts from Eric and Ernie to French and Saunders via Feldman and Moore. What? You haven't heard of Feldman and Moore?

Cannon and Ball Rock on, Tommy? Put a sock in it, Tommy!

Les Dennis and Dustin Gee They weren't very funny, then Dustin died.

Eric and Ernie They were mainstream comedy and alternative comedy in the 1970s. See p320 for more on Eric.

French and Saunders Moments of sublime inspiration – the fat blokes rubbing themselves against the telly when Princess Di was on springs to mind – followed by years of 'contractual obligation'.

Hale and Pace So many shows, so few laughs.

Lennie and Jerry Thousands lost the will to move while watching the jolly permed giant (Lennie Bennett) cracking funnies.

Little and Large Sid looked gormless; not hard because he never had any gorm to begin with. Eddie tried to stop Sid singing with naff impressions.

Mel and Griff They were very funny in the beginning, not so funny in the middle and not at all funny at the end.

Marty and Roger weren't together long but they gave us more laughs than Lennie and Jerry

Mike and Bernie Bernie was a big guy with one joke which put him ahead of his brother Mike who was a small guy with no jokes. When they split, Bernie got custody of the St Bernard called Schnorbitz.

Moore and Feldman Short-lived but frankly hilarious rib-tickling partnership where Marty with the manic eyes did all the sight gags and Roger Moore looked distinctly apprehensive and counted his fee.

The Two Ronnies They were on TV for years and were very funny for five of them. The fork-handles sketch earned them a place in the comedy hall of fame, as did Mr Corbett's pointlessly pleasurable chats in the chair. But they should have said goodnight from me and him a few years earlier.

Vic and Bob Bloody heroes, see p327.

★★★ Dramas ★★★

When there were just 11,000 people in Britain who could receive TV (not so long ago, 1938) TV drama meant Pirandello's *Henry IV*. Since then, the industry has realised that drama has the power to inspire or outrage us in a way that few other things can – apart, of course, from a really atrocious sitcom. Since the 1930s we have had kitchen-sink realism, James-Bond-style campery, left-wing propaganda on *Play For Today*, historical dramas, and seriously ambitious series like **Our Friends In The North** (which tried to say something about the state of the nation but was inferior to **When The Boat Comes In** on several counts: theme tune, the failure of any coal mine roof to fall in and kill the hero's father, and the fact that the 1970s series achieved so effortlessly what its 1990s successor strove so deliberately to do). What does the future hold? The future probably, with more of your *X-Files* style examinations, but there will always be a place for drama as long as we take solace in learning about people worse off than ourselves.

Abigail's Party BBC1 1977

Casting a sharp critical eye over aspiring middle-class social butterflies ('No, I don't like olives either – they're horrid'), **Abigail's Party** was first produced for a Hampstead theatre group (an apt if exquisitely ironic setting) before featuring in a **Play for Today** on the BBC. Confusingly, Abigail was never seen, Beverly's party being the focus, with **Alison Steadman** as a brassy, neurotic hostess, subjecting her guests to the dinner party from hell, a time bomb of tensions, arguments and deteriorating relations. Confirming the talents of writer director **Mike Leigh** and his then wife, Steadman, the play was noted for its improvisation, with Leigh and the cast working without a script. A savagely funny modern classic.

★ Dramatis personae: The writers ★

TV drama would be duller without Jack Rosenthal, Alan Bennett, Alan Bleasdale and Jimmy McGovern. Here's our guide to their ups and downs.

Alan Bennett Best *An Englishman Abroad* Even if Coral Browne did win an award for playing herself. **Worst** *102 Boulevard Haussman* Very watchable but this drama about Marcel Proust probably doesn't say as much about Proust as one of his novels. **Most Underrated** *The Insurance Man* A Kafkaesque journey into unhelpful bureaucracy.

Alan Bleasdale Best *Boys From The Blackstuff* Gritty, sobering yet painfully realistic drama of life on the dole. **Worst** *Melissa* Why, Alan, why? **Most Underrated** *Jake's Progress* A thinking person's *Omen*.

Dennis Potter Best Toss up between *Pennies From Heaven* (with Bob Hoskins) or *The Singing Detective*. **Worst** *Black Eyes* Misogynism by any other name. **Most Underrated** *Blue Remembered Hills* Mainly because it's so bloody long ago. One of his finest early works.

Jack Rosenthal The Best *Eskimo Day* Rosenthal regular (and spouse) Maureen Lipman as one of a set of three parents struggling to cope with the adulthood of their children. **The Worst** *London's Burning: The Movie* Says it all really. **Most Underrated** *P'tang Yang Kipperbang* Simple, comic drama about one boys' mission to ask out the girl of his dreams.

Jimmy McGovern The Best *Hillsborough* A triumph of tension, emotion and control. **The Worst** *The Lakes* Controversial, with residents in Cumbria far from impressed by McGovern's portrayal of life in the Lake District, this just didn't hang together. **Most Underrated** *Dockers* Ken Stott, Ricky Tomlinson and Chrissy Rock in the same drama!

Ally McBeal Channel 4 1998–2002

Loathe it or love it, former lawyer David E Kelly's comedy drama has never been out of the headlines since Ms McBeal first swaggered onto our TV screens. There were the mini skirts at the office, dancing babies and constant whines for the loves of her life, the frankly weak and pathetic, Billy, and the drug-troubled **Robert Downey Jnr** as Larry. There were those who detested the show and its representation of the modern woman, yada yada yada, but someone must have been watching to make it one of the highest rated shows year-in year-out, and make an icon of **Calista Flockhart** (Kelley's original choice was Bridget Fonda), and it probably wasn't men. They could have given Vonda Shepard's singing a rest though.

Attachments BBC2 2000

Having already explored what it's like to work as a copper (**The Cops**), a lawyer (**This Life**) and a priest (**Ballykissangel**), creator **Tony Garnett** tackled the Internet industry. Fortunately for him, *Attachments* aired during the dot.com boom so the idea of pretty young things starting their own company with no business acumen didn't seem so implausible. Amazingly, watching sexy yuppies – Mike, Luce and their band of mismatched employees – type all day whilst spouting technical computer jargon was strangely seductive, and it successfully filled the void, if briefly (it only lasted two seasons), after *This Life* disappeared.

Band Of Gold ITV 1995–97

In a complete change of direction, **Kay Mellor** turned from writing about sick children for the CITV drama **Children's Ward** to life in Bradford's red light district. Displaying her talent for creating strong female characters, *Band Of Gold* centred on four prostitutes, Carol (**Cathy Tyson**), Rose (**Geraldine James**), Anita (**Barbara Dickson**, who also sang the 'Love Hurts' theme tune) and Tracy (**Samantha Morton**, pre–Hollywood), each selling themselves for different reasons. Despite the gritty, disturbingly bleak portrayal of life on the streets, and Mellor's constant message that prostitution was not as glamorous as Julia Roberts would have us believe, police noted an increase in numbers in Bradford's red light district.

Beauty And The Beast ITV 1988–89

A modern retelling of the classic tale, this time featuring lawyer Catherine Chandler (**Linda Hamilton** of Terminator fame) as the beauty living 'Above' in Manhattan and the man-beast Vincent, forced by his appearance to live in the 'World Below'. The psychic bond between them allowed Vincent to rescue Catherine from the clutches of evil many times, though sadly not in the last series when Catherine was killed after giving birth to Vincent's child. The final series centred around Vincent 'finding his true self' while fighting evil throughout the city – but the good versus bad theme could not make up for the loss of the central love story.

Bouquet Of Barbed Wire ITV 1976

Frank Finlay is staring obsessively at his onscreen daughter **Susan Penhaligon** in a manner which is supposed to indicate he is gripped by uncontrollable incestuous lust. Yet such is Finlay's acting that he looks more like he's trying desperately to remember his next line. This **Andrea Newman** drama (scripted from her own novel) was daring for its time, with its adulterous incestuous storyline. It wasn't all Frank's fault – his missus (**Shelia Allen**) was having an affair with son-in-law **James Aubrey**. The title became a cliché at about the same time middle England took this melodrama to its bosom. Newman would achieve a similar success with **A Sense Of Guilt** (1990) starring Trevor Eve as a serial adulterer.

Brideshead Revisited ITV 1981

'Every frame a Rembrandt' was how one fan described it. Granada must have felt it might have been cheaper to go to Sothebys as production costs soared from £4.5m to somewhere closer to £11m. But when you spend £50,000 to film aboard the *Queen Elizabeth II* ocean liner for eight minutes of film, what do you expect? Despite a troubled production, (a technicians' dispute halted filming long enough for star **Jeremy Irons** to be summoned to the set of **The French Lieutenant's Woman**, whilst original director **Michael Lindsay-Hogg** was replaced by **Charles Sturridge**), a beautiful and engrossing drama still emerged. **John Mortimer** stayed true to Evelyn Waugh's novel. Irons played Charles, although producer

Two toffs and a cuddly toy. Called Sebastian and played by Anthony Andrews

Derek Granger initially saw co-star **Anthony Andrews** in the role, the pair swapping on Andrews' recommendation. **Diana Quick** was sublimely sexy. The only thing that can be said against this is that too many young men rushed out to buy teddy bears and give them stupid names.

Budgie ITV 1971–72

Adam Faith is still one of the few singers to successfully carve out an acting career. Starring as the chirpy cockney geezer Budgie Bird, he tried to find the pot of gold which would enable him to escape his menial job as a runner for Glaswegian gangster Charlie Endell (**Iain Cuthbertson**). Budgie was the first TV criminal to be taken to audiences' hearts, which he might never have achieved if the producers had stuck to their original plan and called it *Loser*. Filming ended after two seasons, despite good ratings, when Faith was involved in a car crash. A spin-off series, *Charles Endell Esquire* briefly followed, a strike halting production forever. Surely wins the prize for best character name, Laughing Spam Fritter.

Camomile Lawn Channel 4 1992

Based on the **Mary Wesley** novel about the lives and loves of a group of cousins from World War II to present times, this wasn't your average period drama, being filled with nudity and a frank approach to sex you won't find in an Austen novel. It also marked the controversial nude debut of **Jennifer Ehle** as the young Calypso (her mum Rosemary Harris starred as the elder Calypso). Ehle was something of a sensation – not just because of the bath scene – but hasn't found good roles that easy to come by since.

Cold Feet ITV 1998–

A kind of British take on **Friends**, with a group of thirtysomethings coming to terms with the end of their reckless twenties and trying to behave like proper grown-ups. The original pilot won the coveted Montreux festival Golden Rose award, but poor ratings cast doubt on the show returning. When it did, it quickly became a major success, making household names of **James Nesbitt**, **Helen Baxendale** and **John Thomson** and taking off at the same time **Friends** was losing its way.

Edge Of Darkness BBC2 1985

If there is one cult drama above all others it has to be writer Troy Kennedy's **Edge of Darkness**. Having previously scripted *Z Cars*, Kennedy decided to tackle conspiracy and murder, amidst the setting of nuclear activists. Unable to walk away from the murder of his daughter Emma (**Joanne Whalley**), Ron (**Bob Peck**) investigates, unearthing political intrigues, nuclear waste sites and Knights of St John. This isn't the most cheerful of topics, but Kennedy wove in dark surreal humour (Joe Don Baker as golf-obsessed Jedburgh) and even symbolism, with Whalley making ghostly appearances throughout. Thankfully the original finale, where Ron turns into a tree, was scrapped. The show was repeated on BBC1, just weeks after its debut on BBC2. Eric Clapton and Michael Kamen provided the haunting soundtrack. It's time it was repeated.

Gormenghast BBC2 2000

Although star **Jonathan Rhys-Myers** doesn't go in for the 'Method' school of acting, ('Being an actor is the easiest job. Just say the lines'), in *Gormenghast* he made a superb Steerpike, the kitchen boy with aspirations to rise to the top of the Groan family through whatever means. Based on Mervyn Peake's first two *Gormenghast* novels, the BBC abandoned its staid costume drama ways for full on gothic fantasy.

The History Man BBC2 1981

Christopher Hampton (*Dangerous Liasions, Carrington, Rozprávky z Hollywoodu*) did a fine job adapting **Malcolm Bradbury**'s satire on campus life in the 1970s but his work went almost unnoticed, such were the plaudits for the central trio of performances by **Anthony Sher**, **Geraldine James** and **Isla Blair**. Sher turned in a repellent, sluglike yet

He'll be in a pickle if the minute hand moves

plausible performance as the self-serving Marxist lecturer. A series from which scenes would suddenly pop into viewers' minds years later.

House Of Cards BBC1 1990

Proving writer **Andrew Davies** had fully graduated from writing kids television (he wrote for **Educating Marmalade**), he adapted Conservative Party chief of staff Michael Dobbs' tale of political greed and deception, with **Ian Richardson** as Francis Urquhart, climbing to the top of the party and into 10 Downing Street. Urquhart became such a celebrated figure that MPs began to adopt his expressions, with 'You might well think that I couldn't possibly comment' becoming part of their vocabulary. Richardson based his portrayal on Shakespeare's *Richard III*. First aired as Thatcher was being toppled, the series became the best-selling drama of the early 1990s. Thankfully Davies had the foresight to change Dobbs' ending, reporter Mattie Storn falling to her death rather than Urquhart, otherwise there would have been no sequels. In the third instalment his wife (Diane Fletcher) emerged as even more ruthless than FU.

FU, the initials said it all really

House Of Eliott BBC1 1991–94

Women doing it for themselves in 1920s England. Slightly implausible – most women in this era were doing well if they got to be flappers. Yet **The House of Eliott** – created by the **Upstairs Downstairs** team of Jean Marsh and Eileen Atkins – justified its £6m budget (for the first series alone), with women enjoying the hormone-fuelled drama and costumes, and men the sight of **Louise Lombard**. Minnie Driver also appeared in an early episode.

The Lazarus Man Sky One 1997

Most of us can recall one seriously bad hangover in our lives but surely none have suffered quite as much as **Robert Urich**'s character in this *X-Files*-cum-Western. He wakes up not knowing who he is but with a hell of a headache, several stab wounds and a farmer's wife who wants to know whether he fought for the North or the South in the American Civil War. Sadly, he cannot answer this vital question or, indeed, many others. Too strange to survive long, even in the vastness of US TV, this is one show that the fortunate few who saw it will never forget.

Love Story ITV 1963–67, 1969, 1972–74

Not to be confused with the film about never having to say you're sorry, this was a series of plays commissioned by ATV on the obvious theme but with some striking talent: **Vanessa Redgrave** in **Marguerite Duras**' *La Musica* and Dudley Moore, in a rare straight role, in *The Girl Opposite*, directed by **Roman Polanski**. It wouldn't be allowed today.

Northern Exposure Channel 4 1992–97

Originally commissioned as a replacement show for CBS, this quirky saga set in the remote Alaskan town of Cicely garnered a devout following. **Rob Morrow** played Joel Fleischman, a newly-graduated doctor who is forced to set up surgery in Cicely having paid his tuition fees. Although he spends most of the time grumbling about leaving, he develops a love/hate relationship with landlady Maggie (**Janine Turner**), a risky business given that Maggie's five previous boyfriends had died in tragic circumstances. The Alaskan tourist industry benefited but visitors were disappointed not to meet ex-NASA astronauts (Maurice Minnifield), Steve Irwin-style adventurers (Holling Vincoeur) or Mort the Moose. A lighter **Twin Peaks** – and to say that means no disrespect to either.

Onedin Line BBC1 1971–80

Originally a one-off for *Drama Playhouse* in 1970, it became a regular Sunday night fixture on BBC1 for nine years and a massive hit in Ceaucescu's Romania. **Peter Gilmore**, hitherto known for his *Carry On* roles, starred as determined Captain James Onedin, the series opening with his marriage of convenience to Anne Wester (Sheila Allen) in order to get his own ship. The show also marked the acting debuts of **Jill Gascoine**, **Linus Roache** and **Kate Nelligan**, as well as starring TV queen Jane Seymour. Was given to Romania (along with **Dallas**) in a UK trade deal, so Gilmore is now as big in Romania as Norman Wisdom is in Albania.

Play For Today BBC1 1970–84

With Britain's best writers and directors – including Ken Loach, Dennis Potter, Mike Newell, John Mortimer and Alan Bleasdale – contributing to the series, it's hard to pick one, but Alan Gibson's **The Flipside Of Dominick Hide** (1980) was a fine work. The brilliant **Peter Firth** starred as Hide, a time-traveller from 2130 sent to observe the London Transport system (ironic given that Firth had spent all that time with a bus in **Double Deckers**). Officially forbidden from mixing with people for the usual reasons, Hide naturally does, falling for Jane (Caroline Langrishe).

Queer As Folk Channel 4 1999

On the eve of the new millennium, a series about the lives and loves of three gay men still managed to stir up controversy. Set in Manchester's Canal Street, the series thankfully ignored stereotypes and judgements, making for enticing late-night viewing, with writer **Russell T Davies** (formerly of *Doctor Who*) filling his scripts with such in-your-face lines as, 'Just tell her that you take it up the arse and get out of there!' Also featured ex-*Corrie* star Denise Black, free from Ken Barlow, as Vince's mum.

Six Feet Under Channel 4 2002–

Anyone who began viewing this US series (set in a mortuary business) mid-way through could be forgiven for thinking they were being subjected to a sick joke when a baker was shredded by an industrial-sized bread mixer. **Alan Ball**, writer of the equally dark **American Beauty**, scripts and co-produces this series about a dysfunctional family, comprising prodigal son Nate (**Peter Krause** doing his best HAL impersonation), uptight and in-the-closet David, confused arsonist daughter Claire, and guilt-ridden mum Ruth, who starts running the family funeral parlour after dad is mowed down by a bus. Who'd have thought death could be so funny?

Tutti Frutti BBC1 1987

On the road with a Scottish rock 'n' roll band, with **Robbie Coltrane** as the unlikeliest rock 'n' roll star, and **Emma Thompson** as old flame and singer, Suzi Kettles. Almost as much fun as the Little Richard hit.

The Waltons BBC1 1974–81

Squeaky clean life in the Blue Ridge Mountains of Virginia. The series was based on the life of creator Earl Hamner Jr, who also narrated. What began as a TV movie, **The Homecoming** (with Patricia Neal as the mum), ran for eight years. The closing sequence of good nights varied, often weaving in topical allusions as in the episode 'The Abdication': 'Goodnight Elizabeth' 'Goodnight John Boy' 'Goodnight Mary Ellen' 'Goodnight Duke of Windsor. Too bad about your throne.'

★ ★ ★ Food ★ ★ ★

Few food programmes are truly cult. **Two Fat Ladies** were a manufactured cult, which never works for long (ask Ann Widdecombe). **Food And Drink** had its moments – mainly when Chris Kelly would mumble, 'Hmm, that's nice' before tasting any food. Somebody obviously told **Ainsley Harriott** his personality was infectious, when they meant contagious. And Nigella may be cult among men but her appeal isn't down to food.

Two cheers for **Fanny Cradock**, for putting the British nation off fine food for so long and for **Graham Kerr**, the Galloping Gourmet, the 'Roger Moore of the frying pan', who pioneered the mix of recipes, chat and flirtation which is now the norm. But three cheers for **Keith Floyd** – in his prime, taking one freshly plucked ostrich, cooking it in a wok with some red wine sauce and serving a piece of it to a nearby ostrich. Cruel? Certainly – especially if you're an ostrich. Unexpected? Definitely. Funny? Well, almost as funny as **Delia Smith**'s attack on **Food And Drink** as 'the most disgusting programme on television.'

★★★ Football ★★★

The match of the day on 30 April 1938 was the FA Cup final between Huddersfield and Preston, the first game to be televised live in its entirety by the BBC, which Preston won by the Colemanesque scoreline of 1-0. For all the shift to colour, new technology, fashion in facial hair (Jimmy Hill's beard, Des and Mark's moustaches) and the succession of presenters (Jimmy Hill, Des Lynam, Barry Venison), football coverage hasn't changed much since. Less limited, reverential and generally more fun, however, are the football spin-off shows, where the sofa is king...

Fantasy Football League BBC2 1994–96 ITV 1998

Heir to *Standing Room Only* and grandparent to *The Royle Family*, the **Janet Street-Porter** commissioned show was based on the simple premise that two fairly funny footie-loving blokes sitting on a sofa discussing football's knobs-out-of-shorts sideshows was worth watching. And it was. Starring real-life flatmates **David Baddiel** and **Frank Skinner** making each other laugh in an imitation front room, it also offered countless celebs submitting themselves to interviews, including John Lydon, (so raucous he was removed during an ad break) and a boozed-up Brigitte Nielsen. 'Phoenix From The Flames', where they recreated great football moments, was ingenious while Baggies striker Jeff Astle closed the show with an ironic sing-a-long. Screened on a Friday night. Perfect post-pub TV.

Footballers' Wives ITV 2002–

Though professional footballers were generally outraged by the portrayal of their extravagant, amoral lifestyles, those not quite so close to the action thought it horribly accurate. With cartoon storylines and plastic personalities, it was also horribly compulsive as infidelity, murder and near-necrophilia (a nurse performing unorthodox revival methods on a comatose club chairman) reigned. So bad it was good.

Gazzetta Football Italia Channel 4 1992–

Neatly coinciding with Paul Gascoigne and Des Walker's first seasons in

Italy, Channel 4 snapped up live coverage of what was then officially the world's most glamorous (and unofficially most boring) league. A live Sunday afternoon game was preceded by a Saturday morning magazine, wryly and wittily presented by James Richardson, whose romp through the headlines over a capuccino still makes **Football Focus** seem old hat.

The Manageress Channel 4 1989–91

The drama series starred **Cheri Lunghi** as the manager of a mediocre men's football team. Some convincing plot lines (including a Karren Brady-esque fling with a player) and likeable characters carried it off. **Stephen Tomkinson** and a pre-EastEnders **Steve McFadden** also appeared. Not quite as strange as **The Ticket**, a *La Ronde*-style romp in which a cup final ticket changes hands. A 1968 ITV one-off, it was co-written by **Jimmy Hill** and starred Gabrielle Drake and Bryan (Alf Roberts) Mosley.

Saint And Greavsie ITV 1985–92

Ian St John and Jimmy Greaves formed a classic funny-guy-straight-guy partnership on this Saturday morning preview show. Top of the agenda: Greavsie's one-man mission to discredit all of Scotland's goalkeepers and St John's unwavering response, 'Och, you kill me Greavsie.'

Soccer AM Sky Sports 1997–

Ideal hangover TV for fans, **Soccer AM** is presented by Tim Lovejoy (who also produces the show and DJs on London's Xfm) and ladette Helen Chamberlain. They're joined on the sofas by celebrities from football and Chris Evans as they laugh at the sporting week's quirkier moments before nipping outside to 'Feed The Goat' (kick footballs into a hole). On Saturday afternoon, **Soccer Saturday** is Teletext taken to another level as we watch ex-pros Rodney Marsh, Alan Mullery, George Best et al watch live Premiership games. It shouldn't work, but it does.

Standing Room Only BBC2 1991–94

Child of the fanzine boom **Standing Room Only** was hosted by Simon O'Brien and featured a broad mix of interviews, profiles and issues plus a cartoon strip from The *Guardian*'s Steve Bell. **David Baddiel** and **Rob Newman** chipped in and various footballers (including Pele) talked about golden football moments. Fans were given airtime as they sat on a portaloo to give their two-penneth. Running for six series, the show kept changing its shirt, as Rory Bremner, Kevin Allen and Shelley Webb (wife of 'special special' Neil), and O'Brien again all had stints as presenters.

★★★ Game shows ★★★

Game shows is one genre where the industrial origins of TV are blatant. The trade in game shows is almost as big as the international arms trade and any bright new idea, be it **Blind Date** or **Big Brother**, will be broadcast to within an inch of its life across the globe. In case you were wondering, the difference between a game show and a quiz show is that on a quiz show contestants are asked factual questions, as opposed to the 'Our survey said…' kind. Within game shows is a polite (well, usually) sub-genre called panel shows, whereby celebrity guests (in the 1970s **Patrick Mower**) would enter into frivolous combat. The show with the most stamina in this field is probably **Call My Bluff** but **Shooting Stars**, even with Will Self replacing Mark Lamarr, is still worth tuning in to.

Blankety Blank BBC1 1979–90, 1997–99, ITV 2001–

'Eugene, reveal the legend!' Terry, Les and now Lily have all wrestled with the tackiest quiz show in the history of telly. The music is moronic and irritatingly catchy – and after your first episode the 'supermatch game' riff was printed indelibly on your memory. The prizes were as tacky as the set, the repartee and the celebs (but at least it kept the former members of Bucks Fizz gainfully employed). In other words, it was utterly compelling. A peculiar feature of the show was the unfairness in the contestants' challenges. One would be asked to fill the blank in something like 'Blankety _', the other poor mite would have to guess which word the panelists might think followed 'existentialist'. And when Cheryl, Linda, Barry, Nerys, Beryl, Gareth et al had failed the challenge, the condemned contestant would be given the *Blankety Blank* cheque book and pen and permitted a cheery wave before being rotated off-screen. They call it entertainment – some might call it sadism.

Don't Forget Your Toothbrush Channel 4 1994–95

Chris Evans' shortlived, but compelling, reinvention of the game show, where the winners left the studio for some exotic, mysterious, location. The premise (but not the wit) would later be adopted by the BBC for **Jet Set**. The most memorable episode was probably when Chris put his own new Jag, recently acquired from Jools Holland's brother, on the line with a contestant and lost it. Bowed out while it was still way, way ahead.

Endurance Fuji TV

The contestants are stripped to their pants in the desert, with huge blocks of ice around their waists, and aren't allowed to go to the toilet. There you have **Endurance**, the game show the Japanese turned to when kamikaze went out of fashion. (Don't confuse it with the dismal Paul Ross British cable version.) **Michiyo Saito**, who created one of the show's predecessors, **The Ultra Quiz** (where two contestants wrestled on top of a New York skyscraper) wasn't surprised by *Endurance*. 'The time will come,' he said, 'when the monstrous, insatiable, audience will demand that someone will be killed on a game show.' If only the culling could start with the hosts.

★ Hi, it's Bob from Wolverhampton! ★

One of the most memorable contestants ever must be the '**Bob from Wolverhampton**' who called **The Golden Shot**. He was directing the crossbow so erratically Monkhouse had to stop and ask if Bob could see the target. At this point, Bob admitted he'd had his TV repossessed by Rumbelows. 'You mean you're sitting at home trying to play this game without a television set?' asked an incredulous Monkhouse. 'No,' Bob replied, 'I'm in a phone box in Wolverhampton High Street, opposite Currys. They've got a stack of TVs in the window.' Bob then asked Monkhouse to wave at him. Failing to see it, he groaned: 'Oh bugger, that's not you at all – they've left 'em all tuned into the bloody BBC!' In despair, he cried 'Fire!' at random, hit an apple and won the game.

The Generation Game BBC1 1971–82, 1990–

'Take eight introverted, unattractive members of the British public. Dress the men in brown corduroy trousers and white polyester shirts with flared collars. Give them large, scraggly sideburns. Then give the women sensible tweed skirts, a weight problem and dumpy horn-rimmed spectacles. Do not expose anyone to hair conditioner. Place all of the above in a cheap television studio constructed dangerously out of coloured cardboard. Add a few soldiers, some dancing Russians, a cake decorator… Then add a naïve beautiful female Scottish songstress, give her a pageboy haircut and plop her into a long blue frilly dress. Finally, douse with camp aging game-show host and throw in a clutch of well-known catchphrases. Stir well. Boil. Simmer for 50 minutes.' Paul Baker, author of *www.dollsoup.co.uk*, says it all really. Aficionados only recognise two GG hosts: Bruce and Larry. Jim was just auditioning – for eight years.

Fort Boyard Channel 5 1998–2001

Next time your friends tell you how good **The Crystal Maze** was (and is – in their memory), you can tell them it's a cheap derivative of *Fort Boyard*,

'They're playing their joker!' The sight of this card was enough to send Stuart into ecstasy

the game show which sprang more or less fully formed from the fertile brain of Jacques Anotine, the Gallic genius who also devised **Treasure Hunt** in the time his countrymen take to shrug their shoulders. Ironically, given the stunts contestants are obliged to perform, Anotine died in a diving accident. There's nothing quite like seeing Melinda Messenger berate a policeman for not putting his helmet on properly for putting you in a good mood for a Saturday night. Unless, of course, it's Suggs and his cast of soap dispensees singing up a storm on **Night Fever**

It's A Knockout/Jeux Sans Frontieres BBC1 1966–82/Channel 5 1999–2001

'And here come the Belgians…' First questions first: when **It's A Knockout** went pan-European and became **Jeux Sans Frontieres**, who decided that the impartial arbiters should both be Italian: Gennaro Olivieri and Guido Pancaldi? Not that it helped the Italians much, they only won four JSFs, the same as us, and two less than all-time champs the Germans. The Spanish only won it once but they always fail to live up to expectations in these big international tournaments. One day all border disputes will be settled like this. Or, perhaps, with the Solomon-like judgement of 'World Cup referee Arthur Ellis'. The Channel 5 revamp replaced Stuart Hall's giggles with Frank Bruno's pantomime laugh. Not the same.

Robot Wars BBC2 1998–

Testosterone levels buildi up to simmering point as two teams of robotics obsessives battle it out with the highly elaborate robots they built in their shed from the bits *Blue Peter* didn't want. Works despite **Craig Charles** who has taken over from **Jeremy Clarkson** as chief host.

Whose Line Is It Anyway? Channel 4 1988–

You're probably too young to recall **Impromptu**, the 1964 show in which such luminaries as Lance Percival and Victor Spinetti improvised for their supper. But the precedent doesn't spoil **Whose Line Is It Anyway?**, as good a way as any to waste half an hour on a Friday night after you've sunk a bottle of wine. Host Clive Anderson's scoring was brilliantly unpredictable and unjust, and Tony Slattery was very funny. For a while.

★★★ Historical ★★★

Edward & Mrs Simpson ITV 1978

Ambitious seven-part drama based on Frances Donaldson's account of the love affair between Wallis Simpson and the then Prince Edward. Although most viewers knew the details of the scandal, Simon Raven's adaptation, and **Edward Fox** and **Cynthia Harris** as the respective leads, portrayed the future king as weak and ineffectual and Simpson as a scheming and manipulative woman. Needless to say the real Duchess of Windsor, living in Paris at the time, took great offence, ensuring it was banned in France. **Edward VII** had his own show too. With **Timothy West** (more of a Henry VIII lookalike these days) as the skirt-chasing king, it was a huge hit Stateside where the series was renamed **The Royal Victorians**. A successful spin-off followed the exploits of Edward's mistress, Lillie Langtry, who was played by **Francesca Annis**.

Elizabeth R BBC2 1971

David Bowie, hot pants and the Tudors were all terribly trendy in 1971. **Keith Michell** impressed as Henry VIII in **The Six Wives Of Henry VIII** yet that virtuoso turn was overshadowed by **Glenda Jackson**'s portrayal of the Virgin Queen. With nine hours of screen-time, the 35-year-old Jackson went to great lengths to make the role her own, shaving her head and forehead, wearing a false nose and spending countless hours in the make-up chair to play the queen at every age from 15 to 70. **Elizabeth R** works as a fascinating drama and pedantically accurate historical narrative even if you don't, finally, end up liking the heroine that much.

Heimat BBC2 1984

A milestone in television history, not just for its current 42-hour running time (set to grow with the release of *Heimat 3* in 2004). Telling the story of the townspeople of **Schabbach**, the action focuses particularly on Maria (**Marita Breuer** in her debut) and the events in her life, including both World Wars and the rise and fall of the Nazis. An arty variation on a soap, shot in monochrome but suddenly bursting into colour where appropriate, this is as full of symbolism as many more pretentious TV dramas. Despite the language barrier, this has been a deserved international success. *The Second Heimat: A New Germany* followed in 1992 with writer, director, producer, cinematographer and general odd job man **Edgar Reitz** now working on the third instalment.

I, Claudius BBC1 1976

After Nero (played by a youthful but already ample **Christopher Biggins**) had sex with his skinny mum, you could almost hear Britain gasp in shock. Fortunately, this was ancient Rome and we could console ourselves that that kind of thing didn't happen any more – except in Andrea Newman dramas. **I, Claudius** had everything: a truly stellar cast (Derek Jacobi, John Hurt, George Baker, Ian Ogilvy, Kevin McNally, John Castle, Sian Phillips, Brian Blessed – before he became a big-voiced, bustling, self-parody – and, er, Biggins), some high culture and a woman who organised a 'who can have sex with the most men in one night' contest. And this was when Rome was already in decline – just imagine what

Rome sweet Rome

a crazy place it must have been when it was really popping.

★★★ L!ve TV ★★★

Television channels don't get to say long goodbyes. In November 1999, L!ve TV, the cable channel more talked about than watched, announced simply 'L!ve TV has ceased transmission.' It was a dull way to end it all for a channel which started as Britain's first truly regional TV network for yoof, with **Janet Street-Porter**, but soon mutated into a tabloid fantasy of **Kelvin McKenzie**'s. Now, years

173

later, it's hard to believe that the City news was read by a woman who looked like the secretary in *Reginald Perrin* and was stripped down to her bra, that a dwarf on a trampoline really did introduce the weather, ('It'll be [boing] rainy in [boing] Manchester'), or that a bunny stood behind a newsreader, giving a thumbs up or down depending on whether the news was good or bad. At least you can tell your grandkids it really happened.

Topless Darts L!ve TV

The McKenzie idea which generated the most publicity. But the frantic haste with which the channel changed the setting (on the moon, at the ballet, on the Titanic) highlighted the basic problem. Once you'd sighed with relief that it wasn't Eric Bristow topless and confirmed that yup, they were bare chested and yep, they were throwing darts, you never needed to watch it again. If indeed, you needed to watch it in the first place.

The Weather In Norwegian L!ve TV

Light years ahead of **The Fast Show**'s spoof Channel 9 and even funnier because McKenzie actually meant it.

★★★ Magicians ★★★

Cooper had audiences over a barrel

Tommy Cooper

Funny buggers, magicians. They can pull a rabbit out of a hat but can they make us like them? **Paul Daniels** did at least convince a beautiful young woman to fall in love with him despite serious height and personality issues, so he must have magic of a kind. But **Tommy Cooper**, who rarely pulled anything out of a hat like he was supposed to, is the most likeable of them all. 'I slept like a log last night. I woke up in a fireplace.' Did he have the same scriptwriter as Basil Brush? Somehow, we never tired of hearing, 'Just like that', and watching him fumble through a card trick. He died in 1984 on stage in front of millions of viewers during **Live from Her Majesty's**, having suffered a heart attack during his act. Since his death, **Anthony Hopkins** has admitted Cooper influenced his portrayal of **Hannibal Lecter**. Mind you, Tommy probably knew a few cannibal jokes.

★★★ Mini-series ★★★

The Far Pavilions Channel 4 1984

Spectacular Indian (and Welsh) landscapes by the great cinematographer **Jack Cardiff** and a lush score by **Carl Davis** flavour this ripping yarn of adventure and romance in the British Raj, adapted from MM Kaye's best-selling odyssey of a dashing officer gone native. Ashton Pelham-Martyn was orphaned in the Mutiny and raised by his loyal ayah (nanny) as her son. His identity and class revealed, public-schooled, he is torn between duty, honour and passion, embroiled in deadly palace intrigues and… you can guess the rest. **Ben Cross** stars as Ash/Ashok with Christopher Lee, Omar Sharif, Sir John Gielgud, Benedict Taylor (as valiant comrade Wally) and, controversially, the American and future Mrs Steven Spielberg **Amy Irving** as Anjuli, his Indian princess and forbidden love.

Hollywood Wives ITV 1985

Jackie Collins' bonkbuster novel was trashy enough, but **Aaron Spelling**'s TV mini-series version of it plumbed new lows. It's hard to imagine which of the cast – including **Candice Bergen**, **Angie Dickinson** and **Rod Steiger** – should be most embarrassed by their performances in this tawdry tale of Hollywood types, though **Anthony Hopkins** (as a movie producer who has a heart attack during sex with a bimbo) especially wishes he could erase it permanently from his CV.

Jewel In The Crown ITV 1984

Britain's middle classes hung on every instalment of this epic, the Indian/British production of **Paul Scott**'s *The Raj Quartet* series of novels, as if every week contained a 'Who shot JR?'-style cliffhanger. Four years in the making, at a cost of £5m, the series focused on the lives and disputes of a group of British residents and Indian locals, opening with the false arrest of an English-raised Indian reporter Hari Kumar (**Art Malik**) for the rape of an orphan, Daphne Manners (**Susan Wooldridge**). Famed for its lavish sets, much being filmed on location in India (although Salford Dock did pass for Bombay in some scenes) as well as performances by **Charles Dance**, **Peggy Ashcroft**, **Geraldine James** and **Tim Piggott-Smith**. The series made a star of Dance. Soon he would be omnipresent, despite one critic complaining he 'had the face of a startled haddock'.

Lace ITV 1984

In the early 1980s, Radio 2 DJ Terry Wogan and his listeners were obsessed with **Shirley Conran**'s racy novel *Lace* (including a particular sex scene with a goldfish that we won't get into here). So it came as no surprise when the book was translated into a steamy mini-series, featuring Brooke Adams, Ariele Dombasle and Bess Armstrong as former friends, one of whom may have given birth to the bitchy Lili (Phoebe Cates, aka Mrs Kevin Kline). Hence the famous line 'Which one of you bitches is my mother?' The series is really just an excuse for actresses to wander around in lingerie and groan orgasmically whenever possible. Bad as it is, it's a higher form of life than *Sins*, starring **Joan Collins**, from the same era.

Masada ITV 1981

Peter Strauss, rival claimant for Richard Chamberlain's crown as king of the mini-series, is the inspirational zealot leader Eleazar ben Yair in this stirring adaptation of Ernest K Gann's novel. (It was directed by Boris Sagal, who also directed Strauss in episodes of *Rich Man, Poor Man*.) Based on the real story of Jewish freedom fighters' resistance to ancient Rome, it culminates in the two-year siege by the Roman 10th Legion led by **Peter O'Toole**'s sympathetic but dutiful Roman Legate Flavius Silva. Gorgeous pouting **Barbara Carrera** co-starred as sultry Jewish slave Sheva. Much more stirring than ATVC's **Moses The Lawgiver**, in which Burt Lancaster ignored the 11th commandment: 'Thou shalt not bore.'

North And South ITV 1986

US producers have made some highbrow mini-series about American history (*The Blue And The Gray, Kennedy*, etc) but far more enjoyable was this opulent costume drama set before and during the American Civil War. Southern boy Orry Main (**Patrick Swayze**, in the role that made him a hearthrob) and Northerner George Hazard (**James Read**) meet at Westpoint but their friendship is tested when the war starts and they fight on opposite sides. A $25m adaptation of John Jakes' best-selling novel, the supporting cast included **Lesley Ann Down** as Madeleine (the married love of Orry's life), **Jean Simmons** as his mother, **Elizabeth Taylor** as a local madam, and **David Carradine** as Madeleine's abusive husband. Cracking stuff that continued in a second mini-series *North And South Book II* (which deviated substantially from its source material).

Return To Eden ITV 1985

Eat your heart out, Danielle Steele! Australia got on the mini-series map with this fabulously lurid piffle in which a middle-aged, Plain Jane heiress (**Rebecca Gilling** as Stephanie Harper) is dumped into the gaping maw of a crocodile by her homicidal toy-boy husband (ex-pop singer James Reyne as ex-tennis champion Greg Marsden) in adulterous cahoots with her best friend (Wendy Hughes). Rescued by an Outback type, the heroine (after extensive cosmetic surgery) becomes heartbreaking supermodel Tara Welles out to seduce and exact vengeance. No prizes for art, but just divine. Topped only by an unforgettably absurd 22-part serial that picked up the saga seven years later and saw Gilling's character undergo another death and resurrection as Princess Talita.

Rich Man, Poor Man ITV 1976

The daddy of TV's bestsellers, this 12-parter of **Irwin Shaw**'s opus rivetted audiences to the trials of the dysfunctional Jordache family (is this where Phil Redmond got the name from?), particularly the opposing fortunes and love rivalry of bad boy Tom and his good brother Rudy (**Nick Nolte** and **Peter Strauss** in star-making roles). One of the directors was actor Bill 'Incredible Hulk' Bixby. The 22-episode *Rich Man, Poor Man – Book*

177

II (1976–77) followed up on the survivors, memorably stalked by one-eyed villain Falconetti (William Smith), and set the standard by which sprawling melodramas are now judged. These included Taylor Caldwell's *Captains And The Kings* (1976) – the rags-to-riches saga of Irish US immigrant Joseph Armagh and his tragic obsession with making son Rory president in a very 19th-century Kennedys way – and Jeffrey Archer's *Kane And Abel* (1985) – the rags-to-riches saga of Polish US immigrant Abel Rosnovski (Strauss again) and his tragic obsession (notice a theme here?) with ruining aristocratic William Kane (**Sam Neill**).

Roots BBC1 1977

Historic ratings (more than 100 million viewers in America) greeted the 12-hour first half of **Alex Haley**'s blockbuster. With a 'Who's Who' of African-American actors and icons from poet **Maya Angelou** to Richard 'Shaft' Roundtree to **OJ Simpson** (and music by **Quincy Jones**), it dramatised the gripping story of the African Kunta Kinte (LeVar Burton, John Amos), his abduction and enslavement, and the trials of his plantation slave descendants (Leslie Uggams, Ben Vereen) to emancipation and the end of the Civil War. The 14-hour follow-up *Roots: The Next Generations* (1979) took the story up to Haley's journey to Africa, with **James Earl Jones** as the author, George Stanford Brown, **Pam Grier**, Debbie Allen and Diahann Carroll among the cast, although the real sensation was **Marlon Brando**, collecting an Emmy as a white supremacist leader.

The Thorn Birds BBC1 1984

Colleen McCullough wrote the bestseller on which this mega (but not as raunchy as the ads suggested) mini-series was based. Handsome TV-movie-veteran **Richard Chamberlain** starred as the Catholic priest in deepest Australia who has a forbidden fling with a young woman (**Rachel Ward**) that leads to her giving birth to his child. **Barbara Stanwyck** played Ward's strict mother, while Ward and **Bryan Brown** (her husband in the series) married when filming finished and lived happily ever after. Often overlooked is the contribution of the solitary kangaroo, which managed to conjure up Australia with just one jump.

The Winds Of War ITV 1983

Producer-director **Dan Curtis** ensured his hugely entertaining 12-part adaptation of Herman Wouk's doorstopper had it all. Set among events leading up to World War II, it centred on the Henry family. Globe-trotting patriarch and naval admiral Pug (Robert Mitchum) talked tough with presidents, statesmen and dictators while his wife misbehaved; chip-off-the-block Byron (**Jan-Michael Vincent**) romanced Natalie (**Ali MacGraw**) across Europe, and the other kids reached Hawaii in time for the attack on Pearl Harbor. The equally exhausting sequel, *War And Remembrance* (1989), cast **Jane Seymour** as Natalie, and wove between the Holocaust (Natalie, her son and uncle John Gielgud in a death camp) and the Henry men's naval engagement. It also had the added attractions of young **Sharon Stone** as Janice Henry and **Steven Berkoff** as Adolf Hitler.

★★★ Movie directors' TV series ★★★

Filmmakers used to be a bit snobby about TV, but in recent years this has changed, possibly because TV execs are just so darn grateful to work with Hollywood talent that they'll let 'em get away with moidah (as the Harts'

179

The Henry family made the Kennedys look like a bunch of underachievers

housekeeper Max would say). **Alfred Hitchcock** was one of the earliest film directors to try his hand at a TV series and since then everyone from Steven Spielberg, Robert Altman and Oliver Stone has got in on the act. It's not always successful. **David Lynch** had to reclaim the pilot episode of **Mulholland Drive** (the producers realised it would be too expensive to turn into a full series), then recut it and release it as the movie.

Alfred Hitchcock Presents ITV 1957–62

Hitchcock had been directing movies for 30 years by the time he launched a TV series made up of half-hour mysteries and dramas. What was most famous about them was the opening credits – a line drawing of Hitch's profile that moved to show the face of the great man himself, who then introduced that night's episode with a few witty well-chosen words (Hitchcock also appeared at the end to make a final comment on the episode). Just about every actor you can name – some at the beginning of their careers – appeared in an episode, from **Robert Redford** to **Joanne Woodward** and **Peter Fonda**. The series was resurrected in 1985, five years after Hitchcock's death, but was notable mainly for the creepily colourised versions of Hitchcock's introductions from the original episodes. Not in the best possible taste. But then neither was Hitch.

Hercules: The Legendary Journeys Sky, Channel 5
1996–2000

Sam Raimi, the director responsible for the **Evil Dead** movies, was executive producer for this campy mythological series – so tongue-in-cheek it makes **Conan The Barbarian** look like **Citizen Kane**. Hercules (former model **Kevin Sorbo**), son of god Zeus and a mortal woman, was blessed with rippling muscles and superhuman strength, and had middle-aged women's hearts racing with his displays of strength and sundry good deeds. The series

Hitchcock, not colourised

proved to be so successful that **Xena: Warrior Princess** (also produced by Raimi), starring Amazonian actress **Lucy Lawless**, was spun off from it.

Nightmare Cafe Sci-Fi 1998

Subtler and more satisfying than *Alfred Hitchcock Presents*, **Nightmare Café** was a short-lived series in which people relived an important moment in their life. They did this by telling it to the proprietor (played by Robert Englund – obviously somewhat more friendly than in his role as Freddy Krueger) of a café situated somewhere between life and death (and no, it's not a Wimpy). Wes Craven directed beautifully.

Wild Palms BBC2 1993

Almost as weird as **Twin Peaks**, **Wild Palms** was **Oliver Stone**'s foray into TV (with the help of co-creator Bruce Wagner). This six-hour series was based on a comic strip in US men's magazine *Details*, and was set in Los Angeles in the year 2007. The plot had something to do with sinister goings-on in the world of reality TV uncovered by lawyer Harry (**James Belushi**), but was most notable for striking visuals that made LA look incredibly alien, and a cast that included **Kim Cattrall** and **Bebe Neuwirth**.

★★★ Music ★★★

There is an unfair assumption that **Top Of The Pops** is the be all and end all of televisual musical idiocy. As anybody who saw Whispering Bob Harris introduce 'Brian Ferris' in Roxy Music's *Old Grey Whistle Test* debut knows, this is untrue. But *TOTP* in 1983 when **Dexy's Midnight Runners** played 'Jackie Wilson Said' in front of a giant picture of darts player **Jocky Wilson** remains one of pop on TV's defining moments.

ITV's contribution to pop on the box wasn't much better and includes **Get It Together** (on which **Roy North**, freed from Basil Brush's side, did an even worse job singing the hits than **Peter Glaze**) and **Shang A Lang**.

Most weeks *Top Of The Pops* is efficient (and *TOTP2* is compelling). Jools Holland's **Later** has its moments (although it's not as much fun as **The Tube**) and the **Old Grey Whistle Test** was fantastic in its day. The

★ The pits of the Brits ★

Any musical glitch on TV pales into Dean Friedman-style insignificance compared to the 1989 Brits awards, hosted by Mick Fleetwood and Sam Fox, which plumbed new depths. For those who need their memory jogging, here's a verbatim account of one of their exchanges.

Sam: Well, those are the nominations and with the all-important answer are four guys who went 'Loco In Acapulco'. Here they are...The Four Tops!
Mick: Tonight they're totally compos mentis – whatever that means. I don't know – here in London. The fabulous, the sensational...
Sam: The Four...
Mick: The Four...
Sam: Woooo...
Mick: Tops...
Enter Boy George
Boy George: Hello.
Sam: You don't look like 'em, George!
Boy George: I'm the one Top. The Four Tops have been held up putting on make-up so I'm giving the award for the Best British Group. It's Erasure.
Sam: Wooooo!

baton has been handed now to music channels. Depending on your age, this could be MTV or VH1 Classic, with its mysterious fondness for screening an old clip of Nilsson in reflective trousers singing *Midnight Cowboy*'s 'Everybody's Talkin''. When he gets to the 'waaaah...' bit, he twizzles one hand in a bad approximation of a working windmill.

Perhaps surprisingly given its famed excesses, rock has not provided a rich seam of fictional programmes for TV. **Rock Follies**, with music by Brian Ferris's pal **Andy MacKay**, was a decent drama and gave roles to Rula Lenska and Julie Covington. But, *Tutti Frutti* aside, that's about it.

Here, in the order they occurred to us, are our favourite moments – apart from those already mentioned.

1 Lynne Perrie singing 'I Will Survive' on *The Word*, closely followed by **Paul Shane** (yes, Ted from **Hi-De-Hi!**) singing 'You've Lost That Lovin' Feelin'' on *Pebble Mill*.

2 David Bowie singing 'Heroes' on Marc Bolan's children's TV series *Marc*. Thank you, Granada.

3 Elvis reclaiming his career with a soulful 'If I Can Dream' in 1968.

4 The brothers Gibb's acoustic version of **New York Mining Disaster** on *Parkinson*, before they became the brothers glib.

5 Pan's People as bank robbers dancing to The Clash's 'Bank Robber'.

6 Dave Lee Travis, hosting *The Golden Oldie Picture Show*, a short-lived experiment in which the BBC provided videos to classic songs.

Introducing a video to 'Strawberry Fields Forever', DLT (remember, it's not a sandwich) said: 'We've done something really imaginative and different with this… I think you'll like it.' The screen then cut to a girl in a strawberry field. Post-modern irony by the Hairy Monster?

7 **Boney M**, mainly for Bobby Farrell's costumes and hairdo but also for 'Ra-Ra-Rasputin/Russia's greatest love machine…'

8 **John Peel**'s 'multi-talented' episode of *TOTP*. After describing **Tracey Ullman** as 'multi-talented', Peel proceeded to describe everyone as 'multi-talented' all the way through the show and right to **FR David**, composer and singer of 'Words Don't Come Easy'.

9 John Lydon staring at Noel Edmonds on **Juke Box Jury**. As Paul Morley said, 'They way he would look at Noel Edmonds is eventually how an entire nation would look at Noel Edmonds.'

When Pan's People weren't strutting their stuff, they helped pioneer country line dancing

★★★ Newsreaders ★★★

We don't ask much of our newsreaders. We like them to deliver the news with reasonable efficiency, but not too monotonously, as the lugubrious **Peter Woods** did on the BBC in the 1970s. And we'd prefer it if they don't write best-selling books about cats as **Martyn Lewis** did.

Newsreaders were once mysterious, quasi-official figures (best personified by the likes of **Richard Baker**). They might do the odd voiceover (on such innocuous guff as **Mary, Mungo & Midge**) but they were rarely seen full-bodied until **Angela Rippon** showed off her pins as a chorus-line dancer on the 1976 *Morecambe And Wise Christmas Show*. Like freed slaves, newsreaders then descended on the world of light entertainment with a vengeance, making dubious disco records, hosting strange game shows with Annabel Croft and generally behaving like **Gyles Brandreth**. **Kirsty Young** brazenly walked around the desk on Channel 5 to read the news, thereby becoming the first of her breed to do it standing up, an innovation which sadly was seen as heralding a revolution in news programming.

Honourable mentions must go to **Angela Rippon** and **Jan Leeming**. When Rippon became the first woman newsreader in 1975 the news was, frankly, turning ugly and we needed someone as nice as Angela to break it to us gently. Leeming has become rhyming slang for being drunk (Jan Leeming/steaming) and was last seen sporting an unwise blonde hairdo which made her look like Penny Smith's mum. But nobody could pronounce surnames like 'Nkomo' with her disturbing precision. **Jon Snow** and **Jeremy Paxman**, you'll be glad to hear, are profiled on p323.

Michael Buerk Britain's favourite news agent since he aroused our indignation over the Ethiopian famine in 1984. The nickname 'Des Lynam of TV news' does him no favours because he is one of the few broadcasters on either of the main news bulletins to carry real moral authority. Occasionally, the sharpness behind that world-weary exterior is revealed: when Rosie Millard appeared in a low-cut outfit to report from Cannes, Buerk said after the handover: 'Rosie Millard, best supporting dress at Cannes.' Has recently announced he's going to pack it all in.

In his spare time Reassures us that in the direst emergencies we might, just, be rescued by the kind of real-life heroes who appear on *999*.

Reginald Bosanquet Legendary newsreader who formed half of a John Steed/Emma Peel style partnership with Anna Ford on ITV in the 1970s. Some say his drawling delivery was due to illness but Ford recalls his bosses forcing him to walk a straight line across the studio before letting him go on air. His habitual smirk may have had something to do with the obscene poems, often about the Archbishop of Canterbury, he used to write in the studio and pass to Ford. He was celebrated in the song 'Oh Bosanquet' ('why did you go away?') on **Not The Nine O' Clock News** and was the favourite newsreader of the Pythons' Concrete family (Mrs Concrete: 'I prefer Reginald Bosanquet, there's not so many of them'). **In his spare time** Recorded 1970s disco 'smash' 'Dance With Me'.

Anna Ford British television's pre-eminent news maven and frustrated nightclub singer. Beautiful enough to complain about the media's 'body fascism' and get away with it. There's an aloofness about Ford which, even in the newsroom, makes her more intriguing than her peers. **In her spare time** Throws a full glass of wine over the nearest Aitken.

Sue Lawley Famous for keeping her cool when lesbian protestors were chaining themselves to bits of equipment in the newsroom around her. 'We have been rather invaded,' she noted, drily. Despite such coolness, she was more effective alongside Michael Barrett on **Nationwide**. **In her spare time** Hosts *Desert Island Discs*, rumoured to be the real subject of the Police song 'So Lonely' – 'Sue Lawley, Sue Lawley…'

Kirsty Young Former STV continuity announcer and the only thing on Channel 5 worth watching in the early years – apart from a documentary about St Bernards. Switched to ITV but soon returned to 5. Has credibility partly because she is Scottish, a race the English are inclined to trust as chancellors, Manchester United managers and newsreaders. **In her spare time** Beats Carol Vorderman on *Who Wants To Be A Millionaire*?

★★★ Oriental ★★★

West has always been best for TV schedulers although ITV did try to make amends with **Judge Dee**. a 1969 series in which Michael Robbins (from **On The Buses**) put on yellow make up to star as a 7th century Chinese judge detective. In the 1970s there was a vogue for shows of oriental lavour, the genre's champ chimp being **Monkey** (see p51).

Chinese Detective BBC1 1981–82

David Yip, as Sergeant John Ho, was the first non-Caucasian cop to have his own TV series. The timing seems more than coincidental: although it was light years away from *Monkey,* that cult success can't have harmed this show's prospects. Ho had to battle with both crims and fellow officers

When his master told Grasshopper to jump, Grasshopper would say 'How high master?'

(the Met not chuffed with the idea of a Chinese officer, never mind a Liverpudlian Chinese one). But it wasn't all social commentary: creator **Ian Kennedy Martin** instilled a *Sweeney* style of gung-ho violent action.

Jackie Chan Adventures Fox Kids 2000–

If you had a karate belt for every time Jackie Chan says 'Uncle!' Or 'Jade!' in this animated series, you'd be one of the foremost authorities in martial arts. Chan is a likeable hero, hampered by the need to keep uncle (who is almost as stroppy as Father Jack) and niece (Jade) – who would rather fight baddies than study – out of mischief. It's neatly done (Chan gets knocked out quite a bit) and rounded off with a totally trivial Q&A where kids ask their hero 'Jackie, what's your favourite colour?'

Kung-Fu ITV 1973–74

The concept of this Eastern-Western was **Bruce Lee**'s, but TV executives backstabbed the martial artist and cast **David Carradine** as the meditative warrior monk Kwai Chang Caine, whose flying feet and Zen wisdom were at the service of the oppressed. Flashbacks to his novitiate in the Shaolin monastery, fleeing to America pursued by Imperial assassins, and under-taking the ongoing quest for his caucasian half-brother fascinated audiences and provided comedians with gags ('Snatch the pebble from my hand, Grasshopper') for years. Carradine returned in the 1990s as Caine's descendant for routine coperatics in *Kung Fu: The Legend Continues*.

The Water Margin BBC2 1976–78

A predecessor to **Monkey**, *The Water Margin* was a Japanese reworking of a 14th-century Chinese tale. A kind of kung-fu Robin Hood story, each of its 26 episodes saw a band of 108 knights fighting tyrants and rebels from their base amid the beautiful water margins of Lian Shan Po. The actual kung-fu included at least one sword-fight set piece per episode, with the action working seamlessly alongside exciting, magical storylines and characters. The series was later dubbed into English, featuring the voices of **Bert Kwouk** and, er, **Miriam Margolyes**. Not as popular as *Monkey*, possibly because it wasn't as weird, but pleasurable enough.

★★★ Outside broadcasts ★★★

When **Neville Chamberlain** flew back from Munich in September 1938, a BBC crew rushed to Heston airport in west London to capture the moment. 'I held the microphone,' BBC engineer Keith Edelstein recalled later, 'and this funny old man came out waving a piece of paper: "Peace in our time…" A big cameraman from the newsreel said "Silly old bastard."'

Outside broadcasts are usually more organised. Not that that helps much. ITV's coverage of the 1996 Brit awards was already going wrong, with Michael Jackson surrounding himself with children, when **Jarvis Cocker** burst onto the stage, wiggled his arse at the camera in protest and got wrestled to the floor by security guards. Luckily for ITV, the Brits weren't shown live, so they could edit out Cocker's mooning.

BBC producer **Peter Dimmock** had no such luck. At the Royal Needlework Exhibition at St James's Palace in the late 1940s, the cameras were waiting for the King George VI and the Queen (the late Queen Mother) who were late. In desperation, **Richard Dimbleby** waffled about one of the rugs Queen Mary had donated to the show – for five, ten, 15 minutes until, finally, the producer had another filler ready. A few minutes later, the royal couple arrived. The Queen turned to the producer and said: 'I'm sorry I was late, Mr Dimmock, but the King and I so much enjoyed that sequence with mother's rug we stayed back to watch it.'

★★★ Politics ★★★

Politics and TV usually mix as well as Angie Watts and Dirty Den. There are a few notable exceptions. **The West Wing** is a seductive fantasy of how we'd like America to be run – by a non-womanising John F Kennedy. **The House Of Cards** was camp fun (see p162), and there have been some fine, fact-based drama series, especially **Robert Hardy**'s turn as Winston Churchill in *The Wilderness Years*. But rather than extolling the virtues of **Panorama**, we have simply chosen our favourite moments.

1 John Redwood mouthing the Welsh national anthem. Wrongly.

2 Bill Moyers, press aide to Lyndon B Johnson, kicking off a presidential press conference with the remark: 'I'll take the planted questions first.'

3 Michael Portillo losing his seat in May 1997. Lance Price, then a BBC political reporter who had initially argued against going to the count in **Enfield Southgate** because there would be no story, recalled later: 'When I finally appeared to predict with confidence that Portillo was about to lose his seat, I provoked the single biggest outbreak of mass cheering in Britain since the 1966 World Cup.'

4 Mrs Thatcher being grilled over the *Belgrano* sinking in May 1983. Cheltenham housewife Diana Gould, showing a pertinacity few political interviewers of the time possessed, challenged Thatcher's explanation for the sinking, which killed 300 Argentines. 'It was definitely sailing away from the Falklands,' she told Thatcher flatly, later admitting that she had forgotten by that point that she was on telly.

5 Jeremy Paxman asking Michael Howard the same question 12 times (see p323). And 'Why should the public trust a transient, here one day gone tomorrow, politician rather than a senior naval officer?' **Sir Robin Day**'s question prompted defence secretary **John Nott** to walk out of the studio, complaining 'I've had enough of this interview – it's ridiculous.'

6 Richard Nixon: 'There will be no whitewash in the White House.'

7 Death On The Rock conspicuous political courage by the *This Week* team, investigating the shooting of three IRA members in Gibraltar.

8 'You're no Jack Kennedy.' **Lloyd Bentsen** deflates Dan ('potatoe') Quayle in the only line from a televised vice-presidential debate anyone knows.

9 Julian Clary's apology for being late at the 1993 Comedy Awards: 'I've just been fisting Norman Lamont.'

10 Neil Kinnock falling over on Brighton beach.

★★★ Public information films ★★★

Broadcast for almost three decades, the public information film (PIF) educated a nation to use the Green Cross Code, to clunk-click every trip, and to think once, think twice, think bike.

189

PIFs were TV commercials made by the government's Orwellian-sounding Central Office of Information. And a good job too. For Britain in the 1960s and 1970s was a very hazardous place, with perilous river-banks, power stations, pickpockets, foot and mouth, chip-pan infernos and thermonuclear war all threatening to ruin your day. It's a testament to the COI's genius that we all managed to live so long.

Naturally, road safety was a key theme. *Police Five*'s **Shaw Taylor** and later **Jimmy Savile** promoted seatbelts with Jim illustrating the effects on drivers who failed to clunk-click by rattling an egg around in a box with predictable results. After all, 'a car is a box, a box on wheels!'

Pedestrians weren't safe from the COI's wagging finger, either. In 1973 came **Tufty**, a feeble red squirrel who preached road sense in a series of stop-motion animations voiced by **Bernard Cribbins**, invariably ending in poor Willy Weasel getting run over by an ice cream van.

Later came the impenetrable Splink! safety campaign, endorsed by **Jon Pertwee**, which was succeeded by the Green Cross Code, starring muscular yokel **Dave Prowse** – although Dave's Bristolian burr was dubbed over, a fate that would again befall him in the *Star Wars* trilogy. Dave watched over the nation's kids, beaming down from his Green Cross control centre to dish out some timely advice just as they were about to end up under the wheels of an Austin Maxi.

Swimming, sex and Rolf Harris

Learning to swim was another key message. The backstroke, reckoned the COI in 1972, was a sure-fire route to some nudge-nudge wink-wink, as proved by the siren who was so enamoured by Mike 'who swims like a fish' that she ditched Dave who 'wished he didn't keep losing his birds' and swam like a fish finger. The hirsute duo of Olympic swimming champ **David Wilkie** and **Rolf Harris** were enlisted to the cause, the stylophone maestro revealing that his wobbleboard artistry was nearly lost to the world when he fell into a river when he was seven. But the real star of the water-safety show was Death himself, depicted as a menacing hooded figure ('I am the spirit of dark and lonely water, ready to trap the unwary, the show-off, the fool...') stalking bowl-cutted, flare-wearing kids messing about on riverbanks. Scary.

Thankfully the most famous campaign produced by the COI was never transmitted. The **Protect And Survive** series, made in 1975, was intended for transmission in the prelude to a nuclear war, and consisted of *Blue Peter*-style hints and tips on how to survive Armageddon. All you needed, it reckoned, were a few sandbags, a couple of doors taken off their hinges and a fortnight's supply of tinned luncheon meat. Clearly this was going to be a very British apocalypse. But nearly three decades on, the stentorian tones of narrator **Patrick Allen**, sampled by Frankie Goes To Hollywood on 'Two Tribes', still manage to cast a chill down the spine.

★★★ Puppets ★★★

Say what you will against **Shari Lewis** but anyone who can make a career by sticking a hand in a sock is alright by us. Lamb Chop was, at least, more durable than, say, **Roland Rat**. As for **Sooty**, we can understand why he is revered by Trappists and members of the Corbett family (except, of course, Ronnie) but he was, let's be honest, a bit of a bore.

On children's TV, Sooty was outshone by **Fingermouse**, fingermouse, the never stop to think a mouse; even picnic basket dweller **Andy Pandy**

Michael Bentine: potty most of the time

and **The Woodentops** who were cool, although what was really cool about them were the doors, the top half of which swung open independently of the bottom half. We will hear nothing said against **Basil Brush** (see p292) nor, for that matter, against **Zig and Zag**, probably Irish TV's best export since Johnny Logan. Second best of all, perhaps, is **Fozzie Bear**, the real star of the *Muppet Show*. Kermit, schmermit – no one could tell really bad jokes like Fozzie. No one except Tommy Cooper that is. And best of all were the marionette stars of **Michael**

191

Bentine's Potty Time: seldom has such good use been made of a studio table. All marionated (as opposed to marinated) puppets are dealt with in our supermarionation section (see p239). No ventriloquist's dummies are worshipped in this guide because, quite frankly, they give us the creeps.

★★★ Quiz shows ★★★

Which N of the musical compositions *Nutcracker* and *Nimrod* was written by Grieg? It's just one of the questions set by Hilary Murphy at the rate of 6,000 per series for **Blockbusters**. The smart-alec answer (which no one got) is neither. But then as French philosopher Jean François Lyotard said in 1984: 'Knowledge is merely a matter for TV games.'

A few more question masters like Hilary and we wouldn't find quiz shows as compelling. It's not just the glee involved in watching our peers look foolish. As the monster that is **Who Wants To Be A Millionaire?** has proved, we thrive on the sheer melodrama of it all. Both *Millionaire* and *The Weakest Link* appeared likely to break open the US market but are now struggling. *Millionaire* has proved successful with Arab viewers – after the Sheikh of Cairo's Al-Azhar University overruled a fatwa by the country's Grand Mufti and insisted that quiz shows offering large cash prizes were legitimate. *The Weakest Link* has been just as controversial in Thailand. Some contestants have left in tears, Thailand being a tactful society where the very phrase 'Khun khe jud orn, chern kha!' ['You are the weakest link, goodbye'] is appallingly rude. Even the prime minister confessed to being a bit upset. (Theirs, not ours.)

100 Per Cent Channel 5 1997–

Most quiz shows are hosted by personalities who don't have any. But **100 Per Cent** is hosted by a disembodied voice which asks three contestants 100 multiple choice questions. Whoever gets the most right wins. As simple and as unflashy as you can get – and horribly addictive.

Mastermind BBC1 1972–97

The idea for the set came from producer **Bill Wright**'s experience as a prisoner of war being interrogated by the Gestapo: hence the inspiration to spotlight the contestant on a black chair in a darkened room. The chair was once kidnapped by students in Coleraine, who demanded a £50 ransom for charity for its return. Even the theme tune was designed to add to the air of intimidation: it was entitled 'Approaching Menace'. With all this going on, the selection of **Magnus Magnusson**, an Icelander in Britain just in time for the start of the cod war, was incidental. The worst bit was watching contestants who did badly slink back to their seats. You didn't need Desmond Morris to interpret their body language.

Sale Of The Century ITV 1971–83

A set of garden furniture for £15? The most popular quiz show in the history of Australia and Norwich. The 'quiz of the week', officially hosted by **Nicholas Parsons** although he was always outshone by the announcer **John Benson**, never recovered from the rampant inflation in the 1970s.

★ Quiz questions ★

What has 88 legs and no teeth? The front row of a studio audience. A cruel but apt description of the bussed-in grannies who usually fill the seats at game shows, screeching with delight and according to **Bob Holness**, frequently falling asleep. On ITV's short-lived *Runaway*, host **Richard Madeley** used to enter bounding down the gangway through the audience but the cameras showed dozens of empty seats. The producer ordered 100 shop window dummies and stuck them in the gaps, complete with costumes and wigs. Nobody noticed.

Has anyone ever told a decent joke on a quiz show? Possibly. On the 1950s TV quiz show, *You Bet Your Life*, hosted by Groucho Marx, a contestant announced he was the father of 10 children. As the applause faded, Groucho asked if that wasn't excessive. 'Well, Groucho, I love my children and I love my wife,' beamed the contestant. 'Sure,' replied Groucho. 'I love my cigar, but I take it out occasionally.'

What is the most obscure specialist subject rejected on Mastermind? That must be 'routes from Letchworth to anywhere in mainland Britain'. Others include: 'the banana industry', 'orthopaedic bone cement in total hip replacement', and 'beers of the world'.

The Weakest Link BBC2/1 2000–

The woman in black is the quizmaster, given licence to be as insulting as any Gestapo thug. While the poor contestants worry if their peers will vote them off at the end of the road, we, at home, are wondering how many more euphemisms for 'weakest link' the scriptwriters can produce. After watching 37 shows, purely in the interests of research, this reviewer has noted a slight in-built prejudice against beautiful women, who tend to get voted off first, not necessarily because of their performance. There's probably a deep-seated psychological explanation for this: one that would include the words 'jealous' and 'bastards'. You can't help wondering what is going to happen to **Anne Robinson**'s neck and eye muscles if she keeps flicking her head to one side and winking.

Who Wants To Be A Millionaire? ITV 1998–

A fascinating, addictive show on many levels. As **Chris Tarrant** himself has said, part of this series' appeal is that it's part soap opera. You root for the contestants (the likeable ones anyway) and you get a wonderful insight into the gaps in other people's knowledge. The same contestant who can tell you who invented the hydrogen bomb (Edward Teller) stumbles on the show's equivalent of the *GMTV* question about where sprouts come from. And Tarrant is exactly right for this show. Imagine how awful it would be if it were hosted by Jimmy Tarbuck.

★★★ Reality TV ★★★

Sylvania Waters BBC1 1993

This 12-part warts and all documentary about the life of a typical Aussie family was screened here around the same time we were hooked on **Neighbours** and **Home & Away**. Based on producer **Paul Watson**'s earlier reality show *The Family*, the crew spent six months with the nuclear (meltdown) family of Noeline, husband Laurie, and their respective sons from previous marriages, covering every element of their lives, bar bedroom and bathroom antics. By the end of week one, Noeline was a household name thanks to her loud, brash manner and obvious drink-

★ Here is the (reality) TV news ★

Real reality TV stories from around the globe

USA A contestant who had a knife held to her throat on the TV reality series *Big Brother 2* is suing CBS, alleging the network should not have allowed her assailant on the show because of his past record.

Germany *Big Brother* was almost never shown. The show was attacked by political and religious leaders, who said it would violate a clause in the German constitution that protects human dignity. The producers agreed to turn off the cameras for an hour each day, defusing the row.

Sweden Afraid that he would be seen as a fool, Sinisa Savija committed suicide after being the first contestant voted off *Expedition Robinson*, the Swedish version of *Survivor*, in 1997.

ing problem – mind you, it can't be easy being called Noeline. This, coupled with Laurie's racist comments and the family's rows, led critics to accuse Watson of playing up to British stereotypes of Aussies. Despite the abuse thrown at Noeline – *The Sun* being its usual subtle self: 'Meet Noeline: By Tonight You'll Hate Her Too' – reality TV started here.

★★★ Regional television ★★★

Regional television is like a waiting room to fame. Except that some people (**Mike Neville** and **Tom Coyne**) spend their whole lives in that waiting room, condemned to a Roger Melly-man-on-the-telly twilight world. For every presenter like **Kirsty Young** or **Stuart Hall** who achieves national recognition, there are hundreds like **Kay Alexander** – legendary figures in Sutton Coldfield (or its regional equivalents) who wouldn't be recognised by anyone outside their area. Worst of all, there are those tyros plucked from regional TV only to be parked at BBC *News 24*. If regional telly is a waiting room for fame, *News 24* is its underground car park.

For students of regional TV, there is The Fiona Armstrong Trajectory. This briefly describes the arc in which a presenter rises from the regions (albeit local radio in her case), becomes a household name (for Fiona,

Another nutcase, another Hall

through *ITN News* and *GMTV*) only for the whirligig of fame to send them hurtling back to the regions (Border Television for Fi) and life as an occasional presenter on a Sky Sports fishing programme. And no, we're not making this up – Fiona really does host **Tight Lines** and presents something called **Executive Lifestyles** on NBC.

But the soul of regional TV is represented by the double-headed monster that is Tom Coyne and Mike Neville (if you're wondering who they are, Tom is the Mike Neville of the Midlands and Mike is the Tom Coyne of the north-east). British regional TV would not be what it is today without a constant supply of middle-aged, slightly overweight blokes with fixed receding hairlines whose bonhomie can't quite conceal their secret resentment at not being given a starring role. Sadly, the Coynes of this world are being replaced by quicker, lighter, presenters whose ruthless physical homogeneity seems to suggest a *Stepford Wives* scenario – or some deliberate satirical intent, as if these people were being selected by the people behind **The Day Today**.

Channel TV ITV 1962–

The station that gave us *Around Britain*, *Highway* and *Puffin's Pla(i)ce* – a children's TV show starring the station's mascot – has not been resting on its laurels. The content of the Channel archive, as listed on the station's official website, includes the following desirable shows: 'a 12-episode run of young people's soap *Island*; a cartoon series featuring Bertie the Bat; a documentry [Channel's spelling, not ours] on Roderick Newall – the man who killed his parents and nearly escaped justice; amazing real life pictures of Jambo – the Gorilla who saved a boy who fell into the gorilla compound at Jersey Zoo; and *The Escape*: pictures and interviews with some of the wealthiest people in the world who are now living in the Channel Islands.' This little lot is available from Suzette Hase. And if you ask her very nicely, she'll probably drop them off herself.

HOW Southern 1966–81

Fred Dinenage defines that micro-genre of TV regional presenter whose receding hairline never actually recedes. Maybe there's some kind of restorative cream known only to TV presenters or maybe there's a time thing going on. You know, just as dogs age seven years for every year of human life, maybe regional telly folk only age one year in every seven. **How** was the series where Fred, Bunty, Jack (Hargreaves) and the other bloke nobody remembers (Jon Miller) answered the kind of 'How' questions which vexed us all; questions like, 'How did 11 Americans die in vending machine-related accidents last year?' As this was broadcast in the KP Wigwam era when it was cute for native American characters to say 'heap big' in every sentence, the theme sounded like an edited version of the native American party which followed the Little Big Horn.

Middlemen BBC 1977

Alan Plater (yes that one) wrote this sitcom in which **Frank Windsor** (formerly Detective Sergeant John Watt in *Softly Softly*) is a false toenail salesman and **Francis Matthews** (once crimebusting author Paul Temple and the voice of Captain Scarlet) is his mate. Funny and fondly remembered by fortysomethings in the Midlands region.

Now! TTV 1964

Michael Palin's often overlooked introduction to British TV. He hosted what can only be described as an attempt by TTV (predecessor of HTV) to rival **Ready Steady Go**. Palin was at Oxford at the time and would get a few hundred quid to pop up to the studio at weekends and host a show with few stars and less budget. In desperation, Palin hit upon a Pythonesque linking device where, between songs, cameras cut to footage of him in tails hammering away at a piano in a field. Palin's main memory is the end of series party where Lord Derby, who ran TTV, asked 'Would anybody like some white wine?' To which Tom Jones, who'd been on the show, thundered back in his gravelly voice: 'I'll have a vodka and tonic!'

Star Soccer ITV 1969–73

Huw Johns was the 1966 World Cup final commentator who didn't say 'They think it's all over…' He had his own bon mots though, once saying of a player: 'He owns a flower shop this feller, but he's no daisy.' On ATV every Sunday afternoon, Johns commentated on the live game, usually from Molineux – except for those weeks when they went to St Andrews or the Hawthorns for local derbies – with Wolves. Every ITV region had their own Johns and their own Wolves-type bias. Granada blotted its copybook on its version **Kick Off** when Nottingham Forest beat Liverpool 2-0 on aggregate in the first round of the European Cup in 1978, with **Gerald Sinstadt** intoning 'The party's over, Liverpool' before the screen cut to the song of the same name and a montage of Peter Shilton's saves.

★★★ Religion ★★★

'Be sure to get my best side now'

Religion being something of a cult may explain why not many religious shows have true cult appeal. **Stars On Sunday** might have become cult if they'd let Jess Yates (remember he wasn't Paula's dad, **Hughie Green** was) present it after his affair with a Miss World contestant had been exposed. The ban on the show's presenters sleeping with Miss Worlds does explain why George Best never hosted it. *Stars On Sunday* was as entertaining as **Oh Brother**, the Derek Nimmo monastical sitcom. In other words, not very.

Jesus Of Nazareth stands out for

several reasons: Franco Zeffirelli's direction, **Robert Powell**'s Christ, and for casting **Ian McShane**, future lovable rogue Lovejoy, as not-so-lovable rogue Judas Iscariot. And there's **Revelations**, the kitsch late night ITV soap dissected on p230. After that, it's **Father Ted**. Or Father Jack.

★★★ Repeats ★★★

Since repeats on telly are the second subject Brits most like to whinge about, TV companies have devised several cunning plans to stop us getting that *déjà vu* feeling all over again. The most effective has always been dating a programme with Roman numerals: research shows that only a fraction of us can tell when MCMLXVI was (and even if we can, the show will have started by the time we work it out). Then there's 'first shown on BBC2' and 'first shown on Channel 4' or increasingly 'first shown on Sky' – still a repeat but 90 per cent of the punters won't realise.

A 'classic' usually means the programme's been repeated so often even the broadcasters have lost count while 'historical recording' is a repeat which has been found in the props department – under a pile of straw boaters bought for a never-completed remake of *Three Men In A Boat*.

'Retrospective season' is a string of repeats coinciding with an interview with the writers to give the reruns an intellectual gloss (you know, isn't it time we re-evaluated the work of **Ronald Chesney** and **Ronald Wolfe**, the creators of **Yus My Dear** and **On The Buses**? Answer: no, not really). A 'tribute' is like a retrospective season but shorter (usually a one-off devoted to a recently departed giant of British entertainment), while a 'best of' is a retrospective season without the Chesney and Wolfe edition of *Omnibus* but coinciding with some specious anniversary.

Then there's cable and satellite TV, aka a huge hypodermic needle for pumping repeats into our living rooms. Yet these channels confuse us by announcing 'new episodes', which are of course 'old episodes' – new only in the sense that they have just arrived on that particular channel. Those programme-buyers didn't want to snap up *Yus My Dear,* but now they know you like it, they're going to show that episode where **Arthur Mullard** changes his string vest and his dentures again – and again and again…

★★★ Satire ★★★

Satire and TV have never really had more than a casual affair, for all the hype about the satire boom of the 1960s. Rory Bremner and the two Johns (Bird and Fortune – both involved in *That Was The Week That Was*) have persevered on Channel 4. But their brilliant efforts are marred by a certain self-congratulation which, with the two Johns, has matured into a full-blown smugness. The undisputed sultans of satire are **Chris Morris** (see p321) and **Matt Groening**, whose **The Simpsons** continues to nail society with the precision of a heat-seeking missile.

Not The Nine O'Clock News BBC2 1979–82

'Ayatollah come any closer and I'm going to lose my cool…' Lyrics like that may explain why every university common room was tuned in to BBC2 at 9pm on a Monday when this show launched. The post-Python generation adopted this team as their own. **Rowan Atkinson** could make you laugh simply by saying 'Zob', **Pamela Stephenson** was funny and sexy (the comedy goddess Python lacked), and **Chris Langham** has gone on to greater things like *People Like Us*. The stand-out gags were mostly from the first shows: the Khomeini song, the chat-show gorilla ('Wild? I was absolutely livid'), but they saved one of their best till last: the song 'Kinda Lingers', a cunning tribute to a practice which almost rhymed with it.

Rutland Weekend Television BBC2 1975–76

Lovingly observed homage/spoof of the Beatles phenomenon with **Eric Idle**, **Neil Innes** and, briefly, **George Harrison**. As the album of the series proved, Innes really did fancy himself as a real Beatles songwriter, even if the closest he got was such melodic nonsense as 'The Fool On The Pill'.

Spitting Image ITV 1984–96

'Hold a chicken in the air, stick a deckchair up your nose…' The parody of a mindless summer number one that became, er, a mindless summer number one isn't why we liked *Spitting Image*. Like *TW3*, the series benefited from the Tories being in power. Everyone has a favourite

The Rutles stand back in amazement as a troupe of yogic flyers stage a ceremonial fly past

sketch (the writers included Ian Hislop, Richard Curtis, John O'Farrell, John Lloyd and Alastair McGowan), though some missed the mark by a country mile. Those that didn't included the 'I've never met a nice South African' song, Neil Kinnock's election manifesto where he just said 'Nurses' over and over again, and Thatcher's 'Tomorrow Belongs To Me'.

Tanner 88 Channel 4 1988

Robert Altman directed and produced this satire, co-created by Garry Trudeau, best known for his **Doonesbury** comic strip. Tanner (**Michael Murphy**) is Altman's fictional presidential candidate (and Gary Hart lookalike) but the TV movie features real politicians playing themselves, albeit less winningly than Murphy plays Tanner.

That Was The Week That Was BBC1 1962–63

TW3 was a long time ago. **Bernard Levin** was funny. **David Frost** had yet to rise without trace, and **Dennis Potter** and **Kenneth Tynan** were gag writers. Watched again now, the satire can seem more sharp than funny but Rushton and Frost's attack on Tory home secretary Henry Brooke was

201

probably the most effective demolition of a public servant on TV until Michael Howard got Paxmanned. The show inspired a US version which made **Alan Alda**. The biggest shock is watching Frost. In his heyday, he didn't instinctively Insert. An. Invisible. Full. Stop. After. Every. Word.

★★★ Schools ★★★

The Beiderbecke Affair ITV 1984

On paper Alan Plater's **The Beiderbecke Affair** sounds a risky venture. A six-part comic drama with a touch of mystery and detective work (**James Bolam** and **Barbara Flynn** starred as schoolteachers/amateur sleuths), it also addressed social issues to a jazz soundtrack. But it was this very eccentricity – plus its unusual dialogue and Bolam as an amiable northerner – that made it work. One enduring image had Bolam shouting, 'Haway the lads!' during a critical bedroom moment. It spawned *The Beiderbecke Tapes* and *Connection* where the quirkiness seemed more manufactured.

Grange Hill BBC1 1978–

Phil Redmond – inventor of *Brookside* and *Hollyoaks* – created this kids' drama set in a London comprehensive (the show's filming later relocated to a disused school in Hertfordshire). The series began with characters such as loveable rogue Tucker (**Todd Carty**), chubby Alan and pals (Carty and fellow original cast member Susan Tully would both reappear in *EastEnders*). In later years, after parental complaints, the series became more preachy (the 'Just Say No' anti-drugs campaign) and less popular.

Please Sir! ITV 1968–72

Inspired by the Sidney Poitier film *To Sir, With Love*, this starred **John Alderton** as caring but naïve Bernard 'Privet' Hedges, fresh out of college into Fenn Street Secondary Modern's most unruly class, 5C. At times it was as sickly as a bag of tuck shop sweets, but Derek Guyler provided some comic class as Norman Potter, the janitor. This movie spin-off spun off its own movie in 1971 and a US replica in 1975, *Welcome Back, Kotter*, starring the then-unknown **John Travolta**.

★ The staff room from TV hell ★

Professor James Edwards (Jimmy Edwards) headmaster, Whack-O!
A headmaster who cares about pupils' development and the well-being of the school. That's exactly what James Edwards, head of Chislebury school in *Whack-O!*, isn't. But he is venal, boozy, incompetent and devious.

Eric Slatt (David Bamber) deputy headmaster, Chalk
The education system's Basil Fawlty, bumbling Eric Slatt is a man whose casually insulting ways have somehow failed to endear him to his pupils. 'Are you girls wearing make-up?' 'No.' 'Well, could you borrow some?'

Screech (Dustin Diamond), principal's assistant, Saved By The Bell
Imagine how bad school could have been if your headmaster had been not-so-ably assisted by the rubbery, well-meaning geek Screech (below).

Ken Barlow (William Roache), English teacher, Coronation Street
Decent bloke Ken but in his class you'd probably fall asl... zzzzz.

Doug Digby (Brian Conley), PE teacher, The Grimleys
Doug Digby made millions of us relive our own painful memories of the kind of physical education (and sadistic PE teachers) that made this country what it is today.

Jimmy Corkhill (Dean Sullivan), supply teacher, Brookside
The supply teacher from your mum's worst nightmares. A former junkie, he's forged his credentials and has an unfortunate habit of going violently berserk in the classroom.

Teachers Channel 4 2001–

This Life favourite **Andrew Lincoln** (as Simon, a 27-year-old going on 11) and friends struggle to separate themselves from their pupils – smoking behind bike sheds, bullying the school nerd (head of year, Bob) and chasing girls (Jenny, Penny and Susan). With shades of *Ally McBeal* – including dreams of teaching naked and sudden MGM-style musical settings – and running background gags (students being hurled from a height), *Teachers*, as an end of term report might say, shows promise.

Whack-O! BBC1 1956–60, 1971–72

On one level, this was a fairly inventive sitcom about a low-rent public school run by a headmaster (**Jimmy Edwards**) whose chief interest was raising money from the school to buy beer. On another, it was evidence of just how twisted the British national psyche really is. A consummate comedy of corporal punishment, it played a lot on the cane and Edwards' moustache. The series died after Edwards' co-star **Arthur Howard** was found doing a George Michael: Edwards, whose own affair with a young Australian man would hit the headlines 20 years later, was bitter about what he saw as his co-star's carelessness. The film of the series was called, in dubious taste, *Bottoms Up*. The show was revived in the 1970s, with tall, upper-class twit **Julian Orchard** supporting Edwards.

★ ★ ★ Science ★ ★ ★

Science on television has never quite recovered from the twin ghosts of **James Burke** and *Tomorrow's World*. Burke, a TV boffin much loved by the BBC in the 1970s, could find the hidden connection between the invention of cheese and Einstein's theory of relativity, but could never connect to an audience. **Tomorrow's World** was presented by former officer **Raymond Baxter** (any relation to Biddy? we were never told) as if he was still in the RAF. The show was all about gadgets that were going to change the world but somehow didn't. Occasionally the team made longer documentaries. While filming one on heart surgeon Christian Barnard, the crew sent for a Chinese takeaway. When it failed to arrive, floor manager Joan Marsden ran down the corridor to find two oriental gentleman approaching. 'Are you the food for *Tomorrow's World*?' she asked. 'No, I'm the prime minister of Singapore,' replied one of them.

Science on TV has broadened its wings since then, with the decent **Equinox** (Channel 4), the tabloid thrills of **Savage Skies** (ITV) and, best of all, **Walking With Dinosaurs**. Pedants have quibbled about the scientific accuracy of these shows but whatever the inaccuracies in their recreations, they are probably more intelligent than Burke's connections. The finale of *Dinosaurs*, where the sky is turning ugly with poisonous dust and an asteroid the size of Stephen Hawking's intelligence is about to strike the poor unsuspecting beasts, is hard to watch without a lump in the throat.

★★★ Science-fiction ★★★

Just as science-fiction literature used to be dismissed as pulp and its films as B-movies, so its TV series were seen as cheap children's hokum. The first icon of the genre was the daft but loved 1950s daily serial **Captain Video**. **Rocky Jones, Space Ranger** is best remembered for Rocky's mini-skirted assistant Vena, a forerunner of *Star Trek*'s Lieutenant Uhura. The UK was quicker to see the scope for adult TV fantasy with **Quatermass** and a grim, prophetic drama of a radiation-poisoned Britain, **Off-shore Island**.

Rod Serling's *The Twilight Zone* marked the genre's coming of age in the 1960s. Superheroes superceded thinkers and spacegoers in the 1970s, but the 1980s mini-series **V** and **The Next Generation** heralded a burgeoning taste for sci-fi. **X-Files** mania in the mid-1990s prompted a flurry of offbeat investigators. Although stand-alone stories are still the meat and potatoes of TV sci-fi, a notable development has been ambitious story 'arcs' – *The X-Files*' alien mythology, **Deep Space Nine**'s war with the Dominion and **Babylon 5**'s full five-year remit – followed by savvy, fervent fans. Once unimaginable, there is now a sci-fi channel dedicated entirely to the futuristic and fantastic. Only a niche? No more.

There is also a fine tradition of sci-fi comedy in which aliens are used to comment on human foibles. The best American examples are probably **Mork And Mindy** (which made Robin Williams), and **ALF** (the cuddly alien who sent up his hosts, the Tanners). The great British contributions to this genre are **Hitchhikers Guide To The Galaxy** and **Red Dwarf** which made Chris Barrie in the way Mork had made Williams. Less happily, *Red Dwarf* also gave us Craig Charles. **Come Back Mrs Noah**, in which Mollie Sudgen played a housewife lost in space, is well remembered considering this David Croft/Jeremy Lloyd sitcom only lasted one short series in 1978.

A For Andromeda BBC1 1961

Astronomer **Fred Hoyle** conceived the story for this series, in which radio signals from the Andromeda constellation translate as instructions for a super-computer. Too late, they are found to be the means of conquering Earth. The show introduced **Julie Christie**, fresh from drama school, as the android Andromeda, who decided humanity wasn't so bad after all.

Babylon 5 Channel 4 1993–98

In the 23rd century major races conduct diplomacy and intrigues on space station **Babylon 5**, 'our last, best hope for peace'. Creator and chief

They don't make androids like they used to: Julie Christie shows why Marvin was right to be paranoid

writer **J Michael Straczynski**'s five-year novel for TV was devoted to the ultimate good-versus-evil conflict, the Shadow War. A threat to cancel it hastened victory, leaving the reprieved fifth season in search of a cause, but it was a remarkable 'non-Trek' journey and among the first shows to use CGI to good effect. Highlights include the brilliant 'Babylon Squared' and 'War Without End' chapters, in which the missing Babylon 4 station and key characters slip in and out of a time rift for mega plot revelations. A spin-off series *Crusade* was terminated after 13 episodes.

Battlestar Galactica ITV 1978–79

Although *Star Wars*' producers sued for plagiarism, this dumb odyssey of refugees wandering the galaxy in search of a legendary ancestral Earth had more in common with Westerns. Commander Adama (**Lorne Greene** of *Bonanza*) led the convoy while Cylon robots were in hot pursuit. Sequel series *Galactica 80* (in which they reached Earth) was dire, save for the classic episode 'The Return Of Starbuck'. There is a serious *BG* cult: grown men have paid thousands for those Egyptian headdress helmets.

Farscape SCI FI Channel 1999–

Astronaut John Crichton (**Ben Browder**) is sucked into a wormhole and stranded in a faraway galaxy populated by strange aliens. Aboard the living ship *Moya*, he joins her multi-species crew of escaped prisoners, pursued by an adversary seeking the wormhole technology in Crichton's mind. This Jim Henson Company production (conceived by **Rockne S O'Bannon** of *Alien Nation*) is wildly imaginative. Once audiences got over the Muppet factor (helium-farting Rygel XVIth and Pilot are sophisticated puppets), they realised this was a clever, wittily performed journey.

LEXX Channel 5/SCI FI Channel 1997–2001

This wacko, sex-obsessed creation of Canadians **Paul Donovan**, **Jeffrey Hirschfield** and **Lex Gigeroff**, featured three fugitives – cowardly Stanley Tweedle (Brian Downey), feisty, libidinous Zev (Eva Habermann) who transformed into Xev (Xenia Seeberg), and walking-dead assassin Kai (Michael McManus). Together they steal a genocidal tyrant's organic spaceship (**LEXX**) and set off in search of a home. Four feature-length episodes led to three full, convention-flouting seasons and the unforgettable episode 'Brigadoom' (in which the trio enter a theatre outside time for a musical version of Kai's life). Latterly blighted by juvenile, anarchic grossness, this was one of the most inventive genre shows of the 1990s.

Quatermass BBC1 1953

Author **Nigel Kneale** created Professor Bernard Quatermass, an anti-authoritarian rocket scientist and foe of alien invaders, for the pioneering six-part serial *The Quatermass Experiment*, one of the great popular successes of early British TV. The boffin returned in *Quatermass II* (1955) and *Quatermass And The Pit* (1959) – even more sophisticated adventures which combined chills with mind-expanding ideas (an ancient spaceship buried under London reveals humanity is the result of a Martian experiment). This is the series young **Michael Palin** most liked to be scared by.

Sliders Sky One 1995–2000

Physics student Quinn Mallory (**Jerry O'Connell**) accidentally transports himself, friend Wade (**Sabrina Lloyd**), irate Professor Arturo (cult icon **John Rhys-Davis**) and passing soul singer Rembrandt Brown (**Cleavant Derricks**) on an interdimensional odyssey from which they can't return. They continue to 'slide' to a multiplicity of alternative San Franciscos where they find Soviet rule, the ice age, or fiendish occupying race the Kromagg. By season five, a good idea had long been exhausted.

The Stand Sky One 1994

This superb mini-series is – *The Shawshank Redemption* excepted – the best adaptation of a Stephen King story. In the near future, America is gripped by a superflu that has killed 90 per cent of the population. Those who remain are plagued by dreams of a dark man with red eyes intent on bringing destruction, or an old woman called Mother Abigail who seems their only hope of salvation. **Jamey Sheridan** is creepy as 'the Man', aided by criminal flunkies **Miguel Ferrer** and **Matt Frewer**, while Rob Lowe, Gary Sinise and Molly Ringwald (among others) are on the good guys' side, trying to rebuild society in this hell-on-earth battle. Cool. Proof that there is nothing new under the sun (or even in far away galaxies), **Terry Nation** had spun a similar yarn in the 1975 BBC series **Survivors**, in which a handful of survivors who haven't been killed by a rogue virus rebuild society from scratch, preying on weaker groups for precious supplies…

Tripods BBC1 1984–85

Saturday teatimes saw 21st-century teens Will and Henry (John Shackley and Jim Baker) flee Britain to resist monster conquerors from space, in

★ The aliens have landed ★

The Invaders (1967–68) Seminal Quinn Martin running-man thriller in which architect David Vincent (Roy Thinnes) witness to a UFO incident, is on the run and rights a wrong a week, exposing the presence among us of despoiling aliens who disintegrate without trace on dying.

Space: Above And Beyond (1995–96) 21st-century US Marines in space hold the line against mysterious aliens (The Chigs) after the destruction of Earth colonies. Cool saga from X-Files alumni Glen Morgan and James Wong, inspired by World War II films.

Dark Skies (1996–97) History is a conspiracy of sweethearts encountering invasive aliens (the Hive) and crossing paths with historic figures (the Kennedys, Howard Hughes). The concept of a decade per season was thwarted by cancellation at the 1960s' cliffhanger.

Earth: Final Conflict (1997–2001) Posthumous Gene Roddenberry production, in which resisters discover a hidden agenda for humanity behind the enigmatic Taelon race's seemingly benevolent arrival.

First Wave (1998–2001) Executive-produced by Francis Ford Coppola, the series had rebel experimental subject Cade Foster using the prophecies of Nostradamus and the Net in his battle to expose the invading Gua who, like The Invaders, unhelpfully dissolved when killed.

In an interesting twist, **Ray Bradbury's The Martian Chronicles**, adapted into a three-part mini-series starring Rock Hudson, posited that the alien invaders were us, colonising the Red Planet after germ-carrying astronauts unwittingly wiped out the native Martians.

a serial based on a trilogy of novels by **John Christopher**. (The aliens enslaved humanity by inserting mind control devices in a coming-of-age 'capping' ceremony.) BBC chiefs' lack of enthusiasm for long-run sci-fi doomed it before we could find out what happened after 22 episodes, yet the show foreshadowed a bevy of 1990s teen sci-fi soaps such as *Roswell High* (*Dawson's Creek* with angst-ridden high-school aliens) and Canada's *Deepwater Black* (teen clones in space).

The Twilight Zone and The Outer Limits
ITV 1963–66   ITV 1964, BBC2 1995–99

Rod Serling created a seminal fantasy series when he made **The Twilight Zone**. Its individual freestanding episodes explored many themes of speculative fiction – travels in space and time, alternate realities, nuclear war, Kafkaesque and paranormal mysteries – with humour, horror and high quality. Cue the insistent rhythmic theme music: 'You're travelling through another dimension, a dimension not only of sight and sound, but of mind; a journey into a wondrous land whose boundaries are that of imagination.' The show paved the way for other anthologies of

Quatermass scared Michael Palin, possibly because of its innovative use of BBC cameras

weirdness from **Way Out** to **The Outer Limits**. Writer-producer **Joseph Stefano** (screenwriter of *Psycho*) made the first *The Outer Limits* memorable for stars like **Robert Duvall** and **Martin Sheen**, but Pen Densham and John Watson's solid later series lasted a creditable 154 episodes. A new TV series of *Twilight* from 1985–89 didn't have Serling's magic.

UFO ITV 1970–73

Gerry Anderson's first series with people instead of puppets was set – a tad prematurely – in 1970, when marauding aliens are helping themselves to human bits to aid their reproduction, and Commander Ed Straker (**Ed Bishop**) is in charge of secret agency SHADO (Supreme Headquarters Alien Defence Organization). *UFO* was fun with spiffing vehicle and craft models, groovy gadgets and glam gals in purple wigs scampering around the SHADO Moonbase. The same couldn't be said for Anderson's drab, earnest *Star Trek* wannabe *Space: 1999* (1975–78), watchable only if, like this reviewer, you had a crush on **Barbara Bains**.

V ITV 1984

This dark, thrilling and influential alien-invasion epic from writer-director-producer **Kenneth Johnson** was two mini-series, premiered in Britain over five consecutive nights. The two-part *V* has giant saucers arriving above the world's capitals, heralding the seemingly benevolent 'Visitors', unmasked by skeptical TV news cameraman Mike Donovan (Marc Singer) and scientist Julie Parrish (Faye Grant) as reptilian despoilers with a taste for humans. The three-part *V The Final Battle* sees the resistance try to reclaim the world for humanity. Millions gasped as alien-impregnated teen Robin (**Blair Tefkin**) gave birth – to what turned out to be twins with a gob-smacking genetic inheritance. **Robert Englund**, later Freddie Krueger in *Nightmare On Elm Street*, featured as alien ally Willie.

Voyage To The Bottom Of The Sea ITV 1964–68

Irwin Allen's spin-off from his smashing 1961 movie had secret atomic sub *Seaview* patrol the world's waters, foiling colourful villains every week under the command of Admiral Harriman Nelson (**Richard Basehart**)

★ Mutants, freaks and lab accidents ★

Who needs aliens when science or unnatural selection can thrill us?

The Tomorrow People (1973–79) From a hidden base in the London Underground, young things in flares who were the next step in human evolution used psychic powers, teleportation through hyperspace and biomorphic computer Tim to protect Earth from villains in spandex.

Swamp Thing (1990–93) Arson in the lab turned a scientist into a mucky mess – the comic hero known as Alex to his friends or Swamp Thing (Dick Durock) – but left him at one with the marshlands.

Prey (1998) Homo sapiens became prey to higher-evolved humanoids. Bio-genetic sabotage, serial killing and hints of extra-terrestrial origins challenge the scientists. Can they cope?

Now And Again (1999–2000) This atypical genre charmer from *Moonlighting* creator Glen Gordon Caron had dying slob Michael Wiseman's brain implanted into an engineered superbod (Eric Close) by a maddening scientist (Dennis Haysbert). The resulting top secret commando combined hi-tech anti-terrorism with forbidden pursuit of fatty foods, and renewed ties with his beloved 'widow' and child.

Dark Angel (2000–02) Created by James Cameron (*Terminator*, *Titanic*), mad DNA-mix-and-match Max (Jessica Alba) was bred as a super-soldier by sinister forces but escaped. In the social chaos after a global tech disruption, she gathered other mutants in a battle for justice.

and Captain Lee Crane (**David Hedison**). Sadly it soon dove full speed into cheap and cheerful, childish hooey (killer toys, aliens that looked like veggies and Munchkins). Steven Spielberg's production **SeaQuest DSV** (1993–96) attempted a serious voyage with environmental messages and an underwater *Trek* crew, including boy genius and talking dolphin.

★★★ Sitcoms ★★★

There are few things on television as agonisingly, skin-crawlingly, energy-sapping awful as a really bad sitcom. We know because we've experienced quite a few over the years – **Gimme Gimme Gimme**, **You Rang M'Lord**,

Up The Elephant And Round The Castle – but we've also had more than our fair share of classics such as **Steptoe And Son**, a fine example of the circular sitcom, where characters return to the same point in their lives, or something as quirky as **Black Books**. *The Rough Guide To Sitcoms* could be a book in itself, so the following list is doomed to be partial. A few real gems (Black Adder, Fawlty Towers, Father Ted, Reginald Perrin, The Office, Porridge, Seinfeld) are profiled at length in the cult programmes section on p15, as are more idiosyncratic choices like **Marion And Geoff**.

Absolutely Fabulous BBC2/1 1992–96, 2001–

The classic role-reversal sitcom, with bookish, sensible daughter Saffron Monsoon (**Julia Swahala**) keeping house and a sense of normality despite the antics of her wayward, childish PR mother Eddy (**Jennifer Saunders**) and her best mate, fashion editor Patsy Stone (**Joanna Lumley**). Developed from the 'Modern Mother And Daughter' sketch by French and Saunders, *Ab Fab* was the latter's first major solo project, although one Beeb exec exclaimed on seeing the pilot: 'I don't think women being drunk is funny.' In the US, Roseanne Barr bought the rights to produce a version but it was canned because astonished suits deemed it an assault on motherhood. *Sesame Street* modelled two puppets on Patsy and Eddy. We hope for the sake of our nation's youth the resemblance ends with their running around yelling 'Sweetie!' and 'Darling!'.

Are You Being Served? BBC1 1972–85

The antics of the staff in Menswear and Ladies Fashion at Grace Brothers' department store was first aired as a filler, when the BBC cancelled its scheduled coverage of the Munich Olympics after the murder of 11 Israeli athletes. The camp comedy struck a chord, with Mrs Slocombe's (Mollie Sugden) pussy and Mr Humphries' (**John Inman** was a former window dresser for Austin Reed) 'I'm free!' securing its place in TV history.

Billy Liar ITV 1973–74

Hoping to emulate the success of the 1963 film starring Tom Courtenay, LWT pestered **Keith Waterhouse** to adapt his book for the small screen and cast a young **Jeff Rawle** as Billy, whose fantasy world lets him escape from his hum-drum job. The show, which pioneered the use of the word 'bloody' in sitcoms, lasted just one season, but Rawle later found his niche playing put-upon wimp George Dent in **Drop The Dead Donkey**.

Black Books Channel 4 2000–

Co-written by and starring droll Irish stand-up comedian **Dylan Moran**, *Black Books* is far from the average cheesy sitcom. Moran stars as Bernard Black, the semi-permanently pissed owner of a bookshop who hates book-lovers and customers in general. Original and brilliantly written, each episode sees Black and his two cohorts – laidback yet dim Manny (**Bill Bailey**) and downright stupid Fran (**Tamsin Greig**, the voice of Debbie Aldridge in *The Archers*) – embark on some surreal adventure while trying to accomplish the simplest of tasks, such as going on holiday.

Cheers and Taxi Channel 4 1982–93; BBC1 1980–853

After writing for **M*A*S*H**, Glen and Les Charles developed **Taxi**, starring **Danny DeVito** as the cantankerous boss of a New York taxi firm, who bullies his misfit cabbies. The brothers then shifted to a Boston bar with **Cheers**. Norm is the only character to star in every episode, and in the 2,000th he proved it really is the bar where everybody knows your name – they all yelled 'Norm' as he walked in (even though his real first name was Hillary). What's truly notable about *Cheers* (**Kurt Vonnegut** said he'd rather have written this sitcom than any of his novels) , is that it contains arguably the largest group of really dense characters in any successful sitcom: Sam, Rebecca, Woody, Coach, Cliff, Norm, Carla. Perhaps alcohol really does rot the brain.

Dad's Army BBC1 1968–77

Probably the best investment the BBC ever made. The antics of the Walmington-on-Sea Home Guard are still a ratings-winner 25 years after the final episode. The debut of writers Jimmy Perry and David Croft, who went on to create *Hi-De-Hi* and *It Ain't Half Hot Mum*, it drew on Perry's experiences in his local World War II defence corps and those of ex-Army major Croft. The beauty of *Dad's Army* (and the secret of its longevity) lay in the depth of characterisation, with Arthur Lowe's Captain Mainwaring the perfect pompous fool (the actor insisted in his contract that he would not have to play a scene with his trousers off) opposite John Le Mesurier's laid-back Sergeant Wilson. Most of the stars were typecast by the show, with **Clive Dunn** (chosen over David Jason for Corporal Jones) staying prematurely aged to reach number one with his hit single 'Grandad'.

Desmond's Channel 4 1989–94

Based in a black barber's shop in Peckham, the show's activity centred on Desmond, his family and his philosophising pal Porkpie struggling with their day-to-day existence while dreaming of home (the West Indies). Rarely was a barnet approached, though much time was spent sweeping non-existent hair from the floor while putting the world to rights. The series, which gave rare screentime to Caribbean characters and humour, came to an untimely end with the death of **Norman Beaton** (Desmond).

Frasier Channel 4 1994–

Watching the first episode we expected and/or dreaded a **Cheers** rehash. What we got was a hilarious comedy of manners, with quick wit ('Niles, owning the CD of *Ella Sings Gershwin* does not qualify you as a soul brother!') and a finely-observed cast – finicky Niles, mattress-surfing Roz, Martin the dad (and ex-cop who was shot in the hip by an armed suspect days after giving a lecture about how to deal with armed suspects) and Daphne, the allegedly Mancunian home help. Yet if **Lisa Kudrow** had accepted the role of Roz ahead of **Peri Gilpin**, or if the writers had seen **Jane Leeves** (Daphne) on *Benny Hill*, it could have been so different. The show's central irony, that the hero spends his life sorting out other people's lives when he can't sort out his own, applies to Kelsey Grammer himself, whose off-screen life has been marred by tragedy and scandal.

The Groovy Fellers Channel 4 1989

Jools Holland and **Roland Rivron** wrote this bizarre sitcom. Jools comes across a Martian (Rivron) in a pub in Northumberland (as you do) and the pair strike up a friendship, the Martian (as Holland's touring buddy) learning what life on Earth is like. Surreal in tone and appearance, the show only lasted one season but is cherished for the scene where Jools, Roland and **David Owen** drive around Parliament Square singing the old World War I trenches ditty 'We're here because we're here.'

The High Life BBC2 1995–96

Playing Sebastian Flight, a character he developed at the Scottish Academy of Music and Drama, **Alan Cummings**, along with **Forbes Masson** (Steve McCracken), also composed the music to this camp-as-you-like sitcom set among the cabin crew of Air Scotia. Masson and Cummings played sly stewards, working with, and against, tyrant boss Shona Spurtle (**Siobhan Redmond**). Hollywood called Cummings, while Masson went on to feel the end of Gianni Di Marco's fist in *EastEnders*.

The Larry Sanders Show BBC2 1992–98

Familiar with the inner workings of TV talk shows (he stood in for **Johnny Carson** on *Tonight* and was a candidate to take over from **David Letterman**), Garry Shandling came up with the idea of a sitcom in a chat

As a shrink, Frasier never shrank from dispensing advice, though his dad's dog had a firmer grip on reality

show. With host Larry based on Jerry Langford (**Jerry Lewis**' character in Martin Scorsese's *The King Of Comedy*), the show had a split format. The on-air interviews showed Larry schmoozing with David Duchovny, Sharon Stone, Roseanne Barr et al, while behind-the-scenes Larry was demanding and egotistical. His sidekicks included veteran star **Rip Torn** as producer Artie ('I speak fluent bullshit'), guest booker Paula (comedian **Janeane Garofalo**) and **Jeffrey Tambor** as Hank 'Hey Now!' Kingsley, who was based on Carson's right-hand man, Ed McMahon. Too edgy and arty for some, the show built up a loyal following in the UK, where it was relegated to a late-night BBC2 slot.

The Likely Lads BBC1 1964–66

Mixing comedy with social commentary, **The Likely Lads** focused on the working class heroes of the extrovert, cynical, work-shy Terry ('I'd offer you a beer but I've only got six cans') and his childhood friend, the ambitious, sensible, loyal Bob, as they try to find their feet in the world of work, pubs, football and girls. The lads were reunited in colour in 1973 with **Whatever Happened To The Likely Lads?** when Terry returned from the army with a failed marriage behind

---

★ Normisms ★
(Cheers, 1982-93)

Sam: What's new, Normie?
Norm: Terrorists, Sam. They've taken over my stomach and are demanding beer.

Sam: What'll you have, Normie?
Norm: Well, I'm in a gambling mood, Sammy. I'll take a glass of whatever comes out of that tap.
Sam: Looks like beer, Norm.
Norm: Call me Mister Lucky.

Sam: Hey Norm, how's the world been treating you?
Norm: Like a baby treats a diaper.

Woody: Would you like a beer, Mr Peterson?
Norm: No, I'd like a dead cat in a glass.

Woody: Hey, Mr Peterson, there's a cold one waiting for you.
Norm: I know. If she calls, I'm not here.

Woody: Pour you a beer, Mr Peterson?
Norm: Alright, but stop me at one... make that one-thirty.

Woody: Can I pour you a beer, Mr Peterson?
Norm: A little early isn't it, Woody?
Woody: For a beer?
Norm: No, for stupid questions.

him to find the social gap widening between him and his old chum Bob, who is about to marry the boss's daughter. Although the dialogue was key (such as Terry's tour of the world's nationalities in xenophobic clichés), writers Clement and Le Frenais weren't afraid to drop in broader humour, as when Terry used his fork lift truck to help his locked-out pal.

Married... With Children
ITV 1990–94, Sky One 1994–

Al Bundy is an ex-football star working as a women's shoe salesman, and bitching about his couch-potato wife Peg (**Katey Sagal**, a former backing singer for Bob Dylan and Better Midler) and his miserable kids – party animal Kelly (played by the equally wild **Christina Applegate**) and Bud (David Faustino) who couldn't get enough of his blow-up doll. The surname Bundy referred to the pro-wrestling character, King Kong Bundy. But the real star of this series was the couch, the finest in sitcom land.

Men Behaving Badly   ITV/BBC1 1992–96

Adapted by **Simon Nye** from his novel, *Men Behaving Badly* epitomised laddism while sending it up. Centering on the lives, loves and drunken ramblings of a couple of emotionally-stunted flatmates, the laugh-out-

'In the chocolate box of life, the top layer's already gone': Bob 'Sartre' Ferris waxes philosophical

loud series dealt with everything from lager to sex to lager again. The series improved after dim Dermot (**Harry Enfield**) was replaced as Gary's (**Martin Clunes**) flatmate by the equally dense Tony (**Neil Morrissey**).

Nightingales Channel 4 1990–92

Even if you weren't a fan you had to admire the ambition of *Nightingales*. Director **Tony Dow**, possibly semi-catatonic after directing *Bergerac*, helmed this surreal sitcom in which disparate (and desperate) night-watchmen **Robert Lindsay**, **James Ellis** and **David Threlfall** whiled away the hours in a tiny office, either fighting or spinning bizarre fantasies – a routine disturbed by cameos from (among others) a pregnant Mary on Christmas Eve and Eric the werewolf. Love it or loathe it, it certainly made a refreshing alternative to *The Upper Hand*. Lindsay has some track record in Britcoms, making a debut as Smiff in **Get Some In** before going on to greater glory as **Citizen Smith** and recently starring in the slightly-above-average sitcom of family life, **My Family**.

Only Fools And Horses BBC1 1981–96

Nicholas Lyndhurst was chosen to play 'Plonker' Rodney after his success in *Butterflies*. **David Jason** was, at best, third choice for Del Boy behind Enn Reitel and Jim Broadbent (**Roger Lloyd-Pack** also auditioned before becoming Trigger). Grandad (**Lennard Pearce**) was so closely modelled on Steptoe he would have been **Wilfrid Brambell** if the producers hadn't thought him too stereotyped. And when the trio moved into 368 Nelson Mandela House in 1981, writer **John Sullivan** noted, 'It had an audience of 13, my family.' But Del's catchphrases, the wrong chandelier, and Trigger calling Rodney 'Dave' soon became part of our culture, leading to inevitable Christmas specials. As a general rule, though, the further from Peckham they travelled, the less funny the Trotters became.

The Phil Silvers Show BBC1 1957–60

In its fourth season and at the height of its popularity, CBS pulled the plug on fast-buck Bilko without consulting **Phil Silvers**. This may explain the closing scene of the last episode, which saw Sergeant Bilko switching on a small TV set, connected to a recently-installed CCTV system, to watch his 'favourite programme'. The screen showed Bilko and his henchmen behind bars, and Bilko closed the show with 'Tha-tha-tha that's all folks!' But it wasn't quite over. Bilko's unsuccessful get-rich scams and his love/hate relationship with authority figure Colonel Hall (Phil Ford) were transferred to animation, a New York alley and the love/hate relationship to **Top Cat** and **Officer Dibble** by **Hanna and Barbera** in 1961. To cap it off, Top Cat's Benny the Ball, the cartoon equivalent of Private Doberman, was voiced by the real Doberman, **Maurice Gosfield**.

Sex And The City Channel 4 1999–

The televised version of New York columnist's Candace Bushnell's writing is as formulaic as it gets when it comes to sitcoms. Carrie and friends meet; an issue is introduced that affects one of them directly (infertility, promiscuity, lesbianism, shopping); they discuss it either at brunch, while jogging or during a few Cosmopolitans; Carrie goes home and writes her column (on what must be the most under-used laptop in journalism since she never gets past the first line) before various scenes are played around the theme. And at some point someone – usually Samantha – will have sex. But who cares? It's witty, sharp, well-observed, sexy and gives women a freedom of expression hitherto unheard of on TV. Many men are uneasy about some of the comedy (such as the episode that featured visible evidence of the female orgasm, which, interestingly, came as a result of lesbian sex) but this only serves to delight women even more.

Some Mothers Do 'Ave 'Em BBC1 1973–78

Sometimes accidents are waiting to happen. Sometimes Frank Spencer gives them a helping hand. As the provider for long-suffering wife Betty (and, later, daughter Jessica), he holds a fatal attraction for ladders, roller skates and open paint pots. Many of the visual gags were taken from movie greats Buster Keaton and Harold Lloyd. **Michael Crawford** (third choice for the role of Spencer after Norman Wisdom and Ronnie Barker) did many of the stunts himself. He also ad-libbed so much of the dialogue that after filming on one occasion writer **Raymond Allen** told Crawford

'It was nice of you to use some of my words.' Painfully naïve — the slightest innuendo sent him into shock — he was still rebuked by self-appointed watchdog Mary Whitehouse, who labelled him a 'purveyor of pornography' because of his supposed obsession with his genitals.

How to be a domestic goddess 2: Nigella who?

Steptoe And Son
BBC 1 1962–74

The odd couple of scruffy rag-and-bone man Albert (**Wilfrid Brambell**) and his ambitious but doomed son Harold (Harry H Corbett — to distinguish him from Sooty's handler) were actually just 13 years apart in age. **The Beatles** were so taken by the show — remade in Sweden as Albert And Herbert, America as Sanford And Son and Holland as Stiefbeen En Zoon — they enlisted Brambell to play McCartney's grandpa in **A Hard's Day Night**.

Sykes BBC1 1960–65, 1971–79

Sebastopol Terrace, the very name of the street in which **Eric Sykes** lived with his sitcom sister Hattie Jacques sums up the charm of this everyday yet surreal sitcom. With **Derek Guyler** and **Richard Wattis** as their local constable and uptight neighbour, the pair quietly marked the end of the British empire and the beginning of not much else. Some episodes were written by **Johnny Speight** but Sykes, who had already written for the likes of Tony Hancock and Frankie Howerd, did the lion's share, bringing a warmth to the series that Speight never managed to.

★★★ Sketch shows ★★★

The late 1960s were as revolutionary in TV comedy as they were in rock music. The advent of **At Last The 1948 Show** (1967) and Spike Milligan's **Q5** (1968) heralded a new brand of off-the-wall comedy. Jokes were no longer organised to the point of sterility – the sketches on **Monty Python's Flying Circus** often didn't feature a punch line. Python's crucial (and often overlooked) achievement was to make comedy cool – they were much more credible with adolescent boys in the early 1970s than most rock groups. That legacy is still with us. We watch sitcoms guiltily but we happily publicly parrot catchphrases from our favourite sketch show. But many comedians now seem to see comedy as something you do to earn a shot at being a proper actor. We don't blame them for trying to do something completely different but they shouldn't blame us if we'd rather watch something else, like reruns of **The Fast Show**.

Absolutely Channel 4 1989–93

Surreal Scottish humour (with a hint of Welsh thanks to John Sparkes), with everything from Pythonesque animation to sing-a-long skits and the

Dealing with flying handbags was, Ted realised, a serious omission in his Charles Atlas manual

weirdest collection of characters, including Little Girl, anorak Callum Gilhooley, DIY expert Denzil, and Donald and George McDiarmid (no relation). In retrospect, the show had an unlikely cast, with comediennes **Morwenna Banks** and **Moray Hunter** alongside recent national lottery presenter **Gordon Kennedy** and Channel 5 star **Jack Docherty**. Absolutely, most definitely, the highlight of their career.

The Day Today BBC2 1994

Like many BBC sketch shows, this started on Radio 4 (as *On the Hour*). **The Day Today** was a pastiche of newscasting, with Chris Morris as the abrasive anchorman, prone to yelling out headlines like 'Police chief crushes lizard with whistle' at will. He was supported by Alan Partridge (**Steve Coogan**) Pringle-loving sports reporter, Barbara Wintergreen (**Rebecca Front**), Stateside reporter, and business expert Collaterlie Sisters. In a six-week run, **The Day Today** spawned two shows, **Knowing Me Knowing You** and **Brass Eye**. The credits featured thanks to 'Horses by Will Self, Carpets by Bono, Maps by Faye Dunaway'.

The Fast Show BBC2 1994–97

For a while **Paul Whitehouse** (who devised Stavros and Loads-A-Money) was just that bloke you saw with Harry Enfield. But when he and **Charlie Higson** saw a cut-down press preview of Enfield's work, they had the idea of producing a show comprising fast, straight-to-the-punchline gags. Each episode packed in 25 sketches, almost guaranteeing we'd laugh at something, be it Ted and Ralph, 'Do you like… Tina Turner, Ted?', John Thomson's jazz lover, Competitive Dad or drunken Rowley Birkin, QC, 'the whole thing was made entirely out of rubber!, Snake! Snake! Cairo!!! … poisonous monkey…' **Ted and Ralph** – Higson and Whitehouse's own favourites – starred in their own 1998 spin-off, and **Swiss Toni**, who's smooth lines are written by Bob Mortimer, is set to get his very own show.

The Goodies BBC2 1970–80, ITV 1981–82

Madcap antics in the Python manner, just sillier. Originally called Super Chaps Three, the super chaps were **Tim Brooke-Taylor** (the patriot swathed in a Union Jack waistcoat), **Bill Oddie,** (the hairy cynical socialist) and Graeme Garden (mad-cap professor). Together they tried to save the world from a giant white kitten, on the back of their tandem bike, Buttercup. Sending up politics, pop music ('The InBetweenies') and giving kung-fu movies a new spin with their 'ecky thump' sketch. Despite huge ratings and awards, **The Goodies** were seen by the BBC as children's entertainers and, tiring of not being taken seriously, they moved to ITV. They later went on to voice the characters of cult cartoon **Bananaman.**

Goodness Gracious Me BBC2 1998–

Originally (again) a radio series, this was named after the 1960 Peter Sellers/Sophia Loren novelty hit single from the film **The Millionairess.** The original choice had been the blunter *Peter Sellers Is Dead* but the show was destined to spark debate whatever it was called. Previous ethnic minority shows (**The Real McCoy** had featured three of the *Goodness Gracious Me* team) had struggled in the ratings. But audiences were happy to accept a send-up of British and Asian stereotypes. Favourite characters include the Kapoor family, or Cooper as they prefer to be known to emphasise their English roots; Bollywood columnist Smita Smitten the Showbiz Kitten, and Mr. 'Everything was created by an Indian'. The cast have since created the equally hilarious **The Kumars at No. 42.**

Monty Python's Flying Circus BBC1 1969–74

'As a kid with Monty Python, there were just some of them who were small and did funny old women and John Cleese,' **Charlie Higson** recalled later. 'Well, they thought his name was Monty Python, didn't they?' said **Paul Whitehouse.** 'They'd say "Oh he's funny, that Monty Python with his walk. You know, that walk he does." But in terms of the way it affected kids, it was just everywhere.'

Rowan & Martin's Laugh-In BBC2 1968–73

In the US, it took two nightclub comedians, **Dan Rowan** and **Dick Martin** to change the face of TV comedy forever. Debuting as a one-off special in 1967, the show was such a success it replaced **The Man From U.N.C.L.E.**.

John Cleese, wrongly believing there's a banana skin on the pavement, tries to evade the old sight gag

225

Timing had a lot to do with it – the show was a welcome, anarchic relief from events in Vietnam – but the humour was innovative, a wild version of variety night with stand-up, music, skits, satire, slapstick and recurring sketches including The Flying Fickle Finger Of Fate Award. *Laugh-In* discovered the likes of **Goldie Hawn** (Richard Nixon was one of her big fans) and **Lily Tomlin**, and will go down in TV history as the only show of its kind to star someone called Pigmeat (**Pigmeat Markham** was the name). The show inspired BBC2 and Des O'Connor to do something similar which, to be fair, wasn't the worst thing on TV in the 1970s.

Scotch & Wry BBC Scotland 1978–92

On 31 December 1978, before the midnight watershed that heralded the usual torrent of tartan teuchterama, there appeared on Scottish BBC a clever sketch show that was to offer a grateful nation an antidote to the traditional Hogmanay TV of black bun and Jimmy Logan. Starring light-entertainment veteran Rikki Fulton (b. 1924), it ran for 14 years and has been treasured ever since. Fulton's useless traffic cop and lugubrious Presbyterian minister the Rev I M Jolly (author of *How I Found God, And Why He Was Hiding From Me*) are the show's best remembered characters. Sidekicks included Tony Roper (Jamesie Cotter of *Rab C Nesbitt*). For more fabulous Fulton, see his KGB man in the movie *Gorky Park*, and for *S&W*'s natural successor, check out BBC's **Chewin' The Fat**.

Smack The Pony Channel 4 1999–

Made by TalkBack, which felt there was an opening for an all-girl comedy show, this has been pigeonholed unfairly as a comedy for women, but is slapstick and surreal, with dating agency sketches alongside a woman who inflates her breasts to get attention from barmen. Doon MacKichan, formerly the Collaterlie Sisters from **The Day Today**, stumbled into it when the original third member alongside Sally Philips (better known as the receptionist from **I'm Alan Partridge**) and Fiona Allen (granddaughter of Harry Allen, the last British public executioner), dropped out of the pilot, then called *Spot The Pony*. Many other names were suggested, other contenders being *Planes, Trains And Forks* and *Les Vaches Dangereuses*.

226

★★★ Soaps ★★★

Italian author **Umberto Eco** once noted that a single cliché may be an annoyance but 100 clichés represents a true feast. He had, presumably, just been watching **Dynasty**. Whatever else soaps do (and one thing they do is deliver viewers more cheaply than almost any other genre), they feed what **AS Byatt** calls 'our narrative greed', our hunger for stories. Just reading the plots for **Dallas**, **Howard's Way** or **Sunset Beach** can be an exhausting experience. But there's something cathartic about the effect they have on us, the licence they give us to give vent to our emotions.

Soaps may be popular but are they cult? On the whole, probably not unless they're seriously trashy – **Crossroads** – or hook us with stories like the Ken, Mike and Deirdre triangle and **Brookside**'s body under the patio. Reality TV shows may have made it harder for soaps to captivate us in that way or maybe the main British soaps are just knackered. Many of us watch **EastEnders** in the hope that **Dirty Den**'s death was just one of Sharon's dreams and that he'll pop up phoenix-like behind the bar at the Queen Vic to lend charisma to a series which, at worst, could be compressed into a single exchange: 'Oi, leave it aht!' 'Mind yer own business.'

Albion Market ITV 1985–86

A case of blink and you'll miss it. Unless you were an avid soap nut in 1985, the twice-weekly visits to the covered market in Manchester will have passed you by. What was meant to be a sister to **Coronation Street**, with similar ratings, was axed after 100 episodes, killed by our love of Wogan and *Open All Hours*. The show broke ethnic barriers, blending Vietnamese, Ugandan, Jewish and Pakistani characters alongside roguish **Tony Booth** and 1960s singer **Helen Shapiro**. Unique to say the least.

Black Forest Clinic Channel 4 1988

Known as *Die Schwarzwaldklinik* in its native Germany, where the show was so popular it pulled in 25 million viewers per episode. Sadly, in Britain, botched dubbing and long, inexplicable shots of woodland features meant that **Black Forest Clinic** barely lasted two months. Set in a local

227

surgery, where it was rare to find a stethoscope out of place, the show commendably avoided any sex and nudity despite aiming to focus on the love-lives of local surgeon Professor Brinkmann and his heart-throb son, Dr Udo Brinkman (ex-porn star Sascha Hehn). No drama, no sex and no excitement – who said the Germans have no sense of humour?

Chateauvallon Channel 4 1985

Chateauvallon was, in its day, France's most expensive soap, although to the French it wasn't a soap but a drama in the same vein as the work of Dumas, Balzac and Hergé. With warring families battling for supremacy, it mirrored *Dallas*, but British audiences failed to warm to a soap where they either had to read subtitles or suffer dodgy dubbing. Yet the show did become a cult favourite, largely due to the amount of sex in each episode, forcing even those wild childs at C4 to move it to a late-night slot.

Compact BBC1 1962–65

Countless soaps emerged in the 1960s hoping to emulate *Coronation Street*. The BBC, at least, had the original idea of basing a soap around the lives and loves of the staff at a woman's magazine. Starring **Ronald Allen** (later *Crossroads*' middle-aged sex-symbol David Hunter), the show racked up nine romances, three marriages and an unwanted pregnancy in its first six months. With a mainly female cast, *Compact* explored how its characters struggled to combine work with a personal life and handled prejudice against female bosses and employees. But ratings slumped relatively rapidly and *Compact* ceased publication in 1965. By then co-creator **Hazel Adair** had already begun contemplating Midlands motels.

The Grove Family BBC1 1954–57

The BBC's first adult soap was the result of father-and-son writing team Roland and Michael Pertwee approaching producer Ronnie Waldman with the simple premise, 'Why don't you have a family?' The title was based on the BBC's Lime Grove studio address and audiences related to the characters, who were lower-middle class folk struggling to rebuild their lives after the war. The highlight of the plots was, sadly, advice on

★ Dallas ancestors, spin-offs & rivals ★

The ancestor
The Brothers, a 1970s BBC series, started with a fatal bang as the patriarch died in a moment of passion. The series had feuding brothers and a queen bitch (Kate O'Mara) but ratings were undermined by the decision to have the brothers fighting over a road haulage company.

The spin-off
Knots Landing, dull title, dull Ewing brother (Gary), dull soap.

The clones
Flamingo Road, a retread of a Joan Crawford film, tried to do for Florida what the Ewings had done for *Dallas*. Morgan Fairchild bedded the entire male cast (onscreen) apart from her brother in the first two series.

The rivals
Dynasty was the biggest, spawning its own spin-off *The Colbys*. *Falcon Crest*, despite being the brainchild of Earl (*The Waltons*) Hamner, made room for 19 deaths and 10 attempted murders as the characters feuded over their vineyards. Jane Wyman, ex-wife of *Bonzo* co-star Ronald, was the matriarch, as tough as Miss Ellie was mushy.

Barnes-beating was one of the favourite recreational pursuits at Southfork

preventing burglaries. **The Grove Family** might have trundled on but after three years working solidly on the show, the Pertwees asked for a break. They were sacked, new writers hired and the end of the show was nigh.

Peyton Place ITV 1964–69

Four decades on, producers are still trying to imitate the sex opera that was *Peyton Place*. Gambler-turned-producer Paul Monash wanted to create a show which could emulate the hold which *Coronation Street* had over British audiences, alighting on Grace Metalious' sin-soaked novel of sex, lust and skeletons in every closet. Set in a fictional American town, each of the original 514 episodes involved some scandal – illicit affairs, illegitimate children, murder – and always ended on a corny cliffhanger. The show primed stars such as **Ryan O' Neal** and **Mia Farrow** for Hollywood stardom, with Farrow (the show's demure starlet) managing to remain a virgin for 200 sin-strewn episodes before she became lost on a foggy night. Come on now, we've all done it at some point.

Pobol Y Cwm BBC Wales 1974–

Wales' longest-running soap, *Pobol Y Cwm* is one of the few recorded on the day of transmission (a 1988 episode even referred to that day's Lockerbie disaster). Life in the fictional village of Cwmderi has spiced up since it became a 20-minute daily serial with adultery and toy boys climbing up the fictional agenda. A 1992 network showing foundered on the English audience's point-blank refusal to watch a subtitled soap.

Revelations ITV 1994

Revelations, ITV's 1990s answer to today's late-night soap offering, was only shown in three ITV regions before being nabbed by Sky One, yet it has its devotees who praise its surreal wooden thespianry, comedy and habit of cutting to quick shots of villains and victims. After scripting (inspired by?) **The House Of Windsor**, Russell T Davies offered viewers a unique look at life in the church, with **Paul Shelley** as Edward Rattigan, an Anglican Bishop whose own family's vices, lust, alcohol, drugs and general wayward behaviour prevented him from spending too much time with his parishioners. The show featured **Ben Hull**, who is possibly trying to set a record for starring in the most soaps, having already appeared in **Children's Ward**, **Hollyoaks** and **Brookside**.

Santa Barbara ITV 1984–93

The overall winner in the 'so bad it's good' stakes, *Santa Barbara* crossed the Atlantic as ITV's answer to *Neighbours*. Never as popular, **Santa Barbara** left its Aussie peers standing when it came to bad acting and rickety sets (even though $30m was spent on the show). Once described by a former cast member as 'a lot like improvised theatre' (no rehearsals and a lot of winging it), the show brought you the same character with a new face every year, touched on male prostitution, and offered such classic soundbites as [Lionel Lockridge]: 'Let's talk about trust. We used to have that.' [Augusta Lockridge]: 'Yes. We also used to have a Studebaker.'

Savannah ITV 1996–97

A hit with audiences all over the world yet cancelled mid-way through the second season due to falling ratings, **Savannah**'s main problem was that no one knew when it was to be shown next. Classic **Aaron Spelling** stuff, this was **Dynasty** with younger bitches: Reese (Shannon Sturges) the virginal little rich girl, Peyton (Jamie Luner), her best friend despite being the lowly daughter of the housekeeper and found to be having an affair with Reese's fiancé Travis, and Lane (Robyn Lively), Reese's other best friend and future drug addict and alcoholic. **Savannah** was high on high drama, the pilot introducing us to Peyton (named in honour of *Place*?) who had just murdered Travis. Compulsive viewing, while it lasted.

Sons And Daughters ITV 1981–87

Not as sickly sweet as the title might suggest, especially once the incest plot was revealed. Long before Kat and Uncle Harry were at it, Angela Hamilton was falling for John Palmer, the only problem being he was her twin brother (not identical obviously). Created to bridge the gap between residents of Melbourne and Sydney (the rich Hamiltons were from Sydney, the poorer Palmers from Melbourne), the action alternated

Kate O' Mara, wishing she was in the Bermuda Triangle

between the two cities and families. Despite the incest issue, *Sons And Daughters* is best remembered for its unique brand of bitches. The producers, fearing one wasn't enough, gave us both Pat 'the Rat' Hamilton and Barbara Hamilton. Pat was the female JR Ewing, whilst Cornelia Frances (**Barbara Hamilton**) would terrify as Morag in **Home And Away** and is now the Australian Anne Robinson on **The Weakest Link**.

Sunset Beach Channel 5 1997–2000

'Can you imagine anything more infuriating than someone coming back from the dead, demanding to see you and then not showing up?' No, Olivia (in the lifeguard shorts), we can't. But then, as Dr Estrada said to a patient, we 'haven't seen brain activity like this in ages' – not since the last **Aaron Spelling** (take a bow Aaron) extravaganza. Normally, Spelling's soaps start off with some vague connection to reality and then start spinning madly in a desperate attempt to shore up their ratings. But **Sunset Beach**, a saga of sun, sex and sperm robberies in California, was round the bend when it started and made several more circuits before being axed, to protests from Spelling and fans in Germany, Australia and Britain where its Saturday omnibus edition on Channel 5 is much missed.

Triangle BBC1 1981–83

Nobody has satisfactorily explained why the BBC thought a drama about a ferry company set against a grey, grim and decidedly choppy North Sea was a good idea. Yet, astonishingly, six million British viewers were still watching three years later when **Triangle** was finally axed. But this soap always surprised, right from the opening shot of freezing **Kate O'Mara** trying to persuade us that it wasn't a mistake to sunbathe topless in a 40mph gale. Having initially been hired (along with 1950s film star **Michael Craig**) to add a touch of glitz, O'Mara jumped ship after one season.

The Young Doctors ITV 1976–82

Despite being plagued by shootings, bombings and general nutters, the young doctors of this Australian medical soap were always Daz white since little blood was shed on screen. Producer **Alan Coleman** was so determined not to upset us that a kiss was as far as sex went, and divorce was banned, so full marks for originality, Alan. Should it ever enjoy another repeat run, it's worth watching as a 1970s fashion retrospective, with some shirt collars capable of spanning Sydney Harbour.

★★★ Spies ★★★

FBI double agent Herbert Philbrick inspired the first authentic spy series. His autobiography, *I Led Three Lives*, became a popular television show chronicling the domestic battle against Red subversion in 1950s America. Nods in a similar direction included America's *The Man Called X* (1956) and Britain's *The Man From Interpol* (1960). But it was the James Bond phenomenon that enthused 1960s TV executives.

Secret agents are a nifty way to up the quotient of exotic settings, glamour, high-tech gadgetry and thrills in what are essentially crime and adventure stories. 007's creator himself, **Ian Fleming**, came up with the concept for *The Man From U.N.C.L.E.* over lunch in London with American TV executives. Even children's TV got in the spy game with *Secret Squirrel* and the running battles between *Rocky And Bullwinkle* and Cold War foes, Boris and Natasha. But few of the series outlived Swinging Sixties frivolity, and spies were out in the cold in the cynical 1970s. Proper secret agenting was left to *Danger Mouse* (1981–92). After the Soviet Union's break-up, new contemporary spy escapades emerged with the glamorous, frenetic *Alias* (*La Femme Nikita* meets *Mission: Impossible*, 2001–) and the BBC MI5 drama, *Spooks* (2002–).

233

Danger Man ITV 1960–66

Danger Man, created by **Ralph Smart**, offered a dignified spy who questioned the morality of assignments, drove a Mini-Cooper and relied on his wits, although matter-of-factly heroic John Drake (**Patrick McGoohan**, who twice turned down the role of Bond) had his share of flashbomb cigars, explosive cuff links and microphone fishing rods. After 39 half-hour episodes, globe-trotting Drake (his cover, employee of World Travel) moved from NATO to fictitious MI9 and 47 hour-long adventures – 'A messy job? Well, that's when they usually call on me.' With massive US cult status, it spawned novels, comics, a game and a sound-track album with Eric Clapton instrumentals. McGoohan said that any resemblance to his next series, *The Prisoner*, was coincidental, but the show's offbeat sensibilities anticipated that cult landmark and the latter's setting of Portmeirion in Wales was a favourite *Danger Man* location.

Get Smart BBC1 1965–70

Created by **Mel Brooks** (who used the money to finance *The Producers*) and Buck Henry, this spoofed the spy craze with huge success despite being shunted between all three major American TV networks over the course of its 138 half-hour episode run. Brooks' inspiration was 'I want to centre a show on an idiot. Nobody's ever done that on TV before and I want to be the first.' The zany misadventures of Maxwell Smart, Agent 86 (86 being American bartender slang for a drunk, though he wasn't one), starred deadpan **Don Adams** as the zealous but bungling operative, his more competent, lovely partner and, eventually, bride was never-named Agent 99 (**Barbara Feldon**), his long-suffering Chief Thaddeus (Edward Platt), his foes from KAOS, and his sidekick super-intelligent robot Hymie. The catchphrase 'Sorry about that, Chief' enjoyed currency for years, while favourite gadgets included the much-loved shoe telephone.

Harry's Game ITV 1982

234 Nothing to do with Harry Carpenter, Harry Corbett or Harry Worth, but a three-part thriller based on ITN journalist Gerald Seymour's debut novel, **Belfast Assassin**. The Harry of the more television-friendly title

was a special intelligence operative played by ex-*Z Cars* star **Ray Lonnen**, sent into Northern Ireland by the PM (against more sensible advice, so no change there then) to find the IRA terrorist responsible for killing a government minister. The cat-and-mouse action was more tense and grim than anything previously seen on ITV. Shown in three parts on consecutive nights, it was edited into a feature-length movie, with a suitably stirring soundtrack provided by Clannad, and also starred Derek (*Casualty*) Thompson and Linda (get me out of sitcom hell) Robson.

I Spy ITV 1965–68

This slick drama made broadcasting (and cultural) history in the US by casting black comedian Bill Cosby as equal lead opposite Robert Culp (who wrote for the show). Pentagon agents who pretended to be a tennis player (Culp's Kelly Robinson) and a trainer (Cosby's Alexander 'Scotty' Scott), the hip smoothies were engaging buddies who fitted tournaments in between shoot 'em-ups with the usual nefarious operatives. Race was never an issue or message, with the show focused on glossy romantic adventure. The first season was filmed almost entirely in the Far East; the next year production moved to the Mediterranean. In 2002 Eddie Murphy and Owen Wilson signed up for a film version.

The Man From U.N.C.L.E. BBC1 1964–67

Conceived by **Ian Fleming** and shaped by Sam Rolfe, cool United Network Command for Law Enforcement agents Napoleon Solo (**Robert Vaughn**, dash and seductions) and Russian Illya Kuryakin (**David McCallum**, polo necks and quips) undertook globe-trotting 'affairs' (each with snappy prologue and four acts) at the behest of controller Mr Alexander Waverly (**Leo G Carroll**, unflappable Brit), whose New York HQ was concealed behind a dry cleaner's. International crime syndicate THRUSH threw mad scientists, smugglers and assassins at them, but their speciality was improbable cliffhanger escapes, usually with the secret formula and a pretty girl in tow. Gadgets included pen communicators ('Open Channel D'). Witty escapades, accompanied by cartoonish action and go-go music, saw Vaughn and McCallum idolised as pop stars, but a change of producers and decline into panto did little for the series or silly spin-off *The Girl From U.N.C.L.E.* starring **Stefanie Powers** as April Dancer.

Mission: Impossible BBC1 1966–73

The Impossible Mission Force's Cold War capers became legend for Lalo Schifrin's theme (reprised in the Tom Cruise films) and briefings from the self-destructing tape ('Your mission, should you choose to accept it'). **Peter Graves** as Jim Phelps was usually helped by real-life husband and wife **Martin Landau** (master of disguise Rollin Hand) and **Barbara Bains** (supermodel seductress Cinammon), significant racial equality with **Greg Morris** as the electronics genius Barney Collier, and hunk **Peter Lupus** as muscleman Willie. After Landau and Bains left, **Leonard Nimoy** and Lesley Ann Warren arrived as Paris and Dana Lambert, Nimoy even appearing in the same episode as his future skipper William Shatner.

Reilly: Ace of Spies ITV 1983

Sam Neill starred in the colourful historical exploits of Sidney Reilly (born Sigmund Rosenblum in Russia), legendary British agent before, during and after World War I. The twelve episodes, written by Troy Kennedy Martin (whose cult credits include the nuclear conspiracy serial *Edge Of Darkness*), explored the exotic missions and scandalous sexual intrigues of the handsome enigma up to his lonely, mystery-shrouded execution in revolutionary Russia. Co-stars included Leo McKern as Basil Zaharov and **Tom Bell** as Felix Dzerzhinsky.

Tinker Tailor Soldier Spy BBC1 1979

Spydom was stripped of glamour as

The series born out of an Ian Fleming lunch

Alec Guinness's weary George Smiley was summoned from retirement to catch the highly-placed traitor in *The Circus*. John Le Carre's thriller of deceit and disillusion, dramatised by Arthur Hopcraft and directed by John Irvin, spun out painstaking suspense for seven subtle but labyrinthine instalments, followed in 1982 with *Smiley's People*. A superlative cast (Ian Richardson, Ian Bannen, Hywel Bennett, Beryl Reid) included **Patrick Stewart** as KGB spymaster Karla and concealed the fact that for much of the time nothing really happened. The haunting church choir theme was 'Nunc Dimittis' by Geoffrey Burgon.

Wild Wild West ITV 1965–69

Heroic James T West (**Robert Conrad**) and resourceful master of disguise Artemus Gordon (**Ross Martin**) were 1870s agents in President Grant's Secret Service. In 104 fantastical adventures, favourite nemeses were psychotic dwarf Dr Miguelito Loveless (Michael Dunn), his giant henchman Voltaire (Richard Kiel) and Count Mazeppi (Victor Buono). Travelling between secret frontier lairs by private train (The Wanderer) with a hidden arsenal that included pool-cue rapiers and billiard ball bombs, natty West concealed an array of devices up his sleeve and in his boot heel. Ingenious, audacious fight sequences were a trademark, inspiring Jackie Chan, but led to cancellation after complaints about violence. The film version, with Will Smith and Kevin Kline as Jim and Arte, was a travesty.

★★★ Sports ★★★

Sadly, not everyone can be as glamorous as **Frank Bough**. Just look at **Tony Gubba**. Away from golden greats such as **World Of Sport** lurk legions of long-forgotten programmes. Yet, in their own glorious way, they left their mark, if not always as intended. Follow us then, through the changing room of the mind as we trawl the unseen depths of cult sport on TV.

Gone Fishing ITV 1959–68

For rustic with a capital R, call **Jack Hargreaves**. Think Bob Fleming from **The Fast Show** and you won't be far off. This pipe-smoking veteran angler took to this project like, er, a fish to water, even building his own boat for himself and his sidekick, Ollie Kite. A trawl of the Internet is testimony to Hargreaves' mellow legacy – 30 pages of ruminations on 'today's generation and their 10-second attention span' says it all. A stalwart of Southern Television, he also proved his worth with **Out Of Town** (essential viewing for O-level woodwork students) and **How**. In fishing parlance, a super fly guy, he died in 1994, aged 82.

The Indoor League ITV 1973–79

You didn't mess with 'Fiery' **Fred Truman** when he was ripping through the batting order. You'd have had to be equally crazy to watch his curmudgeonly presidency over **The Indoor League**. Set in a pretend pub, it brought to the masses previously untelevised indoor pastimes such as skittles, arm-wrestling, and shove-ha'penny (and the phrase 'I'll see thee') all washed down with lashings of Yorkshire bitter, homespun political incorrectness and some truly garish knitwear.

Kickstart BBC1 1978–89

Peter Purves, a member of one of *Blue Peter*'s most famous triumvirates (along with John and Val), was your perfect host for this motorbike trials extravaganza in which young turks with wealthy parents strutted their stuff on logs in a quarry in the South Downs. Penalties were incurred for putting two feet on the floor. Oh, the drama, especially in the second round – which was basically the first, only in reverse.

Pot Black BBC2 1969–86 1991–93

This show's success, announced by **Winifred Atwell**'s 'Black And White Rag', whetted our appetite for snooker. Never mind the Crucible and its best-of-365 frame matches, this was the original and best snooker drama, broadcast at a time when colour TV was in its infancy and so was **Stephen Hendry**. One frame live from Pebble Mill for the BBC cameras. Presented by the late Alan Weeks, it came from an age where Bill Werbeniuk could drink 10 pints a night and claim it was medicinal and be believed.

Superstars BB1 1976–83

Never mind where you were when JFK was shot. The real zeitgeist test is where you were when **Kevin Keegan** wobbled for what seemed like years before falling off his bike during a memorable heat of this Friday night ratings-grabber. Skier **Franz Klammer**, Dutch footballer **Ruud Krol** and shot-putter **Geoff Capes**, whose presence seemed required by act of parliament, commenced battle in ten Olympian tests of their clay pigeon shooting and table tennis skills.

We Are The Champions BBC1 1973–87

This remarkable show, hosted first by **Ron Pickering** and latterly **Gary Lineker** (although he wouldn't thank you for reminding him), featured a host of schools in sub-**It's A Knockout** capers. Legions of hyperactive kids would clown about in canoes and on rafts and were rewarded by an incomprehensible points-scoring system that demanded a widescreen TV (hard to come by in those days) just to fit in the scoreboard. 'Well done, you came last, but that's still two billion points for Warblington School.'

★★★ Supermarionation ★★★

You could feel the tingle of electricity in the living room as Mike Mercury ran through his mantra: 'Charging port engine… 5,000…9,000…12,000…15,000; interlock on, fire one!' A roar from the afterburner of the port engine and then, watched from the control room by Prof Popkiss and Dr Beaker, on to the starboard engine: '9,000…12,000…15,000; interlock on, fire two!' The hangar roof doors of the secret laboratory deep in the Nevada desert slid open to reveal a cavernous grey sky. A rasping whoosh of steam, throttle from the vertical engines and then, accompanied by an heroic soundtrack and Barry Gray's inimitable lyrics, up she rose.

In 39 black and white episodes in 1960 and 1961, **Supercar**, a 25 foot, red, yellow, grey and blue marvel that could fly at speeds of 1,500mph or plunge to the depths of the oceans provided enough action and adventure to captivate a nation of children reared on the anodyne *Andy Pandy*. It also introduced to the world a technology that would remain an essential

239

part of children's televisual experience to the present day and created a legacy of British special effects expertise that would prove to be pivotal assets to **George Lucas** and **Steven Spielberg**. The technology was called Supermarionation and its inventor, orchestrator and champion was an unlikely balding man from Hampstead, whose early ambitions to be an architect had been thwarted when he discovered he was allergic to plaster.

Gerry Anderson is one of the greats of British television history, rightly revered for a canon of classics from **Stingray** through **Thunderbirds** and **Captain Scarlet** to **UFO**. Yet it was his earlier work in *Supercar* and *Fireball XL5* that truly defined the genre. When, in 1967, **Peter Cook** and **Dudley Moore** paid homage to Supermarionation in *Not Only But Also*, they bookended Anderson's more enduring characters with a recognition of these roots in their supremely funny spoof 'Superthunderstingcar'.

Where cream buns grow on trees

After an uneventful spell as a dubbing editor at Pinewood and a television director at Polytechnic Studios, Anderson co-founded a commercials company, Pentagon Film. The renamed company, AP Films (APF) was asked by children's author **Roberta Leigh** and Associated Rediffusion executive **Suzanne Warner** to produce a puppet series, *The Adventures Of Twizzle* for ITV. In 1957 and 1958, Anderson and Provis rattled off 52, 15-minute episodes of the adventures of a boy doll with extendable arms (kittens, for the rescuing of) who runs away from a toyshop with his feline friend Footso and builds Stray Town, a haven for toys. Leigh then commissioned **Torchy The Battery Boy**, the story of a different boy doll who time travels by rocket to Topsy Turvy Land where toys can walk, animals can talk and cream buns grow on trees.

Buoyed by these series' success but unhappy with their technical content, APF branched out to make its own show, **Four Feather Falls**. This was the story of Sheriff Tex Tucker who maintains the peace in Four Feather Falls, Kansas with the aid of four magic feathers that allow his dog and horse to talk and his guns to swivel and fire automatically whenever he is in danger. Amongst the voice cast were **Nicholas Parsons**, who played Tucker, Carry On's **Kenneth Connor** and **David Graham** who would famously voice characters like Brains and Parker in *Thunderbirds*.

Anderson was frustrated by his team's inability to make puppets 'walk'. The solution, at once both simple and extravagant, was to place them in vehicles and switch the emphasis from the puppets themselves to a dazzling new array of hardware. His winning notion was a sci-fi adventure series based around an amazing, land, sea and air vehicle located in a secret hideout in Black Rock, Nevada. AFL developed the idea alone, Anderson coming close to bankruptcy before **Lew Grade**, the astute new head of Associated Rediffusion, bailed him out. The production budget was slashed but Anderson persuaded Grade to back the new puppetry technique involving marionettes with extremely fine wires and a solenoid inside their heads. The latter transferred an electronic pulse to the wire that moved the lip so that mouth movements could be synchronised to the vocal tracks. Supermarionation was born and continued, in more sophisticated forms, to be the core technology for Anderson productions until the creation of supermacromation for **Terrahawks** in 1983.

The main premise of **Supercar**, a dedicated team of do-gooders based

Britain wouldn't see anyone this dull on the box until John Major hosted Prime Minister's Question Time

in a remote and mysterious location housing the world's most amazing machine, was to be repeated most notably in *Thunderbirds*. For Black Rock in Nevada read Tracy Island; stammering, confused but brilliant Dr Beaker is the prototype Brains; lantern-jawed test pilot Mike Mercury is Scott Tracy; deep voiced, bald headed villain, Masterspy is The Hood and the vertical take-off all purpose rescue craft Supercar is Thunderbirds One, Three and Four all rolled into one. The stories, more primitive than *Thunderbirds*, were based around a standard formula of five unlikely characters (two scientists, a test pilot, an orphaned boy and his pet monkey), living and working in an isolated laboratory. The more gripping story lines were those that pitted Mike Mercury and Supercar against time and plausibility to pull off a daring rescue often involving other key characters notably mischievous monkey Mitch (a throwback to the days of Torchy, Twizzle, cream buns and talking animals).

The show was a crucial staging post between the cutesy, knockabout fun of *Twizzle* et al and the wizardry of *Thunderbirds* and *Captain Scarlet*. *Supercar* proved Anderson's hunch – that hardware could divert attention from his leaden-footed puppets – was correct.

'I want to be a fireball, a fireball, a fireball'

The lesson was carried forward with **Fireball XL5**, the story of an inter-galactic space cruiser that flies around the universe sorting out massed ranks of evil aliens in a proto *Star Trek* mission of human enlightenment. Grade provided the finance and distribution and took most of the profit, while Anderson assembled the usual suspects including his wife Sylvia, David Graham, technicians like David Lane, John Read and Paddy Searle and music maestro **Barry Gray** who penned the memorable theme.

Gray's heartfelt singalong: 'I wish I was a spaceman/The fastest guy alive/I'd fly you round the Universe in Fireball XL5' pointed us to the dashing hero, Colonel Steve Zodiac and his crew of four including a woman (Venus), the obligatory scientific genius (Matt Matic) and talking robot (Robert the Robot – voiced by Gerry Anderson via a synthesiser). The XL fleet of cruisers belonged to the World Space Patrol, a Starfleet of its day based in Space City under the watchful eye of Jeff Tracy prototype,

★ Supermarionation is go! ★

5! **Fireball XL5** was named after Castrol XL motor oil. 'I saw the ad on TV' said Gerry Anderson, 'and thought it had a good ring to it. I added the '5' to make it a little different.'

4! The **Harlington-Straker** Film Studios, used as a front for Shado in the Anderson live action series *UFO*, now appears as **Holby City Hospital** in the medical drama *Holby City*.

3! **Patrick McGoohan** was to voice world president James Younger in the first *Captain Scarlet* episode. The idea was to have a guest star puppet every week, sculpted to look like its voice artist. But McGoohan couldn't attend the recording, and the plan was killed to cut costs.

2! **Fred Freiberger**, producer of the third *Star Trek* season, replaced **Sylvia Anderson** to try to boost the woeful **Space 1999**'s US appeal.

1! Most of the puppets in the post-Scarlet puppet shows were recycled from *Captain Scarlet*'s large marionette cast. *Joe 90*'s **Sam Loover** is best known as the Supreme Commander of Earth Forces in *Scarlet*; the puppet also appeared as the Lunar Controller in the *Scarlet* episode 'Lunarville 7'. Other puppets turned up in various roles, among the more memorable being **Colonel White** in a dark wig in *Joe 90*.

Commander Zero. From *Stingray*'s mobile Marineville, via the hidden hangars and rocket pads in the crevices and swimming pools of Tracy Island to Spectrum's floating aircraft carrier, *Cloudbase* in *Captain Scarlet*, the sophistication of the programmes was increasingly defined by their improbable locations.

After 39 episodes patrolling Sector 25 of the galaxy in the year 2062, Robert the Robot bleated his catchphrase 'Full Power... on our way home' for the last time and Anderson switched his attentions to the United States market and colour with his new venture, **Stingray**. The rest is pretty much history as the golden age of Supermarionation yielded up its three most enduring series. *Stingray*, the Fireball XL5 of the oceans, followed by *Thunderbirds* and then *Captain Scarlet And The Mysterons*.

APF had now become Century 21 Productions with vast studios in Slough and by the time filming began on the second *Thunderbirds* movie, *Thunderbird 6*, miniaturisation techniques had progressed to allow

A Supermarionated villain, costumes from Liberace, eyebrows styled after Denis Healey

reduction of the size of the puppets' heads to more human proportions. creating greater realism in this and the productions that followed, *Captain Scarlet*, *Joe 90* and *The Secret Service*.

It is hard to imagine, in hindsight, why Grade saw fit to cancel the second series of *Thunderbirds* after just six episodes had been made. *Captain Scarlet* was dark and moody, while, in truth, *Joe 90* and *The Secret Service* were both woeful – *Joe 90* not helped, today, by the hero's curious resemblance to John Major. The last of the Supermarionation series, *The Secret Service*, curiously cast spoonerism's prime protagonist, Dr Stanley Unwin, as Father Unwin the parish priest who secretly worked for secret law enforcement agency BISHOP (British Intelligence Service Headquarters Operation Priest) aided by a miniaturised assistant.

From then on, Gerry Anderson would be a live action man but ironically, in his desperation to escape from puppets, he lost the ability to engender in kids of all ages the wonderful anticipation that 'anything can happen in the next half hour.'

★★★ Talent ★★★

It might be time to get a sense of perspective here. Talent contests are deeply insignificant events which have about as much to do with unearthing talent as Sid Little does with comedy. None of the most famous entertainers of the last 50 years (Elvis, the Beatles, Madonna, Bob Dylan, the Stones) have been unearthed in a TV talent show.

Although the fact that nine million Brits voted in the *Pop Idol* final (compared to the less than seven million of us who vote in local elections) is, as Motty might say, 'quite remarkable', and the contest proved to be as addictive as junk food, it's hard not to pine for the good old days when a contest was won by a device as simple and as unreliable as a clapometer – and we mean that most sincerely folks, yes we really do. And as for Simon 'Mr Nasty' Cowells, those of us who remember *New Faces* can't help feeling he's an inferior knock off of Tony Hatch.

Opportunity Knocks ITV 1956–78

Hughie Greene's show gave us Les Dawson, Peters And Lee (he was blind, they both sang, millions wished they were deaf), the late Lena Zavaroni, Pam Ayres, Mary Hopkin and world famous pianist (say it very carefully) Bobby Crush. They also discovered New World, a trio of middle-of-the-road Mungo Jerry clones ('Sister Jane you gotta get out soon') prosecuted for allegedly trying to fix the vote, an episode which could form a great sequel to *Quiz Show*. The clapometer did its best not to discover **Su Pollard**, who was beaten by a singing dog. The souvenir *Opportunity Knocks Winners* album, promoted under the naïve but appealing slogan 'It's a great gift!' is a collector's item. And we mean that most sincerely folks, we really do. As for **Bob Says Opportunity Knocks**, let's move on. 245

Matthew Kelly, housewives' favourite, with all the patter of a racehorse

Stars In Their Eyes ITV 1990–

Matthew Kelly, as **Half Man Half Biscuit** put it, is the housewives' favourite who should have been a racehorse. Certainly, he seems ill at ease with any social interaction more complex than giving a horse a lump of sugar. His very awkwardness with the contestants he's chaperoning is part of this series' enduring attraction. You can tune in to marvel ('Doesn't he sound like Freddie Mercury?' 'No, not really') at the verisimilitude of some of these contestants. But much of the morbid fascination is watching a host so gauche you think that the Duke of Edinburgh would be more sympatico. As for his jokes, suffice to say they're not as amusing as his wardrobe.

★★★ Talk ★★★

After 20 minutes of **Trisha**, you might wish TV had killed the art of conversation. Although, to be fair you'll feel the same after three minutes of **Kilroy**. At least with Trisha, she's been there and suffered that: her sister committed suicide, her gay HIV-positive husband had an affair with one of her researchers and after throwing him out, she had a breakdown of her own, recovering, meeting and marrying a psychiatrist.

For a compellingly bad talk show, you need Americans – willing participants in the organised cruelty business who will do anything to become famous, even if it means becoming infamous first. The genre's queen (even though she's about to abdicate) is Oprah; Rosie O' Donnell (a white version with no pretensions to acting) has vied for the throne (unlikely now she's come out as a lesbian). Jerry Springer and Geraldo Rivera compete for the honour of the genre's black prince. The truly frightening thing about Springer isn't how successful he became, nor even that (sensing trash talk has had its day) he is rebranding himself as a country singer/songwriter, it's that he was once voted Mayor of Cincinatti.

★★★ Telenovelas ★★★

Telenovelas is more than just a Latin American term for soaps. Although pundits, scholars and even TV execs themselves can't quite agree on the differences. The form dates back to the 1940s when Felix B Caignet's *The Right To Be Born* was made into a radio serial (heard throughout South America), comic book, movie and novel. Novelist Mario Vargas Lhosa later recalled 'It had such a following that it was said that a man in the street could listen to the episodes of *El Derecho De Nacer* [The Right To Be Born] by Felix B Caignet in any area in Lima since every household was listening to it.'

The production of these novelas for radio became industrialised in Cuba but soon, with TV and the backing of advertisers like Colgate, producing a native telenovela became as big a symbol of national pride as having a good football team. Today, telenovelas are one of South America's most lucrative exports. (Venezuela, for example, makes more money selling these series than it does out of exporting pulp, paper or cars.) They thrive on melodrama, narrative closure, elaborate plotting and, unlike many British and American soaps, they thrive in prime-time.

The makers of these telenovelas feel free to indulge in politics. Jose Inoencio, the main character of the Brazilian **Renascer** (*Revival*) actually commented on the corruption scandal in Congress, saying 'The best solution is not to close the Congress but to clean it, get rid of all the crooks and throw them into jail.' It's almost as if Steve McFadden was to stand up in the Queen Vic and declare that it would be a betrayal of our national interest if we joined the euro.

Telenovelas also touch on themes, such as class or racial division, which most north American or British soaps ignore. But the really crucial difference between telenovelas and soaps is that telenovelas like *Renascer* are watched by the whole family, in a way that only *Dallas* and *Dynasty* managed on US prime-time TV. (Even today in the UK, women watch twice as many hours of soaps per week as men, despite the relatively strong pull of *EastEnders* and *Coronation Street*.)

Yo Soy Betty La Fea RCN 2000

Colombian telenovela *I Am Betty, The Ugly One* starring a (comparatively) ugly secretary called Betty who works in an ailing fashion house has ratings British soaps only dream of. Seven out of ten Colombians watch the series which stars a beautiful actress called **Ana Maria Orozco**, who only looks plain after 40 minutes in the make-up chair during which her hair is greased and her teeth are braced. The series hogs the ratings in Chile, Ecuador, El Salvador, Mexico, Panama, Peru and on Spanish language TV stations (such as Telemundo) in the US. In Ecuador, Congress suspended a late night debate for 30 minutes to watch an episode. The first series ran for 18 months until a member of the cast suggested they needed a holiday. Waiting for a sequel, fans are consoling themselves on the Internet: the show currently generates as many searches as *ER*.

★★★ Teletext ★★★

In 1972, the BBC and ITV announced details of a revolutionary television information service, the BBC's offering to be called Ceefax, ITV's, Oracle. Thirty years later, although every terrestrial channel has their own version, it remains an underrated service. For some reason we prefer to make life hard for ourselves, looking to newspapers for world events, the Yellow Pages for the nearest plumber, and the Internet for cheap holidays. But you can find all these things at the click of the text button on your TV remote, and check out petrol prices in Latvia and the location of your nearest chicken farm to boot. The news is presented succinctly, with mispellings but without hype. What more could you want from your TV?

★★★ Themes ★★★

If there's one criterion that marks out a TV theme as a cult classic, it's not its ability to rattle around the head for days on end, nor the fact that it's written by **John Barry** (although that helps). But it is its likelihood to be 'named in one', to use a phrase coined by that TV show within a show, **Name That Tune**. There isn't a **Hawaii Five-O** fan alive who on hearing the clipped opening 'Da' in Mort Stevens' action-packed theme, doesn't pick up a mental paddle. But not all TV themes are as cool as those penned by the likes of Stevens, Barry and **Lalo Schifrin** (*Mission: Impossible*). You certainly wouldn't want to be caught humming anything from the

Tony Hatch/Jackie Trent portfolio, which includes **Neighbours** (no, it counts for nothing with us that he wrote 'Downtown' or 'Don't Sleep In The Subway Darling'). Ironically, Hatch, whose **Crossroads** theme was given a twangy Wings treatment, was the **New Faces** panellist's most outspoken in his musical judgements on the would-be songsters.

★ Ten quite remarkable TV themes ★

Top Cat (William Hanna, Joseph Barbera, Hoyt Curtin and E Timmens) 'The most effec-tu-al Top Cat/Whose intellectual close friends get to call him TC/Providing it's with Dignity...' Tip top lyrics and a swinging big band sound for everyone's favourite alley cat.

The Persuaders (John Barry) 'Dum, dum, di dum, dum' – enough said.

Secret Agent Man (PF Sloan & S Barri) You may not remember the show (as formulaic as its title) but the song was number one in the US charts for 11 weeks in 1966. Writer PF Sloan had had a higher profile hit in 1965 with the epic 'Eve Of Destruction' – but for us this is his signature tune.

Wait Till Your Father Gets Home Kids still like to get their way and, as this theme from this ahead-of-its-time 1970s Hanna Barbera animation proved, what Daddy didn't know usually didn't hurt him.

The X-Files (Mark Snow) 'Duh, duh, duh duh, duh, duh...' Chuck in an eerie whistle and you have one spooky Mulder of a theme.

Twin Peaks/Laura Palmer's Theme (Angelo Badalamenti) Shame the lass didn't hang around long enough to hear her haunting tune.

The Twilight Zone (Marius Constant) As compulsive as a savoury snack.

Hawaii Five-O (Mort Stevens) Deserved to be number one but sadly only made it to number four by The Ventures. Ripe for a remix though, Mr Slim.

Seinfeld (Jonathan Wolff) The perfect spiky anti-theme.

Tales Of The Unexpected (Ron Grainer) As magical as the swaying girl.

You can sample some of TV's finest themes at these sites:

TV Cream Themes http://tv.cream.org/themes
Cult Television Theme Tune Music www.culttelly.co.uk/music.html
Necro's Domain www.necrosdomain.co.uk/tvthemes
MeTV www.tvthemetunes.net

★★★ Time Travel ★★★

A significant strand of science-fiction entertainment offers travels through time rather than space. Nearly every sci-fi series has featured a time tripping episode, despite *Star Trek Voyager* captain **Kathryn Janeway**'s justifiable complaint that the paradoxes involved are stupifying: 'The past is the future, the future is the past... It gives me a headache!' Time travel is a staple of anthology shows like **The Twilight Zone**. And in recent years the 'caught in a time loop' premise of *Groundhog Day* has been borrowed – usually to good effect – for episodes of every genre show worth its salt, from *The X-Files* to *Lois And Clark*, and, in a good twist on a time trap within time travel, *Seven Days*. No wonder several series have been entirely devoted to breeching the fourth dimension.

Crime Traveller BBC1 1997

BBC's short-lived but cult time travelling series teamed cop Jeff Slade (*EastEnders*' **Michael French**) with scientist Holly Turner (*Red Dwarf*'s **Chloe Annett**), who just happened to have whipped up a time machine to go back before the crime took place to solve it. Very handy.

Dr Who BBC1 1963–89, 1996

Doctor Who survived by taking on board the need to change. When **William Hartnell**, cast as the crusty alien time traveller whose ship (the TARDIS) looks like a police telephone box, left the show, it was realised no script had specified he couldn't change into a completely

The best Dr Who even if he had the worst pet, K9

250

different person. Hartnell fell down in battle with Cybermen to spring up again a week later as **Patrick Troughton** and face his worst enemies, the trundling Daleks. Troughton, whose tenure was marked by black-and-white monster shows, was succeeded by **Jon Pertwee**, in dashing colour with *Avengers*-like action in *Quatermass*-like invaded Englands and a strong showing by **Roger Delgado** as the Doctor's Time Lord nemesis, the Master. Tom Baker took over in 1974 and, as the longest-serving Doctor, appeared in arguably the show's high-points. But by the end of Baker's tenure, scariness from concerned busybodies prompted a sad drift to knockabout comedy, with the introduction of a Scrappy Doo-like robot dog K9. In the 1980s, the Doctor was played by **Peter Davison**, **Colin Baker** and **Sylvester McCoy**. The show occasionally flickered into life, but was mostly content to play to fans and trade on recycled monsters. **Paul McGann** was fine in the TV movie, but the story disappointed; the Doctor has been rested since, but seems likely to return eventually.

Quantum Leap BBC2 1989–93

For five seasons the unsuccessful efforts of physicist Sam Beckett (**Scott Bakula**) to return home after his time-is-a-ball-of-string project 'went a little kaka', engaged viewers as his consciousness leapt into a succession of other people's bodies to right wrongs. Typically these were ordinary people in a nostalgic odyssey between the 1950s and 1980s, although Sam did 'become' Elvis, Bigfoot and a serial killer. Aided by holographic Al Calavicci (**Dean Stockwell**) and probability tips from computer Ziggy, Sam tackled racism, sexism (Sam leapt into women in several episodes), disability and revisions of history, most controversially with a disturbing two-parter in which Sam leapt into Lee Harvey Oswald. In the ambiguous final episode, fans were saddened to learn that Dr Beckett never returned home. But Bakula would leap 150 years forward to captain the latest Starship Enterprise.

Sapphire And Steel ITV 1979–82

Shaun O'Riordan's dark suspense telefantasy was ahead of its time (to coin a phrase). Using ESP (**Joanna Lumley**'s sensitive Sapphire), strength (former U.N.C.L.E. agent **David McCallum**'s reserved Steel), an ability to suspend time and the occasional technical expertise of Silver (**David Collings**), the mysterious agents repelled menaces from other realities that broke through weak spots in the corridor of time. Whether the agents were humans from the future or supernatural was ambiguous, but there were 34 half-hour episodes in serial form, most memorably the 'Railway Station story' about a ghost-hunter releasing a horrifying dark power. Unfortunately production company ATV lost its franchise, tragically stranding the duo in a bleak eternal prison.

Timeslip ITV 1970–71

ATV's spiffing children's show was an educationally-friendly, 26-episode science fantasy in which youngsters Simon and Liz (**Spencer Banks** and **Cheryl Burfield**) slipped through a time portal to visit their own pasts and futures. There they learned about the environment, confronted medical experimentation and saw technological advances while having some scary adventures and an aggravating military scientist Traynor (**Dennis Quilley**) to hamper them.

The Time Tunnel BBC1 1968

This seminal venture from king of genre schlock **Irwin Allen** (*Lost In Space, Land Of The Giants,* et al) looms large in aficionados' memories but lasted only 30 episodes after declining into cheesy hokum. Scientists Doug Phillips (**Robert Colbert**) and Tony Newman (erstwhile pop star **James Darren**) became trapped in the swirling Op Art vortex, helplessly observed by lab colleagues as they unwittingly plopped into historic battles and vainly tried to warn disbelieving military personnel of the imminent attack on Pearl Harbour, or disbelieving *Titanic* sailors of the imminent iceberg collision, et cetera. Weirdly, the duo always ended adventures back in the clothes they acquired on the *Titanic* in the first episode (exactly where they wound up in the last, doomed, apparently, to time's spin cycle). Even more weirdly they could always converse with Trojans, Genghis Khan, French revolutionaries and aluminium foil-wrapped invaders from outer space.

★★★ Trash ★★★

One person's trash TV is somebody else's **Panorama**. Okay, not quite, but you get the drift. In Russia, the made-in-Mexico saga *The Rich Also Cry* was seen as the first step on a very slippery slope, at the bottom of which lay Jerry Springer. Yet in America, despite talk of a backlash against Springer's ilk, producers are still coming up with new twists on human misery.

Cheaters Channel 5 2001

'Cheaters chronicles inspirational stories of humankind.' That's what the makers say. Each week, a person asks the show to check up on their significant other, whom they believe is cheating on them. The partner is stalked, filmed (lots of juicy grainy footage), and the results are shown to the poor cuckold. As they stew in their emotional juices, the host asks them if they'd like to talk to their partner. The poor saps usually say yes and they are driven to their rendezvous, once the host has checked that the partner is certain to be caught in flagrante. If the show says anything about human nature, it's in the surprising statistic that nine out of ten couples who are exposed on this show do actually stay together.

Loft Story Endemol/M6 2001–

The French can't see what the big deal was with Helen and Paul in **Big Brother**. In *Loft Story*, the issue was not if the scantily clad young men and women living in a loft for ten weeks would go mattress surfing but how. Even Gallic resignation has limits and 250 people dumped garbage in front of the TV studio's office in May 2001 to protest against trash TV. Yet 52 per cent of the population tuned in to watch the show, obviously encouraged by a government warning that the programme 'undermined human dignity'.

The Pet Psychic Animal Planet 2001–

If you missed **Sonya Fitzpatrick**'s series, fear not, you can still talk to your pet. How? Just chill out and encourage your pet to chill out, say your animal's name telepathically. It helps if you visualise the creature as you're doing this because you can send the picture and the pet's name to them.

253

Having accomplished all that, just ask your pet if there's anything it would like you to do for it. Imagine the pet is sending a reply and accept whatever your imagination thinks the reply is. Acknowledge the answer. Continue to ask questions and trust whatever answers your imagination gives you. We're only telling you this to spare you the pain of watching the show.

★★★ TV movies ★★★

Movies made for TV have a reputation for being bad, and – in the case of those 'disease of the week' true stories – they often are. As a rule of thumb, it's best to avoid any TV movies starring **Cheryl Ladd** or **Jaclyn Smith**, someone from the cast of *Dallas* or *Knots Landing*, or Jack Scalia (a TV movie stalwart who wouldn't know a good script if it slapped him round the face), and any movie whose title includes the words 'Danielle Steele's…'

The Billionaire Boys' Club Channel 4 1987

TV movie director supreme Marvin Chomsky helmed this 1987 drama that's – you guessed it – based on a true story. When a wealthy business-man is murdered, a list of instructions of how to commit the crime is found at the scene, and it emerges that a group of ambitious men led by Joe Hunt (**Judd Nelson**) may be involved. One of the most successful 'true crime' TV movies of the time, this featured a relatively unknown cast (apart from *Breakfast Club* star Nelson and **Ron Silver** as the victim) and sent Nelson on his journey from promising Brat Pack actor to the man reduced to starring as a killer in the dire *Cabin By The Lake* TV movies.

The Day After SCI FI channel 1983

In the early 1980s, TV producers tried to depict the possible aftermath of nuclear war in the graphic British TV film *Threads* (lots of vomiting and hair falling out) and in this glossy American TV movie with **Jason Robards**, **Steve Guttenberg** and **JoBeth Williams** in the cast. The grisly truth of what would actually happen following a nuclear explosion was toned down a bit for American audiences, but this still drew impressive audience figures as it focused on the people trying to rebuild a society after such an event rather than the radiation poisoning (and side effects) that might have turned the tea-time audience's stomachs.

The Deliberate Stranger BBC1 1986

Everyone loves a good serial-killer story, especially when it is based on true events. And there was no subject more fascinating than Ted Bundy, the American serial killer who was a suave, good-looking man, respected by friends, associates and family, all of whom were unaware that he was stalking and murdering young women in his spare time. **Mark Harmon**, best known as a smooth doctor in *St Elsewhere* (and, in 1986, when this was broadcast, *People Magazine*'s Sexiest Man Of The Year), was suitably sinister (and dashing at the same time) as the enigmatic Bundy, who – you'll be glad to know – was finally captured and executed.

Duel BBC1/2 1971

Steven Spielberg's first movie (made when he was 23) was made for TV on a tight budget, yet remains one of his most interesting films. Made in 1971, it stars **Dennis Weaver** as an ordinary man setting off on a long car journey who finds himself pursued by a rusting oil tanker intent on running him off the road (you never see who the driver is). Based on a story by Richard Matheson (whose stories have also been adapted into episodes of *The Twilight Zone*), **Duel** was filmed in just 16 days with a sparse script, yet has been much imitated and debated – are the man's desperate attempts to escape and the lack of help from others a tale about urban alienation or man against machines or simply a terrific chiller?

The Executioner's Song Channel 4 1982

This award-winning 1982 TV movie has an impressive pedigree – it was based on novelist **Norman Mailer**'s best-selling book and starred a young up-and-coming actor by the name of **Tommy Lee Jones**. He plays real-life convict Gary Gilmore, a killer who campaigned to be executed in the electric chair rather than face life imprisonment. It's depressing stuff thanks to the subject matter, but brilliantly performed by Jones and his co-stars **Rosanna Arquette**, **Christine Lahti** and **Eli Wallach**.

My Name Is Bill W BBC1/2 1989

Even better than your average disease of the week movie is a TRUE disease of the week movie, like this well-played film about the forming of Alcoholics Anonymous (cheery stuff, then) starring **James Woods** as the man drinking himself to death until he meets another alcoholic, Dr Bob Smith (**James Garner**) and they decide to kick the booze together.

Take Me Home: The John Denver Story Sky 2000

Few TV movies are as laughably dreadful as this biopic of famed country and western singer **John Denver**, here played by Chad (brother of Rob) Lowe, sporting a career-ending wig and delivering a performance almost as false as his hair. What makes this so funny (in a twisted sort of way) is the dialogue about the beauty of flying, delivered deadpan by Lowe and **Kristin Davis** (of *Sex And The City* fame) as his wife, that takes on new meaning when you remember Denver died at the controls of his plane.

★★★ Variety ★★★

Bruce's Big Night Out ITV 1978

Derek and Clive said it best. Well, Clive did. 'You'll never compete with Bruce Forsyth on a Saturday evening because he's really chummy! Isn't he really chummy?! Really, isn't he?! Innee nice?! I'n' 'e!! Come on, enjoy yourself! Come on, Dudley, ha-a-a-a-a!! Got Dudley on the show, let's have a tune [random plonking on piano]. Ah-ha-ha-ha!! Have a tune, come on!! Ha ha!! Have a tune!! Ha ha ha ha ha!!' Pete and Dud's alter egos also alleged that the national treasure that is Bruce couldn't sing, dance or do anything else. That wasn't quite true, but as this misguided bid for the big-time showed, he isn't Broadway calibre – enter *Play Your Cards Right*.

Sunday Night At The London Palladium ITV 1955–67, 1973, 2000

Sometimes 28 million people (ie more than half the British population) would tune in to watch this (though you have to remember the lack of competition then, especially on a Sunday night). Yet hundreds of viewers would phone **ATV** the next day to say which acts they wanted to shoot. So although the ratings impressed, nobody knows how many were watching to select the victims of their next fantasy homicide. Officially, whenever anyone recalls this **Sir Lew Grade** and **Val Parnell** extravaganza, it is to mention the high-kicking Tiller girls, the comperes (**Leslie Crowther**, **Bruce Forsyth** and **Roger Moore** among them) or the fact that the Beatles and Bob Hope were on. Yet for many of us, it's the details that stick in the memory: the comedians who laughed at their own jokes – often beating the audience to it, **Harry Secombe** falling through a trap door, **Mario Lanza** accidentally punching his bodyguard, and moustachioed slapstick master **Mr Pastry** (Richard Hearne). Eat your heart out, Ceasar's Palace.

Wheeltappers' And Shunters' Social Club ITV 1974–76

'First prize in the raffle is a diving suit… no, it's a divan suite'. Those who saw this variety series, set in a fictional northern working men's club, can still hear the bell, followed by the gormless drawl of pretend chairman **Colin Crompton**: 'We've had a meeting of the committee…' Today,

Her name was Lola – and so was theirs

glimpsed on Granada Plus, the series seems like a social document, a *Saturday Night Sunday Morning* with gags, **Buddy Greco** (with oversized bow tie) and Canadian knife twirler, Tina. Crompton was the chairman and **Bernard Manning** the insulting compere. Of Ronnie Hilton (the singer of 'No Other Love'), he said: 'If there's ever a nuclear war, go to this man's house because he hasn't had a hit in years.' Among the waitresses, who served real beer to the audience, was Our Vera, **Liz Dawn**, from *Corrie*.

★★★ War ★★★

Colditz BBC1 1972–74

Snarling sadistic Germans, one token decent German, stiff upper-lipped British officers getting up to pranks (including the prisoner who pretended to go mad and then really did), Robert Wagner's Canadian accent (when you heard it you realised he'd never sounded completely American anyway), David McCallum, and a fantastic children's board game. Yep, *Colditz* really did have it all.

Hogan's Heroes ITV 1967–71

Billy Wilder's *Stalag 17* with all the edginess smoothed away, the Germans turned into caricatures of incompetence (especially Colonel Klink – his surname, being an allusion to the fact that prisoners were put in the 'clink', set the level for the show's humour) and the Americans running

McCallum recognises a Colditz inmate: 'I say, aren't you Jonathan Hart? Where's Freeway?'

the POW camp for their own ends. Somehow, with all these moronic ingredients, it worked. Mind you, the funniest skit appeared only in one of **Denis Norden's** interminable *It'll Be Alright On The Night*s, when one of the POWs, instead of lighting a colleague's ciggie with his lighter, set fire to the man's nasal hair. Happy days. The sitcom made it onto German TV as *Ein Kaefig Voller Helden* (*A Cage Full Of Heroes*) but it wasn't a hit – not because the Germans can't laugh at themselves – but because the dubbing was as bad as the worst lip synchronisation you ever saw on Top Of The Pops. The cast of German voices was also the same as for **M*A*S*H** which must have given viewers an unsettling feeling of deja vu.

Holocaust BBC1 1978

When shown on the BBC in 1978 over four consecutive nights, writer Gerald Green's **Holocaust** received a mixed reception. The *New York Times*, never short of an opinion, called it 'untrue, offensive and cheap'. The US TV premiere was also marred by some unfortunate juxtapositions between programme and commercials: an ad warning against kitchen odours following a scene where Adolf Eichmann complains that the smell of the crematoria at Auschwitz makes dining there unpleasant. The mini-series introduced viewers to the tragedy of the Jewish Weiss family, who one by one succumbed to Nazi rule and to a young German lawyer Eric Dorf (Michael Moriarty), seduced by the Nazis and the SS. Critics justifiably complained of a certain soapiness yet there were powerful moments, notably when Dorf explains why it is the Nazis' duty to keep killing Jews. The series boasted an impressive cast with **Ian Holm**, **James Woods**, **Sam Wanamaker**, **Tom Bell** and **Meryl Streep**. The mini-series had a very powerful effect in West Germany where half of the adult population watched it. The drama broke a 35-year taboo on public discussion of the subject and the response was so overwhelming that the government cancelled the statute of limitation on Nazi war crimes.

M*A*S*H BBC2 1973–84

'I'd like a dry martini, Mr. Quoc, a very dry martini. A very dry, arid, barren, desiccated, veritable dustbowl of a martini. I want a martini that

Corporal Klinger waves a fond farewell to the Korean war. But only in his dreams

could be declared a disaster area. Mix me just such a martini.' It's the incidental pleasures that surprise when you catch up with the famous mobile army surgical hospital. Like **Captain Hawkeye Pierce** ordering a martini after a bad year at the office. Like **Loudon Wainwright** popping up as a Roland-style balladeer to comment on the action when the nurses are sent to another unit, after threats of bombing. True, the series went off when **Wayne Rogers** (Trapper John) left and the finale was a bit soppy, but how many other sitcoms do you know that could deliver lines like this in prime-time US TV and hold on to a massive audience? 'Every war has its cute things. World War II had nice songs. The War of the Roses had nice flowers. We've got booms, they had blooms. Actually, every war has its 'ooms. You've got doom, gloom, everybody ends in a tomb, the planes go zoom, and they bomb your room.'

The Monocled Mutineer BBC1 1986

The series that made **Paul McGann** and unmade a BBC director general, **Alasdair Milne**. As the monocled mutineer Percy Topliss in **Alan Bleasdale**'s drama, McGann was a revelation. But the press was full of other revelations, claiming that this series, advertised as an 'enthralling true-life story' was riddled with historical inaccuracies and dramatic licence. They had a point. Not a big one – but it would have been better for all concerned if the 'true-life' claim had never been made. Judged as a drama (as even the *Daily Telegraph* admitted), it was probably the best thing on the telly that year. While the portrayal of the officers as upper-class twits is a tad simplistic, the drama had more genuine power and indignation than a hundred *Daily Mail* editorials. In the ensuing row, Milne lost his job. So, as in the Bleasdale drama, the establishment had the final say.

Private Schulz BBC2 1981

Underrated black comedy in which the eponymous German fraudster (**Michael Elphick**) is seconded to the SS to work for mad Major Neuheim (**Ian Richardson**) who wants to flood Britain with used fivers. Rather than telling the Major to grow up and keep his adolescent fantasies to himself,

Schultz does his best to oblige. All this and **Billie Whitelaw** doing her Marlene Dietrich impersonation as good time gal Bertha.

Tenko BBC1 1981–84

This series may have felt like *Bridge On The River Kwai* in drag but it started as an episode of *This Is Your Life*. Creator **Lavinia Warner** was researching the life of a nursing corps officer and decided there was scope for an *Omnibus* programme and then the TV series. The Stephs (Beacham and Cole) are the inmates who remain in the memory. Mercifully **Bert Kwouk**, a brave choice as Major Yamauchi, doesn't choose to jump out of wardrobes or from roofs to attack the POWs unawares when they return to their tents after a long day's march.

★ ★ ★ Weather ★ ★ ★

In the 1980s, thanks to the Tribe Of Toffs' 'John Kettley Is A Weatherman', most of us knew who Kettley and **Michael Fish** were, although on the wrong day we still mixed up Ian McCaskill and Bill Giles (McCaskill is the one who wasn't accused of bullying his colleagues). But these days you'd be lucky to find one person who can distinguish Rob McElwee from David Braine (we only know because we looked it up).

There are two exceptions to the rule. The radical cutting edge **This Morning With Richard And Judy** starred **Fred** (no last name necessary) who shunned the traditional grey suit attire of BBC weather presenters for a line of Noel Edmonds jumpers, many sent in by grannies who thought he'd catch his death on his weather map at Mersey docks. This floating map was the real innovation: Fred recklessly jumping from the north west of England to Ireland, viewers watching to see if he fell in.

Fred set out to flout convention. The BBC's **Michael Fish** hadn't wanted to stand out from the crowd. But in 1987, he proclaimed to the lunchtime news-viewing public that, 'a woman rang the BBC and said that there was a hurricane on the way. Well, if you are watching, don't worry – there isn't.' Twelve hours later the worst storm since 1945 hit the south east of England, in which 19 people died. This ensured that his entire career will be unfairly encapsulated into one remark and confirmed to the entire British nation that weather presenters are not to be trusted.

★★★ Westerns ★★★

The cheaper alternative that killed live drama were filmed series that could build regular audiences and be repeated. And the most American of all genres was a natural to transfer to television. Savvy cowboy star **William Boyd** owned the rights to his movie serials, turning them into instant TV. Hopalong Cassidy blazed the trail for other B-movie cowboy stars and radio stars like **The Lone Ranger**. Women and ethnic minorities got a look in, too: **Annie Oakley** and the famous white-sombreroed Latino champion **The Cisco Kid** with sidekick Pancho (the world's first-ever TV show filmed in colour – even though no one yet had colour). There was cowboy puppet **Howdy Doody** (who had 48 freckles on his face, one for every state in the Union at that time) and 'Out of the night, when the full moon is bri-aye-ight, rode a horseman known as… Zorro.'

In the mid-1950s, adult Westerns suddenly sad-dled up, offering character

Howdy Doody and significant other. Altogether ooky

263

Mean, moody, macho... and that's just Clint Walker's saw

drama along with rootin' tootin' action. Beleaguered film studios like Warner Bros saved themselves by churning out the likes of *Cheyenne*, *Bronco*, *Sugarfoot*, *Colt .45*, and *Maverick*. In 1959 there were 21 Westerns showing on US prime-time every week, many exported globally.

Inevitably, sated audiences tuned to trendier fare. Infrequently, novelty Westerns like **Kung-Fu** captured the popular fancy. The acclaimed 1988 mini-series **Lonesome Dove** reminded people of the missing-presumed-dead genre's pleasures, encouraging new sagebrush saga **The Young Riders** and its spin-offs. But in a sense the Western tradition never died. Many a law man or lone wolf action show is just a Western in modern dress.

The Adventures Of Rin Tin Tin ITV 1954–59

'Yo-oh, Rinty!' Lassie's butch rival, the original German shepherd **Rin Tin Tin** was a puppy rescued from a trench in World War 1 and taken to Hollywood. The handsome wonder pooch became a silent movie sensation and bequeathed star billing to several direct descendants. The 1950s incarnation (actually three dogs) starred with young **Lee Aaker** as orphans Rusty and Rinty, adopted by Lieutenant Rip Masters, Sergeant Biff O'Hara and the cavalry troopers at Fort Apache for fantasy fulfilment heroics that set the tone for such 'boy and his beast buddy' Westerns such as **My Friend Flicka** (1956–59) and **Fury** (1955–60) starring Peter Graves (later **Mission: Impossible**). Other famed Wild West law-enforcing animals for kids include the animated variety: drawling Deputy Dawg and Hanna-Barbera's disaster-prone horse sheriff Quick Draw McGraw with his Mexican burro deputy Baba Looey.

The Adventures Of William Tell ITV 1958–59

Innocent sharpshooter is forced to become an outlaw by the authorities and consoles himself by mounting his trusty steed and leading a mild bunch of buddies to cause much mayhem. Meanwhile the obese villain consoles himself for his failure to catch the bad guy who's really a good guy by tucking into a high cholesterol diet of raw meat followed by more meat. True, William Tell may technically be set in the Swiss Alps (well, Snowdonia, which stood in for the Alps in this series) but this is a Western by any other name, as you can tell from episode titles like 'The Bandit', 'The Killer' and 'The Unwelcome Stranger'. **Conrad Phillips** played Tell in this stirring tale of one man and his crossbow's fight against the Austrians – he still hasn't forgiven them for Falco's 'Rock Me Amadeus'. Created by **Ralph Smart** (who later begat *Danger Man*) the real interest of the series now is in spotting such aspiring thesps as Michael Caine or Frazer Hines.

Bonanza ITV 1959–73

Landmark chronicle of family and land that had the Cartwright menfolk righteously ranching their Nevada spread The Ponderosa. Pa Ben (**Lorne**

★ What we owe to TV Westerns ★

Gunsmoke Without Matt Dillon there might have been no 'mean cup of coffee' references in *Twin Peaks*. Sam Peckinpah also wrote for the show and Burt Reynolds, pre-toupe, was in the cast.

Have Gun, Will Travel Peckinpah and Gene Roddenberry wrote for it.

Maverick Robert Altman and Budd Boetticher were among the directors. Robert Redford and Clint Eastwood guested.

Rawhide Clint began rollin', rollin', rollin', to fame as Rowdy Yates.

Wagon Train Clint earned acting spurs, Aaron Spelling was one of the writers and the series gave Roddenberry the idea of a '*Wagon Train* in space' which became *Star Trek*.

And finally...

Bonanza Gave Robert Altman work, imprinted the image of a burning map on the world's long-term memory and popularised a new kind of rummy.

Greene) and his three sons – cool, upright Adam (**Pernell Roberts**), gentle giant Hoss (**Dan Blocker**) and wild-oats-sowing heart-throb Little Joe (**Michael Landon**) – had Chinese cook Hop Sing and the space to cater for a continuous stream of troubled guests when they weren't tied up with romance or rustlers. In 1964 the stars received record salaries of $10,000 each per episode. *Bonanza*'s spectacular Lake Tahoe locations (captured by directors including a young **Robert Altman**) were credited with selling more colour TV sets than anything else. The series literally lost heart when the much-loved Blocker died.

Branded ITV 1965–66

Not every cowboy had a supportive sidekick. Some roamed the West as lone, two-fisted dispensers of rough justice while clearing their names or seeking revenge, redemption and reward. **Chuck Connors**, as Captain

Jason McCord, is the prototypical such hero, a precursor of **Dirty Harry**, with a grudge against authority – in Chuck's case, because he was wrongly discharged from the US Cavalry. **Steve McQueen** had become a star in a similar role as bounty hunter Josh Randall in **Wanted: Dead Or Alive** (1958–61). While Chuck was dispensing justice, **Wagon Train**'s Robert Horton was roaming the West as a left-for-dead amnesiac in **A Man Called Shenandoah**. This tradition had a final flowering in the 1980s with **Elmore Leonard**'s TV movies, **Desperado**, a hyper-*Fugitive*, where Duel McCall is accused of a mounting series of crimes he didn't commit.

Cheyenne ITV 1958–61

One of the first grown-up Westerns. Pre-eminent 'loner', brooding Cheyenne Bodie (hunky **Clint Walker**), was a half-breed returned from the Civil War, making a stand against injustice, mob rule and bullies. Walker walked (into history as TV's first contract holdout) when Warner Bros declined to raise his salary and put *Bronco*, starring Ty Hardin, on in his slot. Fan uproar forced the studio to capitulate to Walker's demands and return *Cheyenne*, moving *Bronco* elsewhere.

Davy Crockett ITV 1954–55

What can be claimed as the first mini-series was a two-part adventure for the *Frontierland* series in Walt Disney's massive Wednesday night plug-the-theme-park show Disneyland. **Fess Parker** played the famed back-woodsman and was back the next season in a three-parter, blazing trails, whuppin' hostile Indians and river pirates, getting elected to Congress and making a dying stand at the Alamo. The resulting cultural phenom-enon was unprecedented. As episodes repeated several times, America went completely nuts buying over $100m dollars' worth of merchandise – replicas of Davy's trusty rifle 'Betsy', racoonskin caps and hit record 'Davy Crockett, King Of The Wild Frontier' – were everywhere.

Gunsmoke ITV 1955–70

It was one of the first prime-time oaters but when the dust settled, Dodge City's Marshal Matt Dillon (**James Arness**) was the only Western hero left

267

★ Know your heroes ★

Range riders, singing cowboys or masked avengers, where would they have been without their trusty steeds, their faithful companions, their trademark accessories and their signature tunes?

Hopalong Cassidy
Played by: William Boyd.
Rode the range from:1945 to 1952.
Trusty steed: Topper.
His sidekick: Red (Edgar Buchanan).
His look: all black, the biggest ten-gallon hat.
His signature tune: 'Hopalong Cassidy March'.

The Lone Ranger
Played by: Clayton Moore.
Rode the range from: 1949 to 1957.
Trusty steed: Silver.
His sidekick: Tonto (Jay Silverheels).
His look: The famous mask and powder blue duds.
His signature tune: Rossini's 'William Tell Overture'.

Gene Autry
Rode the range from: 1950 to 1956.
Trusty steed: Champion.
His sidekick: Pat (Pat Butram).
His accessory: Guitar.
His signature tune: 'Back In The Saddle Again'.

Roy Rogers
Rode the range from: 1951 to 1957, returning for a reprise in 1962/63.
Trusty steed: Trigger.
His sidekick: Pat (Pat Brady) — who drove a jeep called *Nellybelle*.
His best girl: Wife Dale Evans,

Queen of the West.
Her trusty steed: Buttermilk.
Trigger's buddy: Bullet, the dog.
Their song: 'Happy Trails To You'.

The Cisco Kid
Played by: Duncan Rinaldo.
Rode the range from: 1950 to 1956.
Trusty steed: Diablo.
His sidekick: Pancho (Leo Carillo).
His accessories: white sombrero, mariachi suit.
Exit time: 'Hey Ceesco!'

Wild Bill Hickok
Played by: Guy Madison
Rode the range from:1951 to 1958.
Trusty steed: Buckshot.
His sidekick: Jingles (Andy Devine) — whose mount was Joker.
His look: Fringed buckskin.
Catch phrase: 'Hey, Wild Bill, wait for meee!'

Zorro
Played by: Guy Williams.
Rode the range from: 1957 to 1959.
Trusty steeds: Tornado (black) in Los Angeles and Phantom (white) in Monterey.
His sidekick: Bernardo (Gene Sheldon).
His look: all black, Spanish riding hat, mask, cape and sword
His song: 'Zorro'.

standing tall after a record run. Arness, brother of Peter Graves, was recommended by **John Wayne** (he turned down the part but introduced the premiere episode). He entered myth as Dillon, winning showdowns with miscreants and helping troubled wayfarers with his surrogate family – Long Branch Saloon proprietor Miss Kitty (Amanda Blake), no-nonsense Doc Adams (Milburn Stone) and excitable, limping deputy Chester B Goode (**Dennis Weaver**, later urban cowboy cop McCloud).

Have Gun, Will Travel ITV 1959–62

Richard Boone (later Hec Ramsey) was the hard-faced, highly-principled hero in by far the most sophisticated, highbrow Western series ever. It centred on the exploits of gun-for-hire Paladin (real name a mystery), who quoted Shakespeare, Shelley and Socrates. Paladin, whose past was memorably revealed in a final season episode, lived an elegant, cultured life as linguist, pianist, gourmand, gambler and ladies' man in a San Francisco hotel with a Chinese servant Hey Boy (Kam Tong) to fetch his cigars and brandy. When someone used his business card (a chess knight – also embossed on his holster with the words 'Have Gun, Will Travel' – Wire Paladin, San Francisco') he became the highly paid Man In Black who also did pro bono violence for justice's sake. Creator Sam Rolfe (**The Man From U.N.C.L.E.**) also sang 'The Ballad of Paladin'. Meticulously as the show was crafted, it had its sloppy moments: when Paladin's Chinese servant Hey Boy missed a series he was replaced by a female Chinese assistant called, you guessed it, Hey Girl.

The High Chaparral BBC2 1967–71

Having already written about life on the open range on *Bonanza*, **David Dortort** brought us this Western soap about the Cannon family's struggle with life in Arizona. Headed by John Cannon (**Leif Erickson**, formerly William Anderson, before he renamed himself after a Viking king), he was aided (or not) by dim-witted son Blue (later replaced by a character with the even more risible name of Wind), brother Buck (**Cameron Mitchell**), wife Victoria (**Linda Cristal**) and wily brother-in-law Manolito (**Henry Darrow**). Originally called *Rancho Rivera*, the show fitted the

269

liberal attitude of the 1960s with John Cannon as honest as his back was straight. There are those who insist that this show went downhill after Linda Cristal became obsessive about plucking her eyebrows.

The Life And Legend Of Wyatt Earp ITV 1956–57

Debuting the same season as **Gunsmoke** and destined to spend time in the same storied locale of Dodge City, Kansas, this upbeat, pacy, seminal series (sometimes done in cliff-hanger serial form) earnestly drew on a popular biography of Earp that had enshrined the legend without fussin' about facts. **Hugh O'Brian**'s Wyatt was dapper in fancy waistcoats and string tie, gracefully whipping out his Buntline Specials, pistols with foot-long barrels, to tame wild ones, along with deputy Bat Masterson – later the star of his own hit show (1958–61) in the dandy person of **Gene Barry** – brothers Virgil and Morgan, and gambler Doc Holliday. Two hundred and sixty-six episodes followed Earp's adventures from Ellsworth to Dodge (where he never bumped into Matt Dillon) and, inexorably, Tombstone to take on the Clanton Gang. The Gunfight at the OK Corral provided the climax to the ambitious, must-see five-episode finale. The precursor for many a law man show, including **The Lawman** and the science-fiction fantasy Western **The Adventures Of Brisco County Jr** (1993–94).

Lonesome Dove US 1988

This beloved eight-hour adaptation of **Larry McMurtry**'s Pulitzer Prize-winning novel resurrected the Western genre's TV viability. It also earned seven Emmys (a mini-series record), and gave **Robert Duvall** his all-time favourite role as rascally adventurer Augustus McCrae, memorably buddied up with **Tommy Lee Jones** as terse, tyrannical Woodrow Call. Former Texas Rangers bored with the peaceful life, the craggy duo embark on an epic cattle drive to Montana. Embattled by renegade Indians, desperadoes and nature, entangled with indomitable rancher **Angelica Huston** and traumatised saloon whore Diane Lane, the rootin' tootin' troupers triumphantly negotiated multiple sub-plots of birth, death, hardship, horse thieving, hangings and heroism. Followed by a sequel in which **Jon Voight** took Jones' role, another with **James Garner** as Call, and a prequel (**Dead Man's Walk**) starring David Arquette and Jonny Lee Miller.

Maverick ITV 1957–62

'**Maverick** is the name. Riding the trail to who knows where, luck is his companion, gamblin' is his game…' The theme song applied to dandy, unflappable brothers Bret and Bart Maverick (**James Garner**, who departed for films in 1960, and Jack Kelly), late arrival British cousin Beau (**Roger Moore**) and the surprise younger brother Brent (**Robert Colbert**, later of *The Time Tunnel*) in this jaunty adventure comedy. Wins, losses, scams, fisticuffs, narrow escapes from weddings and hangings, and the oft-quoted teachings of Pappy Maverick ('A man does what he has to do… if he can't get out of it') sent up the genre while fans stripped shops of playing cards to practice 'Maverick solitaire'.

Wagon Train ITV 1958–62, BBC1 1962–63

The great transcontinental saga of pioneers forever bound for the promised land of California, this had the imprimatur of genre master **John Ford**, who directed *The Colter Craven Story* and persuaded John Wayne to cameo (his only TV drama appearance) as General Sherman. Starring was Ford fave **Ward Bond**, as wagon master and Civil War veteran Major Seth Adams, with Robert Horton as frontier scout Flint McCullough and Frank McGrath as cook Charlie Wooster. It also had the influential, ever-changing interest of an anthology with guest stars bringing their tales and title names (such as *The Elizabeth McQueeney Story* for **Bette Davis**) to backdrops like Monument Valley. With Bond's death (on location in 1960) and Horton's departure, **John McIntyre** took charge as Chris Hale, with Robert Fuller scouting. It's a tribute to the resilience of the narrative that the wagons kept on rolling through a mammoth 284 episodes, 32 of them at 90 minutes.

Whiplash ITV 1960–61

Little known kangaroo Western. **Peter Graves** (again) starred as an American trying to establish a stagecoach line in lawless 1850s Australia.

After this mission surprisingly plausible, he spent a lot of time hanging around with self-destructing tape.

★★★ Wildlife ★★★

'And here I am standing in a pile of guano.' **David Attenborough** (we recognised the shorts) was indeed standing in a pile of guano or, to use a less formal term, bat shit. Worse, although David was too polite to mention this, it was probably infested with maggots too, attracted by the fact that David was standing in 1,300 years worth of guano. And as if that wasn't bad enough, Attenborough, with his eye for such details, noted that there were around 3,000 cockroaches per square metre in the cave, and the ammonia fumes were so strong that he almost passed out. That was, he later said, his worst experience in 40 years of natural history broadcasting but it was worth it – for us. A final word from David: 'There

'And there I was standing in a cave in a pile of guano...' Wildlife king David bends a passing lemur's ear

is more meaning and understanding in exchanging a glance with a gorilla than with any other animal I know.' He should know. He had his shoe laces untied by a Rwandan gorilla when making **Life On Earth**.

Witches, wizards and fantastical fables

The Addams Family and The Munsters
ITV 1964–66   BBC1 1965–67

The creepy, kooky, mysterious and ooky family, based on **Charles Addams**' cartoons, didn't even have names until they appeared on TV in 1964. Then the world was introduced to Morticia (**Carolyn Jones**), husband Gomez (**John Astin**), their children Pugsley (**Ken Weatherwax**, whose character was called Pubert until producers decided it may be too rude) and Wednesday (**Lisa Loring**), plus Uncle Fester (**Jackie Coogan**), Lurch (**Ted Cassidy**, who later narrated *The Incredible Hulk*), Cousin It (**Felix Silla**, later an ewok in *Return Of The Jedi*) and Thing (the disembodied hand, also played by Cassidy). The series, which, broke new ground in implying Morticia and Gomez had a sex life, only ran for two years, but was spun off into an animated series (1973) and two hit movies. **The Munsters** depicted another odd family who got strange looks from their 'normal' neighbours. **Fred Gwynne** starred as Frankenstein-like funeral director Herman, **Yvonne De Carlo** as his wife Lily, **Al Lewis** as the Dracula-like Grandpa, **Butch Patrick** as son Eddie and **Beverly Owen** as the pretty black sheep of the family cousin Marilyn (Lily tells her: 'Oh Marilyn, those circles under your eyes – how lovely you look').

American Gothic Channel 4 1995–96

A surprisingly twisted (for American TV) series, co-created by Shaun (brother of David) Cassidy, **American Gothic** mixed supernatural forces of good and evil with tales of ordinary folk in the small South Carolina town of Trinity. **Gary Cole** was deeply sinister as Sheriff Lucas Buck, who thinks nothing of resorting to murder to ensure Caleb (**Lucas Black**), an orphan who is really his son, stays on the side of evil. Caleb has help staying 'good' from his cousin Gail (**Paige Turco**) and his dead sister Merlyn (**Sarah Paulson**) who appears to him in visions to try to help. Incredibly creepy stuff (made even more so by Cole's skin-crawling central performance), this was little seen and only ran for 22 episodes.

Bewitched BBC1 1964–76, Channel 4–

Over 250 episodes were made of this comedy (which was the show airing on 4 April 1968 when it was interrupted by a newsflash announcing the shooting of Martin Luther King). In it a nose-twitching witch named Samantha (**Elizabeth Montgomery**) gets into scrapes while married to poor mortal Darrin (played by **Dick York**, and from 1969, **Dick Sargent**) thanks to Endora (**Agnes Moorehead**), her meddling mother who doesn't approve of the witch/mortal mixed marriage. Incredibly silly but addictive, it spawned a 1977 spin-off about Darrin and Samantha's witch daughter called **Tabitha**, starring **Lisa Hartman** and **Robert Urich**.

Catweazle ITV 1969–70

Odd little British children's series. **Geoffrey Bayldon** (who later played the Crowman in the equally strange *Worzel Gummidge*) played the 11th-century wizard who accidentally ends up in the 20th century, accompanied by his toad Touchwood, and is helped by a young boy in his attempts to return to his own time. The results were so hilarious Catweazle, who must have been the Homer Simpson of Norman wizardry, made the same mistake in a second series.

Fantasy Island ITV 1978

Superbly kitsch Aaron Spelling series which ran for 130 episodes from 1978. Like Spelling's creations *The Love Boat* and *Hotel*, this show – about a tropical island (filming was done in Burbank and Kauai in Hawaii) where the guests get to live out their wildest fantasies – was packed with guest stars each week, from **Leslie Nielsen**, **Peter Lawford** and **Juliet Mills** to **Sonny Bono** and **Cyd Charisse**. But the real stars were **Ricardo Montalban** as the white-suited, slightly sinister Mr Roarke, who ran the resort and granted people's wishes (one episode, *Salem*, featuring

The sheriff in American Gothic looks suspiciously like that nice DJ in Midnight Caller

a couple who end up as witches during the Salem Witch Trials), and his diminutive assistant, Tattoo (**Herve Villechaize**, who died in 1993). Tattoo was best known for alerting his boss to new arrivals by chanting 'Da plane, boss, da plane!' The series idea was unsuccessfully revived in 1998, with **Malcolm McDowell** (honest) as Roarke.

Forever Knight Sky One 1996-97

This drama/action series could be seen as a forefather of Joss Whedon's *Angel*, if it wasn't so terrible (sample dialogue: 'I am what I am, and I don't think Betty Ford takes vampires!'). Welsh-born **Geraint Wyn Davies** starred as mid-life-crisis-suffering vampire Nick Knight, who decides he no longer wants to suck human blood and joins the police. Apparently, there's a bit of a crisis of morale among the vampire work-force what with the monotony of the perks and the unsocial hours.

The consummate hosts of Fantasy Island wave back at Corporal Klinger, in Korea and on p260

I Dream Of Jeannie ITV 1966-71, Channel 4

Larry Hagman stars in this everyday tale of an astronaut who, crash-landing on an island, finds a bottle and uncorks it to discover his very own perky genie, named Jeannie (**Barbara Eden**), whom he takes home. Now considered sexist (Jeannie refers to Tony as 'master'), the series eventually married Tony and Jeannie, and is now a kitsch classic.

Randall & Hopkirk Deceased ITV 1969–70

Much as we love Vic and Bob, the phantasmagorical crime-fighting pair were more fun the first time around. The fact that one half of the partnership was a ghost had both pros and cons; white-suited Hopkirk (Kenneth Cope) was only visible to Randall (Mike Pratt, performing in a style one critic referred to as 'relaxed sleep walking'). Creator **Dennis Spooner**, who also wrote for adventure dramas The Avengers and Man In A Suitcase, originally had **Dave Allen** in mind for the show. Allen went but the comedy stayed. However, when the show was sold to the US under the slightly less original title **My Partner The Ghost**, US audiences didn't really get it. Pratt's other stab at pop culture immortality is as composer of 'Little White Bull', as sung by Tommy Steele: 'very sad because he was...'

Sabrina The Teenage Witch ITV 1996–

Teenage actress and TV mogul **Melissa Joan Hart** (who had previously scored a hit as a tot with **Clarissa Explains It All** and now has her own production company with her mum) stars as Sabrina in this US sitcom. The plot? A teenager discovers she is half-mortal and half-witch when she is sent to live with her two aunts (both witches, with a talking cat called Salem). The postcode for Sabrina's home town is the same as for real-life Salem. Just thought you'd like to know.

Tales Of The Unexpected ITV 1979–88

This British anthology series was originally based on stories by **Roald Dahl** (who hosted the first season, followed by **John Houseman** from 1980 until 1984). Filmed cheaply by Anglia TV, the half-hour episodes (which ended with a twist in the tale) were often noted for the rather wooden

277

acting from all-star casts, who included **Susan George**, **Joan Collins**, **John Gielgud**, **Rod Taylor**, and **Nigel Havers**. Some later episodes were written by Ruth (*Inspector Wexford*) Rendell but sometimes the creepiest thing about the show was **Ron Grainger**'s carousel theme.

★★★ The Wombles ★★★

You've probably already started humming the theme tune so let's all join in: 'Underground, overground, wombling free/The Wombles of Wimbledon Common are we/Making good use of the things that we find/ things that the everyday folks leave behind…' There are those who argue that the Wombles are nothing but a mass-market rip off of **The Clangers**, while many can't forgive all those **Mike Batt**–produced hit singles (the naggingly insidious chorus of 'Remember, member, member, member what a Womble, womble womble you are' is a painful reminder of just how awful the charts were in the 1970s). Doubtless they also gave kids an excuse to drop litter, many likely to respond to Mum's reprimand with, 'Great Uncle Bulgaria will pick it up.'

But having said all that, the Wombles – Bulgaria, Tomsk, Orinoco, Tobermory, Wellington, Bungo and Cholet – are Wimbledon's most famous export after the football club (recently controversially exported to Milton Keynes). And they are bloody hard to dislike, especially Great Uncle Bulgaria (although that Madame Cholet could do with being taken down a peg or two). They weren't initially viewed as a sure-fire hit, what with their goody-two-shoes conservationist ways and their weird names which led parents to demand their kids get out the dreaded atlas in order to prove that yes there is actually a place called Orinoco (if you never had to check, it's a delta in Venezuela – not at all, don't mention it).

Maybe the literary genius of George Bernard Shaw, Somerset Maugham and DH Lawrence rubbed off on creator **Elisabeth Beresford** (the three were friends of her parents). The series launched (on BBC1) in 1973 and seemed to be on for the rest of the 1970s. In 1998 the Beeb brought back the ratings-winner, with four new friends for the original family called Stepney (a Cockney), Obidos (a Brazilian pan piper), Shanshi (Chinese) and Alderney, who lived in a tree house when he wasn't skateboarding. They are fondly remembered by some for rescuing London from a mountain of rubbish, others simply maintain they were rubbish.

★★★ Youth ★★★

While **Teletubbies** and **The Magic Roundabout** are still strangely appealing when you're 15 years older than the target audience (and nursing the mother of all hangovers), TV makers since the 1970s have realised there is a huge teen market who were no longer entertained by **Blue Peter** (shame on them) and wanted their own TV shows.

More Wombles litter

These seem to be divided into four types of mini-genres: gritty (usually British) dramas like **Brookside** spin-off **Damon And Debbie**, teenage angst shows (in which the characters have an impressive adult vocabulary) like **Party Of Five**, teen sitcoms and glossy entertainment (*Beverly Hills 90210*, *Happy Days*) and entertainment shows like the phenomenally successful **SM:TV**. Now, if only someone could get Jason Priestley to present an entertainment show set in a Northern orphanage, we would all be rich.

Beverly Hills 90210 ITV 1991–2000, Sky One

Spoilt, rich and far too pretty to be real people, the kids of Beverly Hills 90210 became an almost instant hit when the series was launched by Aaron Spelling in 1990. The series focused on twins, good guy Brandon (**Jason Priestley**) and slightly less good girl Brenda (**Shannen Doherty**), newly moved to Beverly Hills from Minnesota, and their new (and incredibly wealthy) school friends from West Beverly High, including

279

The original man in black. Okay, apart from Marlon Brando, Elvis, Gene Vincent...

high-school slag with a heart of gold Kelly (**Jennie Garth**), jock Steve (**Ian Zierling**), rich rebel without a cause Dylan (**Luke Perry**, many a teenage girl's pin-up), and creator Spelling's daughter **Tori** as virginal Donna Martin. Apparently glossy and vacuous, the series tackled some serious subjects in the first few years (teen pregnancy, drug addiction) before resorting, like many of Spelling's shows, to sensational plots (Dylan's long -absent dad gets blown up in car bomb) to boost flagging ratings.

The Brady Bunch ITV 1969–73

Altogether now: 'Here's the story, of a lovely lady, who was bringing up three very lovely girls;' (we know you know all the words). Launched in 1969, the series about a widower with three boys who married a widow with three girls (remember it was the 1970s, so there were no divorced families on TV) ran for five years and its mix of squeaky clean family values and cutesy kids became such a hit that it is on TV somewhere in the world at this very minute (scary, huh?). What happened off-screen is slightly more interesting than what happened on it (usually some sibling strife that would make middle child Jan cry) – **Barry Williams** (eldest son Greg) talks of sex and sin in his autobiography, while **Robert Reed** (dad Mike) insists he hated making the show. The usual tempest in a tea cup.

Byker Grove BBC1 1990–

The north-eastern version of **Grange Hill**, Byker Grove (although most of it was filmed in Wallsend) was a slow starter, southern audiences possibly struggling with all the 'why aye man's' in the script. But it wasn't that long before kids across the country were racing home to catch the exploits of Spuggie, Speedy, Nicola and of course PJ and Duncan, at the local youth club (do they still exist?). Storylines included raising money for charity and early forms of breast enlargements with Spuggie choosing tennis balls down her top over plastic surgery. Classic episode: PJ (aka Ant) blinded whilst paint-balling, leading to him doing a bad impression of Stevie Wonder for the rest of the series.

Fame BBC1 1982-85

A spin-off of **Alan Parker**'s hit movie set at the High School of Performing Arts in New York, the 1982 series featured some of the film's cast, including **Lee Curreri** as music student Bruno, **Gene Anthony Ray** as dancer Leroy and choreographer **Debbie Allen** as dance teacher Lydia Grant. Each week, there'd be a moralistic tale and at least one song and dance number, many of which ended up on *Kids From Fame* albums. Not a success in America, *Fame* was huge in the UK, prompting most of the cast to tour in a stage musical version. Madonna notoriously failed an audition to appear as one of the character's girlfriends in the show.

Happy Days ITV 1976–85, Channel 4–

Made in the 1970s but set in the innocent 1950s (the most risqué thing here was Fonzie's leather jacket), **Happy Days** became a huge hit due to the inclusion of 'cool' ladies' man **The Fonz** (Henry Winkler). Despite being short, having a real name of Arthur and a toilet for an office, the Fonz proved a real babe magnet. (Creator **Garry Marshall** – whose pilot for the show inspired George Lucas' **American Graffiti** – had only drafted him in to stop his show getting too gooey.) The series starred **Marion Ross** and **Tom Bosley** as Ma and Pa Cunningham, **Ron Howard** (now a movie director) as son Richie, **Anson Williams** as his dufus pal Potsie, **Donny Most** as chatty Ralph Malph, and **Erin Moran** as little sister Joanie. It ran for 10 years and was spun-off into **Laverne & Shirley** and **Mork & Mindy**. In Thailand, screenings of *Laverne & Shirley* were always prefaced with a warning that the eponymous heroines had just escaped from an asylum. That way, viewers wouldn't worry about the flag-bearer of the free world..

My So-Called Life Channel 4 1994

The team behind **thirtysomething** created this series about tormented teen Angela Chase (**Claire Danes**) and her daily trials and tribulations. Although fans loved it, and Angela's musings were often acclaimed by critics, the series didn't garner huge audiences and was cancelled after one season. Among Danes' young costars was actor **Jared Leto**.

Teletubbies BBC2 1997–

These luminous, linguistically challenged creatures with TV screens stretched unflatteringly over their frankly too ample stomachs have enjoyed their share of controversy. Their habit of saying 'Eh-oh' (not 'hello'), the repetitive film sequences and the fact that Teletubbyland, far from being a mythical enchanted kingdom was really a small hill in Warwickshire, have all exercised the media. Then there is handbag-toting **Tinky Winky**, seen as a trojan horse of homosexuality in those parts of America where the only issue when a stranger walks into a bar is whether it's worth the locals' trouble to murder him. Tinky was 'outed' as a joke by a *Washington Post* writer and the Moral Majority's outrage only served to confirm his iconic status. All of which, of course, made it compulsive, post-modern ironic viewing on the campuses of Britain, thereby freeing students from their infatuation with **Supermarket Sweep**.

That 70s Show Channel 5 2000–2001

The rights to this smash (in the US) sitcom tale of teenagers in the mid-1970s were bought by British TV then turned into an inferior copy called **Friends Like These** that stiffed. The original is a slick, well-played and hilarious take on family life as nerdy kid Eric (**Topher Grace**) deals with his apple-pie mom and gruff dad (**Kurtwood Smith**), while romancing neighbour Donna (**Laura Prepon**) and acting as referee between his dumb friend Kelso (**Aston Kutcher**) and his particular girlfriend Jackie (**Mila Kunis**). Cleverly written, with some nice winks at 1970s popular culture, it has been followed by **That 80s Show**, with different characters and cast.

The Wonder Years Channel 4 1989–95

Daniel Stern narrated as adult Kevin, remembering back to 1968 when he was 12 years old (and played by **Fred Savage**) and life was simple and soft focus in this nostalgic comedy drama. Kevin had all the usual pre-pubescent problems (but narrated them with wry grown-up wit), a gruff dad (**Dan Lauria**) and often oblivious mother (**Alley Mills**), an annoying older sister (**Olivia D'Abo**), much worse older brother (**Jason Hervey**), and a huge crush on Winnie (**Danica McKellar**), the girl across the street.

★ ★ ★ ZZZZZZ ★ ★ ★

There is no excuse for insomnia. Not with the sedative programming now on digital TV. Should you watch the infomercial (do you need a knife you can cut through your shoes with?), the biopic of **Little Richard** (eternally on Sky movies) or turn to Living for 'erotic' stimulation where the screen may fill with such 'revelations' as the 'fact' that human sperm travels at 0.01mph? But does every bloke's sperm travel at the same speed and does it travel at a constant 0.01mph or, like the cars in **The Sweeney**, does it accelerate from a standing start and slam on the brakes when it reaches its destination? Such mysteries are the essence of late-night telly. You're probably better off with baseball, which on Flannel Chive's steady-as-she-goes through-the-night coverage moves at approximately the same speed as the sleep-deprived human brain.

The James Whale Show ITV 1995

If the object of all post-midnight viewing – as far as you the viewer are concerned at least – is to persuade you that the only sane thing to do is to go up the wooden hill to Bedfordshire, this show succeeded admirably. As the website TV Cream out it, 'a rubbish radio chat show on the telly'.

Night Network ITV 1987–89

EastEnders escapee **Tom Watt**, **Emma Freud** interviewing in pyjamas, and **The Partridge Family**. A short-lived treat for viewers in the LWT region.

Oz Channel 4 2000–

This tough US prison drama makes *Prisoner: In Cell Block H* look as menacing as *Porridge*. Presumably, Channel 4 was attracted by the fact that it was created by **Tom Fontana** and **Barry Levinson**, who had given us *Homicide*. And presumably, the fact that episodes were directed by such thesps as Steve Buscemi didn't harm the show's cause. So why oh why (as they used to say on **Points Of View**) screen it in the traditional post 11pm dumping ground for imported shows that have been condemned without a trial? If you can figure out when it's on, it's well worth staying up for.

The Word Channel 4 1990–95

This Friday night show lives on for two reasons only. One, because it's still hard to believe that Terry Christian really did host a network show – even one watched by viewers who were, as **Louis Jordan** would say, 'booted with liquor'. And two, for future 1950s throwback **Mark Lamarr** who, after listening to Jamaican reggae superstar Shabba Ranks say that he agreed with the Bible that all 'batty boys' should be put to death, finally flipped his lid and shouted 'That's crap and you know it.' This kind of unscripted, unpremeditated conflict is really the only reason some of us watch late night TV. That and our inadequate personal lives…

42 cult TV heroes

Kings of the box and Sir Lew Grade

'Would you mind awfully falling into three lovely lines?'

John Le Mesurier as Sergeant Wilson in *Dad's Army*

The process by which we take a TV character or personality to our hearts is as mysterious as that by which we fall in love. Sometimes, we know at first sight – as with **Dr Who**. Sometimes, it takes time: **Basil Fawlty** wasn't a top 20 show until 1985, six years after the second series had ended. Sometimes we're never sure or sure only that we won't be bored (**Chris Morris**). And sometimes it's best if the brutal truth is faced swiftly, as it should have been with **Jeremy Beadle** before he was forced off air by **Dad's Army** reruns. These bearded pranksters – they don't like it up 'em!

So, like the girl in the Boomtown Rats song who loathed Mondays, it's probably pointless to look for reasons because there are no reasons. It's very hard to explain why the way John Le Mesurier brushes his hair back as Sergeant Arthur Wilson is hilarious, it just is. So here is a celebration of 42* of those who have lit up our living rooms. And **Sir Lew Grade**.

*There are, in fact, 44 people listed in this chapter but as TV heroes we felt it was impossible to separate Clement and Le Frenais and Reeves and Mortimer.

★ Caroline Aherne ★

ARGUABLY THE BEST THING TO HAVE EMERGED FROM RADIO STOCKPORT

Mrs Merton began life as an agony aunt to local troubled folk on Radio Stockport. Based on a friend of her mum, **Caroline Aherne**'s alter ego was picked up by the BBC and given her own chat show, performing to an audience of her mum, friends and friends of her doctor's receptionist. Some viewers saw her as a new Parkinson, not realising that beneath the blue-rinse wig was a 31-year-old comedienne with an IQ of 177. The penny might have dropped when she asked **Debbie McGee**: 'What was it that attracted you to multi-millionaire Paul Daniels?'

Aherne insists Merton wasn't a spoof as the guests didn't know what was happening, but the show came to a natural end as celebs queued up to 'prove' their sense of humour. Working with **Craig Cash** (Mrs Merton's son Malcolm), **Dave Gorman** and **Henry Normal** (one of Steve Coogan's conspirators), Aherne next gave us *The Royle Family*. Filmed in real-time, the Royles basically did nothing, but somehow their pointless Christmas gathered around the telly seemed so much more fun than yours did.

The show won awards and fame Aherne found hard to handle. The media pounced on her alcohol addiction and failed relationships (she suggested **Fred West** as the most appropriate person to play her former husband, New Order bassist Peter Hook, in the film *24 Hour Party People*). Nor did she do herself any favours when she heckled the late **Sir Nigel Hawthorne** at the British Comedy Awards, telling him to 'Get on with it.' Presumably, she must have thought she was heckling **Jonathan Ross**.

Fleeing to Australia, Aherne created *Dossa And Joe*, a comedy drama about a middle-aged Aussie couple who have nothing in common. With Mrs Merton, Denise Royle and **The Fast Show** already behind her, Aherne is the most versatile British comedienne since, well, **Yootha Joyce**.

+ + + + + + + + + + + +

★ Dave Allen ★

IRISH COMEDIAN WITH MORE THEMES THAN FINGERS ON HIS RIGHT HAND

Let's clear up the digit business first. He did have half a finger chopped off his right hand. Asked how this particular finger had come to resemble a sawn off shotgun, he told an interviewer: 'My father was cutting wood and I put my hand on a stump, I thought my dad wouldn't chop, and my dad thought I'd move my hand.' Simple as that.

Allen once claimed he only had five themes, but what themes: life, death, drinking, religion and the English. (Actually he was being modest – he certainly had a sixth: sex.) He mused on all these from a long-legged stool, a cigarette in one hand and a drink in the other (whether it was whisky or apple juice has never been established). His monologues were interspersed with sketches he called 'quickies', some of which – such as 101 things to do with a Popemobile – were as funny as his jokes.

Allen was born David Tylan O'Mahony in Dublin in 1936, the son of a local journalist. He decided to become an entertainer when he was 19 but it took a decade and a half of touring (often for Lew Grade) and stints as a Butlins redcoat and host of the *Sunday Night At The London Palladium* before he hosted the BBC2 series, *Dave Allen At Large*, which made him.

His comedy might have struggled to stay on air a few years earlier but in a decade of increasing frankness, freed from the need to tailor his act to a main-stream audience, he became a regular fixture, a friendly but still slightly enigmatic figure who closed each show with raised glass and a quick 'And may your god go with you.'

> **He piled absurdity on absurdity until laughter burst out of you like steam from a kettle**

He drifted off our screens in the 1980s, apart from some entertaining encounters with British eccentrics, returning to ITV in the 1990s with a series of monologues which, although the tabloids focused on the swear words, showed he hadn't lost his touch. He now lives in semi-retirement, trying to cut down on cigarettes and alcohol.

At his best, he brought to his comedy a beguiling blend of journalistic cynicism, slight bewilderment and surprised indignation. His monologues, on such themes as the household manners of his teenage son, piled absurdity on absurdity until the laughter burst out of you like steam from a boiling kettle. But he could also make a point, as when he told the sorry tale of a black American visitor to Ulster who was so upset at being barred from the Reverend Ian Paisley's church that he prayed publicly to God for assistance – only to be told that God too had been petitioning, unsuccessfully, for admission to Paisley's church for many years.

+ + + + + + + + + + + + +

★ Gillian Anderson ★

SEXIER THAN PAMELA ANDERSON, THE MOST DURABLE AGENT ON THE BOX

At high school in Grand Rapids, Michigan, she was voted by classmates as the person most likely to be arrested. When she auditioned for Dana Scully's role (so eager that she lied about her age, claiming to be 27 when she was 24), she seemed the actress least likely to get the part. Producer

Chris Carter liked her but the Fox suits wanted somebody blonder, bigger-breasted, more *Babewatch*. But she got the part, thank God; **The X-Files** needed her sceptical intellectual chic to offset Fox Mulder's paranoid certainties. For almost a decade, she and her partners lived, chased monsters, almost died, and lived again to chase monsters another week.

The plots were so outlandish, the conspiracy so vast and Mulder so eager to apply the most convoluted meaning to the flimsiest evidence, disbelief would not have been suspended without Anderson's laconic quizzical look. Her underplaying served her (and us) as Scully was kidnapped by aliens, shot her trusty partner, and endured the weirdest time any FBI employee had had since the bureau's director **J Edgar Hoover** turned up to Mafia parties in mascara, a little black dress and demanding to be called 'Mary'. Things weren't quite the same after her co-star's dash for freedom but she was still there, looking far more alluring in those dinky FBI suits than she had any right to. Although she has acted to acclaim in such films as *The House Of Mirth*, she may be caught in the same trap as **David Duchovny**. She admitted once, 'There's something vulnerable about having that feeling, hearing people whisper "Scully" as you pass them.' That may, alas, be a whisper she'll hear the rest of her life.

+ + + + + + + + + + + +

★ Tom Baker ★

BRICKLAYER, TIME LORD AND VOICE-OVER KING

The son of a factory worker, Tom Baker was born in Liverpool in 1934. Although he came from a Jewish family, he left school at 15 to become a monk ('The Old Testament

The thinking man's Anderson. Apart from Gerry, of course

is my favourite science fantasy reading,' he once said) but left after six years to do national service in the Medical Corps. A spell as a bricklayer followed before he turned to acting. In the early 1970s he had several big-screen parts (including Rasputin in *Nicholas And Alexandra*) but was back on the building sites when pop-culture immortality beckoned.

In 1974 he took over as **Dr Who** – a role he saw as a cross between the Pied Piper and Jesus Christ (**Jim Dale**, **Michael Bentine** and **Fulton Mackay** had all been rejected for the role). Adopting a floppy hat, a long scarf and a coat as likely to harbour jelly babies as polarity-reversing gadgets, Baker mixed natural clownishness with a genuinely disturbing streak. Baker worked best with fighting babes in bizarre outfits, such as Louise Jameson in animal skins (savage Leela) and Lalla Ward in a St Trinian's outfit as a time lady. (Offscreen, Baker and Ward were briefly married.)

The Baker era produced many of the best-ever Who serials, including 'City Of Death', a Parisian romp involving Leonardo Da Vinci and multiple Mona Lisas penned by **Douglas Adams**. But Baker's tendency to play the fool and a BBC decree to downplay the horror meant he also starred in some of the worst (alongside K-9) with the dodgiest monster suits (were those really Cheerios stuck all over the Zygons?). But because Baker believed in himself he took us with him. For many he still is The Doctor.

After seven years, and evidently expecting to be seen as irreplaceable (a basic error when playing a character who'd already had three different incarnations), he talked of leaving. Bye then, said the BBC. But with his easy handling of lines like 'You are a classic example of an inverse ration between the size of the mouth and the size of the brain,' he left a lot to live up to. Since then, he has played Sherlock Holmes, been a regular in *Medics* and *Randall And Hopkirk (Deceased)* and done many, many voice-overs.

✛ ✛ ✛ ✛ ✛ ✛ ✛ ✛ ✛ ✛ ✛ ✛

★ Frank Bough ★

FAMOUS FOR NATIONWIDE, GRANDSTAND, BREAKFAST TIME, HOLIDAY

It's all true: Frank Bough did it five nights a week and again on Saturday. But enough of his notorious recreational habits: let's talk about the man's standing as the genial overlord of 1970s live TV.

Once a chemical works site manager, Bough launched his broadcasting career fronting BBC's Northeast regional newsreel *Home At Six*, opening each edition by tossing his homburg onto the studio hatstand as if he was **John Steed**. But sport was Bough's passion, and after commentating at the Olympics and World Cup, he started fronting *Grandstand* in 1968. Soon no big sporting event was complete without Frank, who also took custody of the football teleprinter. Viewers in Yorkshire may have thought they detected a smirk on the rare occasions Leeds United lost, but he emphatically denied this on his final programme in 1982.

But that was just Bough's Saturday job. Since 1972, he'd spent weekdays compering the chatty evening news magazine *Nationwide*, interrogating cabinet ministers and meeting championship gurners, dipsomaniac snails and skateboarding wildfowl. Bough, as Clive James pointed out, was a key exponent of the 'I dunno' technique of presentation. ('I dunno what a folly is. Bob Wellings, do you know what a folly is?' 'Well, Frank, we asked...')

Into the 1980s, and Bough hosted the BBC's innovative *Breakfast Time* on a maroon sofa with Selina Scott, and presented *Holiday* too, forever caravanning through the Dordogne in a green Ford Fiesta with his wife Nesta. But then scandal struck, with tabloid charges of Cynthia Payne-style sex and cocaine orgies. His BBC contract in tatters, Frank briefly joined Sky TV but his last major gig, save for an appearance on *Shooting Stars*, was chairing ITV's Rugby World Cup coverage in 1991.

Oh, and lest we forget – he was also one of the all-singing, all-dancing BBC newsreaders who performed 'There Is Nothing Like A Dame' in a sailor suit on the *Morecambe And Wise Christmas Show*.

+ + + + + + + + + + + + +

★ Basil Brush ★

SLIGHTLY OVERDRESSED FURRY FUNSTER AND PUNSTER

There was usually an inverse ratio between the length of Basil Brush's laugh and the quality of the joke. But the 18-inch fox reigned supreme in the chicken coop that was BBC light entertainment, attracting audiences of 13 million at Saturday teatimes. The hand (and boom boom) behind Basil was **Ivor Owen**, who never allowed himself to be photographed in case proof of his existence dismayed Basil's fans (among whom were **Prince William** and **Lord Carrington**, who said 'Basil Brush says things to people that I'd like to say'). **Peter Firmin**, a collaborator of Oliver Postgate, supplied the puppet for just £1 per appearance. The fox made its debut on **David Nixon**'s magic show in 1966 and his first straight man (they were all referred to with mock politeness as Mr) was **Rodney Bewes**.

Between 1968 and 1981 Brush had his own Saturday evening show, but then Ivor and the BBC fell out over talk of more grown-up content. Fame had obviously gone to Owen's hand. The charm of the act lay in the corny jokes, the way Basil never learned that toffee would cement his jaws together, and the schlocky sentimentality with which he'd nudge his best straight man – **Derek Fowlds** – and sing 'I'm shy, Mr Derek, I'm shy.' Basil was surprisingly formally dressed in a jacket, orange waistcoat and green cravat, but perhaps the costume was meant to remind everyone that, as he constantly insisted, 'I am not a dog!'

In the absence of any proper script, Basil would tell terrible jokes in his Terry Thomas voice, wax indignant ('Ali Baba and the 40 thieves – 98 per cent of the leading characters are dishonest!'), humiliate his assistant and guests (who ranged from **Abba** to **Sir Michael Horden**) and then apologise. All this was peppered with as many of his laughs and 'Boom boom!'s as possible. The humour was childish, but not stupid: writing to his cousin Cyril he noted: 'I am writing this letter very slowly because I know you can't read very fast.'

> **In the absence of a script, Basil would tell terrible jokes, wax indignant and humiliate his guests**

His popularity was such that he even made two albums, one inevitably being called *Boom Boom It's Basil Brush*, but like **Samantha Fox** and **Edward Fox**, he never conquered America, a failing which opened the door for Jim Henson's Muppets. Owen died in 2000 of cancer, shortly after Basil had been given a lifetime achievement award by *Loaded* magazine but before talks about his return to the small screen could be finalised. The BBC have since announced plans to brush off Basil and give him his own sitcom on its children's cable channel CBBC.

+ + + + + + + + + + + +

★ Dick Clement and Ian La Frenais ★

THE DYNAMIC DUO OF BRITISH SITCOM

Evelyn Waugh famously observed that asking someone else to help you write was rather like inviting a third party to help you and your wife conceive a baby. The success of **Dick Clement** and **Ian La Frenais**, the kings of British sitcom, suggests otherwise. Together they have penned a string of hits based on sharp dialogue, finely drawn characterisation and a streak of kitchen-sink realism. They joined forces when Clement, a radio producer training as a TV director, needed to mount a sketch for his course. He enlisted a friend, La Frenais, and in 1964 the resulting script became BBC2's first hit, *The Likely Lads*, featuring young blades Bob and Terry sowing their oats on swinging Tyneside.

The pair's finest half-hour, **Porridge** (see page 54), made its debut in 1973; remarkably that same year they also delivered the exquisite **Whatever Happened To The Likely Lads?**, with Terry now aghast at Bob's Berni Inn lifestyle and engagement to Thelma, a hydra in floral polyester.

Le Frenais and Clement in their 10cc meets Bodie and Doyle heyday, sometime in the 1970s

Thick As Thieves misfired in 1974, despite boasting **John Thaw** and **Bob Hoskins**, and *Porridge*'s post-release sequel *Going Straight* also stiffed.

After becoming the only sitcom writers to successfully adapt their work for the big screen – *The Likely Lads* (1976) and *Porridge* (1979) – the duo next tackled one-hour comedy drama with **Auf Wiedersehen, Pet** (1983). Throwing seven potentially dodgy regional stereotypes into a hut in Germany, they came up with a funny, affecting reflection on the working class's lot in Thatcher's Britain. Their *The Commitments* movie script was a hit, but the 1990s were a fallow decade. Remember *Freddie And Max*, *The Old Boy Network* or *Full Stretch*? Thought not.

With C&LF mostly working as Hollywood script 'firemen' (turning others' hopeless screenplays into hits like *The Rock*), it looked very much as if they'd given up on British TV. But an inspired reprise of *Auf Wiedersehen, Pet* was a hit in 2002, while **Ant and Dec** became the Likely Lads trying to avoid the result of the big match. With England still flooded out…

+ + + + + + + + + + + + +

★ David Coleman ★
THE BBC'S SPORTING PERSONALITY OF THE 20TH CENTURY

'She's not Ben Johnson but then who is?' It's the kind of thing David Coleman would say, and such is the myth surrounding the many alleged slips by the BBC's most durable commentator (Colemanballs as *Private Eye* calls them) that whether he actually said it or not is almost irrelevant.

The Colemanballs legend is slightly unfair on a man who commentated on 16 Olympic Games, eight Commonwealth games, sundry World Cups, FA Cup finals and Grand Nationals, bringing what the *Guardian*'s Frank Keating called 'his knowingly passionate prattle' to each event (or, as **Spitting Image** would have it, his 'I think it's impossible tokeepthislevel-ofexcitement… headexploding' style). His finest hour was his description of **David Hemery**'s medal-winning 400m hurdle race at the 1968 Olympics, when he spoke at a quite remarkable rate of 200 words a minute (the normal rate is from 120 to 150 words a minute).

As Hemery himself noted, Coleman 'engenders the adrenaline people identify with and he can create such a spirit of excitement that it helps people to live in the moment.' That may be because he really does share the passion: his own athletic career was cruelly ended by injury.

He hosted 600 or so *Grandstands* and 18 years of *A Question Of Sport* ('all that changed,' said long-term team skipper **Bill Beaumont**, 'when his parting got wider and his sweaters got worse') but it was as a commentator, with or without Colemanballs, he excelled. For those of us who grew up with him and still dream of scoring the winning goal in the FA Cup final, it is Coleman – not Motty – describing our triumph.

Nobody will ever say 'one-nilll!' with Coleman's finality, as though the fact that one side had scored meant the game was over (this was before Fifa took him at his word and invented the golden goal). He got caught once, in the 1978 World Cup, when France played Italy. As the striker, inches from an open goal, measured his shot, Coleman declared 'One-

> **'If that had gone in, it would have been a goal,' blurted Coleman**

nilll!' – only for the ball to rebound off the post. He panicked and blurted out: 'If that had have gone in it would have been a goal.' In the same finals he called hole-in-the-heart Scottish international **Asa Hartford** a 'whole hearted player', apologising just before the

BBC switchboard lit up like a Trafalgar Square Christmas tree.

Coleman was always hunting for the killer line, saying of one long-forgotten athlete, 'And it's Yifter, Yifter the shifter'. There was a fascination about hearing Coleman improvise on a theme, even if that theme was an East German athlete called **Renata Stecher**, who he variously described as 'The big girl... East Germany's powerful... Really very squarely built. Really Square. Very, very strong' before coming clean and blurting out 'The bulky figure of Renata Stecher.'

✛✛✛✛✛✛✛✛✛✛✛✛

⋆ Steve Coogan ⋆

THE NEXT PETER SELLERS?

296 It may be presumptuous to proclaim **Steve Coogan** as a worthy contender for **Peter Sellers**' comedy crown, but then Coogan is presumptuous. And he did turn the simple phrase 'A-ha' into a national institution.

One of six children in a devout Catholic household, Coogan's recurring prayer, 'God, make me rich and famous', was obviously heard. A regular on the Manchester stand-up circuit while studying acting at the local poly, Coogan was spotted by a talent scout, leading to appearances on *A Word In Your Era* and *Paramount City*. Off-screen, Coogan made his mark by providing many of the voices (including **Margaret Thatcher**'s) on **Spitting Image**, and on the Radio 4 show *On The Hour,* where his most famous character, Alan Partridge, made his debut. Based on a radio presenter Coogan had had the dubious pleasure of being interviewed by, Partridge was a pathetic, cringeworthy nerd who became a instant hit, possibly because everyone seems to have a Partridge in their circle of acquaintances.

Until 1993 Partridge had a face for radio, so many didn't spot Coogan as the link between the talk show host and student-basher Paul Calf, who emerged with his sister Pauline (also played by Coogan) in *Paul Calf's Video Diary* on BBC2. As a loud-mouthed, northern slob, Coogan gave us more insight: 'Foreplay is important... put some toast on... have a bit of a nap... get her to give you a shout when she's ready.'

Coogan, with writer **Patrick Marber**, brought Alan Partridge to the small screen on **The Day Today**, with *On The Hour* co-host, **Chris Morris**. Partridge soon earned his own chat show, *Knowing Me, Knowing You* (featuring Minnie Driver before she was famous), and *I'm Alan Partridge*, in which he was relegated to a graveyard show (*Up With The Partridge*) on Norwich local radio and living in a Travelodge.

Coogan has since brought us Duncan Thickett, Ernest Moss, cabaret Euro-crooner Tony Ferrino (pictured, right) and Gareth Cheeseman the travelling sales rep. But at the time of writing it was as Partridge that Coogan is to return, complete with a new Canadian wife – 'and it's love and not for a green card'.

✛ ✛ ✛ ✛ ✛ ✛ ✛ ✛ ✛ ✛ ✛ ✛ ✛

'A Christmas shopping list for a bigamist is a very, very long one indeed, bigamy at Christmas...'

⋆ Peter Cook ⋆

ELVIS PRESLEY WANNABE, WIT, AND RELENTLESS HUMOURIST

When **Peter Cook** died, the newspaper obituaries were full of charges that he had not fulfilled his potential. These claims provoked **Stephen Fry** to complain 'Why commentators have to write and talk about extraordinary people as if they were composing school reports is beyond me: "A fair term's work but Peter must concentrate more on writing stage plays this year." Would his potential have been realised in appearing in more Hollywood films or in having a regular prime-time TV show?'

Almost certainly not – although millions who saw **Not Only But Also** in which Cook co-starred with **Dudley Moore** would have welcomed more than the three series on BBC between 1965 and 1970. Cook was probably the quirkiest of the four Oxbridge graduates (the others being **Jonathan Miller**, **Alan Bennett** and **Moore**) who led the 1960s satire boom.

His great gift, the ability to take flight into fantastic comic fantasy, was not easily placed on television or anywhere else. Moore, recently reunited with Cook in TV heaven, admitted, 'If he had a fault, it was that he was relentless in making people laugh. At parties after the show, he made sure people were laughing but he kept on bludgeoning people with his wit.'

In the Dagenham Dialogues (and on the **Derek and Clive** albums which followed) this worked to Cook's advantage. A certain ruthless comic drive was needed to persuade us that, on some level, he was being stalked by 'bloody Greta Garbo'. (Even then the language proved controversial: after a rerun on BBC1, a researcher noted 'a not inconsiderable number of the sample were unable to make anything of the comedy… the main reason seemed to be the far too liberal use of the expletive 'bloody'. It was felt a great pity these two undoubtedly brilliant young men had chosen to introduce such a sour note into this otherwise refreshingly different show.'

When Dud went to Hollywood, Pete was left without a foil and TV land didn't know what to do with a man who could be so cruelly funny (he once dismissed **David Frost** as a 'bubonic plagiarist'). So he appeared in shortlived US sitcom **The Two Of Us**, made the most talked-about turn on a chat show as four eccentrics opposite **Clive Anderson** and earned an indecent amount for telling **Joan Rivers** she had a nice frock.

Since he believed indolence was bliss, Cook seemed to get roughly what he wanted from life. He probably would have liked to last a bit longer (but not if meant cutting down on booze and fags). David Frost, a colleague and victim of Cook's, once rang him up to invite him to a soiree he was giving for **Prince Andrew** and **Sarah Ferguson**. 'Hang on, I'll just check my diary,' said Cook. After several minutes of loud rummaging noises, Cook returned to the phone to say: 'Oh dear, I find I'm watching television that night.'

> **'I thought the pros outweighed the cons by about two and a half ounces'**

+ + + + + + + + + + + +

★ Jacques Cousteau ★

DID MORE FOR THE SEA THAN VIRGINIA WOOLF

Long before **David Attenborough** (okay, not that long before but you get the idea), a slightly built, personable Frenchman took us to places we had never imagined and documentary film-making to a whole new level.

Jacques-Yves Cousteau had already achieved more than most in a lifetime when he became a TV star at 60. At the age of 11 he built a model crane, at 13 a battery-operated car and in his thirties he helped develop the aqualung. He was also a gunnery officer in the French Navy and a spy for the French Resistance. After World War II, divers used the aqualung to find enemy mines: the same device enabled Cousteau to become a 'manfish' and open all our eyes to a wonderful watery world.

Cousteau started making films to finance his trips and raise public awareness. In 1968, he was asked to make a TV series and for nine years the voyages of the *Calypso* and **The Undersea World Of Jacques Cousteau** brought us face-to-face with sharks, dolphins, whales, giant octopuses and his red woolly hat, as big a trademark as Benny's in **Crossroads**.

Cousteau looked more at ease underwater than **The Man From Atlantis**. His contribution to oceanographic exploration is immense but like many of his countrymen he was not averse to the occasional gnomic pseudo-profound utterance, such as 'If you realise you are only a violin, you can open yourself up to the world by playing your role in the concert.'

Sadly, the man who was usually voted France's most popular figure in opinion polls, spent his later years embroiled in family quarrels over the various Cousteau enterprises and a legal battle with his son Jean-Michael. In 1997, just over a year after his beloved *Calypso* sank in Singapore harbour after being hit by a barge, Cousteau died, aged 87.

+ + + + + + + + + + + +

★ Pete Duel ★

THE JAMES DEAN OF TV WESTERNS

'All have a great show' were **Pete Duel**'s last words to **Roger Davis** as he walked off the set of **Alias Smith And Jones**. The words only sounded significant to Davis, the show's narrator, when he heard that Duel had been found dead and was asked to take the part of Hannibal Heyes.

Duel, 31, had been at home in his West Hollywood apartment with his girlfriend Diane Ray. He'd watched himself in an episode of *Alias Smith And Jones*; Ray said he'd been unhappy with the show but didn't think he was suicidal. That night she was awoken by the sound of a gunshot and found Duel dead on the living room floor, a bullet hole in his head.

Suicide, decreed the coroner. Davis agrees. Some saw Duel as a martyr for the radical causes he supported but his younger brother Geoffrey Duel, says 'If anything, it probably had to do with him screwing around with guns. There was a lot of alcohol in his body.'

Alias Smith And Jones, created by Glen A Larson, was the tale of two sexy, loveable reformed outlaws – a spin-off of **Butch Cassidy And The Sundance Kid** and TV's last prime-time Western hit. Hannibal Heyes and Kid Currie had been given a secret pardon by the Governor of Kansas (as the opening voice-over reminded us, they'd never killed anybody) as long as they stayed

Pete Duel smiles for the camera. Kinda

out of trouble for a year – no easy task for wanted men. The series, far more irreverent than most TV Westerns, set the tone for the later male bonding in the likes of *Starsky And Hutch* and *The Dukes Of Hazzard*.

But Duel soon felt trapped. He was a melancholy figure who liked to camp alone in the wilderness, relax in his rustic apartment and spend time alone with his dog. 'He really didn't handle the highs and lows well,' Davis says, and his habit of driving under the influence led to a ban.

That summer Duel took time off from the show to film a version of the stageplay *The Scarecrow*, alongside Gene Wilder. This was the work he was proudest of, he said, but the exhilaration didn't last. Months later he left the *Alias* set for the last time, bidding that casual goodbye. Yet for a man whose legacy consists of guest-starring roles, some TV movies, two minor sitcoms and 33 episodes of a *Butch Cassidy* rip-off, Duel is well remembered. On the 25th anniversary of his death, British fans paid for a star in the constellation of Ursa Minor to be named Peter Ellstrom Deuel.

+ + + + + + + + + + + +

★ Peter Glaze ★

INVENTOR OF THE TERM 'DOH!', CRACKERJACK CROONER

Only **Matt Groening** knows if he was influenced by **Peter Glaze**'s incessant cries of '**Doh!**' as he went about the serious business of making kids laugh every Friday at five to five. To have Glaze burst into your favourite hit in the final sketch was, in **Crackerjack**'s heyday, a validation, even if the way the songs were introduced was about as subtle as **Don Maclean**'s teeth. Typically, Glaze would enter stage right in a new costume to find Maclean wearing a pair of tigerskin boots. 'I love those!' Glaze would cry and the two would launch into a singalong rendition of Mud's *Tiger Feet*. **XTC**'s Andy Partridge once noted, with perverse glee, that the only person to cover one of their songs was Glaze, jollying up 'Making Plans For Nigel'.

Glaze was born in London in 1924 and had just turned 30 when he first appeared on the show with which he, more even than **Leslie Crowther** or **Michael Aspel**, became synonymous. While the precise appeal of this 'put upon little lump' (in Aspel's words) is mysterious, his presence was vital: as became apparent when he was briefly replaced by **Little and Large**.

In real life Glaze wore contact lenses: the thick black framed glasses he wore on stage contained no glass for safety reasons. When Aspel took over as host, he was astonished to find that his new colleague numbered his facial expressions ('After number 14, I start to bleed'). Like many a great trouper, Glaze went on too long, although those privileged enough to see him sing **Pretty Vacant** still speak of that performance. He also guested as an actor on **Dr Who** and **The Sweeney**. He died, too early, at the age of 59. One can only hope that he was buried with a *Crackerjack* pencil.

✛✛✛✛✛✛✛✛✛✛✛✛

★ Gracie Wyndham Goldie ★

QUEEN OF 1950s BBC WHO LAUNCHED TONIGHT AND ELECTION NIGHT SPECIAL

The name may be unfamiliar, but those six syllables are enough to make male BBC employees of a certain age twitch. Head of the BBC talks department, she influenced all of Auntie's factual coverage, persuading bosses to run a results programme on **election night** (engineers feared the transmitters might blow up if left on overnight), pioneering the launch of **Tonight** and **Panorama**, and persuading Marshal Tito to give her correspondent an interview by playing on the fact that the Yugoslav secret police tapped the Beeb's phones in Belgrade.

'This geezer comes up and says "How'd you like to be secretary-general of the United Nations, mate?"'

She had, as **Denis Norden** has testified, the power to make successful producers and TV stars stand around shuffling their feet. Her reputation as the fiercest dragon at Broadcasting House seemed apter than ever after she gave evidence to Parliament about a second TV channel. Asked about the feasibility of a service like ITV, she replied: 'I can't find nearly enough young men to run one system well, one channel well. The idea that there could be two is absurd.' She retired in 1965, when she was 65. There is an apocryphal story that a **Blue Peter** guide dog was christened Goldie in her honour – coincidentally, the dog retired in 1986, the year of Grace's death.

Probably her finest (well, funniest) moment came in 1961 when *Panorama* was rehearsing an interview with UN secretary-general **Dag**

Hammarskjold. Floor manager Albert Stevens stood in for the UN boss and, when asked how he had got his job, replied: 'I was unemployed at the time and as I was walking down the road, this geezer comes up to me and says "How'd you like to be secretary-general of the United Nations, mate?"' The BBC's first lady stormed down and tore a strip off Stevens for his impertinence. Unknown to them, Hammarskjold was in the studio and, when asked that question for real, replied, in his best Norwegian-cockney: 'I was walking down the road one day and this geezer comes up to me…'

+ + + + + + + + + + + + +

⋆ Larry Hagman ⋆

THE OILIEST TYCOON IN TELEVISUAL TEXAS

If you ever ask **Larry Hagman** for an autograph, be warned: he'll only oblige if you sing a song or do a dance. It's just one of the quirks which make the seventysomething Texan (almost) as colourful as the character he's most famous for playing, JR Ewing.

The son of a district attorney and Broadway starlet **Mary Martin**, Hagman joined mum's musical troupe in *South Pacific*. His first big break on TV came in 1965 with the implausible tale of an astronaut finding a genie in a bottle. **I Dream of Jeannie** was a big hit and ran for five years.

Further success eluded him until **Dallas**. The series ran on prime-time for 14 seasons, the 'Who Shot JR?' episode attracting the second biggest TV audience ever. Nobody tuned in to see nice but dull Bobby – we wanted to see suave, sneering JR make the most of lines like 'It's mind over matter Cliff – I don't mind and you don't matter'.

Off-screen Hagman was drinking almost as much as his onscreen wife (a liver transplant would follow) and indulging in the brinkmanship his alter ego was so adept at. When the producers tried to sack **Linda Gray**, his 'if she goes, I go' ultimatum saved her. He also tried to have **Donna Reed**, Barbara Bel Geddes' stand in as Miss Ellie, replaced by his mum. (He obviously hadn't consulted her. When asked how it felt to have a legend for a son, Martin replied: 'No dear, I'm the legend. Dallas is a bloody cult.'   303

Dallas has bowed out, but there's still the odd made-for-TV movie. Never mind the ludicrous plot (JR himself returns from the dead in the imaginatively titled *JR Returns – The Movie*), just treasure Hagman in those quintessential JR moments. 'You should go to sleep, Sue Ellen – you know how haggard you look when you don't get your full eight hours.'

+ + + + + + + + + + + +

★ Tony Hancock ★

'A PINT? THAT'S VERY NEARLY AN ARMFUL.'

Hancock. Thirty-four years after his death, the surname alone summons up the ghost of one of Britain's great post-war comedians. He was 44 when he committed suicide in Australia. Willie Rushton had the job of escorting Hancock's ashes back to Britain. He and the urn occupied two seats on the flight back to London but he was asked to give up one of them for another passenger. He whispered his predicament to the stewardess who took the urn into first class and a seat of its own. The flight over, Rushton went to pick up the ashes from first class. Next to it was a single red rose and a note which read 'Thank you for making us laugh.'

Anthony John Hancock had thirsted for a career in show biz ever since the first music-hall guests had stayed at his parents' hotel in Bournemouth. (His dad Jack was a semi-pro entertainer too.) In 1941, when he was 17, he naïvely treated a crowd of soldiers and Sunday school teachers to Max Miller jokes, prompting a woman in the audience to tell him he would not be asked back because 'We want to fumigate the hall.'

Dropping the blue jokes, Hancock joined one of impresario Ralph Reader's concert parties during the war. In 1951, he became famous as Archie Andrews' tutor in the BBC radio hit *Educating Archie*, acquiring a catchphrase 'Flipping kids' and meeting scriptwriters **Ray Galton** and **Alan Simpson** who would write his **Hancock's Half Hour** scripts on radio and TV – and then, like many people he met, be rejected by him. Spike Milligan summed up this side of Hancock's character: 'He went around closing doors on everybody and eventually closed the door on himself.'

Hancock didn't impress in two ITV series (scripted by **Eric Sykes**), so he turned to Galton and Simpson to translate their radio success of *Half Hour* to television, famously creating '**The Blood Donor**'. Oddly enough, he'd been admitted to hospital days before following a car crash and had

Before he became a TV star, Hancock told blue jokes and tried his hand as an Easter bunny

not been able to rehearse his lines. The show's start had been nervy: one viewer complained the show was 'senseless bilge from beginning to end'.

Hancock had his hit but he wasn't happy. As **Frank Muir** noted, 'his self-confidence ran out at the height of his career. He began to worry the success was due to Sid James, so he dropped Sid [without telling his partner]. He then worried that the quality of the scripts was the winning ingredient so he moved to ITV without Galton and Simpson.' But by 1963 he could no more escape Railway Cuttings than Chaplin could escape the clown with the moustache and the cane.

His private life had become turbulent: he had intense affairs with (amongst others) **Joan Le Mesurier** and a fatal romance with the bottle. By 1968, things had (as he said) gone wrong too many times and he died of depression, pills and vodka. As **Harry Secombe** said, 'If anyone paid dearly for his laughs, it was the man himself.' Critics said he'd never grown up, a charge Hancock wouldn't necessarily have denied, as he said once, 'We're all moth-eaten kids really.'

+ + + + + + + + + + + +

★ Tony Hart ★

THE NATION'S FAVOURITE ART TEACHER

Tony Hart's white hair, dapper cravat and friendly yet teacher-like manner endeared him to kids and rich conservative American women. The soothing tones of the *Gallery* theme music ushered you into a trance-like world where the unflappable Hart presided with quiet humour, never suggesting there was anything very difficult about this art business.

Having left the 1st Gurkha Rifles of the Indian Army, Hart had earlier bummed around London, painting murals on restaurant walls to earn free meals, and scrawling a fish on a napkin to prove his talent to a BBC producer. This led to a career which saw Tony appear in at least one show a year for the next 50 years. No matter how old you are, you will have grown up with Tony as your art teacher.

After stints on such shows as *Playbox* and *Titch And Quackers*, Hart gained his own shows (*Vision On, Take Hart* and *Hartbeat*) and created the *Blue Peter* ship logo. But the most memorable event of these years had nothing to do with his artistic talents – it came when an inexperienced **Lulu** clasped Quackers to her chest, not realising Hart's hand was inside.

Vision On (1964) ran for 12 years. Famed for its quirky animation and Hart's belief that anyone can do anything with anything and it will be art, the show was sold throughout the world. In America the ultra-conservative Daughters of the Revolution (motto: God, Home and Country) held the programme in such esteem that any TV station transmitting it received a special

> **Lulu clutched Quackers to her breast, not realising that Hart's hand was inside**

plaque. With *Take Hart*, Tony acquired a sidekick – Morph, the plasticine model – and the pair continued on *Hartbeat*, much funnier than Nick Berry's pale imitation. The show attracted five-and-a-half million viewers and 6,000 letters a week: a merry band of OAP's sifted through the fan mail and pictures sent in by aspiring artists. Tony still wears the cravat and pops up on our screens now and then, but his place as national minister for art is now filled by **Neil** *(Number 73)* **Buchanan**.

✢ ✢ ✢ ✢ ✢ ✢ ✢ ✢ ✢ ✢ ✢ ✢ ✢

★ Max Headroom ★

THE ONLY TV HOST TO BE NAMED AFTER A CAR PARK SIGN

Max Headroom is often billed, slightly erroneously, as the first computer-generated TV show host. The face of Channel 4's post-modern ironic TV personality was really Canadian actor **Matt Frewer**, heavily made up and played around with on computer to produce the visual equivalent of the interference you get on your car radio when passing under a bridge.

Frewer also played Headroom's doppelganger, Edison Carter, an investigative reporter killed after investigating his channel's use of 'blipverts' – condensed TV ads – to boost ratings, even though these ads led some of its viewers to explode. Carter's mind is scanned into a computer and reformatted as a character called Max Headroom, named after the last two words Carter ever saw in a multi-storey car park. The show is set 20 minutes into the future when TV dominates everyone's lives – not just those of **Big Brother** contestants.

Max headroom, min airtime - in the US

Headroom was created at the behest of Channel 4 commissioning editor **Andy Park** to link pop videos. He had a wonderful propensity to say things like 'Special bulletin: There is still no news from New Zealand. If they ever have any, we'll be sure to let you know.' In the US, Lorimar, makers of *Dallas*, made the show a sci-fi thriller. This lasted long enough for Headroom to become the spokesman for New Coke, but TV executives, taking post-modern irony to its limits, killed it by running it against **Dallas.**

Max was adored by sci-fi fans who credited him with introducing such cyberpunk terms as 'nano-technology' to the mass audience, while as a talking head between pop videos he was a lot more fun than **Jamie Theakston**. He even had his own brand of humour, a frankly terrifying mix of the quirkily futuristic and the excruciatingly cheesy, as if David Byrne and Bob Monkhouse had had a mind-meld.

✛ ✛ ✛ ✛ ✛ ✛ ✛ ✛ ✛ ✛ ✛ ✛

★ Frankie Howerd ★

'OOH ERR, MISSUS, DON'T TITTER, OH PLEASE YOURSELF'

You need a lifetime's training to deliver lines like 'You can't die here – this is the living room' and get a laugh. Just as well, then, that **Francis Alick Howard** (whose birth coincided with the first Russian revolution in March 1917) was shoved, at the age of four, onto the stage of a working men's club in Eltham, Kent, and told to do something to earn the prize of a bag of sweets. He screamed, won the sweets and an obsession was born. When he was 17 he was invited to apply to Rada but became so nervous during the audition that his left leg shook violently and the cheese sandwiches his mum had given him exploded, showering the tutors with crumbs. Rather than go straight home, he sat in a field trying to decide what he could be if he couldn't act. From somewhere came the idea that he might be a comedian.

And a comedian he became, with gags too obvious to be called double entendres (he once said of his deaf pianist 'She's known to me as madam Vera Roper but she's known to everyone else as the English Open') and by the 1960s his act had become officially obsolete. A nervous breakdown, a doomed marriage (and an even more doomed attempt to seduce **Bob Monkhouse** on the eve of the wedding, just to prove his tackle was in order) left him stranded until **Peter Cook** gave him a slot at his new club, the Establishment. Howerd won the crowd with his opening line: 'If you're expecting Lenny Bruce then you may as well piss off now' – and ignited a second career which led, in 1970, to his most famous role as Lurcio, slave to Ludicrous Sextus, in **Up Pompeii!**.

Lurcio fitted Howerd's camp on-screen persona better than his wig (only half-secured by the hairs he knotted over the top of it). He had always looked (as the *Guardian*'s **Nancy Banks Smith** put it) 'like a moulting moose' but as he aged, the lines, wrinkles and bags accumulated and his physog looked more pitted than the surface of the moon. As his old pal **Eric Sykes** said recently, 'What other job could he have got? Join the fire brigade? Can you imagine? Brass helmet on? Course you can't. There's only one thing he could do well. Go up on stage and have the whole house with tears rolling down their face.'

Only 14 episodes (including the pilot) were made but *Up Pompeii!* lives on in the nation's memory – unlike its 'sequel' **Whoops Baghdad** or the war sitcom *And Churchill Said To Me* which was canned during the Falklands War, resurfacing on cable to little applause. But it didn't matter: Howerd's shtick had become part of British life. To watch him today, a decade after his death, is to be reminded that **Graham Norton** wouldn't be sooooo Graham Norton without Frankie.

At his best, Howerd contrived to suggest that he was appearing against his will and if the audience didn't get his jokes, it was no concern of his. As the man himself used to say, oh please yourself.

+ + + + + + + + + + + + +

★ David Hyde Pierce ★

THE AMERICAN JOHN LE MESURIER

Once when **Kelsey Grammer** was playing Othello, he became so enraged by the way his co-star **Christopher Plummer** hogged the limelight that he grabbed him by the crotch and threw him across the stage. It's a wonder Grammer hasn't done the same to his co-star and sitcom sibling **David Hyde Pierce**. Because as Niles, the anally retentive brother who can make a drama out of ordering a steak ('I'd like a petit filet mignon, very lean, not so lean that it lacks flavour, but not so fat that it leaves drippings on the plate, and I don't want it cooked, just lightly seared on either side, pink in the middle – not a true pink but not a mauve either, something in between, bearing in mind the slightest error either way and it's ruined') and who took seven years to declare his love for the allegedly Mancunian home help, Hyde Pierce has now stolen the sitcom from its official star.

Hyde Pierce learned to play priggish, slightly neurotic sons of privilege the honest way: by growing up in a wealthy family in Saratoga Springs, New Jersey. He originally wanted to be a concert pianist, a profession Niles would approve of, but gave it up to become an actor. Parental disapproval was tempered by the fact that, as he only realised later, his dad and great-grandfather had had similar ambitions.

The show that made Hyde Pierce was **The Powers That Be**, a quickly cancelled sitcom in which he played a comically suicidal Congressman and was spotted as a dead ringer for Grammer by an executive at the time NBC was plotting to spin *Frasier* off *Cheers*.

Since 1994, Hyde Pierce has become the show's most distinguished player. Only an actor as understated as he could say 'I'm pumped, I'm psyched and I'm fairly certain I've just swallowed an entire twist of lemon' and make the comedy believable. He has also played John Dean in Niles-esque fashion (and to good effect) in **Oliver Stone's** Nixon, but the real worry must be whether audiences will ever accept him as anyone but Niles. Mind you, as *Frasier's* ratings wobble after eight years, don't surprised if another Crane brother spins off to top the ratings.

✢ ✢ ✢ ✢ ✢ ✢ ✢ ✢ ✢ ✢ ✢ ✢

★ John Le Mesurier ★

THE ENGLISH JOHN LE MESURIER

John Le Mesurier was one of those actors who had to wait for most of his career before playing the role which really connected with the public. TV history is a bit murky on whether **Dad's Army** creators **David Perry** and **Jimmy Croft** wanted him, as some rumours suggest, to play Mainwaring or that they had another actor – possibly **Jack Douglas** – in mind to play Wilson. But as soon as they met Le Mesurier they would have had to be very stupid not to cast him as Wilson.

Opinions differ on how much Le Mesurier was Wilson and how much he played up to it. His next-to-last words when he died in 1982 ('it's all been rather lovely') certainly sound like the sergeant at Walmington-on-Sea's Home Guard. Croft was once amused to see the make-up girls flocking (as they always did) around Le Mesurier and hear him say – with just the right note of *longueur* – 'Would you mind awfully winding up my watch for me?' Yet his reaction in the 1960s when his third wife, Joan, fell in love with Tony Hancock – he never rebuked her, even after the come-

The Le Mesurier ménage a trois: John, Hattie Jacques and that furry thing

dian's suicide – suggests he might indeed have been as vague, impractical and tight-lipped about his emotions as his character.

He was born John Elton Halliley in 1912, adopting his mother's maiden name when he gave up being a solicitor's clerk for acting. His first marriage was destroyed by his wife's alcoholism and his second wife, **Hattie Jacques**, left him for another man (but not before they had lived together in an amicable menage a trois). He married his third wife Joan after a typically vague proposal – 'I don't suppose you'd take me on for a start.'

> **'Would you mind awfully winding up my watch for me?'**

Le Mesurier's great loves were jazz, alcohol and acting, but he could not abide **Jimmy Savile** – the peroxide one's face on the 'This is the age of the train' poster at John's local station would invariably prompt an expletive. Nor could he abide rough handling by medics, telling an American nurse who was too quick with the needle 'You're not drilling for oil in Texas now, dear.'

On the set of *Dad's Army* he occasionally complained about co-star **Arthur Lowe**'s reluctance to learn his lines, but usually he behaved just as Wilson would have. His lack of pretention often led to him being underestimated as an actor: he was superb as Kim Philby in **Dennis Potter**'s play *Traitor*. He died in 1982, aged 71, famously insisting Joan put an obituary in *The Times* saying he had 'conked out'. Asked once if he had any strong views on show business, he replied 'I don't like women wearing green on stage. That's supposed to be a very bad thing to do.'

+ + + + + + + + + + + +

★ David Letterman ★

THE GOD OF LATE NIGHT TELEVISION

You can't watch **David Letterman** without thinking 'if only'. If only some enterprising British TV executive had screened *Letterman* a decade ago we might have been spared **Crinkly Bottom** and realised what **Danny Baker** was trying to do when he flitted across our screens on Saturday nights.

Who but Letterman would have worn a suit made of rice crispies and jumped into a giant bowl of milk to see if he'd go snap, crackle and pop?

And where but the *Letterman* show, in its week of UK residence on BBC2, would you see **Peter O'Toole** arrive on a camel, before giving his steed a can of Heineken to quench its thirst? His absence from our screens enabled lite entertainers such as **Noel Edmunds** to exploit his ideas. But Edmunds' version of Letterman is like a monkey typing Tolstoy: the words may be in the right order but that doesn't mean the monkey understands them.

Letterman has been doing the late night stint on American telly since 1982 and there are nights when he seems in need of a rest. (The top ten lists were funny, but maybe he should have stopped when he'd done ten of them.) But his mad cackle is a tonic. And you never know if his guests will do a striptease (**Drew Barrymore**) or just say the f-word a lot (thanks **Madonna**). When **Sharon Stone** came on and tried to shock, Letterman looked bored. Then she blurted out: 'I can't put a sentence together… thank God I can take my clothes off' and he turned to the audience and observed coolly: 'It's good to hear somebody call a spade a spade, isn't it?'

Don't bother with cheap imitations (or even expensive ones) – watch the original on ITV2. The sparkle isn't as consistent but on the right night, the show zips by faster than you can say 'Clive Anderson talks back'.

+ + + + + + + + + + + +

★ Jack Lord ★
THE LORD OF HAWAII

Nobody has done as much for hair lacquer or Hawaiian holidays as **Jack Lord**. As Steve McGarrett, head of **Hawaii Five-O**, he seemed as honest as the Hawaiian summer is long. But the actor whose shoulder swerve was the highlight of his show's title sequence, was less one-dimensional than his character or his acting.

King David, even funnier than Richard Gere's film

313

Lord's roots were so Irish even **James Joyce** might have hesitated to include them in a novel. He was born John Joseph Patrick Ryan, the son of an Irish cop, in Brooklyn, New York. He was known as Jack and acquired his stage name after discovering some ancestors called Lord ('not the royal kind' he insisted, 'but fishermen from County Cork').

Before getting his break as an actor, he'd been a car salesman, an artist (he ran a studio in Greenwich Village, and some of his works appeared in in the gallery in the *Hawaii Five-O* episode **How To Steal A Masterpiece**), and an officer on cruise liners and (in World War II) the US Merchant Navy. When he was 19, he married a girl from Buenos Aires whom he'd met on a liner, but he soon found that his new bride (who was carrying his son) didn't want to live in America. They got divorced and the son was killed in a tragic accident at the age of 13.

Steve McGarrett never really believed in dressing down – even on the beaches of Oahu

Lord decided he was a better actor than a painter, and took drama studies by night while selling cars during the day. He took ages to make his mark, but then he was choosy: among the 22 roles he turned down before his debut as cowboy **Stoney Burke** were parts in *Wagon Train* and *The Naked City*. He also refused to reprise his role as **James Bond**'s buddy Felix Leiter because producers wouldn't give him equal billing to **Sean Connery**. After Burke ended, Lord coasted as a guest villain in various series before landing the part of McGarrett.

His on-set nickname 'The Lord' was part tribute to his alleged habit of firing extras for looking at him, but also to the fact that he wasn't just the star but, after **Leonard Freeman**'s death, effectively the producer. Yet he is revered in Hawaii for insisting native actors got a decent percentage of the parts. With his second wife Marie (he met her when trying to buy her cottage), he moved to Hawaii where, during filming, he lived a reclusive existence, waking at 4am for tea and papaya, and a run on the beach during which he always picked a fresh flower for his missus.

As McGarrett, he was as incorruptible as his lacquered hair, apart from the famous forelock, was immobile, bullet repelling. The phrase 'Book him, Danno' with which he closed most shows has entered the popular psyche, even though many people don't know where it originated. Steve McGarrett was the police chief every American city should have had but rarely did. Unlike many other TV cops, McGarrett's onscreen personal life was off limits. He was married to the job, with only the occasional hint that a bachelor of his looks (almost as if Lord's buddy **Elvis** had been redesigned by a marketing department) and status might be quite a catch.

The show ended in 1982 and Lord retired to Oahu (where *Five-O* was set) to write poetry, paint, make jewellery with his wife Marie and never, ever answer the phone. He died in 1998, after turning down a walk-on part in a projected film based on the series. He also rejected the chance to appear in *Magnum P.I.* but in those rare episodes where McGarrett was seen in civvies, he'd already proved he could wear dodgy Hawaiian shirts with a panache that **Tom Selleck** could never hope to match.

+ + + + + + + + + + + + +

★ Ian McCaskill ★
BBC WEATHERMAN

In 1994, **Ian McCaskill** was voted Britain's sexiest weatherman. Admittedly he didn't exactly face stiff competition, but even if the voting was done with tongue firmly in cheek, it proved McCaskill's iconic status.

McCaskill was the weatherman who always managed a sunny disposition, even if it was blowing force ten outside. His aim was to instil a little humour into the weather, once going so far as to appear with **Roland Rat** in the name of entertainment. His sheer irrational bright and breeziness made him a national figure – and one of **Rory Bremner**'s favourite targets.

Initially hoping to be a science teacher, McCaskill had had to leave Glasgow University when he ran out of deferments for national service. After joining the RAF's meteorological division, he auditioned for a BBC presenting vacancy in 1978. Chosen from more than 2,000 applicants, he took over from **Barbara Edwards** and her fine selection of knitted tunics to become the face and voice of BBC weather, though unlike **John Kettley,** he never managed a **Tribe of Toffs** hit single named after him.

For 19 years McCaskill's cheery face reminded us what awful weather we have in Britain. 'There's nothing you can do about it,' he once said, 'so you might as well look for the funny side.' The funny side was McCaskill, willing to laugh at his own ties, safari suits or bumbling mannerisms. Now he's retired, there's no weatherman worthy of a Bremner send-up.

+ + + + + + + + + + + +

★ Quinn Martin ★
KING OF CRIME AND COP SHOWS

There was a time in the 1970s when every US cop show on British TV seemed to be 'a **Quinn Martin** production', those four words said with the kind of gravitas acquired only after several hours gargling with gravel.

Martin (real name Martin Cohn) learned his trade with **Lucille Ball** and **Desi Arnaz**'s company Desilu, developing **The Untouchables** for them with Leonard Freeman (of *Hawaii Five-O*) and giving **Robert Stack** his first big break. His next hit, *The Fugitive*, with **David Janssen**, was one of the 1960s' most popular shows, its success being partly due to Martin's realism and his revolutionary idea of shooting night scenes at night and not, as most of his rivals did, shooting film in the day and darkening it.

His hot streak continued in the 1970s with **Barnaby Jones**, **Cannon** and the **Streets Of San Francisco**. *Cannon* had the definitive sub-*Shaft* theme tune and made **William Conrad** – previously deemed too fat to play Matt Dillon in *Gunsmoke* – famous. There were few sights more thrilling than watching a sweating, panting Cannon chasing a suspect with a dedication which, in his condition, could have triggered an instant coronary.

The Streets Of San Francisco is best known for giving **Michael Douglas** his break as keen, naïve, Inspector Steve Keller. Douglas was the perfect foil for **Karl Malden**, the proud owner of the most distinctive showbiz schnozzle since Jimmy Durante. The series is also cherished for the ludicrous pseudo-Shakespearean titling which divided each episode into four acts and an epilogue, the device spoofed so relentlessly in **Police Squad**.

But in 1980, for the first time in 21 years, there were no Quinn Martin productions on prime-time TV in the US. He had sold his production company two years earlier and was barred from competing with its new owners until 1983. In the 1970s, his shows had been criticised for violence. Ironically, by the time national policy reflected Martin's preference for the certainties of law and order, he was in professional exile. The final Quinn Martin production was his funeral in 1987. He was 65.

✢✢✢✢✢✢✢✢✢✢✢✢✢

★ Rik Mayall ★

AS KEVIN TURVEY, RICK IN THE YOUNG ONES BUT NOT AS HITLER

'Good evening. This is **Kevin Turvey**. There's something different about me this week, isn't there? Can you spot it? I've had a haircut. Nope. That's not it, is it? What can it be then? That's right – I'm not here. I have completely disappeared and become utterly invisible.' So began Kevin Turvey's groundbreaking investigation into the supernatural.

As the fearless anorak-clad investigator from Redditch, Turvey was the real star of the fairly short-lived BBC sketch series **A Kick Up The Eighties** (the other high point being **Richard Stilgoe**'s remark that 'Death, rather like Pot Noodles, is something you only try once').

317

Turvey's monologues piled inconsequential detail upon irrelevant aside upon non sequitur. Analysing the fridge's role in his mum's house, he confided: 'We mainly use it for keeping things cold, y'know. Well, it ain't much good for anything else, really. I mean you can't get Radio One on it.' This worked brilliantly, not just in a slot of a few minutes but also in the mockumentary *Kevin Turvey, The Man Behind The Green Door*.

> **'We're Young Ones! Bachelor Boys! Wild-eyed big bottomed anarchists!'**

But time has not been kind to the man behind the man behind the green door. As Rick in *The Young Ones* he brought the requisite naïve enthusiasm to lines like: 'There'll be plenty of chicks for these tigers on the road to the promised land! Who cares about Thatcher and unemployment? We can do just exactly what we want to do! And do you know why? Because we're Young Ones! Bachelor Boys! Wild-eyed big bottomed anarchists! Look out Cliff!' But after that it all went wrong.

Both *Bottom* and *Filthy Rich And Catflap* were both panned, not entirely fairly – certainly in the former's case. (It's a pity Mayall and Edmondson couldn't call the series *Your Bottom* – they wanted viewers to say 'I saw your bottom on telly last night.') **The New Statesman** wasn't a bad idea but it was naffly done. **Rik Mayall Presents** was doomed by the title – decent series in which the star's name is followed by the word 'Presents' being as rare as funny sitcoms starring Gwen Taylor. His appearance as Lord Flasheart in **Blackadder** showed verve, but his tactless Hitler jibe in the anti-Euro campaign succeeded only in making Kevin Turvey's genius seem more distant than ever. While it could be fun to find out what Turvey is up to now, on current form a sequel could justify the *Friends* gag: 'That's funny. That's painfully funny. No wait, it's just painful.'

+ + + + + + + + + + + +

★ Spike Milligan ★

THE MAN WHO MADE MONTY PYTHON (AND SO MUCH ELSE) POSSIBLE

The starts opening music over a studio silhouette. Fifteen seconds to go before the show is on air and **Spike Milligan** leaps out of his chair, runs behind the cameraman and bites him on the ear. The programme opens to shrieks of studio laughter as Milligan enters, tucking his shirt into his trousers and doing up his flies. As the show ends, the screen darkens and Milligan jumps out of his chair again, grabbing a piece of chalk. As the first closing credit rolls, a hand appears to chalk an exclamation mark after it. The next credit reads 'Editor: Cyril Bennett' over which Milligan chalks '9 out of 10' and as the third caption 'Directed by Peter Morley' comes on screen, Milligan chalks 'Who he?'

Standard madcap fare today, but this was in the 1950s. Milligan had to wait a decade before the box caught up with his anarchic comedy. **The Telegoons**, a children's TV version of the radio show, was a cult 1960s hit, especially in Buckingham Palace where the young **Prince Charles** found the show a blessed relief from the onerous business of having the Duke of Edinburgh as a dad. (The Duke was, in many ways, exactly the kind of establishment figure Milligan – born in India and turned down for a UK passport because he refused to swear the Oath of Allegiance – sent up.)

With the launch of **Q5** in 1969, he paved the way for **Monty Python**, his sketches often missing any combination of an end, beginning or middle. **Q5** to **Q9** were the kind of shows you couldn't comfortably watch with your mum in the same room: apart from the puerile surreal humour, there was always the risk that the screen would, for reasons obvious only to Milligan, suddenly be filled by a pair of voluptuous female breasts.

His other moments of TV immortality include **The Phantom Raspberry Blower Of Old London Town**, a starring role as a Pakistani Dalek in a Q6 spoof of *Dr Who* and various chat show appearances in which his reminiscences often reduced himself, his host and the audience to tears of laughter. He once said the strain of having to write *Goon Show* scripts to order cost him his sanity, but despite frequent bouts of depression he lived until he was 84. He died in February 2002, 12 years after his self-penned obituary had been published in the *Sunday Correspondent*.

Only he could create humour so surreal it still feels ahead of its time today, yet also be responsible for such corny, old-fashioned gags as 'Can you play "The Maple Leaf Forever"?' 'No sir, after an hour I get tired.'

319

+ + + + + + + + + + + +

★ Eric Morecambe ★

'WHAT DO YOU THINK OF IT SO FAR?'

Eric Morecambe could raise a laugh with his silhouette. Or by sticking his hand under **Ernie Wise's** chin and saying 'Get out of that without moving'. He had one of those special voices: you only have to read one of his lines to hear him saying it. With his partner, straight man and owner of two short fat hairy legs **Ernie Wise**, Morecambe bore the heavy responsibility for the quality of Britain's Christmases for many years. That was some achievement for a duo whose first appearance on the box, in the 1954 sketch show **Running Wild**, prompted one critic to write: 'Definition of a TV set: the box in which they buried Morecambe and Wise.'

Morecambe was so upset by the reviews that a plague of boils broke out on his neck. He never forgot the indignity, often worrying obsessively about a joke. In the 1970s, he was so afraid a *South Pacific* spoof might not

'Welcome to Shooting Stars, welcome whoever you are, come along and...'

be funny he came down at midnight to watch it being edited. Hyperactive as ever, he tapped the arm of his chair as the film was loaded. When the sequence had run, he shouted in relief: 'Bloody hellfire – it works!'

The contributions of Wise as the instinctive foil and **Eddie Braben**, who wrote many of their best lines, should not be underestimated. But it was Morecambe who elevated the double act to such a level that **Ben Elton** compared the routines where they were sitting in bed bickering over which of them a teacher had liked better 40 years ago, to Samuel Beckett, a comparison (he also admits) that would have horrified them. The structure of comedy was in Morecambe's genes. **John Thaw** recalled one rehearsal where a line got a huge laugh but Morecambe stepped in saying: 'I'm cutting that laugh, because we've got one too many.'

The idea that behind every successful comedian lies immense emotional pain is something of a cliché. Although Morecambe called his first novel (about a comic) *Mr Lonely*, opinions differ as to whether he nursed a secret melancholy. He did, though, tire of the treadmill, taking time later in his career to appear in a couple of films drawing on the poems of **Sir John Betjeman**. A dodgy heart (he suffered his first attack in 1968) finally claimed him in 1984, when he was just 58.

Eric and Ernie's appeal could cross the genders and generations. This may explain why they left behind a legacy which **Reeves and Mortimer** would openly exploit, a small dictionary of catchphrases, and a trick with a paper bag and invisible stones which adults still use to delight credulous children at birthday parties. Routines like 'The Stripper', in which they made breakfast to the jazz tune, are justly famous (as are the musical spoofs with such guest stars as **Angela Rippon** and **Shirley Bassey**) but it's the inconsequential stuff, the banter with his wannabe playwright partner, which stands up best of all.

✢ ✢ ✢ ✢ ✢ ✢ ✢ ✢ ✢ ✢ ✢ ✢ ✢

⋆ Chris Morris ⋆

'THE MOST LOATHED MAN ON TELEVISION'

Chris Morris was given the title of 'the most loathed man on television' by the *Daily Mail*. Not that the honour would worry a man who had no qualms about falsely declaring live on Radio 1 that **Jimmy Savile** and **Michael Heseltine** were dead. Yet for all his antics, Morris had a fairly average upbringing. The son of two doctors, he was popular at school before heading to Bristol University to study zoology, where his charisma triumphed over acne and a love of garlic (he was once asked by colleagues to work outside the office after eating a chicken stuffed with 20 cloves).

Although notorious for **Brass Eye**, Morris already had a string of angry ex-employers long before Michael Grade booted him off Channel 4. He was sacked from Radio Bristol for adding salacious commentary to news stories. Despite the risks, he was hired to front *On The Hour,* a spoof radio news show whose team included **Patrick Marber, Dave Schneider** and **Steve Coogan**. That became *The Day Today* and Morris was given a new medium to abuse: TV. As a psychotic Paxman, Morris emphasised how absurd news-reporting had become. Ridiculous stories – like the death-row prisoner who wanted to be electrocuted on the toilet as a homage to Elvis – were investigated, interspersed with random outrageous headlines like '"Last one on drugs is a queer," yells Portillo'.

> **Morris was asked to work outside the office after eating 20 cloves of garlic**

This was tame compared to *Brass Eye*, which took satire to its limits, or at least the limits Channel 4 would permit. The show had the feel of *World In Action*, yet came with the warning: 'Watch this programme now, because it will never be allowed a repeat.' Morris managed to induce celebrity guests to comment on fake issues, pop singers to debate the difficulty of reaching the note H, and MP **David Amess** to ask questions in the House of Commons about the imaginary drug, cake. But the show was attacked for its 'investigations' into a Peter Sutcliffe musical and for allowing a scientist to proclaim disabled people were just lazy.

After *Brass Eye's* demise, Morris placed his own obituary in the *Guardian*, his final words being 'After his glorious student years at Bristol he went on to a varied broadcasting career before consumption ailed his later years. A good friend, he will be sorely missed.' Far from dead, Morris is rumoured to be working on a short film, so celebrities beware.

✢ ✢ ✢ ✢ ✢ ✢ ✢ ✢ ✢ ✢ ✢ ✢ ✢

⋆ Jeremy Paxman and Jon Snow ⋆

TELEVISION'S PRE-EMINENT NEWSMEN

For news junkies, there is no better way to top and tail an evening than with these two unfashionably intelligent and passionate performers.

Paxman's place in TV's annals would be secure if he had done nothing else but ask **Michael Howard**, former Home Secretary, the same question ('Did you threaten to overrule the head of the prison service?') 12 times. He later admitted the repetition was prompted partly by the need to fill airtime. Afterwards, he turned to his interviewee and said: 'I think that went very well, don't you?' to which Howard, tearing his mike off in indignation, replied: 'What do you bloody think?' Paxman's other great interview in the prison service scandal was with **Ann Widdecombe**. The revelation that the woman soon to be known as Doris Karloff had sent flowers to Derek Lewis (the man said to have been overruled by Howard) prompted Paxman to ask: 'Are you in love with Derek Lewis?'

Those interviews were in 1997 and it is fashionable to say Paxman has lost his edge since. Certainly, there have been times when his weary exasperation has seemed manufactured, but he remains a national asset. Who else, after **Boris Yeltsin** had sacked his entire cabinet, could begin *Newsnight* with the thought 'Boris Yeltsin's played a blinder today'?

In his spare time Paxman hosts *University Challenge*, thereby achieving an ambition **Jon Snow** has yet to fulfil. The Channel 4 news presenter, who usually enters our living rooms tie-first, once confessed to a secret yen to become a quiz show host.

Snow (or 'that pinko' as he is known by **Denis Thatcher**) has a CV as a correspondent that sounds like a script for an *Under Fire*-style movie – saving Britons from a ship caught in the Iran-Iraq war, braving death threats in El Salvador and getting engaged, briefly, to **Anna Ford**. Maybe one day he'll fulfil another long cherished ambition: to tell the news as it strikes him. He's already rehearsed that bulletin in his head – 'Well, here's another crock of shit from the government, and a helping of utter hypocrisy from the opposition, followed by a meaningless soundbite.' Maybe it could make an appearance on **Comic Relief** one year.

✛ ✛ ✛ ✛ ✛ ✛ ✛ ✛ ✛ ✛ ✛ ✛

★ Pat Phoenix ★

THE FIRST SCARLET WOMAN OF SOAP

Patricia Pilkington, as she was born (she once tried to change her surname to Dean in honour of James Dean), was unfairly dubbed 'the working man's Racquel Welch'. For Pat, when she became Phoenix and played Elsie Tanner, was Britain's leading hussy, 'the sexiest woman on television', according to prime minister **Jim Callaghan**. Soap stars often bleat about how fans confuse them with their characters. Not Pat: there was a lot of Elsie in her. When producer **Tony Warren** asked her to take her coat off at the audition, she replied, 'You'll just have to bloody well guess, won't you?'

> **'I was the first anti-heroine, not particularly good looking and no better than I should be'**

Phoenix's personal life was almost as complex as Liz Taylor's, but for Pat the complications started in childhood. Born in Port Humna, County Galway, her dad had married her mother bigamously. He was jailed and while she was a teenager her mum wed again. Pat wanted to be an actress and moved to London taking, she said, 'the labour exchange by storm'. Too 'big and busty to play an English rose', she played femme fatales in theatre and wrote scripts for comedian **Harry Worth**.

As Elsie Tanner, she was the first sex symbol of British soap and acquired the usual accoutrements of such success: a divorce, a kidney-shaped swimming pool at her new home and four marriage proposals a week by post. In 1972, she married fellow *Corrie* actor **Alan Browning** but he was, like his character, an alcoholic. They divorced and she wed old flame **Tony Booth** (Cherie's dad) as she lay dying from lung cancer in hospital. Her death, at the age of 62, caused tabloid hysteria. Her last message to the fans was disarming: 'Thank you very much, loves, and ta-ra.'

She was an iconic figure, a more accessible **Liz Taylor** with fewer ex-husbands and cheaper jewellery. **Morrissey** interviewed her (and put her on the cover of a Smiths single). 'I was the first of the anti-heroines,' she told him, 'not particularly good looking and no better than I should be.' Which, in a hugely modest way, says it all.

✛ ✛ ✛ ✛ ✛ ✛ ✛ ✛ ✛ ✛ ✛ ✛ ✛

Pat Phoenix, a pin up for James Callaghan – and for Tony Blair's father-in-law

⋆ Oliver Postgate ⋆
WITTY CREATOR OF CHILDREN'S ANIMATION

It's hard to imagine a descendant of today's Labour leadership creating anything as imaginative as **The Clangers**. But Oliver Postgate – the man who created the pink, knitted whistlers from outer space – is a grandson of George Lansbury, a founder member of the party. Along with **Peter Firmin**, his partner in **Smallfilms**, he has produced some of the best-loved and most original animation of the last 50 years.

Born in 1925, Postgate stumbled into animation, having tried his hand as an actor after being imprisoned in Wandsworth jail as a conscientious objector. But it was while working as an ITV stage manager that he uttered the words of many a TV audience: 'I could do better than that.' Postgate, though, acted on his words, joining up with animator Firmin. With Firmin as the artist and Postgate writing and directing, the pair worked from a converted cowshed but never to a formula. With *The Clangers,* cartoon Vikings, a Welsh railway engine desperate to sing in a choir, and a talking wooden woodpecker based on philosopher **Bertrand Russell** on their CV, the pair could hardly have been more diverse.

Despite making innocuous children's television, the pair did attract controversy. The BBC told Postgate to moderate the Clangers' language. An **Ivor The Engine** book was banned by Brent Council libraries on grounds of racial discrimination. Even **Bagpuss** has been subjected to the kind of psychological scrutiny and quest for hidden meanings as *The Magic Roundabout* and *Captain Pugwash*. Postgate, though, says Bagpuss was just a saggy old cloth cat, loose at the seams, which Emily loved.

+ + + + + + + + + + + +

⋆ Fred Quimby ⋆
HEAD OF QUALITY ASSURANCE, TOM AND JERRY

The name might mean nothing to you. A picture of him wouldn't help either. In the most frequently published photo he wears sensible glasses, an eminently respectable haircut and a fade-into-the-background tie, looking very much the stereotypical middle manager at an American corporation. Which is just what he was: except he was not working for

General Motors but **MGM**. As head of short films division, he hired **William Hanna** and **Joseph Barbera** to take on Warner Bros' cartoon clout. Out of this came **Tom And Jerry**, the BBC's eternal schedule filler.

Quimby was born in Minneapolis in 1883. After flirting with journalism, he managed a cinema and became intrigued by films. After landing a job at Pathé, he struck out on his own and then joined Fox, moving to MGM to sell short and animated films. By 1937, he was head of the department. His name as producer on the credits for *Tom And Jerry* is recognised as a guarantee of quality. Yet, he remained what he'd always been, a salesman; as a colleague recalled, 'cartoons were a strange thing to him.' But unlike many bosses in TV and Hollywood, he knew enough to let those who did know what they were doing – **Hanna and Barbera** – get on with it. By the time he retired in 1956, his animated films had won eight Oscars.

After his retirement, changing markets and corporate demands led to a sad decline in quality, with *Tom And Jerry* being briefly and disastrously animated in Czechoslovakia. Hanna and Barbera revived their favourite characters in the 1970s, but budgets and the rise of political correctness made impossible any return to the anarchic violence of the 240 or so shorts made under Quimby, the shrewdest tycoon in toon town.

✛ ✛ ✛ ✛ ✛ ✛ ✛ ✛ ✛ ✛ ✛ ✛ ✛

★ Reeves And Mortimer ★

LEADING EXPONENTS OF NORTHERN DADAIST COMEDY

If you don't like **Reeves and Mortimer**, mere words will not convince. If the idea that a man might live in mortal fear of chives, or that people could be sentenced to spend a year as a cast member of *Jesus Christ Superstar*, doesn't raise a titter. Then that's it. End of story.

Comedy, **Alan Bennett** said, should never be explained because 'if too much explaining goes on… it becomes the sum of all the boring old rubbish that's ever been said.' So this is not the place to explore the debt this duo owe to **Morecambe and Wise** (but it goes deeper than their taste in specs) or to **Bryan Ferry** (when Bob first saw Vic perform, Reeves wore a Ferry mask – he has the same knack for hijacking brand names and popular culture for his own ends as their fellow north-easterner).

The closest anyone has come to defining their humour was to call it 'northern dadaist variety'. Certainly **Vic Reeves' Big Night Out** (which first aired in 1990) was one of those shows which either left you as cold as Mary Whitehouse watching the *Red Shoe Diaries* – or made you laugh out loud. And that has been the story since, be it **The Smell Of Reeves And Mortimer** or **Shooting Stars**, one of the few post-modern ironic quiz shows which was genuinely funny.

> **Miscreants could be sentenced to a year in the cast of Jesus Christ Superstar**

Together they have the ability, in an instant, to conjure up a world of comic idiocy so infectious your stomach muscles just will you to laugh to release the tension. Giving out Bob Hoskins masks as prizes is amusingly appropriate even if it is a homage to the Pythons, whom both Vic (real name Jim Moir) and Bob (real name Bob Mortimer) had adored as schoolkids in Darlington.

They have, at least, experimented and even where they haven't quite worked – like *The Weekenders*, the 1992 sitcom starring several future *Fast Show* regulars (and the Human League's **Philip Oakey**) – their efforts have been original. After a new BBC deal, there was an obvious bid to broaden their appeal with shows like **Families At War** flawed but funnier than most shows in that slot since Basil Brush resigned in a huff.

The idea of reviving *Randall And Hopkirk Deceased* seemed promising until the first episode aired. Although the scripts were by **Charlie Higson**, Mortimer, as the straight man, looked lost while Reeves, as the ghostly partner was guilty mainly of overacting. This was last-resort viewing only but nonetheless this retread has been their only out-and-out failure.

There's nothing intrinsically wrong with **Ben Elton** that surgery to remove the cat-got-the-cream-grin couldn't cure, but the flood of politically conscious comedy which followed often had one fatal deficiency: it didn't make you laugh. *Vic's Big Night Out*, with its improvised dialogue and its sheer strangeness, was a very welcome alternative. And yes, despite New Year's resolutions to the contrary, we still find the pub singer amusing.

328

✦ ✦ ✦ ✦ ✦ ✦ ✦ ✦ ✦ ✦ ✦ ✦ ✦

★ Gene Roddenberry ★

THE MAN WHO HELPED US EXPLORE STRANGE NEW WORLDS

Eugene Wesley Roddenberry led an eventful life, but it is as creator of *Star Trek* that he will be remembered. The Trek cult celebrates him as The Great Bird – a humanist and futurist who took us 'where no man has gone before' – though others, such as the series' composer **Alexander Courage**, take a rather different view (see p366).

Roddenberry (born in Texas, raised in Los Angeles) became a qualified pilot at 19, winning the Distinguished Flying Cross and Air Medal during 89 combat missions over the Pacific during World War II. After becoming a crash investigator for the USAF and a co-pilot for PanAm, he himself crashed in the Syrian desert in 1947, earning a commendation for his supervision of the rescue, despite his broken ribs.

His next career move was to follow his father into the Los Angeles police. After getting his start in TV by selling true stories to the cop series **Dragnet**, he became technical advisor on *Mr District Attorney,* where he also sold his first script. Despite passing his police sergeant's exam, he left to write full-time, becoming head writer for **Have Gun, Will Travel** and creating *The Lieutenant,* a Marine Corps drama show.

Contracted by Desilu to develop action adventure shows, Roddenberry pitched his 'wagon train to the stars' concept and *Star Trek* was born. It lasted just three seasons (1969–71) but the show, its images and phrases have entered 21st-century public consciousness, spawning three spin-off TV series and a lucrative film franchise. Its enduring appeal and extraordinary fandom practically define cult TV.

In 1986 Roddenberry became the first writer-producer honoured with a star on the Hollywood Walk of Fame. He was also feted at universities, Nasa and the Smithsonian Institute, but the ultimate accolade came in 1992, when the space shuttle *Columbia* bore his ashes to the stars.

Two Roddenberry-conceived TV series – *Andromeda* and *Earth: Final Conflict* – have also made it on to our screens posthumously, shepherded by his widow Majel (*Star Trek*'s Nurse Chapel and *The Next Generation*'s Lwaxana Troi) and their son Gene Jr.

＋＋＋＋＋＋＋＋＋＋＋＋

★ Leonard Rossiter ★

NOBODY HAS EVER MADE MIDDLE-AGED DISAPPOINTMENT QUITE SO AMUSING

Over 35 years, Liverpool-born Leonard Rossiter built an impressive career in theatre and played numerous film roles (*2001: A Space Odyssey*, *Oliver!*, *Billy Liar*, *Barry Lyndon*, *Le Petomane* etc), yet the roles with which he will always be associated – along with those wonderful Cinzano commercials with **Joan Collins** – were in TV sitcoms.

Rossiter's TV career started in 1956 with a bit part in a BBC play. During the 1960s he had a stint as Inspector Bamber on **Z Cars** and could regularly be seen playing nefarious, raincoated criminal types (and Robin Hood in one episode of *The Avengers*). The following decade it was his scene-stealing turn as an escaped convict in *Steptoe And Son* (1972) that won him him the part of **Rigsby**, which made him a star.

As the dodgy landlord in ITV's **Rising Damp**, Rossiter succeeded in making a seedy, sarcastic bigot with romantic aspirations ('a man so prejudiced he even hates himself,' quipped the actor) into a lovable anti-hero. On BBC, he was even more dazzling as the frustrated middle-aged exec who fakes his own death in **The Fall And Rise Of Reginald Perrin**.

But even he – a powerful, versatile and a bona fide comedy genius – couldn't save *The Losers* and *Tripper's Day*, two sitcoms that have never been repeated, for good reason. Even so, with his memorable countenance (once compared to 'a hollowed-out turnip, lit from within'), a streak of perfectionism and an incredible capacity for learning vast amounts of dialogue, Rossiter was Britain's best comic actor at the time of his sudden death from a heart attack in 1984. He was just 57.

✦✦✦✦✦✦✦✦✦✦✦✦✦

★ Aaron Spelling ★

THE KING OF GLITZY SOAP

Aaron Spelling may be a tiny, funny guy who looks like a beetle but for the four decades that television has ruled the world, he has ruled the world of television. Or, more precisely, that bit of it devoted to the kitsch, the dreck, the rubbish and the trash. His are the shows which millions adore and define the pop-culture of their time: **The Mod Squad** was cool

'It's that escaped puma again, – the one that delayed the train at Chessington South last week'

1960s; **The Love Boat** funky 1970s; **Dynasty** the bitchin' 1980s; **Melrose Place** the droll, post modern 1990s. And that's before we even touch on *Burke's Law, S.W.A.T, Fantasy Island, Starsky And Hutch, Charlie's Angels, Hart To Hart, TJ Hooker, Beverly Hills 90210* – or myriad TV movies which never made it across the Atlantic – *Satan's School For Girls*, anyone?

Yet none of them might ever have happened – if a World War II sniper's bullets had hit Spelling somewhere deadlier than his left hand and knee. Appropriately, Spelling's life story is a classic mini-series schlock plot. He was born in 1923 in Dallas, Texas of poor immigrant parents – a scrawny kid with the nickname 'Jewbaby'. After his time as a war correspondent, he became a roadie for an all-female band. Once he was in LA, he never left. His televisual hallmarks – lots of hot, foxy, young bodies (and Joan Collins) in tight close-up, telling tales of deception and desire, despair, revenge, lust and heartbreak – have changed little in 30 years.

The Love Boat, his cheesiest show, and **Fantasy Island**, his most offbeat, proved popular in the 1970s, the same decade his *Starsky And Hutch* became the first big buddy-buddy cop show. **Charlie's Angels** was the highest-rated TV programme of the decade, the prime exponent of jiggle TV, but by 1989, Spelling was in trouble. His magnificent bitchfest **Dynasty** had been canned. Spelling was off air, and, in his mid-sixties, looked unlikely to make a comeback now.

> ## In Melrose Place the blind saw, the crippled walked again and the dead stalked the earth

But Fox wanted a new young audience and turned to Spelling who recalls: 'Fox had a script called *Class Of Beverly Hills*. I asked them, what the hell do I know about high-school kids? But they told me, 'You have one. Go look in your daughter's bedroom.''

From the teen-angst, 'Mom, Brandon's hogging the bathroom'-type plots, **Beverly Hills 90210** has reached the point where the 'kids' deal with everything from AIDS to napalm. The show led on to Spelling's classic psycho-drama **Melrose Place**, where blind saw, the crippled walked and the dead returned to stalk the earth.

The grand old man has a personal taste as flashy as his TV output. One Christmas, after his daughter Tori (Donna Martin in *Beverly Hills 90210*) and son Randy said they'd never seen snow, he bought a snow-making machine and filled the garden with the stuff. But he has been married to his second wife Candy, for 28 years. The actress **Suzanne Pleshette** once said to Candy: 'I want you to say the word "shit".' When asked why, Pleshette replied, 'You're so damn pure you're driving us all crazy.'

✛ ✛ ✛ ✛ ✛ ✛ ✛ ✛ ✛ ✛ ✛ ✛ ✛

★ Carol Vorderman ★

HOUSEHUSBANDS' FAVOURITE, GAME SHOW ASSISTANT OF THE YEAR IN 1997

Carol Vorderman is the 122nd sexiest woman in the world (say readers of *Maxim* magazine), the owner of the worst celebrity haircut (according to 1,100 women polled by Tesco, who placed her below **Ann Widdecombe**) and the fifth most overrated presenter on TV (as voted in a Mori poll). Cynics have wondered at her ubiquity – she is no longer content to dish out letters and write sums with a felt tip pen, but wants to improve British homes, improve children's education, clean up the Internet, usurp that place in the nation's affections occupied by **This Is Your Life**, and switch us on to certain loans, detox diets and low-fat spreads.

What the cynics don't realise is that 'our Carol' is in fact part of a unique scientific experiment to determine how much of a person the masses can see without finally and irrevocably getting sick of them. So far, the evidence suggests that despite the occasional backlash (do we really need to know she finds Shakespeare as 'dull as ditchwater'?), she hasn't even begun to become an object of fear and loathing.

Vorderman has been adopted by the Welsh (although she was born in Bedford) because her family relocated to Rhyl. It was here she became adept at maths, partly out of a natural desire to avoid the blackboard duster. Although she belongs to Mensa (and is said to have an IQ of 154), she didn't, as legend has it, get a first at Cambridge when she studied civil engineering. But she was confident enough to apply for a job as maths expert on **Countdown**, where she has shown her acting chops in the ease with which she looks unembarrassed by **Whiteley**'s lame jokes.

Before she revealed her true leather-trouser wearing self, she became a secret object of desire for househusbands and male undergraduates. Vorderman was like an attractive friend of your mum, but then her weight and her necklines plunged and she became officially sexy.

But somehow it's not quite the same. As she turns up to the latest film premiere, her image seems about as subtle as one of Whiteley's jackets. But hopefully the scientific experiment will be over soon and 'our Carol' can focus on her felt tip pens again. Let's face it, we don't need an ageing rival to **Kylie Minogue**, but we do need someone to remind us of the vanishing art of mental arithmetic.

+ + + + + + + + + + + +

'Oh Carol, there will never ever be another...'

★ Paul Whitehouse ★

PATRIARCH OF THE WHITEHOUSE FAMILY

Born in Stanleytown in the Rhondda Valley in 1959, Whitehouse is a master of catchphrases (hence the self-deprecating remarks he normally drops in to interviews) and character-based humour who has shown he can handle darker and richer dramatic work. His writing career began in the mid-1980s when Stavros, a character he and his friend Harry Enfield had developed (in the pub) secured a slot on Channel 4's **Saturday Live**. A plasterer at the time, Whitehouse became an integral part of Enfield's shows in the early 1990s. As Mike Smash, Fred Git, Julio Geordio, Captain Stefan Van der Haast Graacht of the Amsterdam Police and others, he has emerged as one of our most gifted, observant comic actor/writers.

With a team that included **Charlie Higson**, **Graham Linehan** and **Caroline Aherne**, his next project was **The Fast Show**, which aimed to cram as many short sketches into half-an-hour as possible. Running for three series (plus three specials in 2000), it introduced the likes of Arthur Atkinson, Ted & Ralph and Jazz Club, spawning myriad catchphrases and making him a household name. In 2001, he returned with **Happiness**, a bleak comedy drama stocked with rounded – if neurotic – characters in which he played a recently widowed minor celeb in a mid-life crisis.

Whitehouse cites **Peter Cook** and **Dudley Moore** as a major influence, and his own work might be as revered in years to come. Equally funny as low or high born, teenager or old geezer, much of his output has been – as he might say: 'the creme de la bollocks!'

+ + + + + + + + + + + +

★ Edward Woodward ★

'A DEAD SHOT WITH THE COLD NERVE TO KILL', AS CALLAN AND THE EQUALIZER

Edward Woodward is a man of many parts – trumpet player with a jazz combo, singer (with two gold albums in Australia), musical lead, actor, narrator – but for most of us, he'll always be a man of two parts: the world-weary spy David Callan who dispensed his own brand of justice in **Callan**, and Robert McCall, the world-weary ex-spy who dispensed his own brand of justice as **The Equalizer**.

Croydon born and bred, Woodward had wanted to be a journalist until school plays turned his head. Traces of a 'sarf Landon' accent were erased at Rada when he was 16. He appeared in his first musical in 1950, when he was 20 and was almost typecast as a musical lead until he won the part of Callan, originally a one-off TV play in the *Armchair Theatre* series.

As Callan, he was very much the anti-Bond – a collector of toy soldiers who 'didn't make friends and all his enemies are dead', with a petty thief Lonely (Russell Hunter) as his lowlife sidekick. The first two series were shot in black and white, perfectly evoking the seediness of the **Len Deighton** world in which Callan worked.

Woodward never really escaped typecasting as a spy, but he tried. He narrated *In Suspicious Circumstances*, starred in the sub-Orwellian fantasy *1990* and hosted his own variety show. His return to small-screen bigtime came on American TV as McCall, the avenging angel who helped anyone who answered his newspaper ad ('Got a problem? Odds against you? Call The Equalizer') in a part written for **James Coburn**. Woodward was in his fifties as filming began, smoking 40 cigarettes a day and the added toll of shooting

> **As one disgruntled viewer put it, McCall sounded 'like William Shatner with a British accent'**

for 18-19 hours a day in a freezing garage on the east side of New York soon led to a heart attack.

Woodward's father, daughter and second wife (**Michele Dotrice**, best known as Betty in *Some Mothers Do 'Ave Em*) all made guest appearances in the show, but he may not have felt its demise too keenly as it gave him a chance to break the mould, showing off hitherto unsuspected comic talents as gloomy dustbinman Nev in the BBC sitcom **Common As Muck**.

As McCall, he has been described as the sexiest man ever on television (in a US poll) and as the hardest man on TV (in a Channel 4 top ten). The role's enduring appeal is mysterious given that he often sounded, as one disgruntled viewer put it, 'like William Shatner with a British accent'. But his fiftysomething, Jag-driving, flawed dispenser of justice was the perfect fantasy figure for an America gripped by urban paranoia.

✛✛✛✛✛✛✛✛✛✛✛✛✛

★ The first mogul of television ★

Lew Grade wouldn't have known what 'close but no cigar' meant

Lew Grade, the cigar-chomping producer who made television for the masses, was so certain of his ideas that during filming of *Jesus Of Nazareth* he asked if the director could make do with six disciples.

Born Louis Winogradsky in 1906 in a small Ukrainian town, he was brought by his parents at the age of six to live in the East End of London. He found early stardom as a world champion charleston dancer (Fred Astaire was one of the judges), but soon began managing a talent agency with his brother Leslie. The pair had the foresight to embrace television, creating their own production company to showcase the talent on their books. Grade then became managing director of ATV and its production subsidiary, ITC, and commercial television was born.

If there was a deal to be made, Grade made it. A workaholic who never took a holiday, he was shrewd in business, yet arguably his real talent lay in recognising what audiences wanted to see: 'I know what the public want,' he said, 'because I am one of them.'

Enjoyment was his real motive, he said. 'I love the entertainment industry and I love people. Money is almost the least important thing.' Almost. His business techniques were certainly unusual. When Roger Moore agreed to *The Saint*, he thought he was being paid for 26 half-hour shows. Only in the press conference announcing the show did he realise he'd signed for one-hour shows for the same money. The deal went ahead regardless.

Grade and ATV dominated British television from the 1950s to the 1970s. Shows such as *The Prisoner, Stingray* and *Thunderbirds* enjoyed success on both sides of the Atlantic, and there was classic British viewing as well, from *Hancock's Half Hour* to *Crossroads*, and from *The Golden Shot* to *Tiswas*. Each show had one thing in common – they were designed with pure entertainment in mind.

But Grade was never afraid to take chances. Many producers before him had failed to see the appeal of a talking frog puppet and his friends, but Grade snapped up the rights to *The Muppets* as soon as it was put to him. There was the odd failure, like the 1980 movie *Raise The Titanic*, but Grade simply shrugged off the episode with a droll, 'It would have been cheaper to lower the Atlantic.'

He died in 1998 at the grand old age of 92. He had only just announced plans to postpone his retirement for another two years.

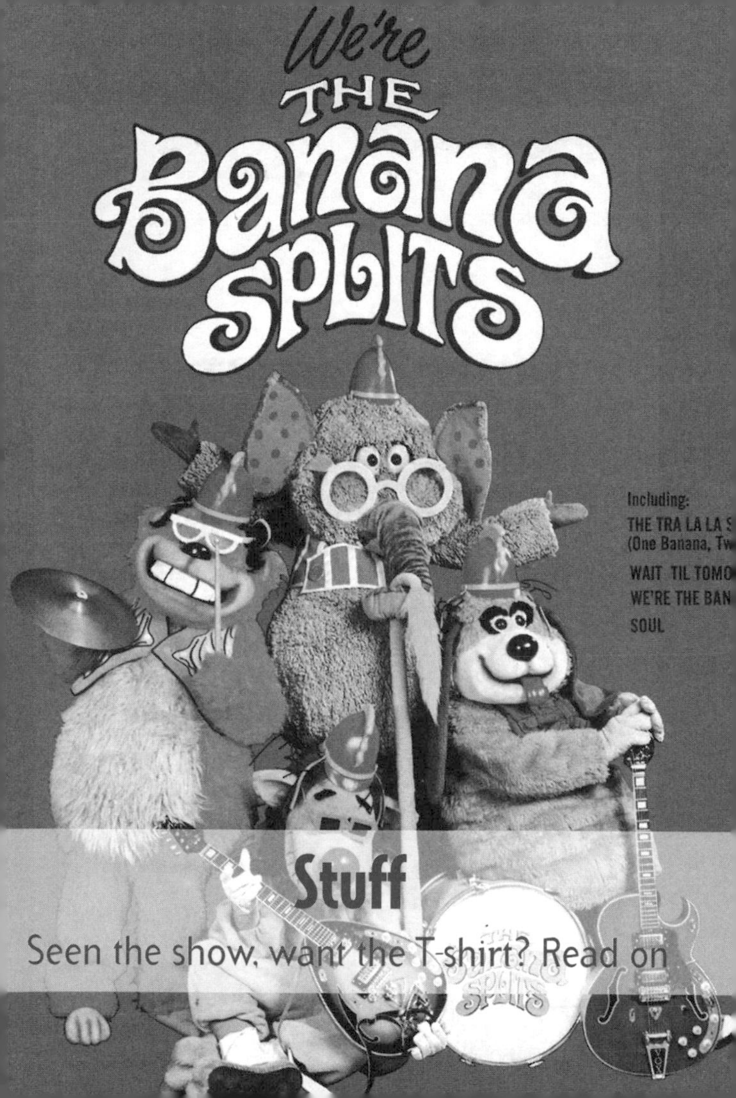

Stuff

Seen the show, want the T-shirt? Read on

'Krusty's brand imitation gruel.
Seven out of ten orphans can't tell the difference!'

The simple fact that you've gone to the trouble of buying a book dedicated to television proves that you have already moved beyond the **Homer Simpson** approach to viewing – that any programme is fine as long as it drowns out the real world.

Companies used to be relatively slow to exploit our affection for all things televisual. But today, while TV merchandise and memorabilia isn't quite up there with movie merchandise, you will be spoilt for choice. The **Hogan's Heroes** fridge magnet could be yours (for the equivalent of $3.50 plus postage) from www.fridgedoor.com. The **X-Files Ken and Barbie**, two of the most sought-after TV dolls, will cost you a slightly less modest $149 (plus the usual add-ons) from www.mykingdomforasource.com. Publishers have offered all kinds of reading matter about TV, a real pioneer title being the **Brand New Monty Python Papperbok**, a must-have in the 1970s. There has recently been a rash of books which try to relate **Kramer** from *Seinfeld* to the teachings of **Aristotle**, or **The Simpsons'** moral universe to the work of **Immanuel Kant**. (This is a free country but generally our advice is that these books aren't worth the time it took some schmuck to decide this was an easy way to make us part with £15.)

This chapter will take you on a tour of the world of TV merchandise and memorabilia ('merch' as they call it in the biz), stopping off to peruse a few relevant books, loiter over a rack of classic TV-related albums (including the work of **Leonard**

Nobody had a silver brass band like the Clangers

Nimoy: believe us, when he sings 'If I Had A Hammer' you'll wish you had one to hand), gawp over products as odd as **Eric Morecambe**'s tie and boldly go on the web to find the best TV sites, including a shrine to the great Gus Hedges from **Drop The Dead Donkey**. Anyway, as Gus might say, this chapter is just meant to be a brief scuba in your think-tank…

Books

Nowadays you need only to star in a soap for a few minutes and your life can be turned into a rags-to-riches tale of hope (step forward, Martine McCutcheon). Mercifully there are more gripping books to read about the folks who made the box what it is today (and was the day before).

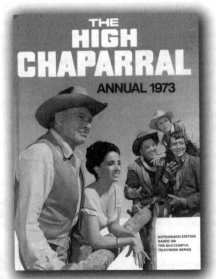

Christmas stockings have never felt as exciting since the Arizona sun set on this Western soap

★ The annual report ★

Let's skip the *Antiques Roadshow* niceties and cut to the chase. That 1980 *Wonder Woman* annual you've spotted in your local Oxfam for £2.20 – is it worth serious money? Sadly, the answer is almost certainly no. Apart from the obvious factors such as condition, the usual tedious law of supply and demand applies.

Most TV-related annuals had large print-runs. The ones which do fetch higher prices – and we're barely talking double figures here – tend to be the likes of *Bagpuss* or *The Clangers*, products of smaller enterprises. Unlike record-collecting, however, there are no incredibly rare annuals that command astronomic prices. (Well, would you put *Wonder Woman* on a par with the Beatles or Elvis?) The annuals we found for sale on our visit to the Vintage Magazine Shop in London ranged from a 1962 *Dr Kildare* annual (comic-style illustrations of the storylines) in perfect condition at £28, to a damaged *Wombles* 1976 item at £3. We left with a slightly tatty *Roy Rogers: King Of The Cowboys* annual (more storybook illustrations) from 1955 for £15 – a bargain to us. A *Dr Who And The Daleks* special, snapped up in a central London secondhand bookshop, cost us £25 but it was worth it for the diagram of the insides of a Dalek.

And therein lies the rub. Most purchases are either by quirky collectors or by people seeking a one-off reminder of their childhood. Higher prices only occur when collectors are trading specific wants, usually based on a particular series (*Star Trek*) or star (mostly film or pop). A typical specialist enquiry might involve Itsy and Bitsy (two puppet spiders from the 1970s lunchtime series *Paperplay*), but that dog-eared *Blue Peter* annual in your loft is not an investment.

If you are interested in buying or selling (and remember professional traders will not be as generous as charity shops), try Sheffield-based Tilleys (**www.tilleys magazines.com**) or the specialist section of the London bookseller Nigel Williams (**0207 836 7757**).

TV comedy at its finest

Biographies

A Jobbing Actor John Le Mesurier (Sphere)
Sadly out of print, this unpretentious little memoir is as quietly stylish and droll as the man himself. The book begins 'My mother had some difficulty in projecting me into the world. Apparently my head was a trifle oversized.' The chapter by his widow on John's foibles, especially his strange ways with tea, is just as amusing.

Blind In One Ear Patrick Macnee (Mercury House)
Star of *The Avengers*, one of the best-loved TV shows, who was brought up by his mother and her lesbian lover, bares all about his stardom and his private life.

Boy Wonder: My Life In Tights Burt Ward (Logical Figments)
This absurd yet humorous kiss-and-tell tale portrays Adam (Batman) West as an egocentric, boozing womaniser, the martial arts equal of Bruce Lee, and on an acting par with Dustin Hoffman. He has a point about Mr Hoffman.

In The Best Possible Taste David Lister (Bloomsbury)
The classic story of funny man Kenny Everett – hilarious on the face of it, sad on the inside. Lister charts Everett's success and unique anarchic brand of humour.

Lucille: The Life Of Lucille Ball Kathleen Brady (Billboard)
Absorbing tale of one of the most revered television actresses of all time and her roller-coaster life both as Lucille Ball and TV's Lucy Ricardo.

Morecambe And Wise Graham McCann (4th Estate)
Hard to go wrong with Britain's funniest twosome and McCann doesn't. His book on *Dad's Army* (also from 4th Estate) is a great fund of insight and anecdotes too.

Pete & Dud Alexander Games (Andre Deutsch)
Provocative but hilarious examination of one of television's most inspiring double acts. *The Dagenham Dialogues* (Mandarin), still obtainable if you're very persistent, would be a wonderful companion.

Polly Wants A Zebra Michael Aspel (Futura)
Reminiscent in tone of Roger Moore's diary of the making of *Live And Let Die*, this rarity is worth buying just for the casual insight into the mystery of Peter Glaze.

The Secret Life Of Sooty Geoff Tibballs (Ringpress)
Probably the biggest revelation is the foreword by George Harrison… never had the quiet Beatle down as a puppet-fancier. Sadly, this doesn't explore the rumour that lovable Sooty took over Harry Corbett's life in a very sinister way.

Seeing Things Oliver Postgate and Peter Firmin (Pan)
Entertaining account of the creation of Smallfilms, who gave us such lasting
joys as *Noggin The Nog*, *Bagpuss*, *The Clangers*, et al. Worth it just for the
accompanying CD-ROM which is not to be played in the office for the simple
reason that you won't want to do any work.

What Made Thunderbirds Go! Gerry Anderson (BBC)
Despite the tabloid slant on Anderson's private life – his obvious disdain for his
ex-wife and voice of Lady Penelope, Sylvia Anderson – there is a wealth of material
on cult classics such as *Fireball XL5*, *Space 1999* and, of course, *Thunderbirds*.

When The Wind Changed Cliff Goodwin (Arrow)
The definitive account of the troubled life of Anthony John Hancock, written by
a man who admits he needs a 'fix' of Hancock to lift him when he's feeling down.

Programmes

Frasier Jefferson Graham (Simon & Schuster)
Character biographies, interviews and, finally, a list of all those radio voices.
The first companion to this fine sitcom, and probably still the best.

The Life And Loves Of Elsie Tanner Daran Little (Boxtree)
Somewhat pedestrian chronology of the brassy *Street* star's life, loves and lodgers
but redeemed by fantastic period photos.

The Life of Python George Perry
(Pavilion)
Hard to find, but an essential guide to
Python's origins and group dynamics.
The most fascinating part deals with their
pre-Python adventures in sitcom land.

Porridge: The Inside Story
Richard Webber, et al (Headline)
Biographies, interviews and insight into
all the inmates, even those without lines.

Worth buying for Pat's period pics. Just

Quotable Star Trek Jill Sherwin
(Star Trek)
'Look, I'm a doctor, not an escalator.' (McCoy to Eleen, needing help
to get her up a mountain). This and many more in a surprisingly broad collection.

Saints & Avengers James Chapman (Ibtauris)
Written for a media studies course, but don't be put off. This is a very accessible, interesting read about cult British 1960s TV series. One of the joys is the reminder of how ropey the plots for *Randall & Hopkirk (Deceased)* were.

The Simpsons Forever Matt Groening (Harper Collins)
Exhaustive guide to characters, quotes and a seemingly inexhaustible supply of clever, witty episode detail. Updates *The Simpsons: A Complete Guide To Our Favourite Family*.

Resistance is useless. **Soap Box** Hilary Kingsley (Papermac)
Almost as much fun   All the inside gossip on every soap known to British TV.
as the series

Welcome To Twin Peaks David Lynch (Pocket Books)
Just don't expect it to make things any clearer.

General (reference, criticism, inside the TV business)

The Encyclopaedia Of Cult Children's TV Richard Lewis (Allison & Busby)
Stop reading, go out now and buy this book. It's that good.

The Encyclopaedia Of TV Science Fiction Roger Fulton (Boxtree)
The good, the bad, and the ugly in sci-fi.

The Penguin TV Companion Jeff Evans (Penguin)
You'll find almost every show in here, dealt with in an authoritative way. The only criticism is that sometimes it could lighten up a bit.

The Ultimate TV Guide Jon E Lewis and Penny Stempel (Orion)
Not as comprehensive as Evans' guide but has some good inside info.

Fuzzy Monsters Chris Horrie (Pocket)
Stories and revelations about various characters working within the BBC.

Inside Prime Time Todd Gitlin (Routledge)
To read this book is to understand American prime-time TV.

Inside the Magic Rectangle Victor Lewis-Smith (Weidenfeld & Nicholson)
Critic's caustic dismantling of a host of dubious UK television shows.

Live TV Chris Horrie & Adam Nathan (Pocket)
Janet Street-Porter versus Kelvin MacKenzie in a cable TV deathmatch.

Mrs Slocombe's Pussy Stuart Jeffries (Flamingo)
Almost the *Fever Pitch* of telly. A very funny read, spoilt only by the occasional bit of pseudery.

Tapehead Jim Shelley (Atlantic)
The funniest book of TV criticism about the 1990s, bar none.

Visions Before Midnight;
The Crystal Bucket;
Glued To The Box
Clive James (Picador)
Wickedly funny reviews by the acid Australian TV critic in his post at *The Observer* 1972–82.

TV Go Home (4th Estate)
Spoof TV listings from the satirical TVGoHome.com website folk. Mick Hucknall's Pink Pancakes indeed.

CDs

Long before soap stars like Kylie and Jason, there were entertainers and actors utterly convinced that their talent for saying their lines on cue in front of a camera made them the next singing sensation.

Charity shops and fund-raising events are a good source of lost treasures like Pinky & Perky's *Wild West* EP or that rare (as in nobody wanted it in 1977 either) *Both Sides Of Bruce* double album by Bruce Forsyth.

★ Songs from the shows ★

Shut That Door, Larry Grayson, 1976
Predictably hackneyed catchphrase cash-in from the *Generation Game* host, including such appalling lines as: 'Shut that door/ It's freezing cold in here/I haven't felt myself all day/I'm feeling rather queer'.

Benny's Theme, Paul Henry, 1978
The woolly-hatted *Crossroads* handyman didn't really disappear to get a spanner – he was talking his way through this 'where is love?' tearjerker as Telly Savalas had done with *If*. Only far less successfully.

Help Yourself/Bigamy At Christmas, Tony Ferrino, 1996
Skip the all-too-accurately bland cover of Tom Jones' old hit by Steve Coogan's Euro-crooner alter ego. Savour instead the savage parody on the flip side, complete with singalong kiddie chorus, jovial talkie bit ('Oven gloves for Mummy') and the plea to think of the man with two wives: 'He's in a pickle when Christmas arrives.'

Fireball, Don Spencer, 1963
'I want to be a fireball,' gushed Spencer enthusiastically. Not exactly a universal sentiment, but the theme from *Fireball XL5* kicked around the charts for three months without cracking the Top 30. A favourite cover by XTC in their early days.

I'm Not A Pheasant Plucker, I'm A Pheasant Plucker's Son, Bill Maynard, 1978
'Oh no – it's Selwyn Froggitt,' said the BBC and banned Bill's potential smasheroo from Radio 1. Life can be so unfair sometimes.

345

But many period items have now been re-released by nostalgia or kitsch-conscious labels. If it's theme tunes you're into, **Television's Greatest Hits 1 & 2** (Cinerama) are a must, though they're usually American. This selection is designed to whet (should that be satiate?) your appetite.

The Best TV Ads... Ever Various (Virgin)
One of many compilations of once-great songs plundered for use in adverts. Still, they are often more entertaining than the shows they're interrupting.

Benny Hill On Top With... (EMI)
Although the title doesn't conjure up a particularly appealing image, Hill could certainly write some clever pop songs.

The Clangers Original Music (Trunk Records)
At the risk of seeming obsesssed, this collection of Vernon Elliot's background music makes a fine chill-out CD.

Crimestoppers Various (Rhino Records)
Well-researched compilation of hip crime TV themes on the excellent Rhino label.

David Hasselhoff The Very Best Of (BMG Import)
How can you resist tracks like 'Do The Limbo Dance' and 'Flying On The Wings Of Tenderness'? But the real masterpiece (aficionados, ie Germans, insist) is the German ballad 'Du'.

Half Man Half Biscuit Back In The DHSS (Probe Plus Records)
Worth buying just for the sleeve notes: Keith Harris – 'bubbly, bestial and boring'. Of the songs, 'God gave us life, but he also gave us... Lionel Blair' is, well, priceless.

Rolf Harris Can You Tell What It Is Yet? (EMI)
Contains all the exasperating favourites – 'Sun Arise', 'Frog Went A-Courting' and slightly less of a classic, a cover of The Beatles' 'Hey Bulldog' (from *Yellow Submarine*) by the now cult-favourite pop festival star.

David McCallum Music Is Part Of Me/A Bit More Of Me (EMI)

A Vulcan's foray onto vulcanite

Bet you didn't know that McCallum (*The Man From U.N.C.L.E.*'s Illya Kuryakin) is classically trained on oboe, cor anglais and piano. In 1966, instead of singing, he made these two albums of jaunty, easy-listening versions of 'Downtown', 'Uptight', 'Satisfaction' and other toe-tapping favourites. Not bad as it 'appens, guys'n'gals.

The Monkees Definitive Monkees (WEA)
What is now revered as classic 1960s pop was viewed at the time as boy bands are today – but at least they manufactured personalities too. Be warned: 'Cuddly Toy' is not to be played when there's more than one feminist in the room.

Leonard Nimoy Highly Illogical (Rev-ola/Creation)
Bizarre set of cover versions ('If I Had A Hammer' with talkover and chorus singing 'America The Beautiful') mixed with Vulcan musings on sex and the madness of mankind. 'With mutual respect people could explore together/The many rooms in the mansion of our lives,' says Len at one point – a Vulcan chat-up line if ever we heard one.

The Partridge Family The Definitive Collection (Arista)
Good-natured, manufactured pop cheese.

Peters And Lee The Best Of (Spectrum)
As the only song of theirs most of us can recall is the cheesy number one 'Welcome Home', you will be staggered to discover that these *Opportunity Knocks* graduates have collated 20 hits for this album, which has also been repackaged (as 'Welcome Home') with added Bontempi organ sounds.

The Rutles The Rutles (Rhino Records)
Still available on import, this is infinitely preferable to *Archaeology*, the box-set spoof of you-know-what, on which the fake fab four sound as if the rock and roll lifestyle has finally caught up with their creativity.

William Shatner The Transformed Man (MCA)
Includes his notorious Shakespearean-style soliloquies of 'Mr Tambourine Man' and 'Lucy In The Sky With Diamonds' while the backing singers do the work. And boy, do they work.

The Simpsons Songs In The Key Of Springfield (Rhino Records)
Includes seven renditions of *The Simpsons* theme tune including Australian, Big Band and Afro-Cuban versions. But the highlight must be Homer's blues spoof 'Born Under A Bad Sign' which fades out with him running through his favourite stage names: 'Blind Lemon Simpson, Blind Strawberry Simpson…'

★ The Good, The Bad & The Just Plain Weird ★

While we understand the need for a *Thunderbirds* model or a *Battlestar Galactica* blaster, we do wonder about some of the things people go for.

1 Eric Morecambe's tie £36 (eBay)
Straight out of the 1970s and bought in the fashion capital that is Blackpool.

2 Spiked collar worn by Diana Rigg in The Avengers £53 (eBay)
One of Rigg's kinkier accessories (worn in the controversial 'Hellfire Club' episode).

3 Battlestar Galactica Blaster Set $249.95 (**www.battlestargalactica.org**)
Complete with a blaster, holster, recharger packs and a handy belt.

4 Clangers knitting patterns £2.20 (inc p&p)
Anyone can buy a replica Clanger but how many people can make their own? Write to Peter Gregory, GKP, Springmill House, Baildon, Shipley, Yorks BD17 6AD.

5 Bump-&-Go Daleks £34.99
There are only 300 of these replica 1960s Daleks available at The Who Shop (**http://thewhoshop.com**). When they're gone, they're gone!

6 The X-Files Ken & Barbie set $149.99
The king and queen of Barbie world – only 4,000 made and no longer in the catalogue. Available at **www.mykingdomforasource.com/barkenxfiltr.html**

7 Babylon 5 character busts $114
Do you really want a bust of G'Kar? Clearly quite a lot of people do – when we last visited **www.uncomyngifts.com** they were sold out.

8 Xena Warrior Princess Wedding Sword $299
'A stunning homage to the strength and beauty of true love', from the official Xena and Hercules store (**www.adarastore.com/cgi-bin/xena-herc**). Yes, but $299?

9 The Young And The Restless faux furs $165
Rather worryingly, this cheesy US soap has enough fans to warrant a website dedicated to selling memorabilia and products 'designed' by the cast. Head to **www.soapoperastore.com/magforsal.html** for Jess Walton faux furs.

10 I Love Lucy cookie jar $140
At $140 you wonder if it doubles as a safe, but no – the California Here We Come cookie jar is one of 'only' 10,000 ever made (**www.destinysfavorites.com**).

The Sopranos Various (WEA/Warner Bros)
A compelling example of how effective atmosphere can be achieved by the judicious use of good music – The Alabama 3's 'Woke Up This Morning' theme, blues man RL Burnside, Frank Sinatra and more.

Autographs

The oldest example of fan mania. If you don't generally bump into Graham Norton in your local Sainsbury's and the most famous person you've ever seen in the flesh was Craig from Big Brother, there are havens for autograph hunters where they can get hold of their heroes' scribbles, without all the legwork. There are a multitude of hardcore autograph websites originating, naturally, in America. Here are a few:

Celebrity Contacts www.celebrity-addresses.com
Celebrity Addresses Database www.celebfanmail.com
Not only will both sites sell you autographs by Mulder, Scully and Ally, but they'll tell you where they live. Membership charges apply, but these give access to thousands of celebrity addresses, which you can then use to request their autograph personally. A disturbingly useful starting point for budding stalkers, but a more exciting way to hunt down autographs than buying them.

Celebrity Email www.celebrityemail.com
Alternatively, if you've completely done away with snail mail, Celebrity Email offers the online addresses of over 15,000 television and movie stars, and this way they won't be able to blame missing correspondence on the post.

Here's a quick sample of top autographs we found for sale on the Net:
1. Gillian Anderson £9.99 A huge Hollywood star, yet never too big for her fans it would seem, considering the bargain price her moniker fetches.

2. Cast of Star Trek £149.99 A fair whack we know, but we are talking about Nimoy, Shatner, et al, so really it's a bit of a steal.

3. Reg Varney £29.99 We think this may become a collector's item.

4. Hannah Gordon £4.50 Although a star of *Upstairs Downstairs*, Hannah is a national institution thanks to the students' favourite *Watercolour Challenge*.

349

5. Cast of Hi-De-Hi £1 One of those programmes that seemed permanently on but no one ever admitted to watching. It seems Su Pollard was just too annoying, as her signature and those of her fellow cast members are in the 'bargain' bin.

Memorabilia

If you're a budding collector, the best place to start your hobby is at one of the many websites dedicated to specific TV shows. Not all of them offer items to buy but they may offer links to sites that do.

The shows

Battlestar Galactica www.battlestargalactica.org
Having been both a film and a television series, there are plenty of collectibles to get your hands on, particularly in the clothing department. This offers actual replica costumes, including a colonial warrior ensemble (minus gun) at $495.95.

Captain Scarlett www.captainscarlet.tv
Kit your kids out with anything and everything from face cloths to action figures.

Charlie's Angels www.charliesangelsfan.com
Only books and videos for sale, but the owner of this site has listed a number of items he's looking to collect, so if you've got anything to sell, this is the place. Alternatively, find out what you should have in your own collection.

Chorlton & The Wheelies www.chorltonandthewheelies.co.uk
Merchandise rather than collectors' pieces – a miniature Wheelie, anyone?

Dr Who http://thewhoshop.com
Apart from the usual array of DVDs and books, they also offer the chance to own your very own Dalek, or at least a half-sized one. A snip at only £495.

Dukes Of Hazzard www.cootersplace.com
No rare collectors' items but plenty of fun stuff to be found in Cooter's Museum, from an autographed Daisy Jeep to Uncle Jessie's finest apple cider.

Green Hornet www.katoman.com
Devoted to the other US 1960s TV series featuring masked men, this specialises in limited edition and unusual collector's items, such as an original 1966 lunchbox and thermos ($270) and a rare boxed Black Beauty car ($125).

Muffin The Mule www.muffin-the-mule.com
One for your granny, with tasteful tea sets, plates and Christmas cards.

The Simpsons www.simpsational.com
Believes itself to be the world's largest *Simpsons* memorabilia shop. Who are we to argue when faced with everything from bubble bath to skateboards?

Star Trek Collectibles www.startrekcollectibles.co.uk
For true Trekkies, there are a number of collectors' items, including a *Star Trek* boxed card set selling at £155 when we visited.

X-Files www.xfilesmerchandise.com
Plenty of *X-Files* gear and all proceeds are donated to charity.
www.thex-filesresource.com
Gotta have an *X-Files* Barbie and Ken? This is the site to head for, but they sell fast.

Xena & Hercules www.xena-herculescatalog.com
Everything from books and videos to luggage and swords.

Where to buy the shows

Tower Records (**www.towerrecords.com**), WHSmith (**www.whsmith.co.uk**) and Amazon (**www.amazon.com**) all sell the basic collected episodes of cult TV shows (and sometimes ephemera such as figures), from The Avengers to The Sopranos. HMV (**www.hmv.co.uk**) do too, and even have their own cult TV section. If you're after something a little more obscure, try these:

Captain Bijou www.captainbijou.com
An American site with a large catalogue of rare shows on both VHS and DVD. If buying, make sure that the video format is compatible with your VCR and, similarly, that your DVD player can handle the US regional coding.

DVD Source www.dvdsource.co.uk
This looks too mainstream for cult TV, and it isn't always bang up-to-date, but stick with it. Go to the deleted and rare section for early episodes of *Buffy* and *X-Files*; somewhat confusingly everything else – from *Morecambe & Wise* to *The New Statesman* – is hidden in the *Friends* section. Good for bargain prices too.

DVD.co.uk www.dvd.co.uk
Easy-to-use site offering cheap prices and a vast catalogue containing, amongst more recent shows, the *Complete Bagpuss* series, *Chorlton & The Wheelies*, and The Collection of Public Information Films including *Charley Says*, for only £12.74.

Rarities

Here are just a few of our favourite rarities, found while trawling the Internet in search of the usual nonsense.

Best Toy Vehicles
A-Team helicopter, 1983
Green Hornet Black Beauty Corgi car, 1966
Man From U.N.C.L.E. Oldsmobile Super 88 Corgi car, 1966
Starsky & Hutch radio-controlled Ford Torino, 1977
Gerry Anderson JR21 Thunderbirds 1 Box Remote, 1960s

Best Board Games
Addams Family, 1964
Columbo, 1973
Dr Who & The Daleks Cutta-Mastic, 1965
California Raisins, 1987
Huckleberry Hound Bumps, 1961

Dolls/Action Figures
Farrah Fawcett Majors (*Charlie's Angel* Jill Munroe), 1977
M*A*S*H (Hawkeye), 1982
Donny Osmond, 1976
ITV Digital Monkey (we kid you not – these are fetching high prices), 2001

Where to buy rarities
If you feel you're ready to move on from simply filling your house with any old memorabilia from your favourite show and would like a few more refined, rare pieces, here are a few useful starting points.

Auction Houses
Contrary to popular belief, you don't need to be a *bona fide* millionaire to bid at an auction house. Sothebys, Bonhams and Christies all deal in entertainment-related memorabilia and act as a useful starting point to

discover what's on the market, a guide to prices and how to recognise true collectors' pieces. Check out their websites for general information or contact one of their experts for more detailed advice.

Bonhams
www.bonhams.com
Useful information about upcoming memorabilia sale events.

Christies
www.christies.com
General information and a sale preview email service to keep ahead of rivals. Worth doing if you don't want to miss the chance to buy the working replica of Captain Blue. Just bear in mind that it'll cost you at least £5,500.

Sothebys
www.sothebys.com
Easy-to-use search facilities and access to live auctions online.

If Bungle's the bear for you...

Websites
If you still find auction houses a bit intimidating, try these sites:

Barter Town UK
www.bartertown.org.uk
A dual site with straight memorabilia sales and bidding auctions.

Heroes for Sale
www.heroes-for-sale.co.uk
Worth wading through the *Star Wars* mass for TV action figures and costumes.

The Prop Store Of London
www.propstore.co.uk
Fan heaven with props, costume and cast items. The site leans more towards movies than television, but it's worth a look if Thor's Hammer from *Xena Warrior Princess* is up your street.

Star Store
www.starstore.com
Comprehensive catalogue with unusual pieces among the standard spin-offs.

TV Memorabilia
www.tv-memorabilia.demon.co.uk
Includes links to memorabilia for classics such as *The Prisoner* and *The Saint*.

VinMag.com
www.vinmag.com
Magazines, T-shirts and stand-up star cut-outs. Collectors' items of the future?
Perhaps. But remember, that Fonz mousepad may take years to increase in value.

Where to buy everything else

Alken M.R.S www.alkenmrs.com
Not necessarily for hardcore collectors but if you have a passion for *Coronation
Street* tea towels, it has one of the best selections this side of Weatherfield.

Destiny's Favorites www.destinysfavorites.com
Quaint store specialising in weird and wonderful nostalgia items for *I Love Lucy*,
Betty Boop, *The Brady Bunch* and *Scooby-Doo*.

Jim's TV Collectibles www.jimtvc.com
Featured shows include *Knight Rider*, *The A-Team*, *The Muppets*, *Starsky & Hutch*
and the *Six Million Dollar Man*. Also offers a useful soundtracks store.

Soap Opera Store www.soapoperastore.com
Love them or hate them, American soaps are here to stay. Here stars of top US
series sell their unique brand of wares, including *The Bold & The Beautiful* star
Dan McVicar's vitamins ($39.95) and a *General Hospital* recipe book ($19.95).

TV Land Store http://store.tvland.com/home/index.jsp
Cult classics from1960s and 1970s, such as *The Munsters* and *Bewitched*.

Virtual Toy Store www.uncomyngifts.com
Specialises in *Babylon 5* and *Farscape* items.

A Wrinkle in Time www.awit.com
Models, action figures and autographs alongside the usual fare, for every
programme from *Beauty and The Beast* to *Highlander*.

General TV sites

There are plenty of websites full of essential info, great jokes, and thoughtful criticism. And there are plenty of websites which, despite having a promising URL, deserve to be arrested for killing time. Here are a few of the best. The details were all correct when we went to press.

★ Teddington, home of the stars ★

It seems highly appropriate that a book about cult TV should be written and designed in Teddington, home of the famous lock which formed part of the address for all those *Magpie* appeals. Teddington may just be an obscure suburb in south-west London but its niche in light entertainment history rests, fundamentally, on the presence of Thames TV studios, one of Britain's greatest TV shrines. In these very studios such classics as *Edward The Seventh* and, er, *Rainbow* were made. Indeed, some of the *Rainbow* cast liked the area so much they stayed here: Geoffrey Hayes is often spotted, and we live in hope of getting Zippy's autograph in the local Café Uno.

Noël Coward grew up in Teddington, but the wit with which the area is most associated is Benny Hill, who lived above a post office here, and could be seen most days lunching at a corner table in a local Italian. He immortalised 'Tedders' in his number one smash 'Ernie The Fastest Milkman In The West': 'Now Ernie had a rival, an evil-looking man/Called Two-ton Ted from Teddington and he drove the baker's van.'

Two-ton Ted won the romantic duel with the aid of a rock cake. Alas, no local bakery has yet launched a Two-ton rock cake, but it can only be a matter of time.

Simply Teddington Lock's finest half-hour

The Alternative Cult TV Directory www.culttelly.co.uk
News, reviews, essential theme tune lyrics and memorabilia to buy.

Awesome 80s www.awesome80s.com/Awesome80s/TV
A guide to the cult, weird and classic shows of the 1980s.

Classic TV Database www.classic-tv.com
Information on US shows from the 1950s onwards; with a theme song section.

EP Guides http://epguides.com
Ideal for fans of American TV, past and present.

★ Celebrity websites ★

Websites created, or commissioned, by the
celebrity themselves are not for the squeamish.

Chuckle Brothers
www.thechucklebrothers.co.uk
Just when you thought it was safe, their official
site reveals they've signed up for panto at Xmas.

Tyne Daly
www.safesearching.com/2k/greenroom/tynedaly
The actress best known as the dark half of
Cagney & Lacey and for being named after the land of Geordies is still working,
as this site proves.

David Hasselhoff
www.davidhasselhoff.com
News of a new feature-length episode of *Knight Rider* is welcome, and news
of a new David Hasselhoff Christmas album will please the Germans.

Nicholas Parsons
www.nicholasparsons.co.uk
He may not have always been everyone's idea of entertainment on television,
but his website offers a race against the clock game to make up for it.

William Shatner
www.williamshatner.com
Very personal site with William's words, his wife's and a lovely family album.

Episode Guides www.EpisodeGuides.com
A guide to the latest popular shows on TV: perfect if you miss an episode.

Kids TV www.kids-tv.co.uk
The perfect trip down memory lane, no matter when you were a kid.

Off The Telly www.offthetelly.co.uk
Reviews and features on popular favourites of today.

TV Chronicles www.tvchronicles.com
Encyclopaedic guide to British classics and forgotten gems.

TV Cream www.tv.cream.org
Info, reviews and ratings of favourite shows and even old TV snacks.

TV Shows www.tvshow.com
Shows, stars, news and reviews covering television around the world.

TV Tome www.tvtome.com
Reviews and cast and crew biographies, as well as show goofs and trivia.

The Ultimate Cult TV Page http://homepages.nildram.co.uk/~culttv
Episode guide to lots of classic shows, from *The Saint* to *Are You Being Served?*

Fan sites for the shows

With so many to choose from, here are just a few of the best.

Alias Smith & Jones www.personalephemera.com/alias/index.html

Auf Wiedersehen, Pet www.aufpet.com/aufhp.htm

The Avengers www.originalavengers.com

The Banana Splits www.thebananasplits.com

Drop The Dead Donkey
www.geocities.com/Hollywood/Hills/9109/DtDD.html

Lost In Space www.lostinspacetv.com.

The Man From U.N.C.L.E. www.manfromuncle.org

M*A*S*H www.bestcareanywhere.net

Monkey www.monkeyheaven.com

Monty Python www.dailyllama.com

The Osbournes www.realitynewsonline.com/page1037.html

Seinfeld http://philco1.home.mindspring.com/seinfeld/seinfeld.htm

The Simpsons http://members.optushome.com.au/jmevans

The Sweeney www.thesweeney.com/swfmain.htm

Taxi www.geocities.com/taxitribute

Thunderbirds www.thunderbirdsonline.com

Trigger Happy TV www.angelfire.com/tv/ronjolly2000

Twin Peaks www.members.tripod.com/~CupidClint/twinpeaks.html

Upstairs, Downstairs www.updown.org.uk

Yogi Bear www.aristotle.net/~cgsports

★ One puddle of water on castors ★

Frank Holland, assistant property master at the BBC in the 1950s, had the fine habit of recording unusual requests for props. Here's a small sample:

Four live husky dogs, able to pull a sledge. (If live husky dogs not available, four stuffed dogs in pulling position)
One hydrogen bomb, non-practical
One puddle of water, on castors
One dead cow, with a tomahawk buried in its skull. (Should have a pleasant expression on its face so as not to frighten children)
One 3ft by 3ft by 6ft deep hole
One chicken with acting experience
One barrel of beer – pale type with nobody in it
One Bible, to be the size of a penguin
One Gordon Blue cookery book
Three dozen apple turnovers, uncooked. Must look like dumplings or female breasts
One live ferret, tame and toothless, to be handled by Bernard Miles

The back stories

TV myths and inspirations exposed

'Wanted: four insane lads, aged between 17–21'

Ad placed by producers of The Monkees. Did Charles Manson really apply?

I Love Lucy co-star **Vivian Vance** was contractually obligated to remain at least 20lbs overweight. **Albert Einstein** once made a guest appearance on **Gunsmoke**. The **Happy Days** spin-off **Joanie Loves Chachi** was the highest-rated American TV show ever in South Korea because 'chachi' is Korean for 'penis'. Sadly, there is no truth in any of these stories, but because they're such good entertainment – and wild enough that they might just be true, such are human failings and quirkiness – we want to believe them, and therein lies the secret of their longevity as urban myths.

The imagination knows few bounds when it comes to inspiration for TV shows either. There are always books to be adapted (from countless detectives to Charles Addams' ghoulish cartoons), real lives to be dramatised (**Michael Crichton** based **ER** on his student years at the Harvard Medical School; **John Sullivan** found the idea for **Just Good Friends** in a letter in the problem pages) and endless spin-off series to be, er, spun-off from hits like *Happy Days* (**Laverne And Shirley**) or *Dynasty* (**The Colbys**).

But the truth is sometimes stranger than fiction. Here are our favourite TV tales – true and false – and weird inspirations for shows.

361

THE URBAN MYTH There was a plot to kill Australia's top TV star

IN FACT... In April 1970, there was a bloody massacre at the home of Australia's most famous and beloved TV star – a senseless slaughter in the kangaroo compound in Waratah National Park.

Filming of **Skippy The Bush Kangaroo** had ended two years earlier, but as the series had been exported to 80 countries, its star was in demand for personal appearances. Pre-*Neighbours*, Skippy was as big as Australian TV got, so the death of its not-so-dumb lead in a scene that Sam Peckinpah would have been proud of was definitely not in the script.

Did they get Skippy? Certainly 13 of his friends – many of whom had been extras in the TV series – would never hop again. The newspapers were certain, however, that Skippy had escaped the slaughter: he had been in his own separate enclosure, and was now in a secret hideaway in case the maniac (man, dogs, dingo, whatever) returned.

But was Skippy really the survivor, and not some stand-in or body double? The authorities were adamant. Yes, this was the real Skippy – the one from Queensland who had starred since the series began in 1966, Sonny's

furry friend and confidant of Clancy the English girl (take a bow, **Liza Goddard**). The 'roo that used to pucker its lips and make that stupid little 'sup sup sup' noise. Yep, that's the one all right.

The big question remains. Why, oh why? Was it a plot to kill Skippy, possibly by some vengeful child who had finally been unhinged by the show's maddeningly catchy tune and implausibly happy endings? A kidnap-and-ransom attempt gone wrong? An Aussie PR stunt? No. The defenceless 'roos were undoubtedly the victims of a wild dog.

Sonny and Skip

THE URBAN MYTH Crew members on Captain Pugwash have smutty names

IN FACT... Wishful thinking. The children's cartoon, which ran on the BBC between 1958 and 1967, is commonly believed to feature characters with less than innocent names, to wit Master Bates, Seaman Staines and Roger the Cabin Boy. A further rumour has it that Captain Pugwash is Australian slang for oral sex. Sadly for schoolboys of all ages, no such nautical naughtiness exists. Crude might well apply to the series' basic animation, but not to its characters. In reality, the crew of the Black Pig consisted of Master Mate, Tom the Cabin Boy, Barnabas and pirate Willy (oh stop it!). No character with the name of Seaman ever appeared in the show.

We know this for a fact because in 1991 **John Ryan**, who created the series, won apologies and damages from the Guardian after the newspaper's youth supplement reiterated this urban myth, suggesting that the BBC had not repeated the series as a result. What had doubtless seemed a harmless giggle to those at the broadsheet was not so funny for Ryan. Much of his income depended on visits to schools, where he gave talks and workshops, and as the erroneous joke spread he was no longer asked to call.

It's difficult to establish where the joke originated. Such puns are hardly new, and in the perpetrators' defence, the semi-strangulated voices of some characters – by **Peter Hawkins**, who also voiced **The Flowerpot Men** and later some of the Daleks – could be difficult to make out. Put the two together...

+ + + + + + + + + + + + +

THE URBAN MYTH Swear words have been spelt out on Countdown

IN FACT... Although it would be nice to watch this popular quiz show in the hope that something more humorous than **Richard Whiteley**'s wardrobe or Richard Stilgoe's annoying anagrams would provide the giggles, the producers are careful to ensure the request for a consonant, a vowel, a consonant and another consonant doesn't spell out anything as controversial as, say, 'fuck'. A spokesman for the programme says that in its 20-year run, the most offensive word to be spelt out has been 'farted'. The producers have also learned, the hard way, to keep a watchful eye on those naive intellectuals in Dictionary Corner after Alice, the non-celebrity lexicographer from Oxford University, lowered the tone in the very first episode by proclaiming that she had done much better than the contestants with an eight-letter word – 'rogering'. (Hopefully Denis Norden will manage to retrieve this gem from cutting-room limbo.) Viewers may also recall a recent Channel 4 late-night show of great TV moments, hosted by **Victor Lewis-Smith,** which showed a clip where one contestant volunteered that they had a seven-letter word – 'wankers'. Sadly, this was an out-take that never made it to the show itself.

+++++++++++++

THE URBAN MYTH That 'Kemo Sabe' – Tonto's name for the Lone Ranger – really means 'horse's ass' in Apache

IN FACT... Nice idea, but sadly not so. The rumour probably originated in a Gary 'Far Side' Larson cartoon which sees the Lone Ranger looking up the term in an Apache dictionary, only to find that it means 'horse's rear end'.

According to website **The Straight Dope** (motto: 'Fighting ignorance since 1973 – it's taking longer than we thought'), the phrase was created by **Jim Jewell**, director of the original *Lone Ranger* radio show until 1938. In an interview Jewell said that he'd taken the term from the name of a boys' camp at Mullet Lake, Michigan called Kamp Kee-Mo Sah-Bee. The camp had been established in 1911 by Jewell's father-in-law, and operated until about 1940. According to Jewell, 'Kemo Sabe' translated as 'trusty scout'.

However, just because some smiling native American told him it meant 'trusty scout' doesn't mean it does. Investigating the matter, the enterprising website found that in the **Concise Dictionary Of Minnesota Ojibwe**, the word 'giimoozaabi' means 'to peek' or 'he who peeks' – the prefix 'giimooj' means secretly. 'Giimoozaabi' is pronounced pretty much as 'kemosabe' and would have been spelled phonetically 'Kee Moh Sah Bee' at the turn of the century.

The site then established that Kamp Kee-Mo Sah-Bee was in an area inhabited by the Ottawa tribe, who spoke a dialect of Ojibwe with the same word 'giimoozaabi'. So while the 'trusty' part may have been decoration, 'kemo sabe' probably really was a Native American term for 'scout'.

+++++++++++++

THE URBAN MYTH Charlie Manson auditioned for The Monkees

IN FACT... Contrary to what at least one Monkees website posts as fact, serial killer Charles Manson did not audition for *The Monkees*. That was **Steve Stills** of Crosby, Stills etc – easily confused, we know, but facts are facts.

The Manson/Monkees rumour came about because veteran Los Angeles DJ and self-publicist **Rodney Bingenheimer** claimed he'd seen Manson at the auditions. Yet a simple check of the dates shows that Manson was in jail from 1961-67 for parole violations (he had earlier convictions for car theft and cheque forgery) and the Monkees auditions were held in 1965.

Manson – an aspiring musician – did, however, have links with the **Beach Boys**, thanks to drummer Dennis Wilson's less-than-sound judgement in making friends. 'Never Learn Not To Love' (on the *20/20* album and B-side of 'Bluebirds Over The Mountain') was allegedly adapted by Wilson from a Manson song called 'Cease To Exist'. But that was in 1968. Anyway, the advert for *The Monkees* auditions had called for 'four insane lads aged between 17–21'. Manson might have qualified on the first count, but at the age of 30 his boy-band potential had long gone.

'Hey hey, it's the Mansons...'

THE URBAN MYTH Mike and Bernie Winters were asked to manage The Beatles

IN FACT... Strange but true. According to their 1976 autobiography *Shake A Pagoda Tree*, in 1962 an agent called **Jack Murray** dropped a picture of four mop-topped lads in to Mike Winters' dressing room at the London Palladium. 'They're big up north,' Murray assured Winters. 'I've got them for 16 to 20 weeks, and I can have a permanent share of their contract if I want to. Do you want to come in with me?' 'I'm not gambling any more,' was Winters' response. 'Bernie and I want to make a go of the act.' And so the shorter (and allegedly smarter) of the Winters brothers turned down the opportunity to manage **John**, **Paul**, **George** and **Ringo**. Ultimately we are all in Mike Winters' debt: the Beatles, rock music, the British public, Schnorbitz.

+ + + + + + + + + + + + +

THE URBAN MYTH The theme music for Star Trek has lyrics too

IN FACT... It's true, though they were never used in the show. TV music composers earn most of their dough from repeats of their work, so when a small studio with a poor track record on pilots wanted a score for a niche – and then unproven – topic like 'serious' science fiction, it hardly seemed like a nice little earner. Luckily for production company Desilu, a gifted arranger from 20th Century Fox called **Alexander Courage** accepted the job, and the imperishable *Star Trek* theme was born.

When *Star Trek* was picked up by NBC, Courage expected to reap his reward – only to find the series' creator **Gene Roddenberry** claiming half the money. In a deal worthy of the music business, Courage had earlier been pressured into giving Roddenberry the option of composing lyrics for his music. Roddenberry had exercised that option, then demanded half the royalties as co-composer.

Legally it didn't make any difference that the lyrics weren't intended for the show or that they'd never been used. 'Hey, I have to get some money somewhere – I'm sure not going to get it out of the profits of *Star Trek*,' was the great humanist's response. Understandably, Courage refused to write any more music for the series. Copyright issues prevent us, alas, from reproducing these controversial lyrics here, but you can find them at: **http://www.snopes2.com/ radiotv/tv/trek1.htm**

+++++++++++++

THE URBAN MYTH Television has a patron saint

IN FACT... Absolutely right: the Vatican has officially appointed **St Clare of Assisi** as the patron saint of television. The honour of having TV execs pray to you for better ratings is often said to belong to St Francis de Sales, presumably because without advertising sales so much TV wouldn't exist. But it is, in fact, St Clare, who was born in Assisi in 1194 and ran away from the palatial family home to serve God and hang around with St Francis of Assisi. She founded the Order of Poor Ladies (Poor Clares) which established itself throughout Europe alongside the Franciscans.

St Clare became seriously ill in her late fifties, too ill to attend mass. It was at this point that an image of the service is reputed to have appeared on the wall facing her sickbed, which probably explains why she became the patron saint of television. She was canonised in 1255, two years after her death. Apart from being the saint of television, she is also the patron of those suffering from eye disease, which seems somehow fitting.

+++++++++++++

THE URBAN MYTH Anti-war sitcom M*A*S*H boosted US Army recruitment

IN FACT... There is no hard statistical evidence that US Army recruitment soared between 1972 and 1983, when the antics of the 4077th Mobile Army Surgical Hospital dominated TV ratings, because of the show. But **Mike Farrell**, (who played BJ Hunnicutt) remembers reading some scary letters from viewers. 'One said, "Boy, you guys sure make war look like fun." I got another that said, "After watching your show I've decided to join up." I wrote back saying, "I don't understand how you came to that conclusion."'

+++++++++++++

EUREKA!

Strange and wonderful are the ideas behind some TV shows. **Robert Graves'** venerable **I Claudius** gave **Esther Shapiro**, ABC's ex-queen of the mini-series, the idea for **Dynasty**. 'I want to write about winners,' she said. 'These Roman families aren't very different from what I see about me.' (Copulating with horses presumably being unremarkable in Shapiro's social circle.) If you're a big enough star, you can make a show about your pet. That's exactly what **Gene Autry** did with **Champion The Wonder Horse**.

And had **Carla Lane**'s mother not met a strange man rummaging through a bucket of dildos in a Paris sex shop, **Nicholas Lyndhurst** might never have become Rodney Trotter. As her mum and the Parisian got acquainted, Carla hovered nearby, thinking maybe she could write a sitcom about a bored housewife who met some man in a café. That became **Butterflies**, which gave Nicholas Lyndhurst his first real 'mature role' after numerous children's shows before moving swiftly on to **Only Fools And Horses**.

One rule which is rarely broken is that you must have an idea before a channel gives you airtime. The exception is the **Monty Python's Flying Circus** chaps, promised a BBC slot although they didn't have a show or a title.

DOSTOYEVSKY, MUMPS, HIPPIES SELLING SOVIET WEEKLY: THE STRANGE BIRTH PANGS OF HIT TV SHOWS

DOSTOYEVSKY'S PETROVICH

A character in a 19th-century Russian literary marathon might seem an unlikely creative spark for a hit US detective show, but the irritating inspector in **Crime And Punishment** was the inspiration for Peter Falk's scruffy **Columbo**.

SCENES FROM A MARRIAGE

The high-brow and gloomy Swedish epic by **Ingmar Bergman** was the model for the low-brow and chirpy **Knots Landing**. David Jacobs, the creator, freely admits it. 'My idea,' he has said, 'was an American equivalent of the Swedish film starring Liv Ullman. The CBS network said it was too middle-class and tame, they wanted something bigger and brasher.' That show was **Dallas**.

NORTH BY NORTHWEST

The Man From U.N.C.L.E., the spy series which ran from 1965–68, was the result of Ian Fleming and producer Norman Felton having a boozy lunch in London. The series used elements of Bond films, and hero Robert Vaughn's job was to emulate **Cary Grant**'s role in *North By Northwest*.

MTV COPS

These two words – in a two-word memo – by NBC boss Brandon Tartijoff to Anthony Yerkovich and Michael Mann gave rise to Crockett and Tubbs roaming the Florida coast to the sound of rock music in **Miami Vice**.

THEY DON'T LIKE IT UP 'EM!

When Jimmy Perry served in the Home Guard, his instructor told him that the enemy 'didn't like it up 'em'. Remembering this, he took his idea for **Dad's Army** to BBC producer David Croft, who showed it to Michael Mills, head of comedy. Mills said: 'This could run forever.' So far it's 27 years and counting.

A HIPPIE AT A WIMPY BAR

John Sullivan grew up in south London where he remembered 'men selling *Soviet Weekly* and *The Morning Star* outside a Wimpy bar.' One night in a pub, the Nelson Arms, he saw one of these men, a 'gangling hippie', singing away on an ancient guitar and realised he'd found his **Citizen Smith**.

A SUMMER JOB

When 17-year-old Californian **Gregory J Bonnan** got a summer job as a lifeguard, it changed his life – he went on to create **Baywatch**. The show was actually cancelled after its first season because ratings were so low, but **David Hasselhoff** and three others put up their own money to finance more episodes.

NAZI FIRING SQUAD

The Golden Shot was originally a German show (catchphrase 'Heinz, the bolt!'). ATV bought the idea and Bob Monkhouse was asked to host it by his old friend and ATV producer Colin Clews with the words: 'Would you like to join me in a Nazi firing squad?'

MUMPS

Stuck in bed with mumps, Troy Kennedy Martin was fiddling around with a radio when he found the police wavelength. What he heard was nothing like the cosy world of *Dixon Of Dock Green* and it gave him the idea for a more realistic series. **Z Cars** was screened on BBC1 for 16 years.

FRANK SINATRA

Fred Silverman, head of daytime programming for CBS TV, had no name for a cowardly dog with a minor role in a new cartoon series. Happening to hear Ol'Blue Eyes singing 'Strangers In The Night' on the radio, he was struck by the phrase 'scooby-dooby-doo'. Duly christened, Shaggy's snack-loving sidekick went on to become the show's lead character.

★ Meet the first Basil Fawlty ★

A certain rude hotelier made his debut on British TV on 3 February 1973 – in an episode of *Doctor At Large* on LWT. It wasn't Basil Fawlty, but it was John Cleese's first attempt to capture the real-life Torquay hotel-keeper he recalled as 'the most wonderfully rude man I've met in my life.' This was the hotelier who had told *Monty Python*'s Terry Gilliam that his table manners were too American and thrown Eric Idle's briefcase into the street in case it contained a bomb.

The character made his debut in the episode called *No Ill Feelings*. (Cleese, just out of Cambridge, wrote occasionally for the series, which was based on Richard Gordon's books.) In fact, the episode provided several clues to *Fawlty Towers* – the miserable, henpecked owner, his bespectacled, patronising hen of a wife, the old ladies giggling, the dining room, the scene where the hotelier pours food over the head of guest Roy Kinnear – all are obvious pointers.

But, as played by Timothy Bateson, the hotelier was querulous and resigned, with none of the manic majesty of Fawlty. In one scene a character orders a kipper for breakfast because he thinks it will be quick. By the time it arrives, he is fleeing the room because of a fellow guest – a cousin of Eric Idle's Nudge Nudge Wink Wink Say No More. 'Wasn't that kipper quick enough for you?' cries Clifford. In Cleese's mouth this line would have been filled with loathing for the customer and his own miserable life. Bateson sounds merely disgruntled.

After the episode had been shot, however, producer Humphrey Barclay said to Cleese: 'You could probably build an entire series around that character.' A year later Cleese treated Barclay to a very expensive lunch and announced that, with his then wife, Connie Booth, he'd done just that.

Probably not what Mr Sinatra had in mind when he scatted on 'Strangers In The Night'

TV LISTINGS

Enter the twilight world of the TV programme buyer

It must be hell buying foreign TV shows from a catalogue. Try this: 'The Kingdom: the inner workings of a Scandinavian, focusing on Swedish neurosurgeon Stig Helmer, who isn't happy about working in Denmark.' Tempted? Us neither, but in fact this is **Lars von Trier**'s cult mini-series, about a mad Dane-hating Swede presiding over Denmark's most technologically-advanced hospital where all sorts of spooky and devilish things are going on. Now if they'd said Twin Peaks meets Chicago Hope… Here are a few more strange TV shows to tickle your fancy. Or not.

The Angel, The Bicycle and The Chinaman's Finger

When a Japanese businessman makes his investment in the South African Postal Office dependent on a display of racial harmony, a randomly selected rural office does its best to comply by staging a heart-warming nativity play.

Beast

An American resort is terrorised when architeuthis dix, a giant squid, is driven to the ocean's surface in its search for food.

373

Cloud Burst

Twin brother scientists – one good, one evil – fight over ownership of a cloudburst gun that can create rain instantly.

Colombo's Quotes

Quotations-themed quiz show for high school students hosted by Canadian poet and quote-compiler John Robert Colombo. Each edition comes from a different city and most quotations focus on Canada.

Danger Team

The adventures of an inexperienced female private eye who solves crimes with the help of three animated clay figures.

Electric Blanket

A day in the life of three loveable low-life types: a pimp, a whore, and their moronic friend.

Family Trilogy

Three powerful dramas that are available with, or without, flashbacks to Biblical times.

Fun At The Funeral Parlour

The father of a family funeral business employs his three sons because of his phobia of dead bodies. One son, an escaped convict, harbours secret desires to be a rock star; another adores actor Brian Blessed, and the third is just plain weird. Each episode focuses on the strange death of one of their clients.

K-9000

An irreverent cop is telepathically linked to his talking, bionic police dog, a canine partner who also doubles as a cellular phone.

A Gutter

A 10-year-old and a man try to retrieve a banknote from a drain.

Kresky
Terence Michael Matterly plays an undercover cop who infiltrates LA's low life and gangs of criminals while disguised as a disco dancing lothario.

Lisa
A pianist falls in love with a woman who falls into his hotel room.

The Message
A struggling fine-art dealer unwittingly becomes a Harlem drug lord's target when his answering machine develops a mind of its own.

Obakie No Samba, Mon Non Monster
Musical, horror or sitcom? Frankenstein's monster, Wolf Man and Count Dracula play happy families in a fake haunted house. Only from Japan.

The Orchestra
1980s Israeli situation comedy poking fun at the various aspects of life in an orchestra.

Pests
The misadventures of a Nebraska man sharing a New York apartment with three three-foot-tall talking cockroaches.

Reptila Opera
On the shore of Golden Lake, our merry friends live a turbulent life, disturbing the lake monster who cannot bear their boisterous music.

Taxi Driver
From Ghana. Each episode sees our hero becoming embroiled in the problems of his passengers, but for budgetary reasons you generally only see the back of actor Psalm Adjetifio's head.

The Visit
A special love story about four women who lived 2000 years apart.

INDEX

7 Up 152
21 Jump Street 127
24 128
77 Sunset Strip 143
100 Per Cent 192

A

A for Andromeda 206
Abigail's Party 155
Absolutely 222
Absolutely Fabulous
    213
Adam Adamant Lives!
    86
Addams Family, The
    273
Adventure Game 118
Adventures Of Rin Tin
    Tin, The 265
Adventures Of
    Robinson Crusoe, The
    114
Adventures Of Sherlock
    Holmes 144
Adventures Of William

Tell, The 265
Adverts 91
Aherne, Caroline 287
Airwolf 86
Albion Market 227
Allen, Dave 288
Ally McBeal 157
American Gothic, 273
Anderson, Clive 106
Anderson, Gerry 240
Anderson, Gillian 289
Animal Magic 119
Anne Of Green Gables
    133
Are You Being Served?
    213
Ascent Of Man, The 152
Aspel & Company 105
A-Team, The 86
Attachments 157
Attenborough, David
    272
Autry, Gene 268
Avengers, The 15

B

Babylon 5 206
Bagpuss 17
Baker, Tom 290
Banacek 135
Banana Splits 18
Band Of Gold 157
Barbapapa 93
Basil Brush 292
Batman 19
Battlestar Galactica 207
Baywatch 369
Beatles, The 366
Beauty And The Beast
    158
Beavis And Butthead 96
Beiderbecke Affair, The
    202
Belle And Sebastian 142
Bennett, Alan 156
Beverly Hills 90210 279
Bewitched 274
Big Breakfast, The 103
Big Brother 195
Billionaire Boys' Club,

The 254
Billy Liar 213
Bionic Woman, The 87
Black Adder 22
Black Books 214
Black Forest Clinic 227
Blake's 7 23
Blankety Blank 168
Bleasdale, Alan 156
Blockbusters 119
Blue Peter 120, 302, 306
Bod 107
Bonanza 265
Boney 144
Borgias, The 24
Bosanquet, Reginald 185
Bough, Frank 291
Bouquet Of Barbed Wire 158
Box Of Delights 114
Brady Bunch, The 280
Branded 266
Brass Eye 322
Brideshead Revisited 158
Brit Awards 182
Brookside 203
Brothers, The 229
Bruce's Big Night Out 256
Budgie 160
Buerk, Michael 184
Buffy The Vampire Slayer 25

Bumfights 140
Byker Grove 281

C

Cagney And Lacey 128
Callan 334
Camomile Lawn 160
Cannon 144
Captain Pugwash 363
Captain Scarlet 26,
Car 54, Where Are You? 128
Casualty 151
Catweazle 274
Chalk 203
Champions, The 87
Champion The Wonder Horse 94
Channel TV 196
Charlie's Angels 146
Chateauvallon 228
Cheaters 253
Cheers 214
Cheggers Plays Pop 121
Cheyenne 267
Chicago Hope 151
Children Of The Stones 114
Chinese Detective 186
CHiPs 129
Chorlton And The Wheelies 121
Cisco Kid, The 263, 268
Citizen Smith 369

Clangers, The 27
Cleese, John 370
Clement, Dick 294
Clerks 96
CNN International 29
Cold Feet 160
Colditz 258
Coleman, David 295
Columbo 129, 368
Como, Perry 127
Compact 228
Coogan, Steve 296
Cook, Peter 298
Coronation Street 203, 324
Countdown 333, 363
Cousteau, Jacques 299
Cows 103
Cracker 30
Crackerjack 121, 301
Crane 135
Crime Traveller 250
Critic, The 97
Crossroads 31
Crown Court 142

D

Dad's Army 214, 311, 369
Daktari 114
Dallas 303
Danger Man 234
Dangermouse 107
Dark Angel 212

Dark Season 115
Dark Skies 209
David Cassidy – Man
Undercover 136
Davy Crockett 267
Day After, The 254
Day Today, The 223, 322
Deliberate Stranger, The
255
Demon Headmaster,
The 115
Dempsey And
Makepeace 129
Department S 87
Deputy Dawg 95
Desmond's 215
Dimbleby, Richard 188
Dinenage, Fred 197
Do Not Adjust Your Set
122
Doctor Snuggles 108
Dogtanian And The
Three Muskehounds
108
Don't Forget Your
Toothbrush 169
Dr Katz 97
Dr Quinn Medical
Woman 150
Dr Who 115, 250, 291
Duckman 97
Due South 130
Duel 255
Duel, Pete 300
Dukes Of Hazzard, The

136
Dynasty 32, 229

E

Earth: Final Conflict
209
Ed Sullivan Show, The
101
Edge Of Darkness 161
Edward & Mrs Simpson
172
Elizabeth R 172
Endurance 169
Equalizer, The 334
ER 151
Executioner's Song, The
255

F

Fall And Rise Of
Reginald Perrin, The
35
Fall Guy, The 88
Fame 281
Family Fortunes 101
Family Guy 98
Fantasy Football League
166
Fantasy Island 274
Far Pavilions, The 175
Farscape 207
Fast Show, The 223,
334

Father Ted 36
Fawlty Towers 37, 370
Fireball XL5 242
First Wave 209
Fish, Michael 262
Flamingo Road 229
Flash, The 88
Flashing Blade, The 39
Flowerpot Men, The
143
Floyd, Keith 165
Flumps, The 122
Follyfoot 115
Footballers' Wives 166
Ford, Anna 185
Forever Knight 275
Fort Boyard 170
Fortunes And
Misfortunes Of Moll
Flanders 134
Frasier 215, 310
Fugitive, The 136

G

Galaxy High 108
Gangster Show, The 138
Gazzetta Football Italia
166
Generation Game, The
170
Get Smart 234
Ghost Story For
Christmas, A 126
Glaze, Peter 301

God, The Devil And Bob 98
Going Live 120
Golden Shot, The 169, 369
Gone Fishing 237
Goodies, The 223
Goodness Gracious Me 224
Gormenghast 161
Grade, Lew 336
Grange Hill 202
Grimleys, The 203
Groovy Fellers, The 215
Grove Family, The 228
Grushko 130
Gulliver's Travels 134
Gunsmoke 266, 267

H

Hagman, Larry 303
Hamish Macbeth 40
Hancock, Tony 304
Hanna Barbera 111
Happy Days 281
Hardwicke House 104
Harry O 41
Hart, Tony 306
Hart To Hart 148
Hartman, Phil 97
Harty, Russell 107
Have Gun, Will Travel 266
Hawaii Five-O 249, 313

Hazell 148
Headroom, Max 307
Hector's House 95
Heimat 172
Herbs, The 122
Hercules: Legendary Journeys 180
Here Come The Double Deckers 116
Hergé's Adventures Of Tin Tin 109
High Chaparral, The 269
High Life, The 216
Hill Street Blues 130
History Man, The 161
Hitchcock, Alfred 180
Hogan's Heroes 258
Holland, Frank 358
Hollywood Wives 175
Holocaust 259
Homicide: Life On The Streets 43
Hopalong Cassidy 268
House Of Cards 162
House Of Eliott 162
How 197
Howdy Doody 263
Howerd, Frankie 308
Hyde Pierce, David 310

I

I, Claudius 173
I Dream Of Jeannie 102, 277
I Love Lucy 361
Impossible Job, The 152
Incredible Hulk, The 88
Indoor League, The 238
Inside The Actor's Studio 100
Inspector Morse 131
Interceptor 44
Invaders, The 209
I Spy 235
It's A Knockout 171

J

Jackie Chan Adventures 187
Jackanory 122
Jackson Five, The 109
James The Cat 109
James Whale Show, The 284
Jamie And The Magic Torch 110
Jewel In The Crown 175
John Craven's Newsround 123
Jonny Briggs 116
Jossy's Giants 104

K

Kickstart 238
Kids From 47A 116
Kilroy 246

King Of The Hill 98
Knight Rider 88
Knots Landing 229, 368
Knowing Me Knowing
  You 106
Kojak 131
Kolchak The Night
  Stalker 45
Kung-Fu 187

L

La Frenais, Ian 294
Lace 176
Land Of The Giants 116
Larry Sanders Show,
  The 216
Lassie 95
Last Of The Mohicans
  117
Law And Order 139
Lawley, Sue 185
Lazarus Man, The 163
League Of Gentlemen,
  The 46
Le Mesurier, John 311
Letterman, David 312
LEXX 207
Life And Legend Of
  Wyatt Earp, The 270
Likely Lads, The 217
Little House On The
  Prairie 117
Littlest Hobo, The 117
Lizzy Dripping 117

Loft Story 253
Lone Ranger, The 48,
  268, 364
Lonesome Dove 270
Lord, Jack 313
Love Story 163
Ludwig 110

M

McCaskill, Ian 316
McGoohan, Patrick 243
McGovern, Jimmy 156
MacGyver 90
Maelstrom 139
Magic Roundabout, The
  49
Magnum, PI 148
Man From Atlantis, The
  90
Man From U.N.C.L.E.,
  The 235, 347, 369
Manageress, The 167
Manimal 90
Manson, Charles 365
Marine Boy 111
Marion And Geoff 50
Married… With
  Children 218
Martian Chronicles, The
  209
Martin, Quinn 316
Mary, Mungo And
  Midge 111
Masada 176

M*A*S*H 259, 367
Mastermind 192
Maverick 271
Mayall, Rik 317
Men Behaving Badly
  218
Miami Vice 139, 369
Middlemen 197
Milligan, Spike 318
Minder 140
Mission: Impossible 236
Monkees, The 365
Monkey 51
Monocled Mutineer,
  The 261
Monty Python's Flying
  Circus 224
Moomins 111
Moonlighting 148
Morecambe, Eric 320
Morris, Chris 321
Mr Benn 112
Munsters, The 273
Murder One 140
Murun Buchstansangur
  112
My Name Is Bill W 256
My So Called Life 282
Mythical Monsters 153

N

Nationwide 185, 291
Night Network 284
Nightingales 219

Nightmare Café 181
North And South 177
Northern Exposure 163
Norwegian Weather 174
Not the Nine O' Clock News 200
Now! 197
Now And Again 212
Number 73 120
NYPD Blue 131

O

Office, The 52
One Man And His Dog 53
Onedin Line 163
Only Fools And Horses 219
Opportunity Knocks 245
Outer Limits, The 210
Oz 284

P

Palin, Michael 197
Panorama 188, 302
Partridge, Alan 297
Paxman, Jeremy 323
Pennis, Dennis 143
Persuaders, The 249
Pet Psychic, The 253
Peyton Place 230
Phil Silvers Show, The 219
Phoenix, Pat 324
Pingu 112
Pink Panther Show, The 112
Play For Today 164
Pobol Y Cwm 230
Poldark 134
Police Squad 104
Porridge 54
Postgate, Oliver 326
Pot Black 238
Potter, Dennis 156
Presley, Elvis 101
Prey 212
Pride And Prejudice 135
Prime Suspects 132
Prisoner, The 55
Prisoner Cell Block: H 56
Private Schulz 261
Professionals, The 59
Public Information Films 189

Q

Quantum Leap 251
Quatermass 208
Queer As Folk 164
Quimby, Fred 326

R

Rainbow 123
Randall & Hopkirk Deceased 277
Rawhide 266
Record Breakers 123
Red Hand Gang, The 118
Reeves And Mortimer 327
Reilly: Ace of Spies 236
Remington Steele 149
Ren And Stimpy 60
Renascer 247
Rentaghost 123
Reputations 153
Return To Eden 177
Revelations 230
Rich Man, Poor Man 177
Right To Be Born, The 247
Ripping Yarns 61
Robot Wars 171
Rockford, Files, The 41
Roddenberry, Gene 329
Rodgers, Roy 268
Rolf On Art 100
Roobarb 62
Roots 178
Rosenthal, Jack 156
Rosie 132
Rossiter, Leonard 330
Rowan & Martin's Laugh-In 224
Royle Family, The 64
Rugrats 113

Runaround 125
Rutland Weekend
Television 200

S

Sabrina The Teenage
Witch 277
Saint, The 141, 336
Saint And Greavsie 167
Sale Of The Century
193
Santa Barbara 231
Sapphire And Steel 251
Savannah 231
Saved By The Bell 203
Scooby Doo 113, 370
Scotch & Wry 226
Secret Agent Man 249
Seinfeld 65, 249
Sex And The City 220
Shoestring 149
Simpsons, The 66
Singing Detective, The
67
Singing Ringing Tree,
The 118
Six Feet Under 164
Six Million Dollar Man,
The 19
Skippy The Bush
Kangaroo 362
Sliders 208
Smack The Pony 226
Small Summer Party, A

50
SMTV: Live 120
Snow, Jon 323
Soap 68
Soccer AM 167
Some Mothers Do 'Ave
'Em 220
Sons And Daughters
231
Sopranos, The 46, 69
South Park 98
Space 1999 243
Space: Above And
Beyond 209
Spelling, Aaron 330
Spitting Image 200
Springhill 104
St Clare Of Assisi 367
St Elsewhere 152
Stand, The 208
Standing Room Only
167
Star Soccer 198
Star Trek 70, 325, 366
Stars In Their Eyes 246
Starsky And Hutch 132
Steptoe And Son 221,
330
Stingray 240
Sunday Night At The
London Palladium
256
Sunset Beach 232
Supercar 239
Superstars 239

Swamp Thing 212
Sweeney, The
59, 73
Sykes 221
Sylvania Waters 194

T

Take Me Home: The
John Denver Story
256
Tales Of The Riverbank
125
Tales Of The
Unexpected 249, 277
Tanner 88 201
Taxi 214
Teachers 203
Teddington 339
Teenage Mutant Ninja
Turtles 99
Teletext 248
Teletubbies 282
Tenko 262
TFI Friday 107
That 70s Show
283
That Was The Week
That Was 201
Theroux, Louis 153
thirtysomething 74
This Life 75
This Morning With
Richard And Judy 262
Thorn Birds, The 178

Thunderbirds 240
Time Tunnel, The 252
Timeslip 252
Tinker Tailor Soldier
  Spy 236
Tiswas 76
Tommy Cooper 174
Tomorrow People, The
  212
Tomorrow's World 204
Top Cat 249
Topless Darts 174
Triangle 232
Tripods 209
Trisha 246
Trumpton 78
Tutti Frutti 165
Twilight Zone, The 210,
249
Twin Peaks 79, 249

U

UFO 211

V

V 211
Vegas 149
Very Peculiar Practice, A
  150
Vorderman, Carol 332
Voyage To The Botto
  Of The Sea 211

W

Wacky Races 113
Wagon Train 266, 271
Wait Till Your Father
  Gets Home 249
Walking With
  Dinosaurs 204
Waltons, The 165
Water Margin, The 187
Watercolour Challenge
  100
We Are The Champions
  239
Weakest Link, The 194
Whack-O! 204
Wheeltappers' And
  Shunters' Social Club
  256
When Louis Met 153
Whiplash 271
White Horses 95
Who Wants To Be A
  Millionaire? 194
Whoops! Apocalypse 81
Whose Line Is It
  Anyway? 171
Why Don't You? 125
Widows 141
Wild Bill Hickok 268
Wild Palms 181
Wild Wild West 237
Willo The Wisp 113
Winds Of War, The 179
Wise, Ernie 320

Wiseguy 133
Without Walls – Dennis
  Potter 100
Wokenwell 105
Wombles, The 278
Wonder Woman 90
Wonder Years, The 283
Woodward, Edward 334
Word, The 284
World At War, The 153
World Cup 102
World Of Sport 82
Worzel Gummidge 125
Wyndham Goldie,
  Gracie 302.

X

X-Files, The 45, 205,
  249, 290

Y

Yarwood, Mike 127
Yo Soy Betty La Fea 247
Young Doctors, The 233
Young, Kirsty 185
Young Riders, The 264

Z

Z Cars 370
Zorro 268

'Well, I'll just get your hors d'oeuvres. Hors d'oeuvres which must be obeyed at all times'